REA: SERIOUS PREP FOR THE GRE

GRE® CHEMISTRY TEST

Edited by
Susan D. Van Arnum, Ph.D.

Research & Education Association
Visit our website at: www.rea.com

Research & Education Association
61 Ethel Road West
Piscataway, New Jersey 08854
E-mail: info@rea.com

**GRE® Chemistry Test
with TestWare® on CD-ROM**

Printed in the United States of America

Library of Congress Control Number 2009935435

ISBN 13: 978-0-7386-0658-3
ISBN 10: 0-7386-0658-8

Contents

Preface

This preparation book with TestWare® on CD-ROM for the GRE Chemistry Subject Test is designed to provide you with five complete practice tests based on the tests most recently administered by the Educational Testing Service (ETS). Each of our tests matches the official test in format and degree of difficulty. Accompanying each test is a complete answer key as well as detailed and clear explanations to every question. Students can benefit the most by taking the practice test under actual test-center conditions. After grading the tests, the explanations will provide a means of refreshing the student with the material before going on to the next practice test.

About This Test

The GRE Chemistry Test is one tool used by graduate school admissions departments to evaluate prospective students. The test is used in conjunction with a number of other factors, including undergraduate record, faculty evaluations, and the GRE General Test. The GRE Chemistry Test is administered three times a year by ETS under the direction of the Graduate Record Examinations Board. Be sure to take note of graduate school application deadlines when registering to take the GREs. When choosing the test date, allow enough time for your scores to be processed and received by the graduate schools before their application deadline passes.

The GRE Chemistry Test is prepared by a committee of experts recommended by the American Chemical Society. Committee members are selected from various undergraduate faculties. The test questions submitted by the committee are organized into a standard format consisting of about 130 multiple-choice questions with emphasis placed on the traditional areas of chemistry. The following is an approximate breakdown of the test's areas of concentration:

Organic Chemistry—30%
Physical Chemistry—30%
Inorganic Chemistry—25%
Analytical Chemistry—15%

A number of questions will come in set form, based on an experiment or a descriptive paragraph provided on the exam. All of the questions in the practice tests are based on material commonly covered in an undergraduate curriculum; therefore, the material is wide-ranging. A realistic approach to the exam is to determine your strengths and weaknesses in these practice tests and use the explanations to hone your skills for the actual exam. A list of topics covered on the test follows this preface.

Random guessing on the test is not recommended because there is a deduction for wrong answers. If you are able to eliminate one or more of the answer choices, then an educated guess probably would be to your advantage. The scoring system is as follows: correct answer—one point; incorrect answer—one-quarter point deduction; omission—no deduction.

The result of this scoring system will give you a "raw score." From this "raw score" a scaled score can be obtained by using the conversion table provided in this book. It is this scaled score that is used by graduate school admissions officers to compare your performance with those of other applicants. Be aware, however, that, for statistical and other reasons, your score on the actual test would be expected to vary from your practice-test score.

Further information on the GRE Chemistry Test is available by contacting:

Graduate Record Examinations
Educational Testing Service
P.O. Box 6000
Princeton, NJ 08541-6000
Phone: (866) 473-4373
Website: *www.gre.org*

SSD ACCOMMODATIONS FOR STUDENTS WITH DISABILITIES

Many students qualify for extra time to take the GRE Chemistry Test. For information on how ETS meets disability needs, contact:

ETS Disability Services
Educational Testing Service
P.O. Box 6054
Princeton, NJ 08541-6054
Phone: 1-866-387-8602 (toll free)
Monday–Friday 8:30 a.m. to 5:00 p.m.
Eastern Time (New York)
TTY: 1-609-771-7714
Fax: 1-973-735-1892
E-mail: stassd@ets.org

Our TestWare® can be adapted to accommodate your time extension. This allows you to practice under the same extended-time accomodations that you will receive on the actual test day. To customize your TestWare® to suit the most common extensions, visit our website at *www.rea.com/ssd*.

About this Book and TestWare®

Do not take all of the practice tests in rapid succession. It is also not a good idea to peek at the material in tests that you have not attempted yet. Once you have taken the two practice tests on CD-ROM, you should have a good sense of the areas that require the most review. Now use the explanations and materials from your coursework to strengthen your knowledge in these areas as well as to refresh yourself in the areas in which you feel confident. After you feel better prepared, you should attempt another practice test and check your progress. Repeat this process until you have completed all of the practice tests in the book.

Be sure to take these practice tests under conditions identical to those you will face at the test center on the day of the examination. Remove yourself from all distractions and work in a quiet place where you will not be interrupted. Remember—no books, calculators, rulers, slide rules, or study aids of any kind will be allowed in the test center.

GRE Chemistry, Score Conversions and Percents

TOTAL SCORE					
Raw Score	Scaled Score	%	Raw Score	Scaled Score	%
133–135	980	99	68–69	690	52
131–132	970	99	65–67	680	50
129–130	960	99	63–64	670	48
126–128	950	99	61–62	660	45
124–125	940	98	59–60	650	43
122–123	930	97	56–58	640	40
120–121	920	96	54–55	630	37
118–119	910	95	52–53	620	34
115–117	900	94	49–51	610	31
113–114	890	92	47–48	600	29
111–112	880	90	45–46	590	26
109–110	870	88	42–44	580	24
106–108	860	87	40–41	570	21
104–105	850	85	38–39	560	19
102–103	840	83	35–37	550	16
100–101	830	81	33–34	540	14
97–99	820	79	31–32	530	11
95–96	810	77	28–30	520	10
93–94	800	76	26–27	510	8
91–92	790	74	24–25	500	6
88–90	780	72	21–23	490	5
86–87	770	70	19–20	480	3
84–85	760	64	17–18	470	2
82–83	750	66	14–16	460	2
79–81	740	64	12–13	450	1
77–78	730	61	10–11	440	1
75–76	720	59	7–9	430	1
72–74	710	57	5–6	420	1
70–71	700	55	3–4	410	1
			0–2	400	1

Important Chemistry Review Topics

The following outline of topics represents the subject areas covered on the GRE Chemistry Subject Test. The questions on the test stem from these topics and are at the same level as those presented in college chemistry courses.

INTRODUCTORY CHEMISTRY

Properties of Matter
Elements, Compounds, and Mixtures
Laws of Conservation of Mass and Definite Proportion
Dalton Atomic Theory
Stoichiometry

ATOMIC THEORY

Fundamental Particles
Atomic Structure
Evidence for the Existence of Atoms
Determination of Atomic Weights (From Mass Spectrograph and X-ray Data)
The Atomic Nucleus, Isotopes, Radioactivity
Electronic Structure
The Periodic Law and the Periodic Table
The Variation of Properties with Atomic Structure
Chemistry of the Families of Elements
Properties and Reactions as a Function of the Electronic Structure
Alkali and Alkaline Earth Metals
Nonmetals, Transition Elements

CHEMICAL BONDING

Ionic and Covalent Bonds
Valence Bond Theory
Hybrid Orbitals, Multiple Bonds
Resonance
Bond Order
Electronegativity, Dipole Moments, and Polar Molecules
Molecular Structure, the Valence Shell Electron
Repulsion Theory
Oxidation and Reduction

GASES

Boyle's Law, Charles's Law, Dalton's Law of Partial Pressures, Gay-Lussac's Laws, Avogadro's
    Law, the Mole Concept
The Ideal Gas Law
The Kinetic Theory of Gases
Real Gases, the Van der Waals Equation

LIQUIDS AND SOLIDS

Crystalline Solids, Lattices
Amorphous Solids
Phase Diagrams
Phase Rule

SOLUTION CHEMISTRY

Electrolytes, Ionic Reactions
Acids and Bases (Arrhenius Definition of Acids and Bases; Brønsted-Lowry Acid-Base
    Definition)
Density and Formality
Normality, Molarity, and Molality
Neutralization Reaction
Balancing of Redox Equations
Colligative Properties of Solutions

THERMODYNAMICS

Temperature, State Variables
Heat and Work Equations of State
The First Law of Thermodynamics
Reversible and Irreversible Processes
Heats of Reaction: Thermochemistry
Hess's Law
Standard States
Bond Energies
Spontaneity of Chemical Reactions
Entropy
The Second Law of Thermodynamics
Free Energy and Equilibrium
Standard Entropies and Free Energies
Third Law of Thermodynamics
Applications of the Principles of Thermodynamics

CHEMICAL EQUILIBRIUM

The Equilibrium Constant
Equilibrium Calculations
Le Châtelier's Principle
Heterogeneous and Solution Equilibria
Ionization of Water and pH Scale
Neutralization and Titration: Titration Curves
Equilibria in Weak Acids and Bases
Indicators
Hydrolysis
Buffers
Phase Equilibria, Phase Rule

CHEMICAL KINETICS

The Rate Law
The Order and Molecularity of Reactions
The Arrhenius Equation, Variation of Reaction Rates with Temperature
Opposing Reaction, Chain Reactions, and Competing Reactions

ELECTROCHEMISTRY

Electrode Reactions
Galvanic Cells
Current Flow in Cells, Electrolysis
E.M.F. and Free Energy Nernst Equation
Oxidation-Reduction Reactions

QUANTUM CHEMISTRY

Early Experimental Basis of Quantum Mechanics and Chemistry (e.g., Black Body Radiation, Heat
   Capacities, Photoelectric Effect, etc.)
Atomic and Molecular Spectra
The Bohr Atom
The Wave Nature of Matter: The de Broglie Equation
Wave Function: Uncertainty Principle
Pauli Exclusion Principle, Hund's Rule
Molecular Orbital Theory

NUCLEAR CHEMISTRY

Spontaneous Radioactive Decay
Nuclear Transformations
Nuclear Stability
Nuclear Fission and Fusion

ORGANIC CHEMISTRY

Hydrocarbons (Saturated and Unsaturated)
Nomenclature
Isomerism: Structural Isomerism
Stereoisomerism (Geometrical, i.e., Cis and Trans)
Optical Isomerism
Cyclic Hydrocarbons
Conformations of Organic Molecules
Functional Groups: Alcohols, Aldehydes, Ketones, Acids and Derivatives, Amines, etc.
Aromatic Compounds
Interconversion of Functional Groups
Organometallic Reagents
Electrophilic Aromatic Substitution
Nucleophilic Displacement Reactions
Elimination Reactions
Natural Products (Terpenes, Steroids, etc.)

About Research & Education Association

Founded in 1959, Research & Education Association (REA) is dedicated to publishing the finest and most effective educational materials—including software, study guides, and test preps—for students in elementary school, middle school, high school, college, graduate school, and beyond.

REA's Test Preparation series includes books and software for all academic levels in almost all disciplines. Research & Education Association publishes test preps for students who have not yet entered high school, as well as high school students preparing to enter college. Students from countries around the world seeking to attend college in the United States will find the assistance they need in REA's publications. For college students seeking advanced degrees, REA publishes test preps for many major graduate school admission examinations in a wide variety of disciplines, including engineering, law, and medicine. Students at every level, in every field, with every ambition can find what they are looking for among REA's publications.

REA presents tests that accurately depict the official exams in both degree of difficulty and types of questions. REA's practice tests are always based upon the most recently administered exams, and they include every type of question that can be expected on the actual exams.

REA's publications and educational materials are highly regarded and continually receive an unprecedented amount of praise from professionals, instructors, librarians, parents, and students. Our authors are as diverse as the fields represented in the books we publish. They are well known in their respective disciplines and serve on the faculties of prestigious high schools, colleges, and universities throughout the United States and Canada.

We invite you to visit us at *www.rea.com* to find out how "REA is making the world smarter."

Acknowledgments

We would like to thank Susan D. Van Arnum, Ph.D., for her technical edit of this edition; Larry B. Kling, Vice President, Editorial, for his overall direction; Pam Weston, Vice President, Publishing, for setting the quality standards for production integrity and managing the publication to completion; Michael Reynolds, Managing Editor, for coordinating revisions; and Caragraphics for typesetting this edition.

Practice Exam 1

Practice Exam 1 is also on CD-ROM in our special interactive GRE Chemistry TestWare®. It is highly recommended that you first take this exam on computer. You will then have the additional study features and benefits of enforced timed conditions and instant, accurate scoring. See page v for guidance on how to get the most out of our GRE Chemistry software.

Answer Sheet: Practice Exam 1

1. Ⓐ Ⓑ Ⓒ Ⓓ Ⓔ
2. Ⓐ Ⓑ Ⓒ Ⓓ Ⓔ
3. Ⓐ Ⓑ Ⓒ Ⓓ Ⓔ
4. Ⓐ Ⓑ Ⓒ Ⓓ Ⓔ
5. Ⓐ Ⓑ Ⓒ Ⓓ Ⓔ
6. Ⓐ Ⓑ Ⓒ Ⓓ Ⓔ
7. Ⓐ Ⓑ Ⓒ Ⓓ Ⓔ
8. Ⓐ Ⓑ Ⓒ Ⓓ Ⓔ
9. Ⓐ Ⓑ Ⓒ Ⓓ Ⓔ
10. Ⓐ Ⓑ Ⓒ Ⓓ Ⓔ
11. Ⓐ Ⓑ Ⓒ Ⓓ Ⓔ
12. Ⓐ Ⓑ Ⓒ Ⓓ Ⓔ
13. Ⓐ Ⓑ Ⓒ Ⓓ Ⓔ
14. Ⓐ Ⓑ Ⓒ Ⓓ Ⓔ
15. Ⓐ Ⓑ Ⓒ Ⓓ Ⓔ
16. Ⓐ Ⓑ Ⓒ Ⓓ Ⓔ
17. Ⓐ Ⓑ Ⓒ Ⓓ Ⓔ
18. Ⓐ Ⓑ Ⓒ Ⓓ Ⓔ
19. Ⓐ Ⓑ Ⓒ Ⓓ Ⓔ
20. Ⓐ Ⓑ Ⓒ Ⓓ Ⓔ
21. Ⓐ Ⓑ Ⓒ Ⓓ Ⓔ
22. Ⓐ Ⓑ Ⓒ Ⓓ Ⓔ
23. Ⓐ Ⓑ Ⓒ Ⓓ Ⓔ
24. Ⓐ Ⓑ Ⓒ Ⓓ Ⓔ
25. Ⓐ Ⓑ Ⓒ Ⓓ Ⓔ
26. Ⓐ Ⓑ Ⓒ Ⓓ Ⓔ
27. Ⓐ Ⓑ Ⓒ Ⓓ Ⓔ
28. Ⓐ Ⓑ Ⓒ Ⓓ Ⓔ
29. Ⓐ Ⓑ Ⓒ Ⓓ Ⓔ
30. Ⓐ Ⓑ Ⓒ Ⓓ Ⓔ
31. Ⓐ Ⓑ Ⓒ Ⓓ Ⓔ
32. Ⓐ Ⓑ Ⓒ Ⓓ Ⓔ
33. Ⓐ Ⓑ Ⓒ Ⓓ Ⓔ

34. Ⓐ Ⓑ Ⓒ Ⓓ Ⓔ
35. Ⓐ Ⓑ Ⓒ Ⓓ Ⓔ
36. Ⓐ Ⓑ Ⓒ Ⓓ Ⓔ
37. Ⓐ Ⓑ Ⓒ Ⓓ Ⓔ
38. Ⓐ Ⓑ Ⓒ Ⓓ Ⓔ
39. Ⓐ Ⓑ Ⓒ Ⓓ Ⓔ
40. Ⓐ Ⓑ Ⓒ Ⓓ Ⓔ
41. Ⓐ Ⓑ Ⓒ Ⓓ Ⓔ
42. Ⓐ Ⓑ Ⓒ Ⓓ Ⓔ
43. Ⓐ Ⓑ Ⓒ Ⓓ Ⓔ
44. Ⓐ Ⓑ Ⓒ Ⓓ Ⓔ
45. Ⓐ Ⓑ Ⓒ Ⓓ Ⓔ
46. Ⓐ Ⓑ Ⓒ Ⓓ Ⓔ
47. Ⓐ Ⓑ Ⓒ Ⓓ Ⓔ
48. Ⓐ Ⓑ Ⓒ Ⓓ Ⓔ
49. Ⓐ Ⓑ Ⓒ Ⓓ Ⓔ
50. Ⓐ Ⓑ Ⓒ Ⓓ Ⓔ
51. Ⓐ Ⓑ Ⓒ Ⓓ Ⓔ
52. Ⓐ Ⓑ Ⓒ Ⓓ Ⓔ
53. Ⓐ Ⓑ Ⓒ Ⓓ Ⓔ
54. Ⓐ Ⓑ Ⓒ Ⓓ Ⓔ
55. Ⓐ Ⓑ Ⓒ Ⓓ Ⓔ
56. Ⓐ Ⓑ Ⓒ Ⓓ Ⓔ
57. Ⓐ Ⓑ Ⓒ Ⓓ Ⓔ
58. Ⓐ Ⓑ Ⓒ Ⓓ Ⓔ
59. Ⓐ Ⓑ Ⓒ Ⓓ Ⓔ
60. Ⓐ Ⓑ Ⓒ Ⓓ Ⓔ
61. Ⓐ Ⓑ Ⓒ Ⓓ Ⓔ
62. Ⓐ Ⓑ Ⓒ Ⓓ Ⓔ
63. Ⓐ Ⓑ Ⓒ Ⓓ Ⓔ
64. Ⓐ Ⓑ Ⓒ Ⓓ Ⓔ
65. Ⓐ Ⓑ Ⓒ Ⓓ Ⓔ
66. Ⓐ Ⓑ Ⓒ Ⓓ Ⓔ

67. Ⓐ Ⓑ Ⓒ Ⓓ Ⓔ
68. Ⓐ Ⓑ Ⓒ Ⓓ Ⓔ
69. Ⓐ Ⓑ Ⓒ Ⓓ Ⓔ
70. Ⓐ Ⓑ Ⓒ Ⓓ Ⓔ
71. Ⓐ Ⓑ Ⓒ Ⓓ Ⓔ
72. Ⓐ Ⓑ Ⓒ Ⓓ Ⓔ
73. Ⓐ Ⓑ Ⓒ Ⓓ Ⓔ
74. Ⓐ Ⓑ Ⓒ Ⓓ Ⓔ
75. Ⓐ Ⓑ Ⓒ Ⓓ Ⓔ
76. Ⓐ Ⓑ Ⓒ Ⓓ Ⓔ
77. Ⓐ Ⓑ Ⓒ Ⓓ Ⓔ
78. Ⓐ Ⓑ Ⓒ Ⓓ Ⓔ
79. Ⓐ Ⓑ Ⓒ Ⓓ Ⓔ
80. Ⓐ Ⓑ Ⓒ Ⓓ Ⓔ
81. Ⓐ Ⓑ Ⓒ Ⓓ Ⓔ
82. Ⓐ Ⓑ Ⓒ Ⓓ Ⓔ
83. Ⓐ Ⓑ Ⓒ Ⓓ Ⓔ
84. Ⓐ Ⓑ Ⓒ Ⓓ Ⓔ
85. Ⓐ Ⓑ Ⓒ Ⓓ Ⓔ
86. Ⓐ Ⓑ Ⓒ Ⓓ Ⓔ
87. Ⓐ Ⓑ Ⓒ Ⓓ Ⓔ
88. Ⓐ Ⓑ Ⓒ Ⓓ Ⓔ
89. Ⓐ Ⓑ Ⓒ Ⓓ Ⓔ
90. Ⓐ Ⓑ Ⓒ Ⓓ Ⓔ
91. Ⓐ Ⓑ Ⓒ Ⓓ Ⓔ
92. Ⓐ Ⓑ Ⓒ Ⓓ Ⓔ
93. Ⓐ Ⓑ Ⓒ Ⓓ Ⓔ
94. Ⓐ Ⓑ Ⓒ Ⓓ Ⓔ
95. Ⓐ Ⓑ Ⓒ Ⓓ Ⓔ
96. Ⓐ Ⓑ Ⓒ Ⓓ Ⓔ
97. Ⓐ Ⓑ Ⓒ Ⓓ Ⓔ
98. Ⓐ Ⓑ Ⓒ Ⓓ Ⓔ
99. Ⓐ Ⓑ Ⓒ Ⓓ Ⓔ

Continued

100. (A) (B) (C) (D) (E)
101. (A) (B) (C) (D) (E)
102. (A) (B) (C) (D) (E)
103. (A) (B) (C) (D) (E)
104. (A) (B) (C) (D) (E)
105. (A) (B) (C) (D) (E)
106. (A) (B) (C) (D) (E)
107. (A) (B) (C) (D) (E)
108. (A) (B) (C) (D) (E)
109. (A) (B) (C) (D) (E)
110. (A) (B) (C) (D) (E)
111. (A) (B) (C) (D) (E)
112. (A) (B) (C) (D) (E)

113. (A) (B) (C) (D) (E)
114. (A) (B) (C) (D) (E)
115. (A) (B) (C) (D) (E)
116. (A) (B) (C) (D) (E)
117. (A) (B) (C) (D) (E)
118. (A) (B) (C) (D) (E)
119. (A) (B) (C) (D) (E)
120. (A) (B) (C) (D) (E)
121. (A) (B) (C) (D) (E)
122. (A) (B) (C) (D) (E)
123. (A) (B) (C) (D) (E)
124. (A) (B) (C) (D) (E)
125. (A) (B) (C) (D) (E)

126. (A) (B) (C) (D) (E)
127. (A) (B) (C) (D) (E)
128. (A) (B) (C) (D) (E)
129. (A) (B) (C) (D) (E)
130. (A) (B) (C) (D) (E)
131. (A) (B) (C) (D) (E)
132. (A) (B) (C) (D) (E)
133. (A) (B) (C) (D) (E)
134. (A) (B) (C) (D) (E)
135. (A) (B) (C) (D) (E)
136. (A) (B) (C) (D) (E)

Practice Exam 1

Time: 170 Minutes
       136 Questions

Directions: *Choose the best answer for each question and mark the letter of your selection on the corresponding answer sheet.*

1. A covalent bond is unlikely to exist in the product of which of the following reactions?

    (A) $CH_4 + 2O_2 \rightarrow CO_2 + 2H_2O$ (D) $Si + 2F_2 \rightarrow SiF_4$
    (B) $Br^- + Br^- \rightarrow Br_2$ (E) $Ca + \frac{1}{2}O_2 \rightarrow CaO$
    (C) $Se + H_2 \rightarrow SeH_2$

2. Which of the following is not a member of the transition metals?

    (A) Scandium   (C) Vanadium   (E) Beryllium
    (B) Titanium   (D) Iron

3. Which of the following can function as a Lewis acid?

    (A) 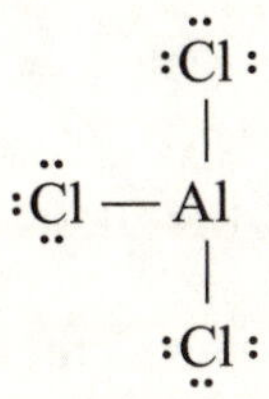
    $$
    \begin{array}{c}
    \ddot{:}\!\overset{\displaystyle :\ddot{Cl}:}{\underset{\displaystyle :\ddot{Cl}:}{\overset{|}{\underset{|}{\ddot{Cl}-Al}}}}
    \end{array}
    $$

    (C) $CH_3 - \ddot{\underset{..}{O}} - CH_3$ (E) $:\!\ddot{Br}\!:^-$

    (B) $:CN^-$ (D) $:NH_3$

4. Which of the following substances has the least ionic character in its bond?

    (A) CCl_4 (C) $MgCl_2$ (E) $BaCl_2$
    (B) KCl (D) $NaCl$

5. Which of the following best describes ionization energy?

    (A) Energy needed to remove the most loosely bound electron from its ground state.
    (B) It is represented by

    $$x + e^- \rightarrow x^- + energy.$$

    (C) It decreases from left to right across a period.
    (D) It increases down the periodic table.
    (E) None of the above.

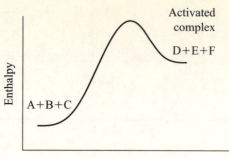

6. The enthalpies associated with the reaction A + B + C → D + E + F is shown above. The fact that the enthalpy of D + E + F is higher than that of A + B + C tells us that

(A) the reaction is exothermic
(B) the reaction is endothermic
(C) the activation energy required for the reverse reaction is higher than for the forward reaction
(D) a catalyst for the reaction is unnecessary
(E) the activated complex for the reverse reaction is a different species from that of the forward reaction

7. Every atom consists of electrons, protons, and neutrons *except*

(A) helium atom
(B) sodium atom
(C) hydrogen atom
(D) boron atom
(E) calcium atom

8. Which of the following is true for isotopes of an element?

(A) They are atoms of the same atomic number with different masses.
(B) The only difference in composition between isotopes of the same element is in the number of neutrons in the nucleus.
(C) The atomic weight of an element is an average of the weights of the isotopes of the element in the proportions in which they normally occur in nature.
(D) (A) and (C) only
(E) (A), (B) and (C)

9. Natural chlorine occurs as a mixture of isotopes. If a mixture contains 75% $^{35}_{17}Cl$ and 25% $^{37}_{17}Cl$, determine its atomic weight.

(A) 34.50
(B) 35.50
(C) 72.00
(D) 70.00
(E) None of the above

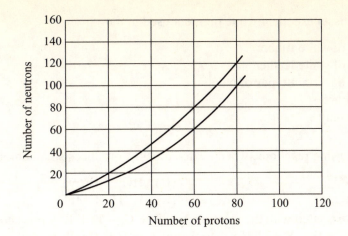

10. Which of the following is (are) true for the above nuclear stability graph?

    (A) Isotopes that fall to the left or right of the stability curve have unstable nuclei and are referred to as being radioactive.
    (B) All isotopes with atomic number higher than 83 are radioactive.
    (C) The curve indicates that the lighter, stabler nuclei tend to have equal numbers of protons and neutrons.
    (D) None of the above
    (E) All of the above

11. Which of the following best characterizes electron affinity?

    (A) Neutral atoms with unfilled orbitals having repulsion for electrons.
    (B) Neutral atoms of noble gases having attraction for electrons.
    (C) Neutral atoms with unfilled orbitals having attraction for electrons.
    (D) Atoms that lie to the upper left of the periodic table.
    (E) Atoms with low ionization potential.

12. The type of precipitate that is most difficult to filter in quantitative analysis is

    (A) curdy
    (B) insoluble
    (C) isomorphous
    (D) crystalline
    (E) gelatinous

13. Which of the following represents the same net reaction as the electrolysis of aqueous sulfuric acid?

    (A) Electrolysis of water
    (B) Electrolysis of aqueous HCl
    (C) Electrolysis of aqueous NaCl
    (D) Electrolysis of molten NaCl
    (E) All of the above

14. Which of the following is most acidic?

    (A) $HClO_4$
    (B) HF
    (C) H_3PO_4
    (D) HCN
    (E) HCl

15. Titanium dioxide is an excellent white pigment used in the

    (A) preparation of white rubber
    (B) preparation of white leather
    (C) preparation of certain types of paints
    (D) All of the above
    (E) (A) and (B) only

16. Which of the following reactions, when heated quickly, produces small amounts of chorine gas?

    (A) $NaCl + HNO_3$
    (B) $NaCl + MnO_2$
    (C) $NaCl + H_2SO_4$

    (D) $HCl + Br_2$
    (E) $HCl + KMnO_4$

17. The compound $CH_3CH \equiv CH_2$ has a bond formed by the overlap of which of the following hybrid orbitals?

    (A) $sp^2 - sp^3$
    (B) $sp - sp^2$
    (C) $sp - sp^3$

    (D) $sp^3 - sp^3$
    (E) All of the above

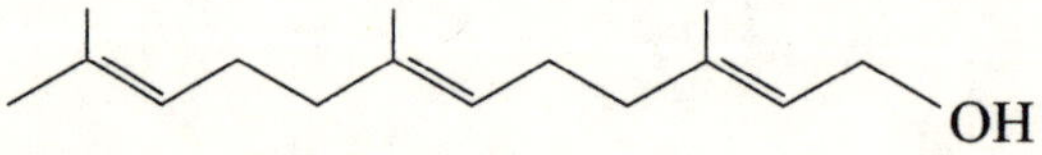

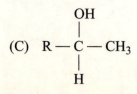

18. The formula above represents a member of the class of compounds known as

    (A) vitamins
    (B) alkaloids
    (C) carbohydrates

    (D) terpenes
    (E) steroids

$$R - \overset{\overset{\displaystyle O}{\|}}{C} - CH_3 \xrightarrow[3OH^-]{3Br_2} R - \overset{\overset{\displaystyle O}{\|}}{C} - CBr_3 + 3H_2O \xrightarrow{OH^-} ?$$

19. When the above reaction takes place, which of the following is the major organic product?

    (A) $CHBr_3$

    (B) $HOCBr_3$

    (C) $R - \overset{\overset{\displaystyle OH}{|}}{\underset{\underset{\displaystyle H}{|}}{C}} - CH_3$

    (D) $R - \overset{\overset{\displaystyle OH}{|}}{\underset{\underset{\displaystyle OCH_3}{|}}{C}} - CH_3$

    (E) None of the above

20. For a certain second-order reaction A + B → C, it was noted that when the initial concentration of A is doubled while B is held constant, the initial reaction rate doubles, and when the initial concentration of B is doubled while A is held constant, the initial reaction rate increases fourfold. What is the rate expression for this reaction?

    (A) $r = k[A][B]$
    (B) $r = k[A]^2[B]^3$
    (C) $r = k[A]^1[B]^2$

    (D) $r = k[A]^3[B]^1$
    (E) $r = k[A]^2[B]^1$

$$2Al(S) + 3Cl_2(g) \longrightarrow 2AlCl_3(S)$$

21. For the above reaction the entropies of Al(s), Cl_2(g) and $AlCl_3$(s) are 28.3 J/Kmol, 222.96 J/Kmol, and 110.7 J/Kmol, respectively. Calculate the standard entropy change for the reactive system.

    (A) -221.4 J/Kmol
    (B) 725.48 J/Kmol
    (C) -668.88 J/Kmol

    (D) -504.08 J/Kmol
    (E) -56.6 J/Kmol

22. How would you express the absolute temperature at which a reaction occurs in terms of the free energy change of the reaction ΔG, the enthalpy change ΔH, and the entropy change ΔS?

    (A) $\dfrac{\Delta G - \Delta H}{\Delta S}$

    (B) $\dfrac{\Delta H - \Delta S}{\Delta G}$

    (C) $\dfrac{\Delta H - \Delta G}{\Delta S}$

    (D) $\Delta H - \Delta G + \Delta S$

    (E) None of the above

23. For a quantized energy system, which of the following is (are) implied by Bohr's postule(s) of the theory of hydrogen atom:

    (A) A normal hydrogen atom in its ground state is a stationary proton and a revolving electron with an energy of -21.79×10^{-12} erg.
    (B) The energy of the electrons can take only the values given by -21.79×10^{-12} erg/n^2.
    (C) The hydrogen atom can emit or absorb only photons whose energy is equal to the difference between the two energy levels.
    (D) For an electron moving between any two levels, the difference in the energy of the two levels equals the energy of the radiation absorbed or emitted by the electron.
    (E) All of the above.

24. Which of the following represents the real gas law?

    (A) $nRT = (P + a/V^2)(V - b)$
    (B) $nRT = (P - a/V^2)(V - b)$
    (C) $PV = nRT$

    (D) $nRT = (P - a/V^2)(V + nb)$
    (E) $nRT = (P + n^2a/V^2)(V - nb)$

25. Which of the following compounds shows splitting of peaks in its ^1H nuclear magnetic resonance spectrum?

    (1) $ClCH_2CH_2Cl$

    (2) $BrCH_2CH_2Br$

    (3) ICH_2CH_2I

    (4) FCH_2CH_2F

    (5) $(CH_3)_3 - C - Br$

    (A) (1), (2), and (3) only

    (B) (1), (3), and (4) only

    (C) (1) and (4) only

    (D) (2) only

    (E) (5) only

26. Acid-catalyzed esterification of carboxylic acids produces which of the following as its final product?

    (A) $\overset{O}{\overset{\|}{R}}COR'$

    (B) $\overset{O}{\overset{\|}{R}}CCl$

    (C) $\overset{O}{\overset{\|}{R}}CNH_2$

    (D) $\overset{O}{\overset{\|}{R}}CNHR'$

    (E) $\overset{O}{\overset{\|}{R}}CBr$

27. Which of the following is the major product of the reaction below?

    $$\text{Reaction: } C_5H_5CH = CH_2 \xrightarrow[\text{Br}_2/\text{CH}_3\text{OH}]{\text{dilute solution}} \text{?}$$

    (A) $C_6H_5CHBr - CH_2Br$

    (B) $C_6H_5\overset{OCH_3}{\overset{|}{C}} - HCH_2Br$

    (C) $C_6H_5CH_2 - CHBr_2$

    (D) $C_6H_5\overset{OCH_3}{\overset{|}{C}}Br - CH_2Br$

    (E) None of the above

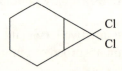

28. The hydrocarbon shown above is

    (A) 7,7 dichlorobicyclo [4.1.0] heptane

    (B) 1,1-dichlorobicyclo [2.7.0] hepatine

    (C) 7,7-dichlorobicyclo [5.6.0] heptane

    (D) 3,3-dichlorobicyclo [4.1.0] heptane

    (E) None of the above

29. A secondary alcohol is formed through oxymercuration-demercuration of which of the following?

    (A) 1-hexane
    (B) hexane
    (C) 2-methyl-1-bromopropene
    (D) 1, 2-dimethyl-propene
    (E) 1-hexanal

30. Which of the following is a characteristic of an isothermal change?

    (A) The enthalpy is constant.
    (B) No heat enters or leaves the system.
    (C) The system is maintained at the same temperature throughout the experiment.
    (D) The system is maintained at the same pressure throughout the experiment.
    (E) None of the above

31. The equation $\Delta G = \Delta H - T\Delta S$ tells us that a spontaneous reaction will be associated with which of the following?

    (1) Negative ΔH

    (2) Positive ΔH

    (3) More disordered positive ΔS

    (4) Negative ΔG

    (5) More ordered negative ΔS

    (A) (1) and (5)
    (B) (2) and (5)
    (C) (2) and (3)
    (D) (1), (3) and (4)
    (E) None of the above

32. In a methanol-ethanol-propanol solution (consisting of a mixture of 42.0g methanol, 35.0g ethanol, and 50.0g propanol), the partial molar volumes are respectively 16.0 ml, 20.0 ml, and 50.0 ml. The volume of 1.00 mole of the solution is: (take the mole fraction of CH_3OH, C_2H_5OH, and C_3H_7OH to be 0.452, 0.260, and 0.287, respectively):

    (A) $(0.452)(16.0) + (0.26)(20.0) + (0.287)(50.0)$

    (B) $(0.26)(160) + (0.452)(20.0) + (0.287)(50.0)$

    (C) $(0.26)/(16.0) + (0.452)/(20.0) + (0.287)/(50.0)$

    (D) $\dfrac{(0.452)(10.0) + (0.26)(20.0) + (0.287)(50.0)}{(0.287)(0.26)(0.287)}$

    (E) $(0.26)(20.0) + (0.452)/(16.0) + (0.287)/(50.0)$

33. In order for Hψ to be defined, which of the following is acceptable?

(A)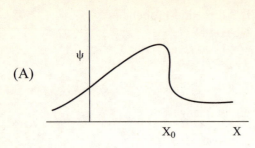

(D)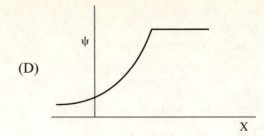

(B)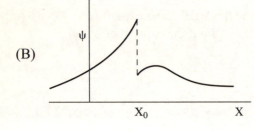

(E)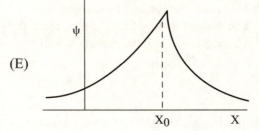

(C)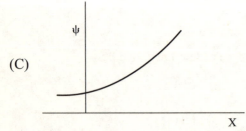

34. For a certain first-order reaction, the time required for half of an initial amount to decompose is 3 minutes. If the initial concentration of A is 1 molar, the time required to reduce the concentration of A to 0.25M is (take ln2 to be 0.693 and ln4 to be 1.39):

    (A) 4.5 mins   (D) 8.0 mins
    (B) 6.0 mins   (E) 6.6 mins
    (C) 12.0 mins

35. Which of the following is closest to the pH of 10^{-4}M NaOH?

    (A) 11   (D) 7
    (B) 10.2   (E) 12
    (C) 9

36. What is the major product for the reaction below?

$$\text{H}_3\text{C} \overset{\text{CH}_3}{\underset{\text{CH}_3}{\bigcirc}} \xrightarrow[\substack{(\text{CH}_3\text{CO})_2\text{O} \\ 20°}]{\text{fuming HNO}} \ ?$$

(A) 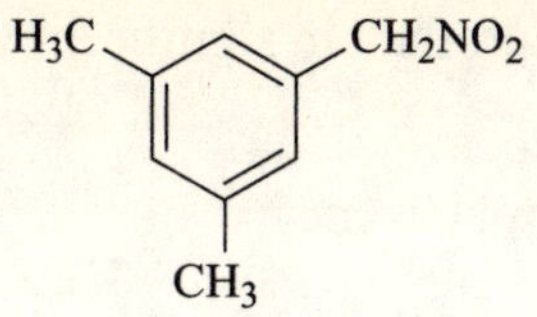 [structure: benzene ring with H₃C, CH₂NO₂, and CH₃ substituents]

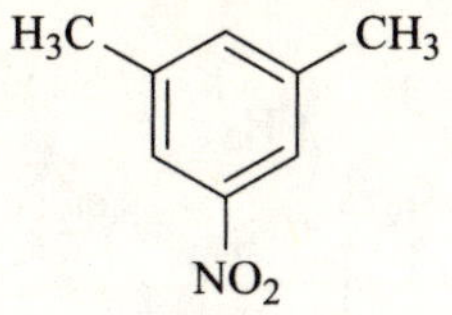

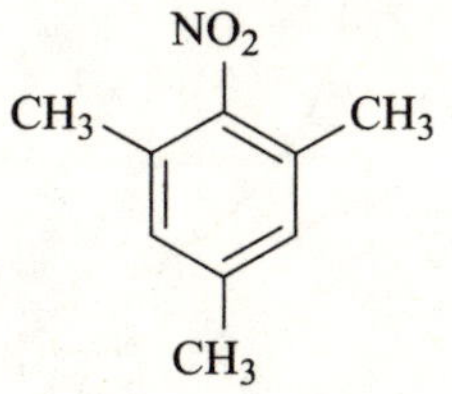

(D) 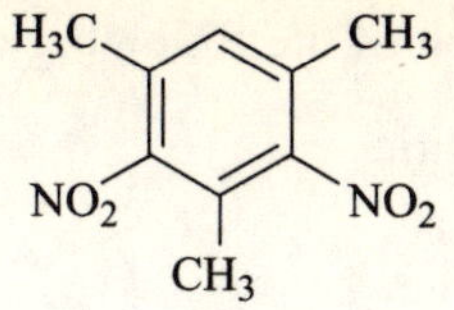 [structure: benzene ring with H₃C, CH₃, NO₂, NO₂, and CH₃ substituents]

(B) [structure: benzene ring with H₃C, CH₃, and NO₂ substituents]

(E) 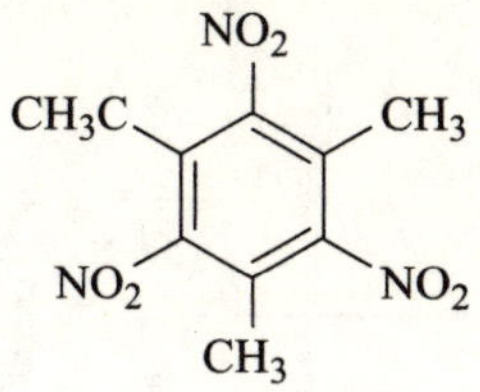 [structure: benzene ring with CH₃C, NO₂, CH₃, NO₂, NO₂, and CH₃ substituents]

(C) [structure: benzene ring with NO₂, CH₃, CH₃, and CH₃ substituents]

37. If a copper bearing material weighing 40 grams yielded 5 grams of CuO (MW 79.55), the percentage of copper (atomic weight 63.55) in the sample is:

(A) $5/40 \times 100$
(B) $5/40 \times 79.55/63.55 \times 100$
(C) $5/40 \times 63.55/79.55 \times 100$
(D) $40/5 \times 79.55/63.55 \times 100$
(E) None of the above

38. What is the normality, N, of a 1M solution of H_2SO_4, given the following reaction?

$$H_2SO_4 + 2KOH \rightarrow K_2SO_4 + 2H_2O$$

(A) 4N
(B) 3N
(C) 2N
(D) 1N
(E) None of the above

39. The reaction below is generally called:

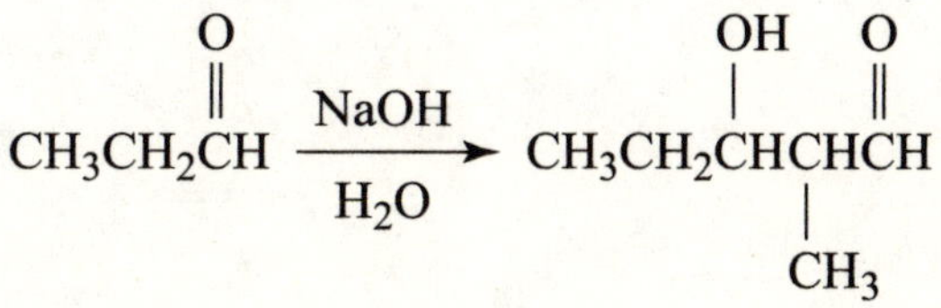

(A) Oxymercuration-demercuration
(B) Oxidation
(C) Reduction
(D) Aldol condensation
(E) Clemmensen reduction

40. During nitration, which of the following can form more than one product in significant yield?

(A) Methoxyacetanilide
(B) Mesitylene
(C) P-dichlorobenzene

(D) P-nitrotoluene
(E) 1,3,5 Trichlorobenzene

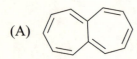 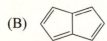  

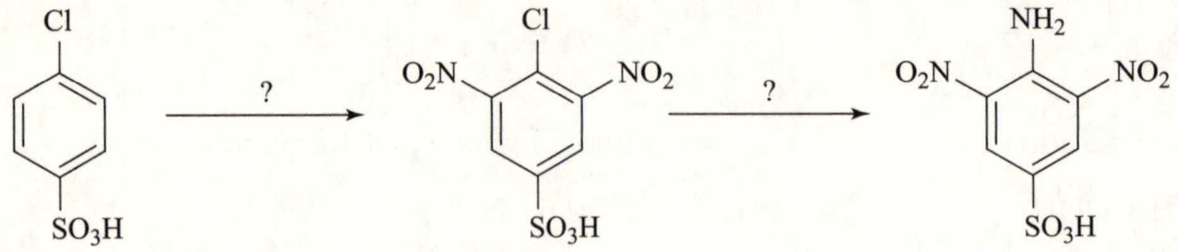

41. What are the missing reactants in the above equation?

(A) NH_3 followed by H_2SO_4
(B) H_2SO_4/HNO_3 followed by NH_3/NH_2^-
(C) $NaNO_2/HCl$ followed by NH_3/NH_2^-
(D) $(CH_3CO)_2O$ followed by NH_3/NH_2^-
(E) None of the above

42. Which is the most acidic of the following compounds?

(A) CH_3OH
(B) C_2H_5OH
(C) $(CH_3)_3COH$

(D) C_6H_5OH
(E) CH_3COOH

43. Which of the following molecules can be considered aromatic?

(A) [structure]

(D) [structure]

(B) [structure]

(E) [structure]

(C) [structure]

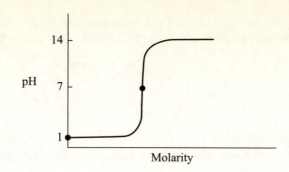

44. The above titration curve shows HCl being titrated with which of the following?

    (A) CH_3COOH
    (B) NaOH
    (C) H_2SO_4 (dilute)
    (D) NH_3
    (E) CH_3NH_2

45. $NH_3(aq) + H_2O(l) \rightleftharpoons NH_4^+(aq) + OH^-(aq)$

    For the above equation, calculate the ionization constant if the $[NH_4^+]$ is 10^{-4}M, $[NH_3]$ is 1.0M and $[OH^-]$ is 0.18M respectively.

    (A) 1.8×10^{-5}
    (B) 1.8×10^{-4}
    (C) 10^{-5}
    (D) 1.8
    (E) 1.8×10^{-3}

46. Which of the following instruments may be used to measure the optical activity of compounds?

    (A) Infrared spectrometer
    (B) Polarimeter
    (C) Nuclear magnetic resonance spectrometer
    (D) Atomic absorption spectrometer
    (E) Flouroscope

47. A solution contains 0.01 mol KI, 0.10 mol KBr, and 0.10 mol KCl per liter. $AgNO_3$ is gradually added to this solution. Which will be precipitated first, AgI, AgBr, or AgCl?

    (Solubility products are $K_{AgI} = 1.5 \times 10^{-16}$, $K_{AgBr} = 3.3 \times 10^{-13}$, $K_{AgCl} = 1.8 \times 10^{-10}$)

    (A) AgI
    (B) AgBr
    (C) AgCl
    (D) Both AgBr and AgCl
    (E) Cannot solve with given information

48. The excitation of outer electrons in atoms and molecules is associated with which of the following bands of radiation?

    (A) X-rays
    (B) Gamma rays
    (C) Ultraviolet
    (D) Infrared
    (E) Microwave and radio

49. At standard conditions 45 liters of oxygen gas weighs about 64g, whereas 45 liters of hydrogen weighs only about 4g. Which gas diffuses faster? Calculate how much faster.

    (A) Hydrogen, $4r_{O_2}$
    (B) Hydrogen, $2r_{O_2}$
    (C) Oxygen, $8r_{H_2}$

    (D) Oxygen, $3r_{H_2}$
    (E) None of the above

50. The unit cell cube edge length for LiCl ($NaCl^-$-like structure, face-centered cubic) is 5.14 Å. Assuming anion-anion contact, what is the ionic radius for chloride ion?

    (A) $\sqrt{2}(5.14\text{Å})$

    (B) $\dfrac{\sqrt{2}}{2}(5.14\text{Å})$

    (C) $\dfrac{1}{2}(5.14\text{Å})$

    (D) $\dfrac{\sqrt{2}}{2}(2.57\text{Å})$

    (E) $\sqrt{2}(2.57\text{Å})$

51. Which of the following is *not* true for metalloids?

    (A) They are borderline elements that exhibit both metallic and nonmetallic properties to some extent.
    (B) They usually act as electron donors with nonmetals and as electron acceptors with metals.
    (C) Some of these elements are Boron, silicon and Germanium.
    (D) They are all solids at room temperature.
    (E) All of the above.

52.
$$\overset{\displaystyle O}{\overset{\displaystyle \|}{CH_3C}}OCH_2CH_3 + OH^- \rightarrow CH_3CO_2^- + CH_3CH_2OH$$

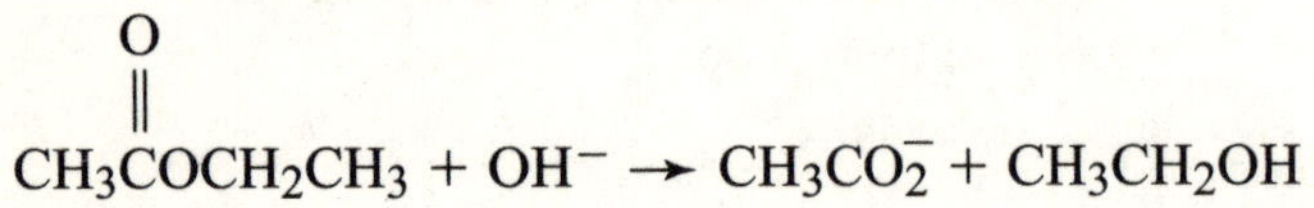

A mechanism proposed for the above reaction is as follows:

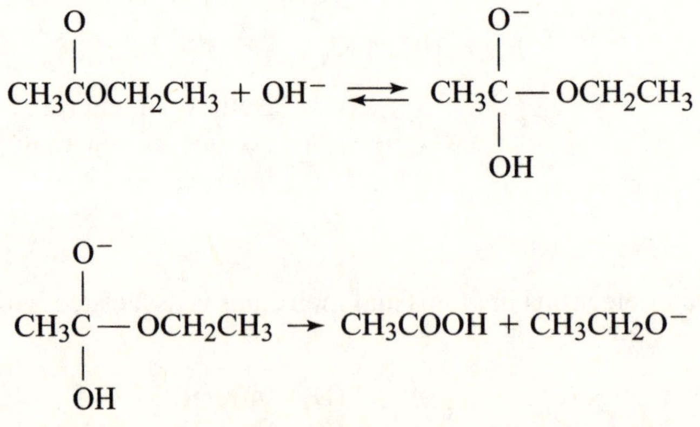

$$\overset{\displaystyle O}{\overset{\displaystyle |}{CH_3C}}OCH_2CH_3 + OH^- \rightleftharpoons \underset{\underset{\displaystyle OH}{\displaystyle |}}{\overset{\overset{\displaystyle O^-}{\displaystyle |}}{CH_3C}}-OCH_2CH_3$$

$$\underset{\underset{\displaystyle OH}{\displaystyle |}}{\overset{\overset{\displaystyle O^-}{\displaystyle |}}{CH_3C}}-OCH_2CH_3 \rightarrow CH_3COOH + CH_3CH_2O^-$$

$$CH_3COOH + CH_3CH_2O^- \xrightarrow{\text{fast}} CH_3CO_2^- + CH_3CH_2OH$$

Predict the rate law for the reaction if the rate constant is given to be 0.1M.

(A) Rate = $0.1[CH_3COO^-][CH_3CO_2OH]$

(B) Rate = $0.1[CH_3\overset{\overset{\textstyle O}{\|}}{C}OCH_2CH_3][OH^-]$

(C) Rate = $0.1[CH_3COO^-][OH^-]$

(D) Rate = $0.1[CH_3CH_2O^-][CH_3COOH]$

(E) Rate = $0.1[OH^-][CH_3COOH]$

53. A 0.10M solution of aqueous ammonia, also containing ammonium chloride, has a hydroxide ion concentration of 3.6×10^{-6}M. What is the concentration of the ammonium ion in the solution if the ionization constant of the following reaction is 1.8×10^{-5}?

$$NH_3 + H_2O \rightleftharpoons NH_4^+ + OH^-$$

(A) 0.50   (D) 0.34

(B) 0.94   (E) 0.74

(C) 0.64

54. Which of the following has the highest boiling point?

(A) CH_3OH

(B) $CH_3CH_2CH_2CH_2CH_3$

(C) $CH_3CH_2\overset{\overset{\textstyle OH}{|}}{C}HCH_3$

(D) $CH_3CH_2(CH_3)OH$

(E) $CH_3(CH_2)_4OH$

55. In a Born-Haber cycle, the total energy involved in the preceding hypothetical preparation of NaCl is equal to the experimentally determined heat of formation (Q) of the compound from its elements. Which of the following thermochemical values is not used to calculate the total energy of formation of NaCl?

(1) Heat of fusion and vaporization (S)

(2) Dissociation energy of molecular chlorine (D)

(3) Ionization energy of sodium atom (I)

(4) Electron affinity of chlorine atom (E)

(5) Lattice energy of NaCl (U)

(A) (1) and (2)   (D) (1), (2), (3), and (5)

(B) (2), (3), and (5)   (E) All of the above

(C) (1), (2), (3), and (4)

56. Which of the following ions can act as both a Brønsted acid and base in water?

(A) HCO_3^- (D) CN^-

(B) SO_4^{2-} (E) PO_4^{3-}

(C) NO_3^-

57. Which of the following represents the equation of standing waves?

    (A) $\psi(x) = A\sin(2\pi x/\lambda) - B\cos(2\pi x/\lambda)$
    (B) $\psi(x) = A\sin(2\pi x/\lambda) + B\cos(2\pi x/\lambda)$
    (C) $\psi(x) = A\cos(n\pi x/L)$
    (D) $\psi(x) = B\cos(n\pi x/L)$
    (E) $\psi(x) = A\sin(2\pi x/L)$

58. Calculate ΔS^0_{298} for the reaction below.

    $$2H_2(g) + O_2(g) \rightarrow 2H_2O(l)$$

    Given that $S^0_{H_2}(g) = 31.21$ eu, $S^0_{O_2}(g) = 49.00$ eu, and $S^0_{H_2O}(l) = 16.72$ eu

    (A) $+122.86$ eu   (D) -77.98 eu
    (B) -122.86 eu   (E) -63.49 eu
    (C) -33.44 eu

59. Which of the following oxidizing titrants would most likely be used as its own indicator in acid solution?

    (A) H_2O_2 (D) $KMnO_4$
    (B) $(NH_4)_2Ce(NO_3)_6$ (E) I_2
    (C) $K_2Cr_2O_7$

60. If the ionization energy for an electron in the first quantum state of a hydrogen atom is 13.6 eV, what is the ionization energy for an electron in the second quantum state?

    (A) $(13.6/e)$eV   (D) $3(13.6)$eV
    (B) $(13.6/4)$eV   (E) $(13.6/2)$eV
    (C) $2(13.6)$eV

61. Calculate the ionic strength of a 0.01M barium chloride solution.

    (A) 0.03   (D) 0.02
    (B) 0.04   (E) 0.005
    (C) 0.01

62. A compound $C_4H_7Cl_3$ has the following ^{1}HNMR spectrum: δ, ppm: 0.9(t,3H); 1.7(m, 2H); 4.3(m, 1H); 5.8(d, 1H). Which of the following compounds represents the above?

    (A) $CH_3 - CCl_2 - CH_2 - CH_2Cl$
    (B) $CH_3 - CH_2 - CHCl - CH_2Cl_2$
    (C) $CH_3CH_2 - CCl_2 - CH_2Cl$
    (D) $CH_3 - CHCl - CH_2 - CHCl_2$
    (E) $CH_2Cl - CH_2 - CHCl - CH_2Cl$

63. Which of the following will *not* show cis-trans isomerism?

(A)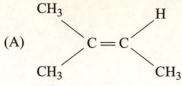

(B)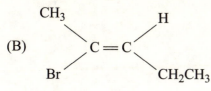

(C)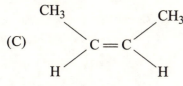

(D)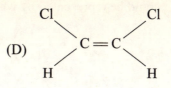

(E)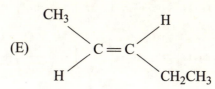

64. Which of the following is the strongest oxyacid?

(A) $HClO_4$
(B) $HClO_3$
(C) $HClO_2$

(D) $HOCl$
(E) ClO^-

65. The activation energy of a reaction can be determined from the slope of which of the following graphs?

(A) $\ln K$ versus T

(B) $\dfrac{\ln K}{T}$ versus T

(C) $\ln K$ versus $\dfrac{1}{T}$

(D) $\dfrac{T}{\ln K}$ versus $\dfrac{1}{T}$

(E) $\dfrac{\ln K}{T}$ versus $\dfrac{1}{T}$

66.

[X]	[Y]	rate
1.0	1.0	0.01
1.0	2.0	0.02
3.0	1.0	0.09

The rate data for the net reaction $X + Y \rightarrow Z$ was obtained at 25°C. The initial rate of increase in [Z] is

(A) second order in both X and Y
(B) first order in X and second order in Y
(C) second order in X and zero order in Y
(D) second order in X and first order in Y
(E) first order in both X and Y

67. By the linear combination of atomic orbitals, the Hamiltonian for the electronic and nuclear repulsion energies of H_2^+ could be represented by which of the following?

(A) $\hat{H}(r_A, r_B, r_1) = \frac{1}{2}\bar{V}_1^2 - \left(\frac{1}{r_{A_1}}\right) - \left(\frac{1}{r_{B_1}}\right) + \frac{1}{R}$

(B) $\hat{H}(r_A, r_B, r_1) = \frac{1}{2}\bar{V}_1^2 - \left(\frac{1}{r_{A_1}}\right) + \left(\frac{1}{r_{B_1}}\right) - \frac{1}{R}$

(C) $\hat{H}(r_A, r_B, r_1) = \frac{1}{2}\bar{V}_1^2 + \left(\frac{1}{r_{A_1}}\right) - \left(\frac{1}{r_{B_1}}\right) + \frac{1}{R}$

(D) $\hat{H}(r_A, r_B, r_1) = \frac{1}{2}\bar{V}_1^2 + \left(\frac{1}{r_{A_1}}\right) + \left(\frac{1}{r_{B_1}}\right) + \frac{1}{R}$

(E) $\hat{H}(r_A, r_B, r_1) = \frac{1}{2}\bar{V}_1^2 - \left(\frac{1}{r_{A_1}}\right) - \left(\frac{1}{r_{B_1}}\right) - \frac{1}{R}$

68. A solution contains the following ions: Ag^+, Hg^{2+}, Al^{3+}, Cd^{2+}, Sr^{2+}. The addition of dilute HCl will precipitate

(A) Ag chloride only
(B) Al and Cd chlorides
(C) Ag, Cd, and Sr chlorides
(D) Al and Sr chlorides
(E) Ag and Hg chlorides

69. Consider the reaction $2N_2O_5 \rightarrow 4NO_2 + O_2$. What is the order of this reaction from the following straight-line plot?

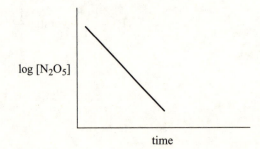

(A) third
(B) fourth
(C) first
(D) zeroth
(E) second

70. Which of the following ions shows no resonance stabilization?

(A) RCO_2^-

(B) $\underset{\displaystyle R}{R_2C = C - O^-}$

(C) CO_3^{2-}

(D) $(CH_3)_3C^+$

(E) $CH_2 = CH - C^+H_2$

71. Which of the following reactions of alkenes is incomplete?

(A) 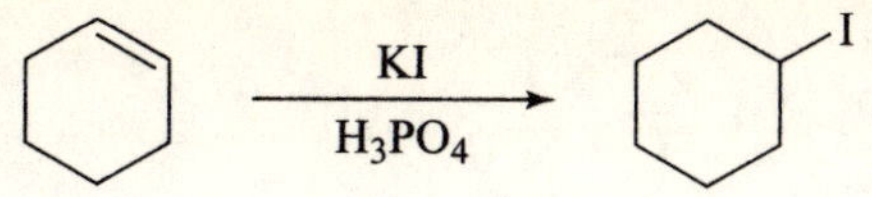 [cyclohexene] $\xrightarrow[\text{H}_3\text{PO}_4]{\text{KI}}$ [cyclohexane with I]

(B) 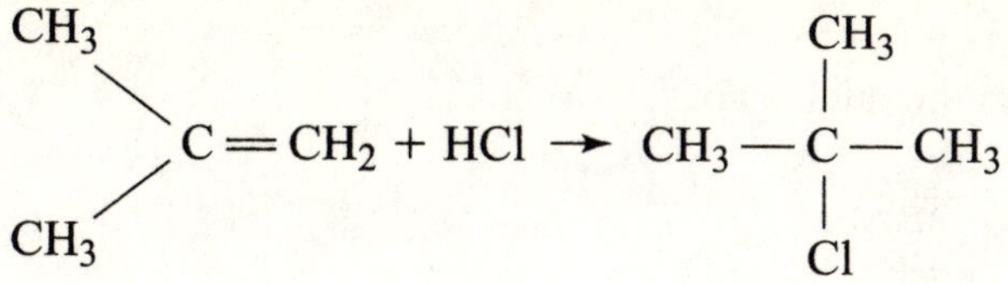 $(CH_3)_2C=CH_2 + HCl \rightarrow CH_3-C(CH_3)(Cl)-CH_3$

(C) $CH_3CH_2CH=CHCH_3 + HBr \rightarrow CH_3CH_2CH(Br)CH_2CH_3$

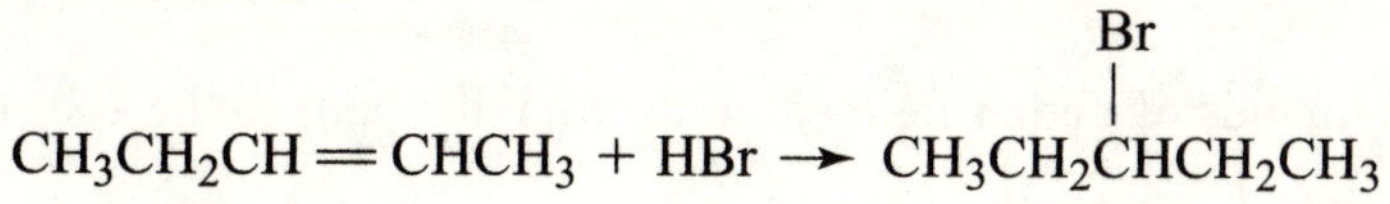

(D) 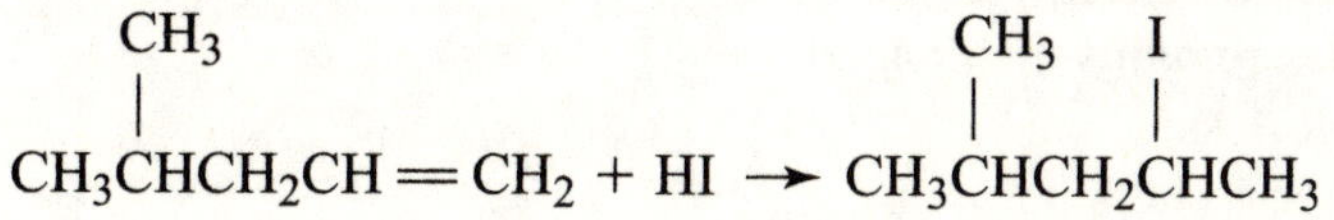 $CH_3CH(CH_3)CH_2CH=CH_2 + HI \rightarrow CH_3CH(CH_3)CH_2CH(I)CH_3$

(E) 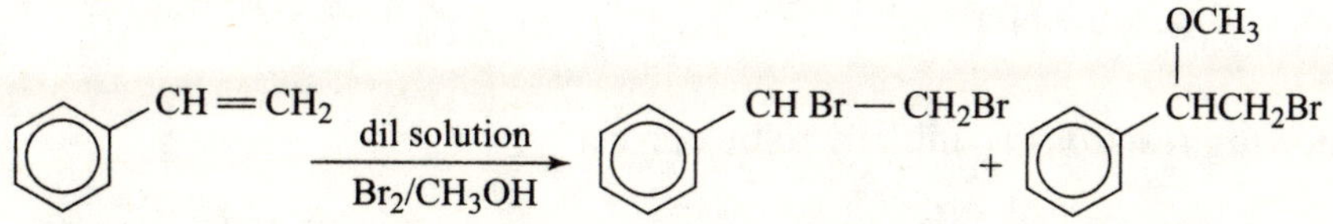 [benzene]$CH=CH_2$ $\xrightarrow[\text{Br}_2/\text{CH}_3\text{OH}]{\text{dil solution}}$ [benzene]$CHBr-CH_2Br$ + [benzene]$CH(OCH_3)CH_2Br$

72. Which of the following free radicals is most stable?

(A) CH_3
(B) $(CH_3)_3C$
(C) C_2H_5
(D) $(CH_3)_2CH$
(E) $(CH_3)_2CHCH_2$

73. The gas that will liquefy with the most difficulty is

(A) He
(B) CO_2
(C) NH_3
(D) SO_2
(E) H_2O

74. Treating benzaldehyde with acetone in 20% NaOH at 100°C gives which compound as the main product?

(A) 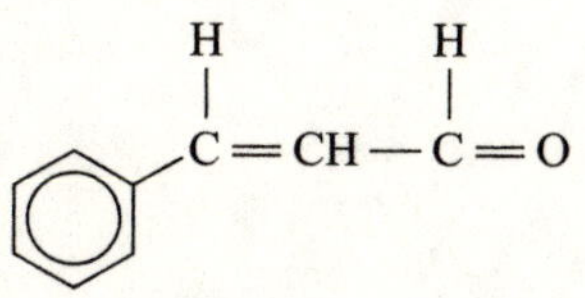 [benzene]$C(H)=CH-C(H)=O$

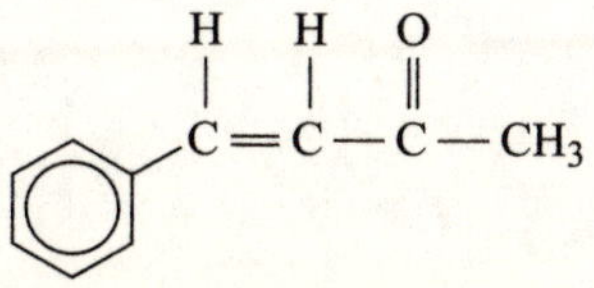

(B) [benzene]$C(H)=C(H)-C(=O)-CH_3$

(C) $CH_3-C(CH_3)=C(H)-C(=O)-CH_3$

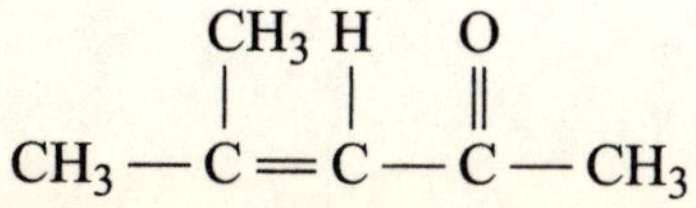

(D) 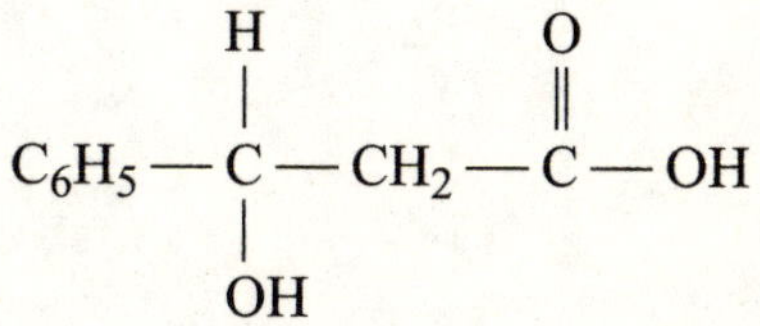 $C_6H_5-C(H)(OH)-CH_2-C(=O)-OH$

(E) 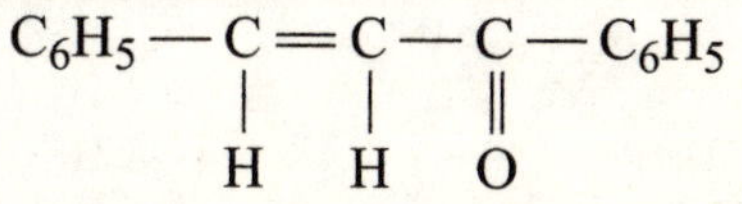 $C_6H_5-C(H)=C(H)-C(=O)-C_6H_5$

75. What is the potential of a half cell consisting of a platinum wire dipped into a solution 0.01M in Sn^{2+} and 0.001M in Sn^{4+} at 25°C?

(A) $E^0_{oxid.} + 0.059$

(B) $E^0_{red} - 0.059/2$

(C) $E^0_{red} + 0.059/2$

(D) $E^0_{oxid.} - 0.059$

(E) E^0_{red}

76. The emission of an alpha particle from the nucleus of $^{226}_{88}Ra$ will yield

(A) $^{223}_{86}Rn$

(B) $^{222}_{86}Rn$

(C) $^{223}_{87}Fr$

(D) $^{222}_{87}Fr$

(E) $^{222}_{88}Ra$

77. If Mn^{2+} ion is coordinated to ligands of higher field strength, what happens to the complex?

(A) Electrons are forced into higher energy (e_g) level.
(B) The stability of the complex remains unchanged.
(C) The complex would be colorless.
(D) The complex will become less stable.
(E) The complex will become more stable.

78. Which of the following reactions is unlikely to be correct?

(A)

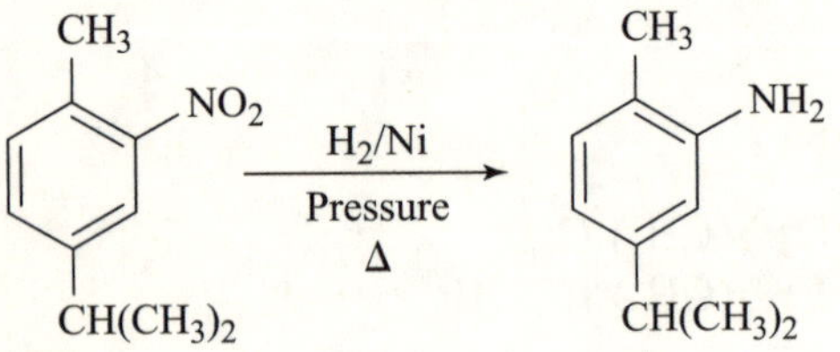

(B)

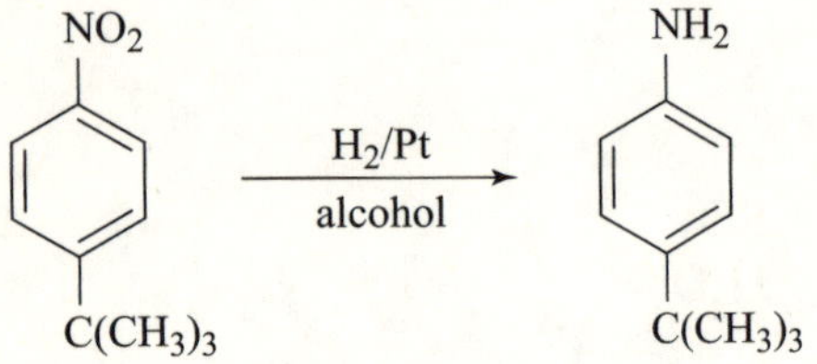

(C)

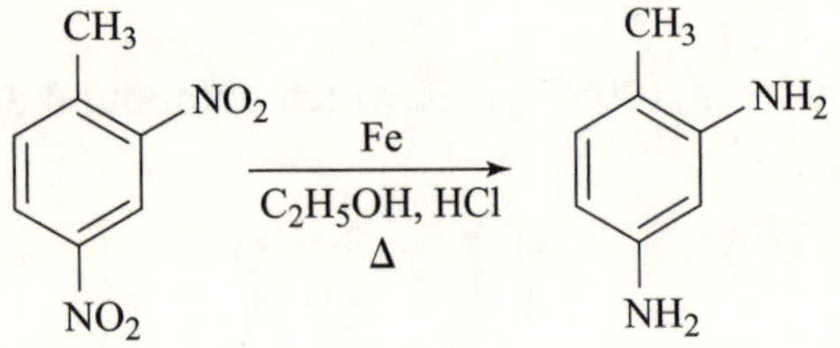

(D)

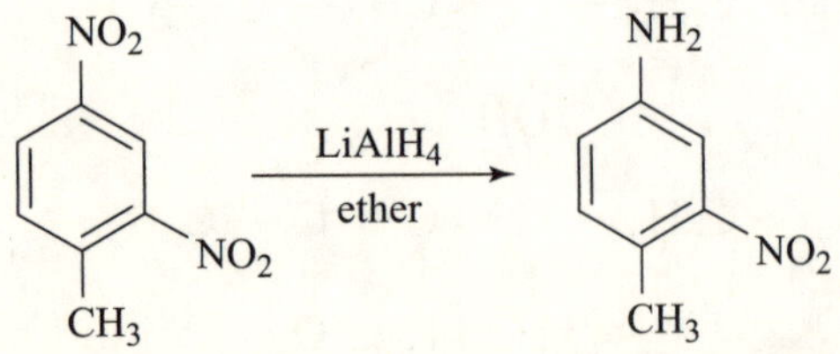

(E)

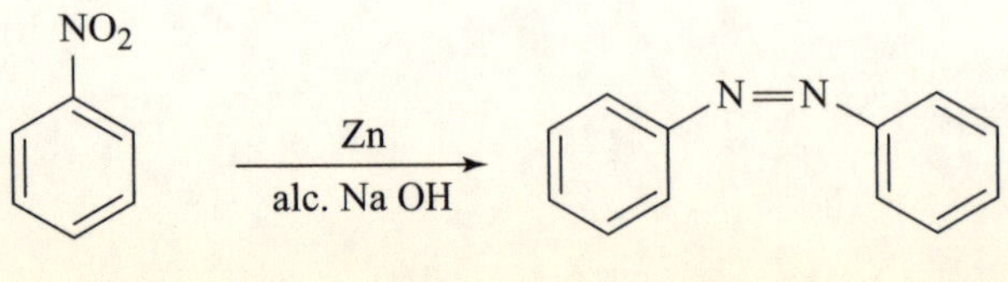

79. Which of the following functional groups is not ortho, para directing, and activating?

   (A) R
   (B) NH_2
   (C) NR_2

   (D) OH
   (E) COR

80. Gabriel's synthesis is used frequently in the preparation of which of the following?

   (A) Primary amines
   (B) Tertiary amines
   (C) Primary alcohols

   (D) β-amino carboxylic acids
   (E) Azide compounds

81. Consider the following series of reactions:

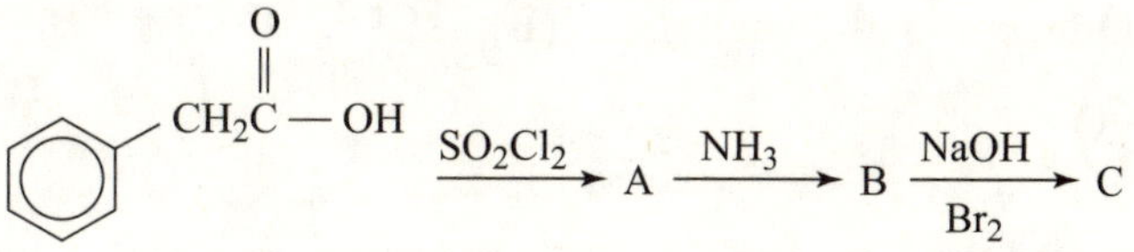

$$\text{C}_6\text{H}_5\text{CH}_2\overset{\overset{\displaystyle O}{\|}}{\text{C}}-\text{OH} \xrightarrow{\text{SO}_2\text{Cl}_2} \text{A} \xrightarrow{\text{NH}_3} \text{B} \xrightarrow[\text{Br}_2]{\text{NaOH}} \text{C}$$

Compound C is:

   (A) acidic
   (B) basic
   (C) bromoketone

   (D) neutral
   (E)

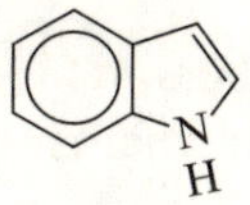

82. Which of the following reactions will *not* take place?

   (A) $CH_3C \equiv C - CH_3 + H_2 \xrightarrow{\text{Pd}}$

   (B) $CH_3C \equiv CH + H_2O \xrightarrow[\text{HgSO}_4]{\text{H}_2\text{SO}_4}$

   (C) $CH_3 - C \equiv C - C_2H_5 + CH_3MgBr \longrightarrow$

   (D) $CH_3 - C \equiv C - CH_3 + (1)B_2H_6(2) \xrightarrow[0°C]{\text{CH}_3\text{COOH}}$

   (E) $CH - C \equiv CH + (1)[(CH_3)_2CHCH]_2 \ \underset{\underset{\displaystyle CH_3}{|}}{\quad} \ BH(2) \xrightarrow[\text{OH}^-]{\text{H}_2\text{O}_2}$

83. The orbitals providing the most efficient overlap are

   (A) $s - s$
   (B) $p - p$
   (C) $sp - sp$

   (D) $sp^2 - sp^2$
   (E) $sp^3 - sp^3$

84. What is the bond order of F_2 according to the molecular orbital theory?

(A) 1   (C) 4   (E) $2\frac{1}{2}$

(B) 2   (D) 3

85. Layers of carbon atoms in graphite are held together by

(A) Van der Waals forces   (D) covalent bonds

(B) free electrons   (E) coordinate covalent bonds

(C) double bonds

86. Which of the following is bent?

(A) $H - C \equiv C - H$

(B) $\ddot{:}\ddot{O} = C = \ddot{O}\ddot{:}$

(C) $[:\ddot{O} = N = \ddot{O}:]^{+}$

(D) $[:\ddot{O} = N - \ddot{O}:]^{-}$

(E) $:\ddot{C}l - Be - \ddot{C}l:$

87. One would expect to find the term *isotactic* used in conjunction with which of the following?

(A) Crystals   (C) Textiles   (E) Plastics

(B) Dyes   (D) Metals

88. There are three quantum numbers, n, l, and m (all integers), characterizing each solution of the Schrodinger equation. If n = 3, what is the range of possible values for m?

(A) 0   (C) ± 2 (E) Any positive number from 0 to (n − 1)

(B) $\pm\frac{1}{2}$ (D) ± 3

89. For the reaction $A + C \rightarrow C$ the change in [A] with time is shown in the graph below. What is the rate law for this reaction?

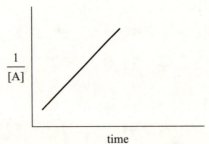

(A) $\dfrac{-d[A]}{dt} - K[A]$

(B) $\dfrac{-d[A]}{dt} - K[A]^2$

(C) $\dfrac{-d[A]}{dt} - K[A]^2[B]$

(D) $\dfrac{-d[A]}{dt} - K[A][B]$

(E) $\dfrac{-d[A]}{dt} - K[A][B]^2$

90. A device in which incident radiation is converted to electric current is called

    (A) a phototube
    (B) a voltaic cell
    (C) an amplifer

    (D) an ammeter
    (E) None of the above

91. In the quantum theory, which of the following tells us that the predictions of quantum mechanics must pass smoothly into those of classical mechanics whenever we progress in a continuous way from the microscopic to the macroscopic?

    (A) Correspondence principle
    (B) Uncertainty principle
    (C) Probability distribution
    (D) Probability density theory
    (E) Electronic configuration theory

92. Which of the following reactions will *not* yield (completely) a carboxylic acid?

    (A) $CH_3(CH_2)_9CN + 2H_2O \xrightarrow[C_2H_5OH]{KOH} \xrightarrow{HCl}$

    (B) $CH_3CH_2CHClCH_3 + Mg \xrightarrow[CO_2]{ether}$

    (C) 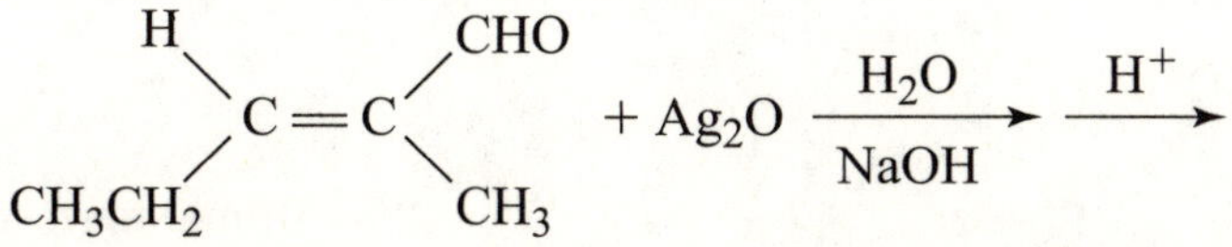
$$\begin{array}{c} H \\ \diagdown \\ C = C \\ \diagup \\ CH_3CH_2 \end{array} \begin{array}{c} CHO \\ \diagup \\ \diagdown \\ CH_3 \end{array} + Ag_2O \xrightarrow[NaOH]{H_2O} \xrightarrow{H^+}$$

    (D)
$$CH_3(CH_2)_3CHCHO + KMnO_4 \xrightarrow[NaOH]{H_2O} \xrightarrow{H_2SO_4}$$
$$\qquad\qquad |$$
$$\qquad\quad CH_2CH_3$$

    (E) 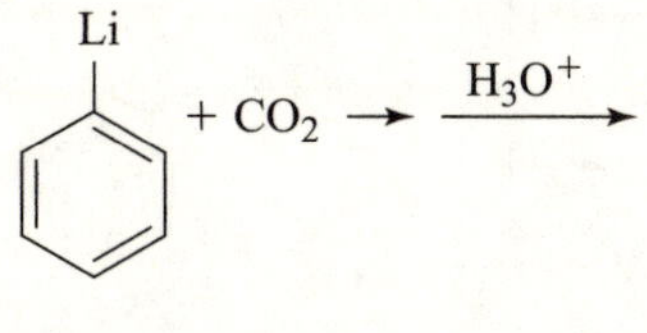
    $+ CO_2 \rightarrow \xrightarrow{H_3O^+}$

93. The system $CaCO_3:CaO:CO_2$ has

    (A) 3 components, 1 phase, and 2 degrees of freedom
    (B) 2 components, 2 phases, and 1 degree of freedom
    (C) 3 components, 3 phases, and zero degree of freedom
    (D) 3 components, 2 phases, and 3 degrees of freedom
    (E) 2 components, 3 phases, and 1 degree of freedom

94. A cyclic ester is called a

    (A) lactone
    (B) semicarbazone
    (C) lactose

    (D) diglyme
    (E) dioxane

95. Periodic acid oxidation of D-glucose in aqueous solution gives

    (A)
    $$4 \, H-\overset{\displaystyle O}{\overset{\|}{C}}-OH + 2 \, H_2C=O$$

    (B)
    $$4 \, H_2C=O + 2 \, H\overset{\displaystyle O}{\overset{\|}{C}}-OH$$

    (C)
    $$CO_2 + 5 \, H\overset{\displaystyle O}{\overset{\|}{C}}-OH$$

    (D)
    $$5 \, H-\overset{\displaystyle O}{\overset{\|}{C}}-OH + H_2C=O$$

    (E)
    $$5 \, H_2C=O + H-\overset{\displaystyle O}{\overset{\|}{C}}-OH$$

96. Consider the following Fisher projections:

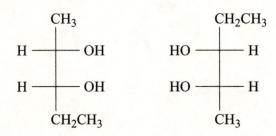

    These compounds are

    (A) identical
    (B) enantiomers
    (C) diastereomers

    (D) stereoselective
    (E) meso

97. Which of the following structures does not represent an optically active compound?

(A)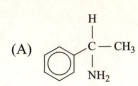

(D)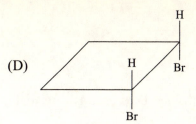

(B)

(E)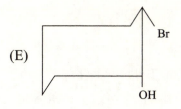

(C)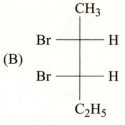

98. Which of the following nuclear reactions is *incorrect*?

(A) $^{14}_{7}N + ^{4}_{2}He \rightarrow ^{17}_{8}O + ^{1}_{1}H$ (D) $^{3}_{1}H \rightarrow ^{3}_{2}He + ^{0}_{-1}e$

(B) $^{9}_{4}Be + ^{4}_{2}He \rightarrow ^{12}_{6}C + ^{1}_{0}n$ (E) None of the above

(C) $^{30}_{15}P \rightarrow ^{30}_{14}Si + ^{0}_{+1}B$

99. Brass is an alloy of

(A) copper and tin   (D) aluminum and copper
(B) copper and zinc   (E) lead and tin
(C) aluminium and nickel

100. The structure of ClO_3F is closest to:

(A) tetrahedral   (D) trigonal-bipyramidal
(B) trigonal-planar   (E) linear
(C) square-planar

101. In a trigonal-bipyramidal crystal field, the d orbitals of a metal will be split into

(A) six levels   (D) three levels
(B) five levels   (E) two levels
(C) four levels

102. The least polarized anion is

(A) SO_4^{2-}
(B) IO_4^-
(C) ClO_4^-

(D) $C_2O_4^{2-}$
(E) NO_3^-

103. A compound that has been used as a rocket fuel is

(A) NH_2OH
(B) NH_2NH_2
(C) N_2F_2

(D) NO_2
(E) NF_3

104. The weakness in the Bohr model of an atom is

(A) the electron was treated as a wave rather than a particle
(B) the model worked only for hydrogen atom
(C) the neutron was not considered
(D) it neglected the radiation emitted by accelerating charged bodies
(E) None of the above

105. The most basic species among the following is

(A) H_2O
(B) CH_3^-
(C) NH_2^-

(D) OH^-
(E) F^-

106. The height to which a liquid will rise in an open capillary tube is inversely proportional to:

(A) temperature of liquid
(B) density of liquid
(C) air pressure

(D) surface tension
(E) viscosity of the liquid

107. Calculate $\Delta H°$ for the reaction

$$2Ag_2S(s) + 2H_2O(l) \rightarrow 4Ag(s) + 2H_2S(g) + O_2(g)$$

if $\Delta H°_{H_2S(g)} = -20.6$ kJ/mol, $\Delta H°_{Ag_2S(s)} = -32.6$ kJ/mol, $\Delta H°_{H_2O(l)} = -285.8$ kJ/mol

(A) 595.6 kJ
(B) 495.6 kJ
(C) 585.6 kJ

(D) 485.6 kJ
(E) 600 kJ

108. How long will it take for a sample of radioactive material to disintegrate to the extent that only 2% of the original concentration remains if the material has a half-life of 5.2 years? Note that $\ln(C_o/C) = kt$.

(A) $\dfrac{\ln 2}{\ln(5.2)}$

(D) $\dfrac{(\log 50)(5.2)}{(\log 2)(2.303)}$

(B) $\left(\dfrac{\ln 50}{\ln 2}\right) 5.2$

(E) $\left(\dfrac{\ln(0.02)}{\ln 2}\right) 5.2$

(C) $(\ln 0.02)(5.2)$

109. Which of the following cations has the highest mobility?

(A) Be^{2+}

(D) H^+

(B) Mg^{2+}

(E) Ca^{2+}

(C) Rb^+

110. The first scientist to publish on the periodic table was

(A) Moseley

(D) Dalton

(B) Fisher

(E) Gay-Lussac

(C) Mendeleev

111. Which of the following compounds has the highest melting point?

(A) NaCl

(D) CsCl

(B) KCl

(E) CsBr

(C) RbCl

112. What is the IUPAC name of the compound 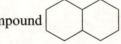 ?

(A) (5.5.1)-bicyclodecane

(D) (5.5.0)-bicyclodecane

(B) (4.4.1)-bicyclodecane

(E) (5.4.1)-bicyclodecane

(C) (4.4.0)-bicyclodecane

113. What is the heat flow under isobaric conditions for a chemical reaction performed in a "solution" calorimeter?

(A) $\Delta H = \Delta E + \Delta(Pv) = \Delta E + W$

(B) $\Delta E = \Delta H - \Delta(Pv) = \Delta H - RT\Delta n$

(C) $\displaystyle\int_{P_1}^{P_2} v dP = nRT \ln\frac{P_1}{P_2} = nRT \ln\frac{v_2}{v_1}$

(D) $q = W \displaystyle\int_{v_1}^{v_2} P dv = P\Delta v = P(v_2 - v_1)$

(E) $\Delta H = \Delta E = q_v$

114. Work can be defined as the product of an intensity factor (force, pressure, etc.) and a capacity factor (distance, electrical charge, etc.). Which of the following expressions for thermodynamic work (below), is *incorrectly* defined?

   (A) Mechanical work $d_w = fdl$
   (B) Surface work $dw = \gamma dA$
   (C) Electrical work $dw = \varepsilon dl$
   (D) Gravitational work $dw = mgdl$
   (E) None of the above

115. Which of the following Maxwell relations is *incorrect*?

   (A) $dE = Tds - Pdv$
   (B) $dH = Tds + vdP$
   (C) $dG = -SdT + vdP$
   (D) $dA = -SdT - Pdv$
   (E) None of the above

116. Ethanol boils at 78.5°C. If 34.2g of sucrose (M · W = 342) is dissolved in 200g of ethanol, at what temperature will the solution boil? (Assume K_b = 1.20°C/m for the alcohol.)

   (A) 79.1°C
   (B) 77.9°C
   (C) 0.60°C
   (D) 78.56°C
   (E) 84.5°C

117. 2.3g of ethcnol (C_2H_5OH, M · wt = 46g/mole) is added to 500g of water. Determine the molality of the resulting solution.

   (A) 0.01 molal
   (B) 0.1 molal
   (C) 1.0 molal
   (D) 10.0 molal
   (E) 1.1 molal

118. The molecular weight of nicotine, a colorless oil, is 162.1, and it contains 74.0% carbon, 8.7% hydrogen, and 17.3% nitrogen. Calculate the molecular formula of nicotine.

   (A) C_5H_7N
   (B) $C_{30}H_{14}N_2$
   (C) $C_{20}H_{28}N_4$
   (D) $C_4H_{14}N$
   (E) $C_8H_{28}N_2$

119. Which of the following electrophilic aromatic substitution(s) is (are) correct?

(A) (1) and (3) only

(B) (2) and (4) only

(C) (1), (2), and (3) only

(D) (1), (2), and (4) only

(E) (1), (2), (3), and (4)

120. A chemist dissolves an excess of $BaSO_4$ in pure water at 25°C. If its $K_{Sp} = 1 \times 10^{-10}$, what is the concentration of the barium in the water?

(A) $10^{-4}M$

(B) $10^{-5}M$

(C) $10^{-6}M$

(D) $10^{-10}M$

(E) $10^{-20}M$

121. Determine the K_{Sp} of MX_2 if a saturated solution contains .02mole/100 ml of water.

(A) .20

(B) .0034

(C) .08

(D) .032

(E) .016

122. Calculate the e.m.f. of a cell with the given standard electrodes: Cu; $Cu^{2+}\|Ag^+$; Ag [use the table below].

Half reaction	Standard reduction potential, v
$e^- + Ag^+ \rightarrow Ag(s)$	$+0.80$
$2e^- + Cu^{2+} \rightarrow Cu(s)$	$+0.34$

(A) $-4.6v$

(B) $-0.46v$

(C) $+0.46v$

(D) $+1.14v$

(E) $-1.14v$

123. Which of the following is *true* for the behavior of lysine during electrophoresis? (Note for lysine $pK_1 = 2.16$, $pK_2 = 9.20$, $pK_2 = 10.80$.)

(A) Lysine will migrate toward the negative electrode in a buffer of pH = 10.0.

(B) Lysine will migrate toward the positive electrode in a buffer of pH = 10.0.

(C) Lysine will not migrate in a buffer of pH = 10.0.

(D) Lysine will not migrate in a buffer of pH = 2.00.

(E) Lysine will migrate toward the positive electrode in a buffer of pH = 3.00.

124. Calculate the wave number ($\overline{v}$) of a photon emitted by a hydrogen atom with an electronic transition from the tenth to the fifth electronic energy level. (Note $R_H = 1.1 \times 10^5 cm^{-1}$.)

(A) $1.3 \times 10^5 cm^{-1}$

(B) $3.3 \times 10^7 cm^{-1}$

(C) $3.3 \times 10^3 cm^{-1}$

(D) $3.3 \times 10^{-5} cm^{-1}$

(E) $2.3 \times 10^5 cm^{-1}$

125. The four dissociation constants of the acid (edta)(H_4Y) are as follows:

$$H_4Y + H_2O \rightleftharpoons H_3O^+ + H_3Y^-; \quad K_{a1} = 1.02 \times 10^{-2}$$

$$H_3Y^- + H_2O \rightleftharpoons H_3O^+ + H_2Y^{2-}; \quad K_{a2} = 2.14 \times 10^{-3}$$

$$H_2Y^{2-} + H_2O \rightleftharpoons H_3O^+ + HY^{3-}; \quad K_{a3} = 6.92 \times 10^{-7}$$

$$HY^{3-} + H_2O \rightleftharpoons H_3O^+ + Y^{4-}; \quad K_{a4} = 5.50 \times 10^{-11}$$

Determine the expression for the total concentration of the edta.

(A) $C_Y = [Y^{4-}] + [HY^{3-}] + [H_2Y^{2-}] + [H_3Y^-] + [H_4Y]$

(B) $C_Y = [HY^{3-}] + [H_2Y^{2-}] + [H_3Y^-] + [H_4Y]$

(C) $C_Y = [Y^{4-}] + [HY^{3-}] + [H_2Y^{2-}] + [H_3Y^-]$

(D) $C_Y = [y^{4-}] + [Hy^{3-}] + [H_2y^{2-}] + [H_3Y^-] + [H_3O^+]$

(E) $C_Y = [Y^{4-}] + [HY^{3-}] + [H_2Y^{2-}] + [H_3Y^-] + [H_4]$

126. The fraction of edta in the Y^{4-} form can be expressed in terms of the dissociation constants of the various species above (in question 125) as

(A) $[Y^{4-}]/C_Y = [K_{a1} + K_{a2} + K_{a3} + K_{a4}]/[H_3O^+]^4 + [H_3O^+]^3 K_{a1} + [H_3O^+]^2 K_{a1} K_{a2} + [H_3O^+] K_{a2} K_{a2} K_{a3} + K_{a1} K_{a2} K_{a3} K_{a4}$

(B) $[Y^{4-}/C_Y = K_{a1} K_{a2} K_{a3} K_{a4}/\{[H_3O^+] + [H_3O^+]^3 K_{a2} + [H_3O^+]^2 K_{a1} K_{a2} + [H_3O^+] K_{a1} K_{a2} K_{a3} + K_{a1} K_{a2} K_{a3} K_{a4}\}$

(C) $[Y^{4-}]/C_Y = K_{a1} K_{a2} + K_{a3} K_{a4}/\{[HY^{3-}] + [H_2Y^{2-}] + [H_3Y^-] + [H_4Y]\}$

(D) $[Y^{4-}]/C_Y = (K_{a1} K_{a2} K_{a3} K_{a4})/\{[Y^{4-}] + [HY^{3-}] + [H_2Y^{2-}] + [H_3Y^-] + [H_4Y]\}$

(E) None of the above

127. Ion exchange chromatography falls into which of the following categories?

(A) Liquid-solid
(B) Gas-solid
(C) Solid-solid

(D) Liquid-liquid
(E) Gas-liquid

128. What is the product of the following reaction?

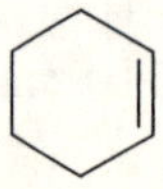

+ cold dilute KMnO$_4$ $\xrightarrow{\text{H}_2\text{O}}$?

(A)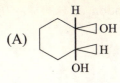

(D)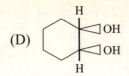

(B)

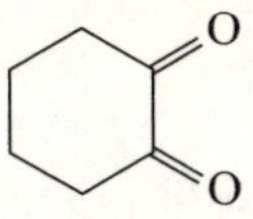

(E)   All of the above

(C)

129. The following reaction is performed at 298°K.

$$2NO(g) + O_2(g) \rightleftharpoons 2NO_2(g)$$

The standard free energy of formation of NO(g) is 86.6 kJ/mole at 298°K. What is the standard free energy of the formation of $NO_2(g)$ at 298°K $K_p = 1.6 \times 10^{12}$?

(A) $R(298)\ln 1.6 \times 10^{12} - 86.6$

(B) $86.6 + R(298)\ln 1.6 \times 10^{12}$

(C) $86.6 - \dfrac{\ln 1.6 \times 10^{12}}{R(298)}$

(D) $86.6 - R(298)\ln 1.6 \times 10^{12}$

(E) $\dfrac{1}{2}[2(86.6) - R(298)\ln(1.6 \times 10^{12})]$

130. Exactly one mole of gaseous methane is oxidized at fixed volume and at 25°C according to the following reaction:

$$CH_4(g) + 2O_2(g) \rightarrow CO_2(g) + 2H_2O(l)$$

If 212 kcal is liberated, what is the change in enthalpy, ΔH?

(A) $-212 - 2R(25)$kcal   (D)   212 kcal

(B) $-212 - 2R(298)$kcal   (E) $212 - 2R(298)$kcal

(C) -212 kcal

131. Calculate the minimum concentration of Br^- ion necessary to bring about precipitation of AgBr from a solution in which the concentration of Ag^+ ion is 1.0×10^{-5} mole per liter (K_{Sp} for AgBr $= 4.0 \times 10^{-13}$).

(A) 4.0×10^{-10}M   (D) 4.0×10^{-11}M

(B) 4.0×10^{-9}M   (E) 4.0×10^{-6}M

(C) 4.0×10^{-8}M

132. If the hydrolysis constant of Al^{3+} is 1.4×10^{-5}, what is the concentration of H_3O^+ in 0.1M $AlCl_3$?

(A) $\sqrt{1.4 \times 10^{-5}M}$ (D) $1.4 \times 10^{-4}M$

(B) $\sqrt{1.4 \times 10^{-4}M}$ (E) None of the above

(C) $\sqrt{1.4 \times 10^{-6}M}$

133. How many moles of Al_2O_3 can be formed when a mixture of 0.36 moles of aluminum and 0.36 moles of oxygen gas is ignited?

(A) 0.72 moles   (D) 0.12 moles

(B) 0.28 moles   (E) 0.46 moles

(C) 0.18 moles

134. Aldehydes may be distinguished from ketones by the use of

(A) Hoffman reagent   (D) Grignard reagent

(B) Tollens' reagent   (E) Cannizzaro reagent

(C) concentrated H_2SO_4

135. What is the maximum weight of SO_3 that can be made from 40.0g of SO_2 and 8.0g of O_2 in the reaction below?

$$2SO_2 + O_2 \rightarrow 2SO_3$$

(A) 40.0g   (D) 20.0g

(B) 31.3g   (E) 52.5g

(C) 25.0g

136. Which of the following reaction(s) involve(s) a protection group?

(1)

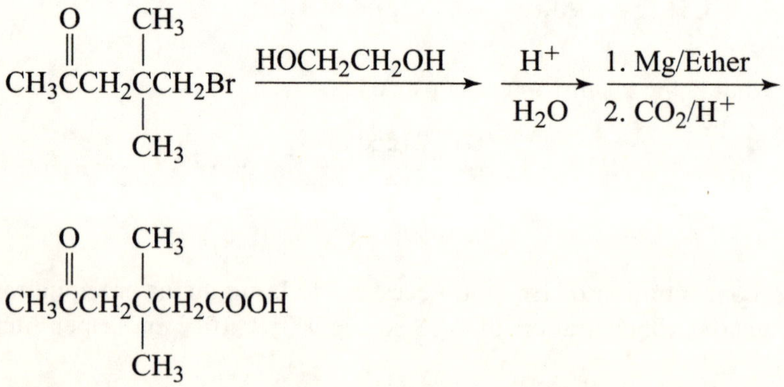

$$CH_3\underset{\|}{\overset{O}{C}}CH_2\underset{\underset{CH_3}{|}}{\overset{\overset{CH_3}{|}}{C}}CH_2Br \xrightarrow[H_2O]{HOCH_2CH_2OH} \xrightarrow[2.\ CO_2/H^+]{H^+ \quad 1.\ Mg/Ether}$$

$$CH_3\underset{\|}{\overset{O}{C}}CH_2\underset{\underset{CH_3}{|}}{\overset{\overset{CH_3}{|}}{C}}CH_2COOH$$

(2)

$$\text{(structure)} \quad OH + (CH_3)_3SiCl \xrightarrow[\text{ether}]{(C_2H_5)_3N \quad CH_3MgBr} \xrightarrow{H_3O^+} + (CH_3)_3SiOH$$

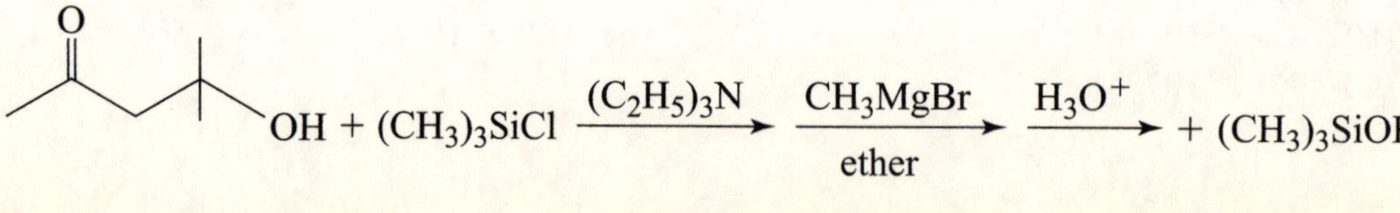

(3)

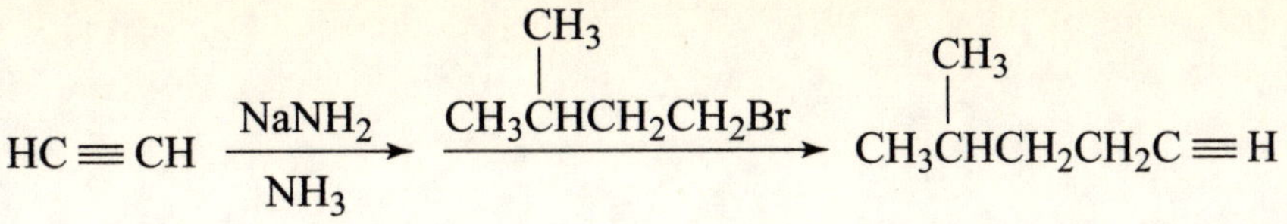

$$HC \equiv CH \xrightarrow[NH_3]{NaNH_2} \underset{\substack{| \\ CH_3}}{CH_3CHCH_2CH_2Br} \longrightarrow \underset{\substack{| \\ CH_3}}{CH_3CHCH_2CH_2C} \equiv H$$

(A) (1) only
(B) (1) and (2) only
(C) (1) and (3) only

(D) (2) and (3) only
(E) All of the above

Answer Key

1. E	24. E	47. A	70. D	93. E	116. A
2. E	25. D	48. C	71. C	94. A	117. B
3. A	26. A	49. A	72. B	95. D	118. B
4. A	27. B	50. D	73. A	96. A	119. E
5. A	28. A	51. E	74. B	97. D	120. B
6. B	29. A	52. B	75. B	98. E	121. D
7. C	30. C	53. A	76. B	99. B	122. C
8. E	31. D	54. E	77. E	100. A	123. C
9. B	32. A	55. E	78. D	101. D	124. C
10. E	33. E	56. A	79. E	102. C	125. A
11. C	34. B	57. B	80. A	103. B	126. B
12. E	35. B	58. D	81. B	104. B	127. A
13. A	36. C	59. D	82. C	105. B	128. D
14. A	37. C	60. B	83. C	106. B	129. E
15. D	38. C	61. A	84. A	107. A	130. B
16. E	39. D	62. B	85. A	108. B	131. C
17. A	40. A	63. A	86. D	109. D	132. C
18. D	41. B	64. A	87. E	110. C	133. C
19. A	42. E	65. C	88. C	111. A	134. B
20. C	43. C	66. D	89. B	112. C	135. A
21. D	44. B	67. A	90. A	113. A	136. B
22. C	45. A	68. E	91. A	114. E	
23. E	46. B	69. C	92. B	115. E	

Practice Exam 1

Detailed Explanations of Answers

1. (E)

To solve this problem, one must know the differences between ionic bonding, which is sometimes called electrovalency, and covalent bonding, called covalency. Electrovalency is the transfer of electrons from one atom to another, which gives rise to ionic bonding, while covalency is the sharing of electrons between two atoms, both of which tend to gain electrons (e.g., nonmetals). In this question, H, Br, Se, Si, F, C (in CH_4), and O are all nonmetals; thus, their combination with each other yields covalent bonds. $Ca \cdot + \cdot \ddot{O}\!: \longrightarrow Ca^{+2} \; :\!\ddot{O}\!:^{2-}$ is not a covalent bond but involves a transfer of electrons, which is termed an ionic bond.

2. (E)

Transition elements occur between calcium and gallium. They are all metals, their ions are mostly colored and they mostly form complexes, e.g., $CuCl_2^-$, $NiCl_4^{2-}$, $CO(NH_3)_6^{3+}$. Beryllium is not a transition element, but rather a neighbor of the transition elements.

3. (A)

A Lewis acid, called an electrophile, can accept a pair of electrons; a Lewis base, called a nucleophile, can donate a pair of electrons. In this question, it could be easily noted that $:CN^-$, $CH_3 — \ddot{O} — CH_3$, $:NH_3$ and $:\ddot{Br}-$ can each donate a pair of electrons; thus, they are Lewis bases. A Lewis acid is a species that can accept an electron pair. Lewis acids include molecules, such as $AlCl_3$, that have less than an octet around their valence shells.

4. (A)

Ionic character is greatest in a combination between a metal and a nonmetal, e.g., KCl, $MgCl_2$, $CaCl_2$, $BaCl_2$. Carbon is not classified as a metal. It is a hard, brittle, dull, and rather amorphous element. It will have the weakest ionic character because the tendency to produce positive ions decreases rapidly across a period and increases downward within a group.

5. (A)

The best choice is (A) because ionization potential is best described as the energy needed to remove completely the most loosely bound electron from an atom in its ground state. This change may be expressed by

$$X + \text{Energy} \rightarrow X^+ + e^-$$

Choice (B) is wrong because it describes the expression

$$X + e^- \rightarrow X^- + \text{energy}$$

which represents the electron affinity. Choice (C) is also wrong because ionization energy increases from left to right across the period rather than decreases. Finally, choice (D) is incorrect because ionization potential decreases down the rows of the period rather than increases.

6.   (B)

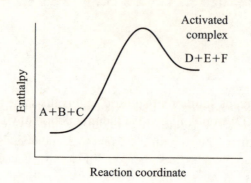

In the above reaction, heat is gained; thus the reaction is endothermic.

7.   (C)

The three basic particles present in an atom are the electrons, protons, and neutrons, with the exception of the hydrogen atom, which contains one proton, one electron, but no neutron.

8.   (E)

The properties of isotopes are represented by all three choices (A), (B), and (C).

9.   (B)

1 mole of chlorine = 0.75 mole of Cl_{17}^{35} + 0.25 mole of Cl_{17}^{37}. Therefore, the atomic weight = 0.75 (35 g/mol) + 0.25 (37 g/mol) = 35.50 g/mol, the atomic weight is the weighted average of the naturally occurring isotopes of that particular element.

10.   (E)

All of the choices are correct.

11.   (C)

Electron affinity is characterized by atoms with unfilled orbitals that gain electrons readily, e.g. nonmetals like F, Cl, Br, I, O and S.

12.   (E)

Gelatinous precipitate, e.g., $Al(OH)_3$, are among the most difficult to filter.

13.   (A)

In the electrolysis of sulfuric acid, the reaction at the anode can be either:

$$2SO_4^{2-} \rightarrow S_2O_8^{2-}$$

or:

$$2H_2O \rightarrow O_2(g) + 4H^+ + 4e^-$$

The reaction at the cathode is

$$2H^+ + 2e^- + H_2$$

The net reaction is the sum of the anode and the cathode reactions, which gives:

$$\text{anode:} \quad 2H_2O \rightarrow O_2 + 4H^+ + 4e^-$$

$$\text{cathode:} \quad 4H^+ + 4e^- \rightarrow 2H_2$$

$$\text{net:} \quad 2H_2O(l) \rightarrow 2H_2(g) + O_2(g)$$

Hence the electrolysis of an aqueous solution of sulfuric acid is the same net reaction as the electrolysis of water. Choices (B), (C) and (D) would all involve the production of Cl_2 gas.

14. (A)

The greater the extent of its ionization in water, the stronger the acid. Thus,

$$HClO_4 + H_2O \rightarrow H_3O^+ + ClO_4^- \text{ (complete in dilute solution)}$$

$HClO_4$ dissociates especially well because of the stability of the ClO_4^- ion. This results from the ability of the ion to delocalize its negative charge over all four oxygen atoms. Though HCl is also considered a strong acid, $HClO_4$ has a higher Ka and a higher dissociation, which makes it the stronger acid.

15. (D)

All of the choices are correct.

16. (E)

$$2KMnO_4 + 16HCl \rightarrow 2KCl + 2MnCl_2 + 8H_2O + 5Cl_2$$

$KMnO_4$ is a stronger oxidizing agent and oxidizes chlorine ion to chlorine gas.

17. (A)

The compound $CH_3CH=CH_2$ has $sp^2 - sp^3$ hybrid orbitals because in CH_3^- there are 4 σ bonds that consist of sp^3 orbitals, while in $-CH=$ there are 3 σ bonds that consist of sp^2 orbitals. ($=CH_2$ also has 3 σ bonds.)

18. (D)

The above compound is called farnesol and is an example of a terpene. Terpenes are built from isoprene units.

An isoprene unit

19. (A)

$$R - \overset{\overset{\displaystyle O}{\|}}{C} - CH_3 \xrightarrow[3OH^-]{3Br_2} R - \overset{\overset{\displaystyle O}{\|}}{C} - CBr_3 \xrightarrow{OH^-} R - \overset{\overset{\displaystyle O}{\|}}{C} - OH$$

$$+ CHBr_3$$
Major product

20. (C)

For the second-order reaction $A + B \rightarrow C$, when (B) is held constant while [A] is doubled, the reaction rate doubles. This means that the rate is directly proportional to [A], so $a = 1$. Then when [A] is held constant and [B] is doubled, the reaction rate increases four times. This means that the rate is proportional to $[B]^2$.

$$\therefore \quad \text{rate} = K[A]^a[B]^b = K[A]^1[B]^2$$

21. (D)

$$2Al(s) + 3Cl_2(g) + 2AlCl_3(s)$$

$$\Delta S° = 2(S°[AlCl_3(s)]) - 2(S°[Al(s)]) - 3(S°[Cl_2(g)])$$

$$= 2 \times 110.7 - 2 \times 28.3 - 3 \times 222.96$$

$$= 221.4 - 56.6 - 668.88 = -504.08$$

22. (C)

Using the fact that the change in Gibbs free energy is related to ΔH and ΔS by the equation

$$\Delta G = \Delta H - T\Delta S$$

$$\therefore T = \frac{\Delta H - \Delta G}{\Delta S}$$

23. (E)

All the four possible choices are implied by Bohr's postulates of the theory of the hydrogen atom.

24. (E)

The ideal gas law is $PV = nRT$.

25. (D)

Choices (1), (2), and (3) each have four equivalent protons and display a single peak. In addition

$$CH_3 - \overset{\overset{\displaystyle CH_3}{|}}{\underset{\underset{\displaystyle CH_3}{|}}{C}} - Br$$

has nine equivalent hydrogens, resulting in a single peak. On the other hand ^{19}F has a spin of $\frac{1}{2}$ and splitting patterns are observed due to spin-spin couplings between protons and ^{19}F nuclei. Thus, FCH_2CH_2F will show peak splitting.

26. (A)

The acid-catalyzed esterification of a carboxylic acid is as follows:

$$\overset{\overset{\displaystyle O}{\|}}{RC}OH + R'OH \xrightarrow{H^+} \overset{\overset{\displaystyle O}{\|}}{RC}OR' + H_2O$$

27. (B)

$$C_6H_5CH = CH_2 \xrightarrow[CH_3OH]{Br_2} \underset{\text{(Minor)}}{C_6H_5CHBr - CH_2Br} + \underset{\text{(Major)}}{C_6H_5\overset{\overset{\displaystyle OCH_3}{|}}{C}HCH_2Br}$$

This is because, in hydroxylic solvents, the solvent itself is nucleophilic and can react in competition with the bromide ion. The relative amounts of dibromide and bromoether produced depend on the concentration. Generally, for dilute solutions, the product is almost exclusively the bromoether.

28. (A)

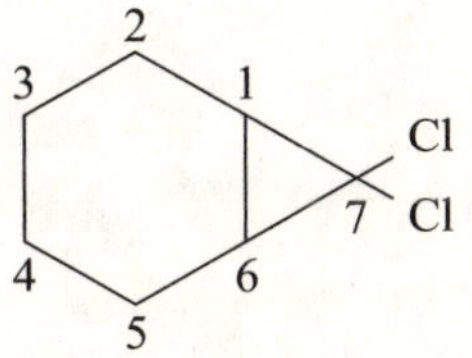

Here the longest arm on each side is 4 and 1, thus the compound is

7,7-dichlorobicyclo[4.1.0]heptane.

29. (A)

$$n-C_4H_9CH=CH_2 \frac{Hg(OOCCH_3)_2}{aq.\ THF} > \frac{NaBH_4}{NaOH} >$$

$$n - C_4H_9\overset{\overset{\displaystyle OH}{|}}{C}HCH_3 + Hg$$

96% 2-hexanol

The product is a secondary alcohol.

30. (C)

An isothermal change involves a system that is maintained at the same temperature throughout an experiment.

31. (D)

A spontaneous reaction is one in which the Gibbs free energy is negative. A negative ΔG can be possible only if ΔH is negative and ΔS is positive.

32. (A)

$$\text{Mole fraction } X_{CH_3OH} = 0.452$$

$$\text{Mole fraction } X_{C_2H_5OH} = 0.260$$

$$\text{Mole fraction } X_{C_3H_7OH} = 0.287$$

Therefore, the volume of 1.00 mole of this solution is

$$0.452(16.0) + 0.260(20) + 0.287(50)$$

33. (E)

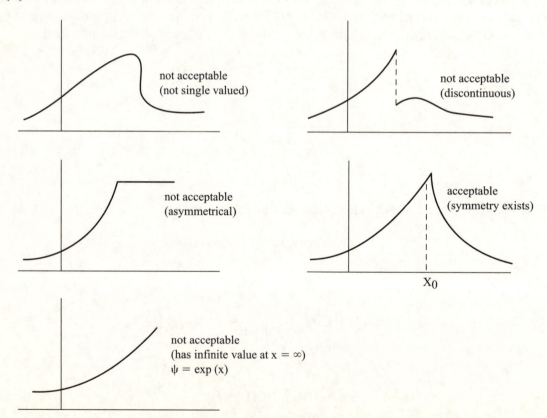

not acceptable
(not single valued)

not acceptable
(discontinuous)

not acceptable
(asymmetrical)

acceptable
(symmetry exists)

X_0

not acceptable
(has infinite value at x = ∞)
$\psi = \exp(x)$

34. (B)

$$t_{\frac{1}{2}} = \frac{\ln 2}{K} = 3 \text{ min. Therefore, } K = \frac{0.693}{3} \text{ min.}^{-1}$$

$$t \ln\left(\frac{[A]_0}{[A]}\right) \times \frac{1}{K} = \ln\left(\frac{1 \text{ mole}}{.25 \text{ mole}}\right) \times \frac{3}{0.693}$$

$$t = \frac{1.39 \times 3}{0.693} \cong 2(3) = 6 \text{ min.}$$

35. (B)

Because pH is defined in terms of hydrogen ion concentration, it is first necessary to find the concentration of this ion by substituting in the ion-product expression for water. The $[OH^-]$ from the NaOH is given as $10^{-4}M$.

$$K_W = [H][OH] \text{ because } K_W = 10^{-14}$$

$$\therefore 10^{-14} = [H^+][10^{-4}], \text{ so } [H^+] = 10^{-14}/10^{-4}$$

$$= 10^{-10}; \text{ because pH} = -\log[H^+]$$

$$\therefore \text{pH} = -\log[10^{-10}] = 10.0$$

The answer closest to 10.0 is 10.2.

36. (C)

This is one of the methods used in the preparation of nitroarenes.

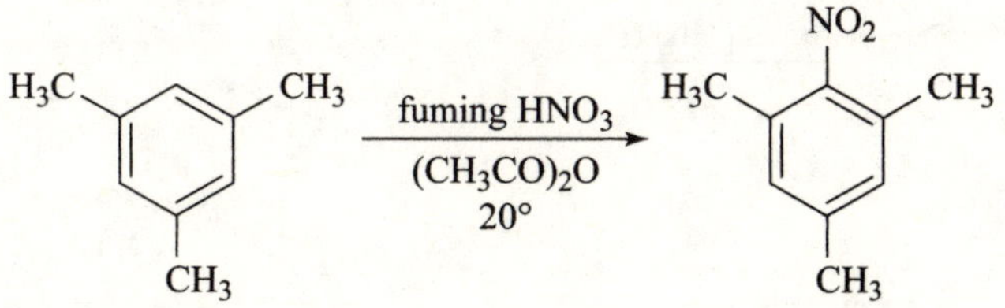

37. (C)

$$\frac{5g \text{ CuO}}{40g \text{ material}} \times \frac{63.55g \text{ Cu}}{79.55g \text{ CuO}} \times \frac{100}{1}$$

38. (C)

$$N = \frac{\text{equivalents of solute}}{\text{liters of solution}} \quad \text{while } M = \frac{\text{moles of solute}}{\text{liters of solution}}$$

It should be evident that 1M solution of HCl is also 1N because a gram-equivalent weight of HCl is the same a the gram-molecular weight. However, a 1M solution of H_2SO_4 is 2N because one mole of H_2SO_4 is equal to two equivalents of H_2SO_4, if both hydrogens react.

e.g. $\quad H_2SO_4 + 2KOH + K_2SO_4 + 2H_2O$

$$\therefore \quad N = \frac{\text{moles of solute}}{\text{liters of solution}} \times \frac{\text{equivalents of solute}}{\text{moles of solute}}$$

$$= M \times \frac{\text{equivalents}}{\text{moles of solute}}$$

$$= \frac{1 \text{ mole of solute}}{1 \text{ liter of solution}} \times \frac{2 \text{ equivalents } H_2SO_4}{1 \text{ mole of solute}}$$

$$= \frac{2 \text{ equivalents}}{\text{liter of solution}}$$

39. (D)

The reaction is known only as aldol condensation. The term *aldol* is used both as a trivial name for 3-hydroxybutanol and as a generic name for β-hydroxyaldehydes and ketones in general.

40. (A)

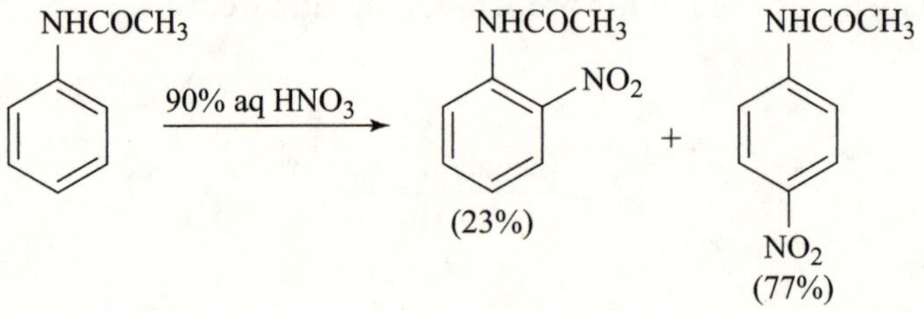

41. (B)

The reaction is

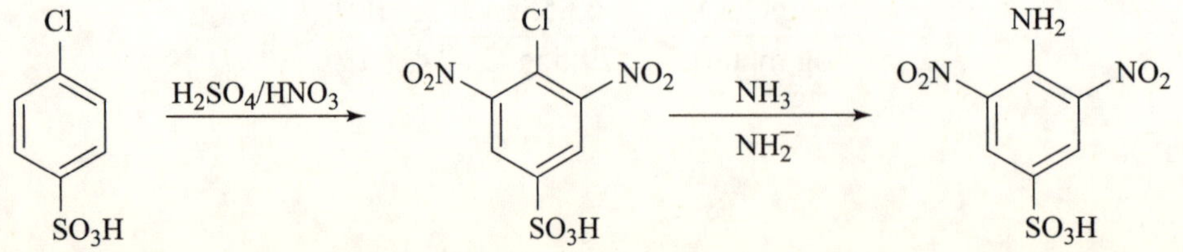

42. (E)

A carboxylic acid is more acidic than the alcohols.

43. (C)

The solve this problem we apply the $4n + 2$ Hückel rule. (A) consists of a 12 electron system that does not satisfy the $4n + 2$ rule because no integral value of n can give us 12. The same applies to all of the other choices except answer choice (C), which consists of a 6 electron system. For $n = 1$, $4n + 2 = 6$.

44. (B)

This shows the simplest acid-base neutralization reactions, which is typical for titrations involving a strong acid and a strong base. From the plot we can see that only a strong base would neutralize an acid with pH of 1 to pH of 13. Choices (D) and (E) are weak bases and choices (A) and (C) are acids.

45. (A)

$$NH_3(aq) + H_2O \rightleftharpoons NH_4^+ + OH^-(aq)$$

We use the formula

$$K_i = \frac{[NH_4^+][OH^-]}{[NH_3]} = \frac{(10^{-4})(0.18)}{(1)} = 1.8 \times 10^{-5}$$

46. (B)

Polarimeter is an instrument used to measure the optical activity of enantiomeric compounds.

47. (A)

The best approach to solve this problem is to first write out the equations of the reactions.

$$AgNO_3 + Kl \rightarrow KNO_3 + Agl \downarrow$$

$$AgNO_3 + KBr \rightarrow KNO_3 + AgBr \downarrow$$

$$AgNO_3 + KCl \rightarrow KNO_3 + AgCl \downarrow$$

So

$$K_{sp} = [Ag^+][x^-]$$

$$\therefore K_{AgI} = [Ag^+][I^-] = 1.5 \times 10^{-15} \text{ where } \frac{0.01 \text{ mol}}{\text{liter}}$$

$$= 0.01M, \text{ so}[Ag^+] = \frac{1.5 \times 10^{-15}}{[0.01]}$$

$$= 1.5 \times 10^{-14} \frac{\text{mol}}{\text{liter}}$$

This is the minimum concentration of Ag^+ necessary for precipitation of AgI.

$$K_{AgBr} = [Ag^+][Br^-] = 3.3 \times 10^{-13} \text{ where } 0.1\frac{mol}{liter} = 0.1M$$

So
$$[Ag^+] = 3.3 \times 10^{-13}/[0.1] = 3.3 \times 10^{-12}\frac{mol}{liter}$$

$$K_{AgCl} = [Ag^+][Cl^-] = 1.8 \times 10^{-10} \text{ where } 0.1\frac{mol}{liter} = 0.1M$$

So
$$[Ag^+] = \frac{1.8 \times 10^{-10}}{[0.1]} = 1.8 \times 10^{-9}\frac{mol}{liter}$$

From the above results, it can be noted that a greater concentration of Ag^+ is necessary to cause the precipitation of AgBr and AgCl, so AgI will precipitate first.

48. (C)

Ultraviolet instruments are used to measure the excitation of outer electrons in atoms and molecules, whereas X-ray instruments are used to measure the excitation of tightly held electrons.

49. (A)

Analysis:

Rate	Density (g/45 liters)
r_{H_2}	$d_{H_2} = 4$
r_{O_2}	$d_{O_2} = 64$

According to Graham's law, a logical statement is: The hydrogen will diffuse faster because it has the lower density. The factor is

$$\frac{r_{H_2}}{r_{O_2}}\frac{\sqrt{d_{O_2}}}{d_{H_2}} \Rightarrow r_{H_2} = r_{O_2} \times \frac{\sqrt{64}}{\sqrt{4}} = r_{H_2} \times \frac{8}{2}$$

$$= 4r_{O_2}$$

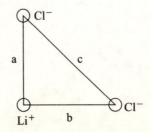

50. (D)

For a face-centered cubic structure, the distance between the center of a lithium ion is one-half the edge length of the cubic unit cell.

$$a = 5.14 \text{ Å}/2 = 2.57 \text{ Å}, b = 5.14 \text{ Å}/2 = 2.57 \text{Å}$$

$C = \sqrt{2}(2.57\text{Å})$; because we assume $Cl^- - Cl^-$ contact, the ionic radius for $Cl2$ is: $\frac{\sqrt{2}}{2}(2.57\text{Å})$.

51. (E)

Metalloids are compounds that exhibit both metallic and nonmetallic properties to some extent. They also act as electron donors with nonmetals and as electron acceptors with metals. They are all solids at room temperature.

52. (B)

$$CH_3COCH_2CH_3 + OH^- \rightleftharpoons CH_3C - OCH_2CH_3$$

(with O double bond on left carbonyl, O^- and OH on right intermediate carbon)

$$CH_3C - OCH_2CH_3 \rightarrow CH_3COOH + CH_3CH_2O^-$$

(with O^- and OH on the intermediate carbon)

The reaction is effectively irreversible because the strong base, $CH_3CH_2O^-$, reacts immediately with acetic acid to produce ethyl alcohol and acetate ion.

$$CH_3COOH + CH_3CH_2O^- \xrightarrow{\text{fast}} CH_3COO^- + CH_3CH_2OH$$

The first step is the rate-determining step. Thus, the rate for the reaction is

$$CH_3COCH_2CH_3 + OH^- \xrightarrow[H_2O]{25°} CH_3CO_2^- + CH_3CH_2OH$$

$$\text{rate} = 0.1[OH^-][CH_3COOCH_2CH_3]$$

53. (A)

To solve this problem, we use the equation for the ionization of ammonia

$$NH_3 + H_2O \rightleftharpoons NH_4^+ + OH^-$$

$$Kb = \frac{NH_4^+ + OH^-}{NH_3}$$

$$\therefore 1.8 \times 10^{-5} = \frac{x[3.6 \times 10^{-6}]}{[0.10]}$$

Solving for x, we find

$$x = \frac{[0.10][1.8 \times 10^{-5}]}{[3.6 \times 10^{-6}]} = \frac{1.8}{3.6} = 0.50$$

54. (E)

$CH_3(CH_2)_4OH$ has a higher number of carbons than the answers in (A) and (C). Branched isomers tend to have lower boiling points than their straight-chain counterparts. Alcohols have higher boiling points than alkanes with equal numbers of carbons.

55. (E)

All of the choices because

$$Q = S + \tfrac{1}{2}D + I - E - U.$$

56. (A)

HCO_3^- is an amphoteric electrolyte acting as either a base or an acid (accepting or donating a proton):

$$H_2O + HCO_3^-(aq) \rightleftharpoons H_3O^+(aq) + CO_3^{2-}(aq)$$

$$H_2O + HCO_3^-(aq) \rightleftharpoons OH^-(aq) + H_2CO_3(aq)$$

57. (B)

The general standing-wave equation is

$$\psi(x) = A\sin(2\pi x/\lambda) + B\cos(2\pi x/\lambda)$$

58. (D)

$$\Delta S° = 2S°_{H_2O}(l) - (2S°_{H_2(g)} + S°_{O_2}(g))$$

$$= 2(16.72) - [2(31.21) + 49.00]$$

$$= 33.44 - 111.42 = -77.98 \text{ eu}$$

59. (D)

The first drop of MnO_4 into a colorless solution produces an easily observable pink color.

60. (B)

The energy of an electron in quantum state n is $E_n = \dfrac{E}{n_{\frac{1}{2}}}$; where E_1 is the energy for $n = 1$ (the ground state).

61. (A)

$$I = \tfrac{1}{2}\Sigma m_i z_i^2 \text{ because 1 mol } BaCl_2 \text{ gives 1 mol } Ba^{2+} \text{ and}$$

$$2 \text{ mol } Cl^-,$$

$$I = \tfrac{1}{2}[(0.01)(2)^2 + 0.02(1)^2]$$

$$I = 0.03$$

62. (B)

To solve the problem, we generate hypotheses of structural units from the information given about δ values and put the units together with the help of the splitting information. The peak at $\delta = 0.9$ ppm clearly corresponds to a methyl group; the number of hydrogens indicated fits this hypothesis. The group at $\delta = 4.3$ ppm corresponds roughly to $H—C—Cl$ but is somewhat shifted downfield, and $\delta = 5.8$ ppm is so far downfield that it corresponds to $—CHCl_2$. We are left with a $—CH_2—$ group to assign to $\delta = 1.7$ ppm. Our structural units are:

$$—CH_3—; \ —CH_2—; \ —CHCl—; \ —CHCl_2—$$

Because the methyl group is a triplet, it must be attached to the $—CH_2—$ group. Because $—CHCl_2—$ is a doublet, it must be attached to $—CHCl—$. The entire structure then becomes

$$CH_3—CH_2—CHCL—CHCl_2.$$

The CH_2 and CHCl protons show complex multiples because of the unequal coupling constants to their adjacent neighbors.

63. (A)

Cis-trans isomerism of the carbon-carbon double bond cannot occur when one carbon of the double bond is bonded to two identical groups.

64. (A)

When a series of oxyacids has the same central atom, acid strength increases as the number of oxygens surrounding the central atom increases. Thus, perchloric acid is the strongest acid.

65. (C)

The Arrhenium Law states that

$$K = A \exp(-E_a/RT)$$

This can be rearranged to:

$$\ln K = \ln A - E_a/RT$$

If we plot ln K versus 1/T, the slope of the graph is $-E_a/R$.

66. (D)

$$Rate = K[X]^m[Y]^n$$

Comparing experiments 2 and 1, we see that holding [X] constant while doubling [Y] doubles the rate of reaction. Hence the rate is proportional to [Y] and m = 1. Comparing experiments 3 and 1, we see that, by holding [Y] constant and tripling [X], the rate goes up by nine times. Thus, the rate is proportional to the square of [X], and n = 2.

$$\therefore rate = K[X]^2[Y]^1$$

67. (A)

The Hamiltonian for the electronic and nuclear repulsion energy for a given internuclear separation R is

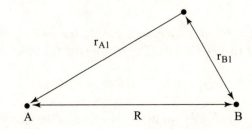

$$\hat{H}(r_A, r_B, r_1) = -\tfrac{1}{2}v_1^{-2} - (1/r_{A_1}) - (1/r_{B_1}) + (1/R)$$

68. (E)

Only three metallic ions, Ag^+, Hg_2^{2+} and Pb^{2+} form insoluble chlorides. Thus, choice (E) is correct.

69. (C)

Integrating the first-order rate law

$$d[N-2O_5]dt = k[N-2O_5] \text{ gives}$$

$$-\ln[N_2O_5] = kt + constant$$

$$\log[N_2O_5] = \frac{constant}{2.3} - \frac{kt}{2.3}$$

70. **(D)**

Although the t-butyl cation shows hyperconjugation, it shows no true conjugation or resonance-stabilization. The other ions exist in several resonance forms:

(A)

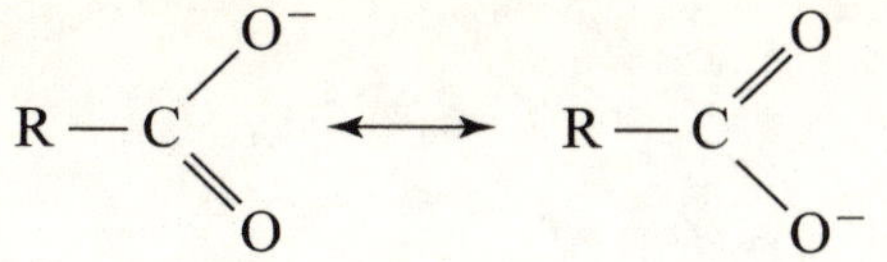

$$R-C \overset{O^-}{\underset{O}{\diagdown}} \longleftrightarrow R-C \overset{O}{\underset{O^-}{\diagdown}}$$

(B)

$$R_2C = C - O^- \longleftrightarrow R_2C^- - C = O$$
$$\quad\quad\quad | \quad\quad\quad\quad\quad\quad\quad | $$
$$\quad\quad\quad R \quad\quad\quad\quad\quad\quad\quad R$$

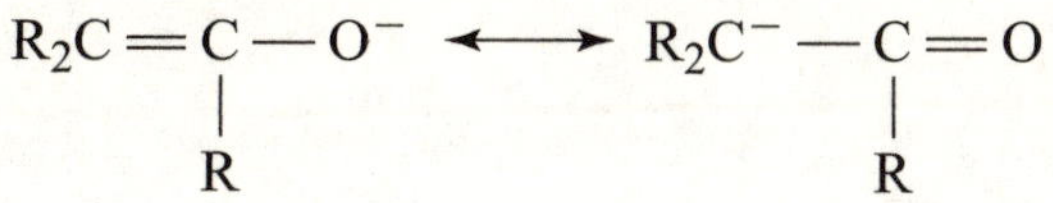

(C)

$$O^- - C \overset{O^-}{\underset{O}{\diagdown}} \longleftrightarrow O^- - C \overset{O}{\underset{O}{\diagdown}} \longleftrightarrow \overset{O}{\underset{O^-}{\diagdown}} C \overset{O^-}{\diagup}$$

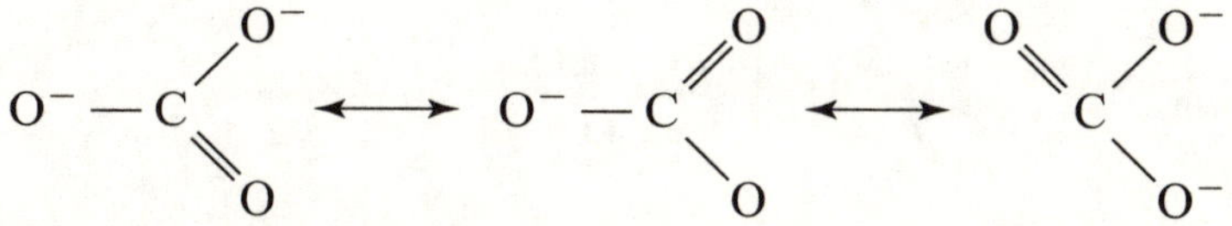

(E) $CH_2 = CH - C^+H_2 \longleftrightarrow C^+H_2 - CH = CH_2$

71. **(C)**

In this reaction, two intermediate carbonium ions of comparable stability can be formed, and this would result in a mixture of products, as shown below.

$$[CH_3CH_2^+CHCH_2CH_3Br^-] \rightarrow$$

$$CH_3CH_2CHBrCH_2CH_3 \quad \text{3-bromopentane}$$

$$CH_3CH_2CH = CHCH_3 + HBr$$

$$[CH_3CH_2CH_2^+CHCH_3Br^-] \rightarrow$$

$$CH_3CH_2CH_2CHBrCH_3 \quad \text{2-bromopentane}$$

72. **(B)**

The relative stability of alkyl radicals depends on the number of alkyl groups attached to the radical carbon; alkyl radicals have the order of stability:

$$(3°)\text{tertiary} > (2°)\text{secondary} > (1°)\text{primary} > (\text{me})\text{methyl}$$

Because answer choice (B) is 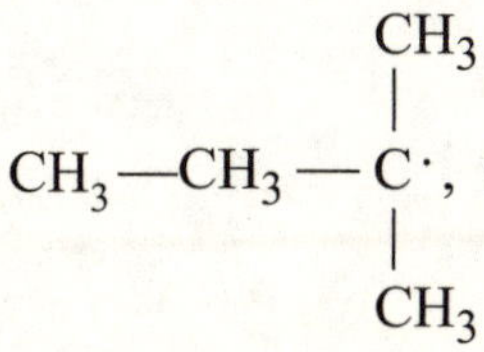
$$\begin{array}{c} CH_3 \\ | \\ CH_3 - CH_3 - C\cdot \\ | \\ CH_3 \end{array}$$
i.e., 3°, it will be the most stable.

73. **(A)**

He has a critical temperature of 5.3K and this is much lower than the other gases. He gas must be cooled to 5.3K before it can liquefy. This is due to its low molecular weight and the difficulty in polarizing the He atom.

74. (B)

This is an example of Claisen-Schmidt reaction known as crosses aldol condensation. The reaction is as follows:

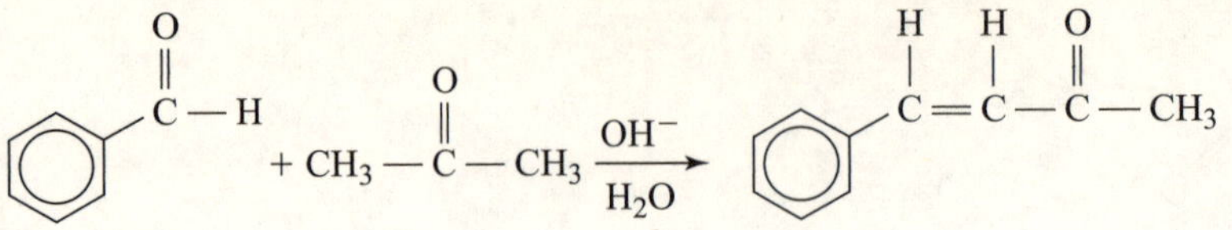

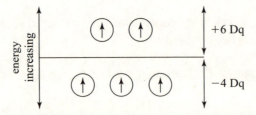

75. (B)

Use the Nernst equation to calculate the potential.

$$E_{red} = E_{red}^{\circ} - \frac{0.059}{n} \log \left[\frac{(Products)}{(Reactants)} \right]$$

$$E_{red} = E_{red}^{\circ} - \frac{0.059}{2} \log \left(\frac{0.01}{0.001} \right)$$

$$E_{red} = E_{red}^{\circ} - \frac{0.059}{2} \log 10; \text{ but } \log 10 = 1$$

$$\therefore E_{red} = E_{red}^{\circ} - \frac{0.059}{2}$$

76. (B)

An alpha particle is a helium nucleus having atomic number 2 and mass number 4.

$$_{88}^{226}Ra \rightarrow _{2}^{4}He + _{86}^{222}Rn$$

77. (E)

Mn^{2+} with low field strength ligands (weak field).

Ligand Field Stabilization Energy

$$= 2(+6Dq) + 3(-4Dq) = 0$$

If, however, the Mn^{2+} ion is coordinated to ligands of high field strength, all five electrons will be forced into the lower energy nonbonding t_{2g} level and none will be at the higher, e_g level.

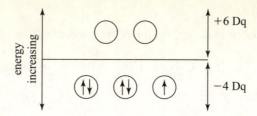

Mn^{2+} with high field strength ligands (strong field)

$$LFSE = 5(-4Dq) = -20Dq$$

Finally, the more negative the value of LFSE, the more stable the complex. As we would expect, a complex of Mn^{2+} with ligands of high field strength is more stable than one with ligands of low field strength.

78. (D)

LiAlH$_4$ is much too strong a reducing agent to select between the two nitro groups.

79. (E)

COOH, COOR, CHO, and COR are meta-directing and deactivating functional groups.

80. (A)

Gabriel synthesis is frequently used in the preparation of primary amines, as shown below:

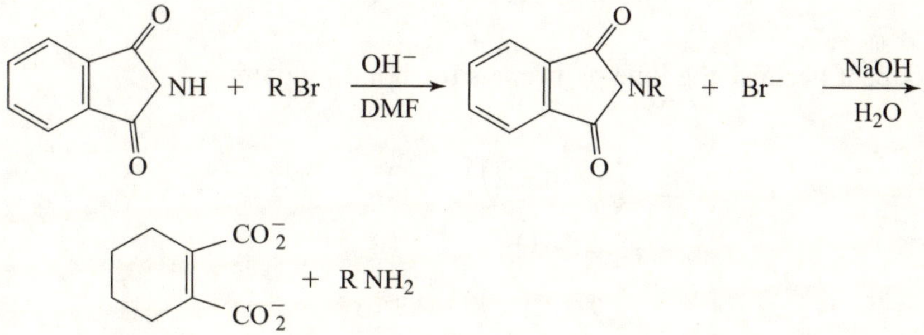

81. (B)

The reaction sequence is as follows:

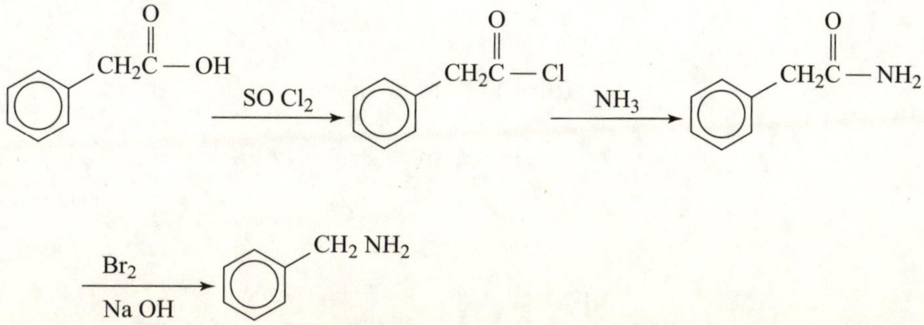

82. (C)

Because a terminal hydrogen is absent on the alkyne, no reaction will take place.

$$CH_3 - C \equiv C - C_2H_5 + CH_3MgBr \longrightarrow \text{No reaction}$$

but

$$CH_3C \equiv CH + CH_3MgBr \longrightarrow CH_3C \equiv CMgBr + CH_4$$

83. (C)

$sp - sp$ is the most efficient.

84. (A)

$$\text{Bond order} = \frac{\text{Number of bonding electrons} - \text{Number of antibonding electrons}}{2}$$

$$\text{Bond order} = \frac{6-4}{2} = 1$$

85. (A)

Van-der-Waal forces exist between the layers of carbon atoms holding graphite together.

86. (D)

Nitrite ion is bent because the lone pair repels the bonding pairs.

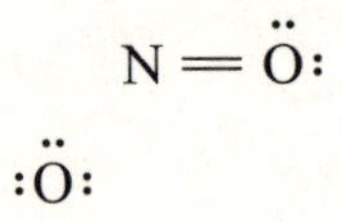

$$N = \overset{..}{O}:$$

$$:\overset{..}{O}:$$

87. (E)

Isotactic is a term used in plastics and polymer sciences.

88. (C)

When $n = 3$, $0 \leq (n - 1)$;

$$\therefore -(n-1) \leq m \leq (n-1)$$

$$\therefore -2 \leq m \leq 2$$

89. (B)

$$\text{If we integrate } \frac{-d[A]}{dt} = K[A]^2, \text{ we get } \frac{1}{[A]} = Kt + \frac{1}{[A_0]}.$$

If we graph $\frac{1}{[A]}$ against t, we will see a straight line with slope K and y-intercept $\frac{1}{[A_o]}$. This is the graph that is given in the question. None of the other answers would yield a straight line for a plot of $\frac{1}{[A]}$ versus t.

90. (A)

The cathode of the phototube is coated with alkali metal. When this is bombarded by radiation, the radiation energy forces the alkali electrons to migrate to the anode one by one.

91. (A)

The correspondence principle states that the predictions of quantum mechanics must pass smoothly into those of classical mechanics whenever we progress in a continuous way from microscopic to the macroscopic realm.

92. (B)

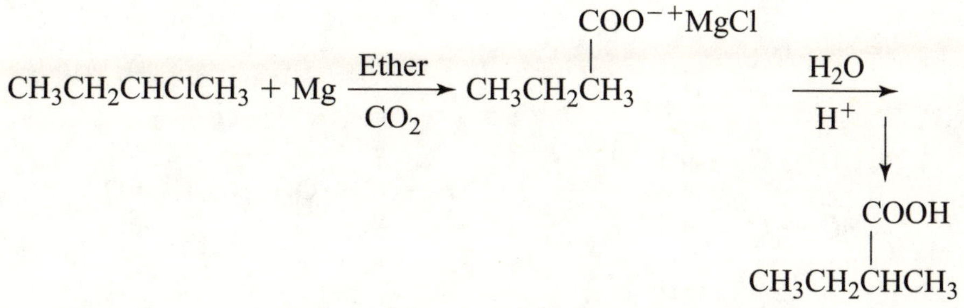
COO⁻⁺MgCl
CH3CH2CHClCH3 + Mg
Ether
CO2
CH3CH2CH3
H2O
H+
COOH
CH3CH2CHCH3

Without protonation, carboxylic acid cannot be produced. As for others

$$CH_3(CH_2)_9CN + H_2O \xrightarrow[C_2H_5OH]{KOH} \xrightarrow{HCl} CH_3(CH_2)_9COOH + NH_3$$

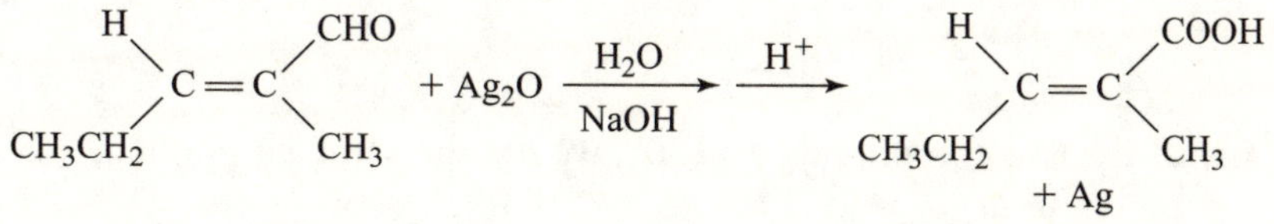
H
CHO
C=C
CH3CH2
CH3
+ Ag2O
H2O
NaOH
H+
H
COOH
C=C
CH3CH2
CH3
+ Ag

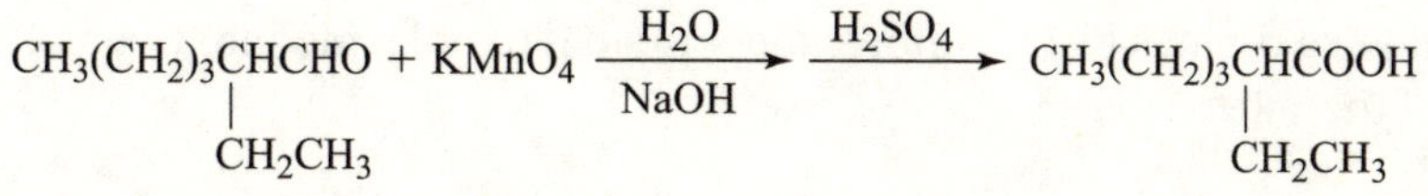
CH3(CH2)3CHCHO + KMnO4
CH2CH3
H2O
NaOH
H2SO4
CH3(CH2)3CHCOOH
CH2CH3

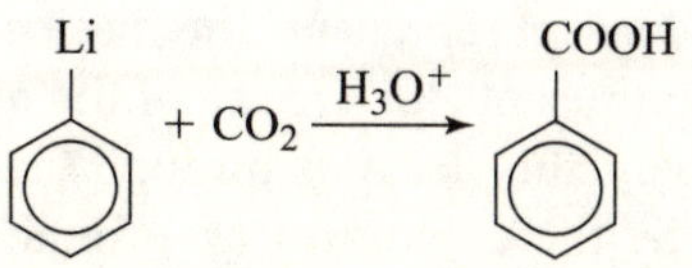
Li
+ CO2
H3O+
COOH

93. (E)

For the equilibrium reaction $CaCO_{3(s)}$ $CaO_{(s)} + CO_{2(g)}$, there are two components because the concentration of calcium oxide is not independent. This also can be seen from the rule $C = S - R$: number of components = number of species − number of relationships between those species. In this case, there are three species ($CaCO_3$, CaO, and CO_2) and one relationship (the equilibrium), giving $C = 2$. The system has three phases, two solids, and one gas, by the definition that a phase must be uniform throughout in terms of both physical state and composition. Using the Gibbs phase rule, $F = C - P + 2$, where F is the number of degrees of freedom, C is the number of components, and P is the number of phases, $F = 2 - 3 + 2 = 1$ degree of freedom.

94. (A)

Lactone is any of a group of cyclic compounds derived by intramolecular loss of water leading to the formation of a cyclic ester.

95. (D)

96. (A)

If we rotate any of the two compounds by 180°, we get the same compound.

97. (D)

A plane of symmetry divides cis-1,2-dibromocyclobutane molecule into two halves, each of which is the mirror image of the other.

98. (E)

In a symbol such as $^{14}_{7}N$, the superscript represents the mass number (the sum of neutrons and protons) of the nucleus and the subscript represents the charge of the nucleus. Nuclei are capable of spontaneous radioactive decay. Most commonly, this decay is through the emission of an α-particle, a positive or negative β-particle, or a γ-ray, or by the capture of an orbital electron. Nuclei can also be altered through bombardment. (A) is an example of α-particle bombardment that produces $^{17}_{8}O$ and a proton. (B) is another example of α-particle bombardment, but this time a neutron is emitted. (C) is an example of positive β-emission through positron decay. (D) is an example of negative β-emission through electron decay. Therefore, all choices are possible responses and (E) is the correct answer.

99. (B)

Brass is an alloy composed of copper and zinc.

100. (A)

101. (D)

In a D_{3h} symmetry, the five d-orbitals will split into a nondegenerate a_1^1 level, a twofold degenerate e^1 level, and a twofold e^{11} level.

102. (C)

Nitrogen and chlorine have very close electronegativities to oxygen so they have the least charge separation in compounds NO_3^- and ClO_4^-, but ClO_4^- will be the least polar of the two because the negative charge is shared among four oxygen atoms.

103. (B)

Hydrazine burns in air with the evolution of great heat.

104. (B)

The Bohr model worked well only for the hydrogen atom.

105. (B)

Among HF, H_2O, NH_3, CH_4, and H_3O^+, CH_4 is the least acidic; therefore, CH_3^- is the most basic.

106. (B)

$$h = \frac{2\gamma}{\rho gr} \text{ where }$$

γ = surface tension
r = radius
ρ = density
g = gravity

Thus, height is inversely proportional to density.

107. (A)

$$2Ag_2S(s) + 2H_2O(l) \rightarrow 4Ag(s) + 2H_2S(g) + O_2(g)$$

$$\Delta H^\circ = 4\Delta H^\circ_{fAg(s)} + 2\Delta H^\circ_{fH_2S(g)} + \Delta H^\circ_{fO_2(g)} - 2\Delta H^\circ_{fAg_2S(s)} - 2\Delta H^\circ_{fH_2O(l)}$$

$$= 4 \text{ mol Ag(s)} \times 0 + 2 \text{ mol } H_2S \times (-20.6 \text{kJ/mol}) + 1 \text{ mol } O_2 \times 0 - 2 \text{ mol } Ag_2S \times (-32.6 \text{kJ/mol}) - 2 \text{ mol } H_2O \times (-285.8 \text{kJ/mol})$$

$$= [-41.2 - (-65.2) - (-571.6)] \text{kJ} = 595.6 \text{kJ}$$

108. (B)

$$\ln\left(\frac{1}{.5}\right) = kt_{\frac{1}{2}}; \text{ therefore } K = \frac{\ln 2}{t_{\frac{1}{2}}}$$

$$\ln\left(\frac{1}{.02}\right) = \left(\frac{\ln 2}{t_{\frac{1}{2}}}\right) \times t$$

$$t = \frac{\ln 50}{\ln 2} \times t_{\frac{1}{2}} = \frac{\ln 50}{\ln 2} \times 5.2 \text{ yrs.}$$

109. (D)

H^+ has by far the greatest mobility of the cations.

110. (C)

Mendeleev first published the arrangements of elements for the periodic table in 1870.

111. (A)

NaCl has the greatest difference in electronegativity. In general, the greater the difference, the higher the melting point.

112. (C)

113. (A)

Isobaric means constant-pressure conditions. Thus, the heat flow or the heat of reaction for a chemical reaction performed in a solution is

$$\Delta H = \Delta E + P\Delta V = \Delta E + W = \Delta E + P(V_2 - V_1)$$

Choice (B), which is $\Delta H = \Delta E - RT\Delta n$, is for ideal gases under constant-pressure conditions, not solution. Choice (C), which is

$$\Delta H = P\Delta V = \int_{V_1}^{V_2} PdV = nRT \ln\frac{V_2}{V_1},$$

represents the equation for reversible isothermal conditions, i.e., constant temperature. Choice (D), which is

$$\Delta H = P\Delta V = \int_{V_1}^{V_2} PdV = P(V_2 - V_1),$$

represents irreversible isothermal conditions, i.e., at constant temperature. Choice (E), which is $\Delta H = \Delta E = q_v$, is for isochoric conditions, i.e., under constant volume.

114. (E)

All the thermodynamic work functions are correctly expressed.

115. (E)

The Maxwell relations for closed reversible systems in which only PV-work is considered can be derived from the four variables T, S, P, and V such that

$$\left(\frac{\delta S}{\delta V}\right)_T = \left(\frac{\delta P}{\delta T}\right)_V$$

116. (A)

$$\Delta T_b = K_b n$$

M-wt of sucrose: Mw = 342

$$\text{moles of solute} = \frac{\text{grams of solute}}{\text{m-wt. of solute}} = \frac{34.2g}{343g/mole}$$

$$= 0.10$$

$$200g \text{ of solvent} = \frac{200g}{1000g} \times 1kg = 0.20 \text{ kg}$$

$$\text{Molality} = \frac{\text{moles solute}}{1kg \text{ solvent}} = \frac{0.10 \text{ moles}}{0.20kg} = 0.5m$$

Therefore, the elevation of the boiling point is

$$\Delta T_b = K_b n = (1.20°C/m)(0.5m) = .60°C.$$

Thus, the boiling point of the solution is 78.5°C + 0.6°C = 79.1°C

117. (B)

In this case, solute is ethanol; solvent is water.

$$\text{Molality} = \frac{\text{moles of solute (ethanol)}}{\text{kg of solvent (water)}}$$

$$\text{mole of ethanol} = \frac{2.3g}{46g/mole} = 0.05 \text{ mole}$$

$$\therefore \text{ molality} = \frac{0.05 \text{ mole}}{0.5 \text{ kg}} = 0.1 \text{ molal}$$

If we need the molarity,

$$\text{molality} = \frac{\text{moles of solute}}{\text{liter of solvent}} = \frac{0.05 \text{ mole}}{0.5\text{kg}/1\text{kg}/\text{m}^3} = \frac{0.05 \text{ mole}}{0.51}$$

$$= 0.1 \text{ Molar}$$

118. (B)

Atomic weights are $C = 12\text{g/mole}$, $H = 1.01\text{g/mole}$, $N = 14.0\text{g/mole}$.

$$\text{moles of C} = \frac{74.0\text{g}}{12\text{g/mole}} = 6.17 \text{ moles}$$

$$\text{moles of H} = \frac{8.7\text{g}}{1.01\text{g/mole}} = 8.61 \text{ moles}$$

$$\text{moles of N} = \frac{17.3\text{g}}{14.0\text{g/mole}} = 1.241 \text{ moles}$$

Ratio C:H:N is 6.17:8.61:1.24, which is the same as

$$\frac{6.17}{1.24} : \frac{8.61}{1.24} : \frac{1.24}{1.24} = 5 : 7 : 1$$

Thus, the empirical formula is $C_5H_7N = 81.05$, but the molecular weight of nicotine = 162.1.

Therefore, the whole number $= \dfrac{162.1}{81.05} = 2$

Thus, the molecular formula $= (C_5H_7N) \times 2 = C_{10}H_{14}N_2$

119. (E)

All the choices are correct.

120. (B)

$$BaSo_4 \rightleftarrows Ba^{2+} + SO_4^{2-}$$

$$K_{Sp} = [Ba^{2+}][SO_4^{2-}] = 1 \times 10^{-10}$$

Because both ions Ba^{2+} and SO_4^{2-} exist in equimolar amounts,

$$K = [Ba^{2+}][SO_4^{2-}] = X^2$$

$$\therefore x^2 = 10^{-10}$$

$$x = \sqrt{10^{-10}} = 10^{-5}\text{M}$$

121. (D)

$$Mx_2(s) \rightleftharpoons M^{2+}(aq) + 2x^-(aq)$$

$$K = [M^{2+}][X^-]^2$$

$$\text{molarity} = \frac{0.02 \text{ mole}}{100ml} \times \frac{1000 \text{ ml}}{1 \text{ liter}} = .2 \frac{\text{mole}}{1}$$

thus

$$[M^{2+}] = 0.2 \frac{\text{mole}}{1} \text{ and } [X^-] = .4 \frac{\text{mole}}{1}$$

$$K = (.2)(.4)^2 = 0.032$$

122. (C)

From the given cell

$$Cu; Cu^{2+} \| Ag^{2+}; Ag$$

$$Cu \rightarrow Cu^{2+} + 2e^- \text{ oxidation}$$

$$2Ag^+ + 2e^- \rightarrow 2Ag \text{ reduction}$$

$$Cu + Ag^{2+} \rightarrow Cu^{2+} + Ag$$

$$E^\circ_{cell} = -(E^\circ_{red} Cu) + (E^\circ_{red} Ag^{2+})$$

$$= -0.34 + 0.80 = 0.46V$$

123. (C)

Lysine exists in its Zwitterionic form at pH 10 and hence would not migrate.

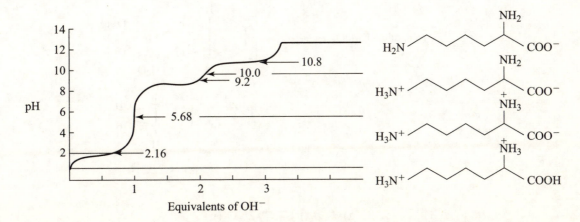

124. (C)

$$\bar{v} = R_H \left[\frac{1}{n_1^2} - \frac{1}{n_3^2} \right] = 1.1 \times 10^5 cm^{-1} \left[\frac{1}{5^2} - \frac{1}{10^2} \right]$$

$$= 3.3 \times 10^3 cm^{-1}$$

125. (A)

The total concentration of the edta is

$$C_Y = [Y^{4-}] + [HY^{3-}] + [H_2Y^{2-}] + [H_3Y^-] + [H_4Y]$$

126. (B)

$$\frac{Y^{4-}}{C_Y} = \frac{K_{a_1} K_{a_2} K_{a_3} K_{a_4}}{[H_3O^+]^4 + [H_3O^+]^3 + [H_3O^+]^2 K_{a_1} K_{a_2}}$$

$$+ K_{a_1} K_{a_2} K_{a_3} + K_{a_1} K_{a_2} K_{a_3} K_{a_4}$$

127. (A)

An example of this is

$$A + RB \qquad RA + B$$

| Solu-tion | Resin phase | Resin phase | Solution |

128. (D)

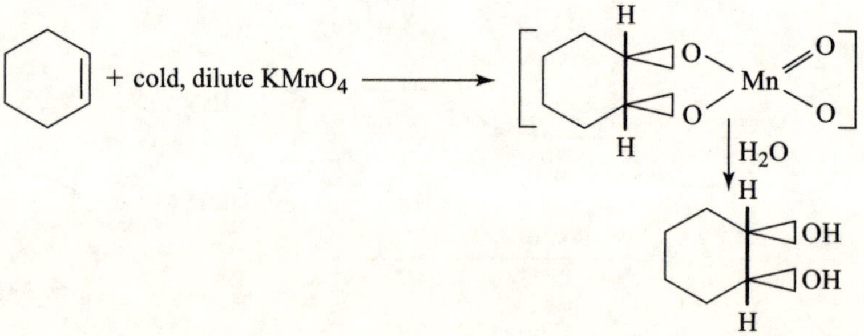

129. (E)

$$2NO(g) + O_2(g) \rightleftharpoons 2NO_2(g)$$

$$\Delta G^\circ_{reaction} = -RT \ln K_p = -R(298)\ln(1.6 \times 10^{12})$$

also

$$\Delta G^\circ_{reaction} = 2\Delta G^\circ_{NO_2} - 2\Delta G^\circ_{NO} - \Delta G^\circ_{O_2}$$

$$\Delta G^\circ_{NO_2} = \frac{\Delta G^\circ_{react} + 2\Delta G^\circ_{NO} + \Delta G^\circ_{O2}}{2}$$

$$\Delta G^\circ_{NO_2} = \tfrac{1}{2}[2(86.6) - R(298)\ln(1.6 \times 10^{12})]$$

130. (B)

$$CH_4(g) + 2O_2(g) \rightarrow CO_2(g) + 2H_2O(l)$$

$$\Delta H = \Delta E + \Delta nRT$$

$$= -212 \text{ kcal} + (-2 \text{ mole})(1.987 \text{ cal/deg-mole})(298°K)$$

$$= -212 \text{ kcal} - 1180 \text{ cal}$$

$$= -213 \text{ kcal}$$

131. (C)

$$AgBr \rightleftharpoons Ag^+ + Br^-$$

$$K = [Ag^+][Br^-] = 4 \times 10^{-13}$$

$$\therefore [10^{-5}][Br^-] = 4 \times 10^{-13}$$

$$[Br] = \frac{4 \times 10^{-13}}{10^{-5}} = 4 \times 10^{-8} M$$

132. (C)

$$AlCl_3 \rightarrow Al^{3+} + 3Cl^-$$

$$Al^{3+} + 2H_2O \quad AlOH^{2+} + H_3O^+$$

$$K_{hyd.=1.4\times10^{-5}} - \frac{[H_3O^+][A]OH^{2+}}{Al^{3+}}$$

$$1.4 \times 10^{-5} = \frac{[x][x]}{.1}$$

$$x = \sqrt{1.4 \times 10{-6}M}$$

$$x = 1.2 \times 10^{-3} M$$

133. (C)

$$4Al + 3O_2 \rightarrow 2Al_2O_3$$

$$\frac{4 \text{ moles Al}}{3 \text{ moles } O_2} = \frac{0.36 \text{ moles Al}}{x \text{ mole of } O_2}$$

$$x \text{ mole } O_2 = \frac{3(0.36)}{4} = 0.24 \text{ moles } O_2$$

Thus, there is an excess of 0.09 mole O_2.

$$\frac{4 \text{ moles Al}}{2 \text{ moles Al}_2O_3} = \frac{0.36 \text{ moles Al}}{x}$$

$$\therefore x = \frac{2 \times 0.36}{4} = 0.18 \text{ moles Al}_2V_3$$

Because Al is the limiting reagent, we calculate the amount of Al_2O_3 produced from the amount of Al available.

134. (B)

Tollen's reagent is used to distinguish aldehydes from ketones.

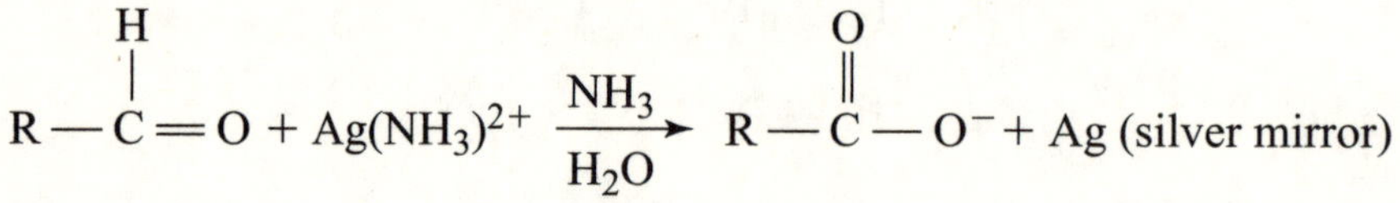

$$\underset{\text{H}}{\overset{\text{H}}{R-C}}=O + Ag(NH_3)^{2+} \xrightarrow[\text{H}_2O]{\text{NH}_3} \overset{O}{R-C}-O^- + Ag \text{ (silver mirror)}$$

135. (A)

$$2SO_2 + O_2 \rightarrow 2SO_3$$

$$\frac{8.0g \; O_2}{32.0g/\text{mole } O_2} = 0.25 \text{ mole } O_2$$

$$\frac{40.0g \; SO_2}{64.0g/\text{mole } SO_2} = 0.625 \text{ mole } SO_2$$

O_2 is the limiting reagent. Because two moles of SO_3 are produced for every mole of O_2 consumed, the maximum yield of SO_3 is 0.50 mole. This weighs $(.50 \text{ mole } S_{O3})(80g/\text{mole } SO_3) = 40.0g \; SO_3$.

136. (B)

$$HC \equiv CH \xrightarrow[\text{NH}_3]{\text{NaNH}_2} \xrightarrow{\underset{\text{CH}_3\text{CHCH}_2\text{CH}_2\text{Br}}{\overset{\text{CH}_3}{|}}} \underset{\text{CH}_3\text{CHCH}_2\text{CH}_2\text{C}}{\overset{\text{CH}_3}{|}} \equiv H$$

has no protection group.

In (1), the protected form of the reactant is

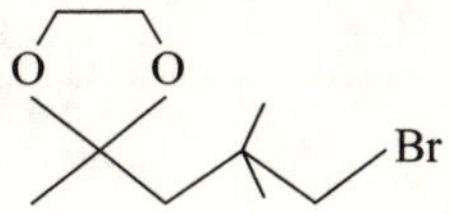

In (2), it is

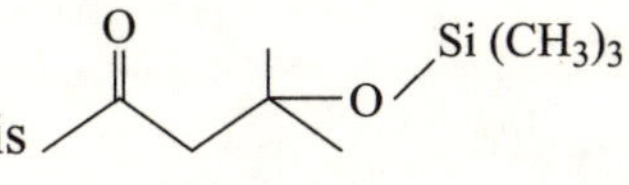

Practice Exam 2

Practice Exam 2 is also on CD-ROM in our special interactive GRE Chemistry TestWare®. It is highly recommended that you first take this exam on computer. You will then have the additional study features and benefits of enforced timed conditions and instant, accurate scoring. See page v for guidance on how to get the most out of our GRE Chemistry software.

Answer Sheet: Practice Exam 2

1. Ⓐ Ⓑ Ⓒ Ⓓ Ⓔ
2. Ⓐ Ⓑ Ⓒ Ⓓ Ⓔ
3. Ⓐ Ⓑ Ⓒ Ⓓ Ⓔ
4. Ⓐ Ⓑ Ⓒ Ⓓ Ⓔ
5. Ⓐ Ⓑ Ⓒ Ⓓ Ⓔ
6. Ⓐ Ⓑ Ⓒ Ⓓ Ⓔ
7. Ⓐ Ⓑ Ⓒ Ⓓ Ⓔ
8. Ⓐ Ⓑ Ⓒ Ⓓ Ⓔ
9. Ⓐ Ⓑ Ⓒ Ⓓ Ⓔ
10. Ⓐ Ⓑ Ⓒ Ⓓ Ⓔ
11. Ⓐ Ⓑ Ⓒ Ⓓ Ⓔ
12. Ⓐ Ⓑ Ⓒ Ⓓ Ⓔ
13. Ⓐ Ⓑ Ⓒ Ⓓ Ⓔ
14. Ⓐ Ⓑ Ⓒ Ⓓ Ⓔ
15. Ⓐ Ⓑ Ⓒ Ⓓ Ⓔ
16. Ⓐ Ⓑ Ⓒ Ⓓ Ⓔ
17. Ⓐ Ⓑ Ⓒ Ⓓ Ⓔ
18. Ⓐ Ⓑ Ⓒ Ⓓ Ⓔ
19. Ⓐ Ⓑ Ⓒ Ⓓ Ⓔ
20. Ⓐ Ⓑ Ⓒ Ⓓ Ⓔ
21. Ⓐ Ⓑ Ⓒ Ⓓ Ⓔ
22. Ⓐ Ⓑ Ⓒ Ⓓ Ⓔ
23. Ⓐ Ⓑ Ⓒ Ⓓ Ⓔ
24. Ⓐ Ⓑ Ⓒ Ⓓ Ⓔ
25. Ⓐ Ⓑ Ⓒ Ⓓ Ⓔ
26. Ⓐ Ⓑ Ⓒ Ⓓ Ⓔ
27. Ⓐ Ⓑ Ⓒ Ⓓ Ⓔ
28. Ⓐ Ⓑ Ⓒ Ⓓ Ⓔ
29. Ⓐ Ⓑ Ⓒ Ⓓ Ⓔ
30. Ⓐ Ⓑ Ⓒ Ⓓ Ⓔ
31. Ⓐ Ⓑ Ⓒ Ⓓ Ⓔ
32. Ⓐ Ⓑ Ⓒ Ⓓ Ⓔ
33. Ⓐ Ⓑ Ⓒ Ⓓ Ⓔ

34. Ⓐ Ⓑ Ⓒ Ⓓ Ⓔ
35. Ⓐ Ⓑ Ⓒ Ⓓ Ⓔ
36. Ⓐ Ⓑ Ⓒ Ⓓ Ⓔ
37. Ⓐ Ⓑ Ⓒ Ⓓ Ⓔ
38. Ⓐ Ⓑ Ⓒ Ⓓ Ⓔ
39. Ⓐ Ⓑ Ⓒ Ⓓ Ⓔ
40. Ⓐ Ⓑ Ⓒ Ⓓ Ⓔ
41. Ⓐ Ⓑ Ⓒ Ⓓ Ⓔ
42. Ⓐ Ⓑ Ⓒ Ⓓ Ⓔ
43. Ⓐ Ⓑ Ⓒ Ⓓ Ⓔ
44. Ⓐ Ⓑ Ⓒ Ⓓ Ⓔ
45. Ⓐ Ⓑ Ⓒ Ⓓ Ⓔ
46. Ⓐ Ⓑ Ⓒ Ⓓ Ⓔ
47. Ⓐ Ⓑ Ⓒ Ⓓ Ⓔ
48. Ⓐ Ⓑ Ⓒ Ⓓ Ⓔ
49. Ⓐ Ⓑ Ⓒ Ⓓ Ⓔ
50. Ⓐ Ⓑ Ⓒ Ⓓ Ⓔ
51. Ⓐ Ⓑ Ⓒ Ⓓ Ⓔ
52. Ⓐ Ⓑ Ⓒ Ⓓ Ⓔ
53. Ⓐ Ⓑ Ⓒ Ⓓ Ⓔ
54. Ⓐ Ⓑ Ⓒ Ⓓ Ⓔ
55. Ⓐ Ⓑ Ⓒ Ⓓ Ⓔ
56. Ⓐ Ⓑ Ⓒ Ⓓ Ⓔ
57. Ⓐ Ⓑ Ⓒ Ⓓ Ⓔ
58. Ⓐ Ⓑ Ⓒ Ⓓ Ⓔ
59. Ⓐ Ⓑ Ⓒ Ⓓ Ⓔ
60. Ⓐ Ⓑ Ⓒ Ⓓ Ⓔ
61. Ⓐ Ⓑ Ⓒ Ⓓ Ⓔ
62. Ⓐ Ⓑ Ⓒ Ⓓ Ⓔ
63. Ⓐ Ⓑ Ⓒ Ⓓ Ⓔ
64. Ⓐ Ⓑ Ⓒ Ⓓ Ⓔ
65. Ⓐ Ⓑ Ⓒ Ⓓ Ⓔ
66. Ⓐ Ⓑ Ⓒ Ⓓ Ⓔ

67. Ⓐ Ⓑ Ⓒ Ⓓ Ⓔ
68. Ⓐ Ⓑ Ⓒ Ⓓ Ⓔ
69. Ⓐ Ⓑ Ⓒ Ⓓ Ⓔ
70. Ⓐ Ⓑ Ⓒ Ⓓ Ⓔ
71. Ⓐ Ⓑ Ⓒ Ⓓ Ⓔ
72. Ⓐ Ⓑ Ⓒ Ⓓ Ⓔ
73. Ⓐ Ⓑ Ⓒ Ⓓ Ⓔ
74. Ⓐ Ⓑ Ⓒ Ⓓ Ⓔ
75. Ⓐ Ⓑ Ⓒ Ⓓ Ⓔ
76. Ⓐ Ⓑ Ⓒ Ⓓ Ⓔ
77. Ⓐ Ⓑ Ⓒ Ⓓ Ⓔ
78. Ⓐ Ⓑ Ⓒ Ⓓ Ⓔ
79. Ⓐ Ⓑ Ⓒ Ⓓ Ⓔ
80. Ⓐ Ⓑ Ⓒ Ⓓ Ⓔ
81. Ⓐ Ⓑ Ⓒ Ⓓ Ⓔ
82. Ⓐ Ⓑ Ⓒ Ⓓ Ⓔ
83. Ⓐ Ⓑ Ⓒ Ⓓ Ⓔ
84. Ⓐ Ⓑ Ⓒ Ⓓ Ⓔ
85. Ⓐ Ⓑ Ⓒ Ⓓ Ⓔ
86. Ⓐ Ⓑ Ⓒ Ⓓ Ⓔ
87. Ⓐ Ⓑ Ⓒ Ⓓ Ⓔ
88. Ⓐ Ⓑ Ⓒ Ⓓ Ⓔ
89. Ⓐ Ⓑ Ⓒ Ⓓ Ⓔ
90. Ⓐ Ⓑ Ⓒ Ⓓ Ⓔ
91. Ⓐ Ⓑ Ⓒ Ⓓ Ⓔ
92. Ⓐ Ⓑ Ⓒ Ⓓ Ⓔ
93. Ⓐ Ⓑ Ⓒ Ⓓ Ⓔ
94. Ⓐ Ⓑ Ⓒ Ⓓ Ⓔ
95. Ⓐ Ⓑ Ⓒ Ⓓ Ⓔ
96. Ⓐ Ⓑ Ⓒ Ⓓ Ⓔ
97. Ⓐ Ⓑ Ⓒ Ⓓ Ⓔ
98. Ⓐ Ⓑ Ⓒ Ⓓ Ⓔ
99. Ⓐ Ⓑ Ⓒ Ⓓ Ⓔ

Continued

Answer Sheet: Practice Exam 2 (Continued)

100. Ⓐ Ⓑ Ⓒ Ⓓ Ⓔ
101. Ⓐ Ⓑ Ⓒ Ⓓ Ⓔ
102. Ⓐ Ⓑ Ⓒ Ⓓ Ⓔ
103. Ⓐ Ⓑ Ⓒ Ⓓ Ⓔ
104. Ⓐ Ⓑ Ⓒ Ⓓ Ⓔ
105. Ⓐ Ⓑ Ⓒ Ⓓ Ⓔ
106. Ⓐ Ⓑ Ⓒ Ⓓ Ⓔ
107. Ⓐ Ⓑ Ⓒ Ⓓ Ⓔ
108. Ⓐ Ⓑ Ⓒ Ⓓ Ⓔ
109. Ⓐ Ⓑ Ⓒ Ⓓ Ⓔ
110. Ⓐ Ⓑ Ⓒ Ⓓ Ⓔ
111. Ⓐ Ⓑ Ⓒ Ⓓ Ⓔ
112. Ⓐ Ⓑ Ⓒ Ⓓ Ⓔ

113. Ⓐ Ⓑ Ⓒ Ⓓ Ⓔ
114. Ⓐ Ⓑ Ⓒ Ⓓ Ⓔ
115. Ⓐ Ⓑ Ⓒ Ⓓ Ⓔ
116. Ⓐ Ⓑ Ⓒ Ⓓ Ⓔ
117. Ⓐ Ⓑ Ⓒ Ⓓ Ⓔ
118. Ⓐ Ⓑ Ⓒ Ⓓ Ⓔ
119. Ⓐ Ⓑ Ⓒ Ⓓ Ⓔ
120. Ⓐ Ⓑ Ⓒ Ⓓ Ⓔ
121. Ⓐ Ⓑ Ⓒ Ⓓ Ⓔ
122. Ⓐ Ⓑ Ⓒ Ⓓ Ⓔ
123. Ⓐ Ⓑ Ⓒ Ⓓ Ⓔ
124. Ⓐ Ⓑ Ⓒ Ⓓ Ⓔ
125. Ⓐ Ⓑ Ⓒ Ⓓ Ⓔ

126. Ⓐ Ⓑ Ⓒ Ⓓ Ⓔ
127. Ⓐ Ⓑ Ⓒ Ⓓ Ⓔ
128. Ⓐ Ⓑ Ⓒ Ⓓ Ⓔ
129. Ⓐ Ⓑ Ⓒ Ⓓ Ⓔ
130. Ⓐ Ⓑ Ⓒ Ⓓ Ⓔ
131. Ⓐ Ⓑ Ⓒ Ⓓ Ⓔ
132. Ⓐ Ⓑ Ⓒ Ⓓ Ⓔ
133. Ⓐ Ⓑ Ⓒ Ⓓ Ⓔ
134. Ⓐ Ⓑ Ⓒ Ⓓ Ⓔ
135. Ⓐ Ⓑ Ⓒ Ⓓ Ⓔ
136. Ⓐ Ⓑ Ⓒ Ⓓ Ⓔ

Practice Exam 2

Time: 170 Minutes
136 Questions

Directions: *Choose the best answer for each question and mark the letter of your selection on the corresponding answer sheet.*

1. For an ideal solution, which of the following is/are *true*?

   I. $\Delta H_{mixing} = 0$

   II. $\Delta S_{mixing} = 0$

   III. $p_{solution} = \overset{components}{\underset{i}{\Sigma}} p_i$

   IV. $\Delta G_{mixing} = -R \overset{components}{\underset{i}{\Sigma}} n_i \ln x_i$

   (A) I, III, and IV
   (B) III and IV
   (C) I, II, and III
   (D) I and III
   (E) I only

2. Select the correct product of the following reaction:

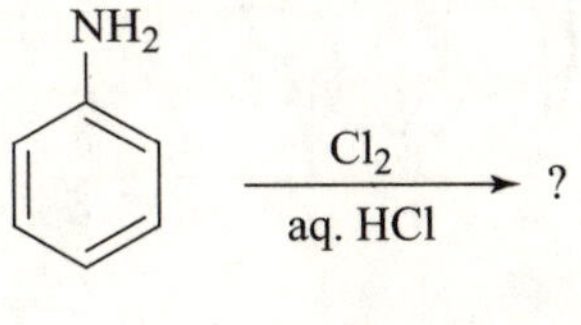

   (A) o-chloroaniline
   (B) 2,6-dichloroaniline
   (C) p-chloroaniline
   (D) 2,6-dichlorobenzene
   (E) 2,4,6-trichloroaniline

3. Choose the number of fundamental vibrational modes in a molecule of nitryl chloride.

   (A) 6
   (B) 0
   (C) 3
   (D) 4
   (E) 2

4. Arrange the following hydrogen bonds in order of increasing strength: O—H . . . Cl; O—H . . . N; F—H . . . O and N—H . . . .

    (A) O—H . . . Cl < F—H . . . O < O—H . . . N < N—H . . . O
    (B) O—H . . . N < O—H . . . Cl < N—H . . . O < F—H . . . O
    (C) O—H . . . Cl < N—H . . . O < O—H . . . N < F—H . . . O
    (D) N—H . . . O < O—H . . . N < F—H . . . O < O—H . . . Cl
    (E) F—H . . . O < N—H . . . O < O—H . . . Cl < O—H . . . N

5. Which substance has the greatest lattice energy?

    (A) AgCl   (D) KI
    (B) NaF   (E) MgO
    (C) CuBr

6. The product of the reaction below was subject to an infrared spectral analysis. Based on its IR spectra pictured below, one can deduce that the product is:

    $$\text{Reaction}: \ CH_3CH_2Cl + Mg \xrightarrow{\text{ether}} \xrightarrow{CO_2} \xrightarrow[H_2O]{H_2SO_4} \text{product}$$

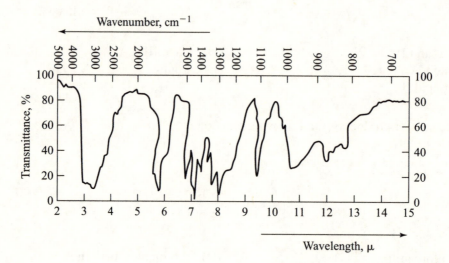

    (A) acetaldehyde   (D) acetone
    (B) propanol   (E) propionic acid
    (C) ethanoic acid

7. A chromatogram obtained using a differential detector would most closely resemble which one of the following diagrams?

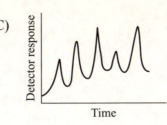

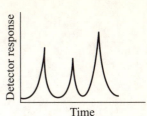

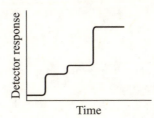

8. Water has a vapor pressure of 23.76 torr at 25°C. What is the vapor pressure of a solution of sucrose, if the mole fraction of sucrose is 0.250?

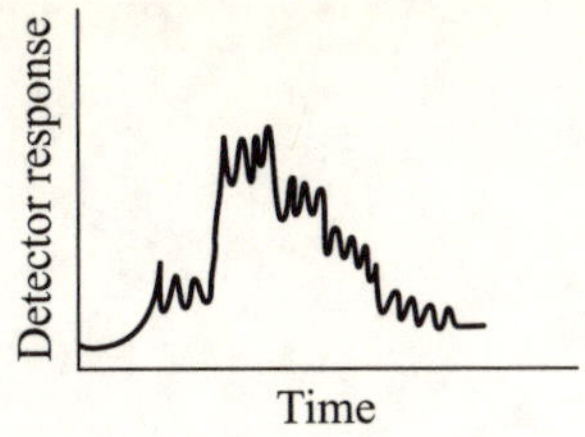

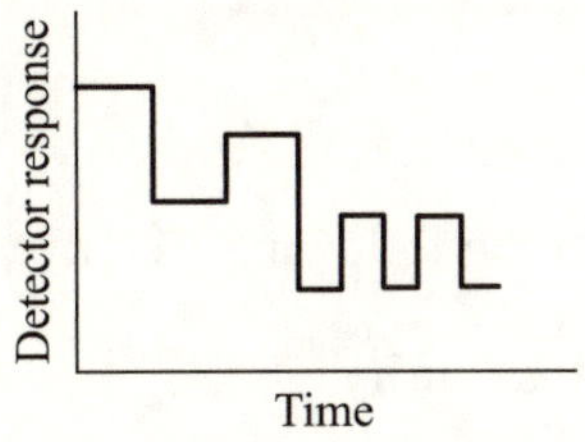

(A) 15.2 torr
(B) 23.8 torr
(C) 29.7 torr
(D) 5.9 torr
(E) 17.8 torr

9. Which one of the following characteristics is *not* usually attributable to ionic substances?

(A) High melting point
(B) Fragility
(C) Crystalline (in the solid state)
(D) Deform when struck
(E) Well-defined three-diensional structure

10. Indicate the reagents and/or compounds required to carry out the transformation show below:

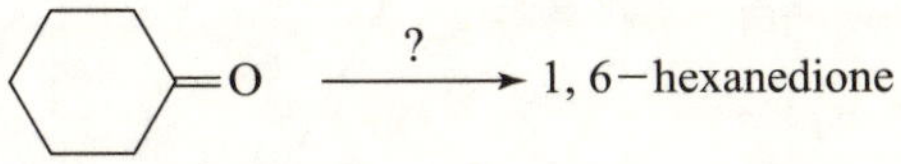

$$\text{cyclohexanone} \xrightarrow{?} 1,6-\text{hexanedione}$$

(A) H_2O; H_2SO_4; heat; $KMnO_4$; O_3; Zn
(B) $LiAlH_4$; $K_2Cr_2O_7$, H_2O; NH_2OH
(C) $LiAlH_4$; NaOH, heat; $KMnO_4$
(D) H_2O, H^+; $K_3Cr_2O_7$; NH_2OH
(E) $LiAlH_4$; H_2SO_4, heat; O_3; Zn

11. In an adiabatic system, if work is done, the temperature must:

(A) increase.
(B) decrease.
(C) remain the same.
(D) increase, then decrease.
(E) decrease, then increase.

12. The Perkin reaction, in which o-chlorobenzaldehyde is heated with acetic anyhydride and its salt sodium acetate, results in the production of:

(A) CHO — Cl (benzene ring)

(C) CH=CH$_2$OH — Cl (benzene ring)

(E) CH$_3$CHOH — Cl (benzene ring)

(B) CH$_2$CHCOOH — Cl (benzene ring)

(D) CH=CHCOOH — Cl (benzene ring)

13. The quality of a particular monochromator depends on which of the following characteristics?

   I.   Light-gathering power
   II. Spectral band width
   III. Radiant output purity
   IV. High signal-to-noise ratio

   (A) I, II, and III
   (B) I and IV
   (C) II, III, and IV
   (D) II and IV
   (E) All of the above (I–IV)

14. In the plot below of $\Lambda_m/\Omega^{-1}cm^2mol^{-1}$ versus $\sqrt{c/mol\,dm^{-3}}$, the slope is equal to:

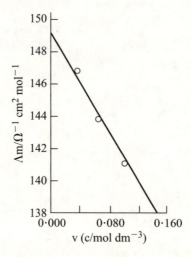

v (c/mol dm^{-3})

   (A) Λ_m°
   (B) the Kohlrausch coefficient
   (C) the molar conductivity
   (D) κ
   (E) ρ

15. To distinguish among primary, secondary, and tertiary alcohols, one would use the following experimental method.

    (A) Sandmeyer reaction   (D) Lucas test
    (B) Wittig reaction   (E) Tollen's reagent
    (C) Ninhydrin test

16. Members of this group (of the periodic table) are used in the manufacture of plastics and insecticides. They are used to produce aerosol propellants and to prepare gasoline additives. The name of this group is

    (A) alkaline earth metals.   (D) halogens.
    (B) noble gases.   (E) alkali metals.
    (C) actinides.

17. The coordination number for cobalt in $[Co(H_2NCH_2CH_2NH_2)_3]^{3+}$ is:

    (A) 3   (D) 1
    (B) 6   (E) 4
    (C) 2

18. If each of the following reagents were added to benzene, only one of them would react for all the others, there would be no reaction. Which reagent is the one that would react?

    (A) $O_3/Zn,H^+$ (D) free radicals
    (B) HI   (E) cold Br_2/CCl_4 solution
    (C) hot $KMnO_4$ solution

19. The following three analytical methods—spectrophotometry (S), photoluminescence (P), and fluorometry (F)—have differences in their respective sensitivities. Arrange them in order, from the least to the most sensitive, and then choose the corresponding answer.

    (A) $P < F < S$ (D) $P < S < F$
    (B) $S = F < P$ (E) None of the above
    (C) $F > P > S$

20. In a galvanic cell, the following reaction takes place:

$$2H_2O \rightleftharpoons O_2(g) + 4H^+ + 4e^-$$

It occurs at the:

    (A) cathode.   (D) external conductor.
    (B) anode.   (E) None of the above
    (C) cathode and anode.

21. Which of the addition reactions below will not proceed under ordinary circumstances?

I. $CH_2{=}CH_2 + HCl \rightarrow$

II. $CH_2{=}CH_2 + HOSO_3H \rightarrow$

III. $CH_2{=}CH_2 + NaOH \rightarrow$

IV. $CH_2{=}CH_2 + Br_2 \rightarrow$

(A) I and II
(B) IV only
(C) III only
(D) I, II and III
(E) I, II, and IV

22. Which of the compounds below is the product of the following reaction?

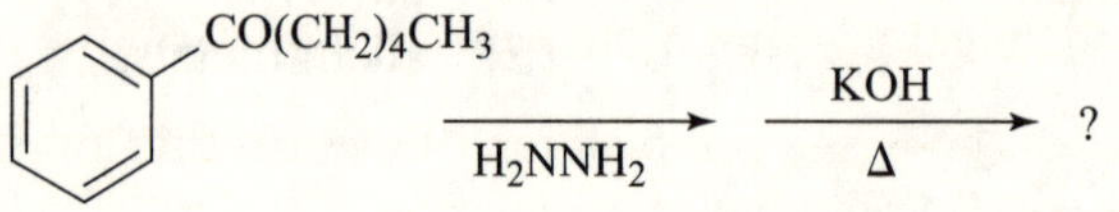

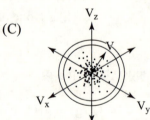

CO(CH2)4CH3
H2NNH2
KOH
Δ
?

(A)
COH(CH2)3CH3

(B)
COH(CH2)4CH3

(C)
OC(CH2)4CH3

(D)
(CH2)4CH3

(E)
(CH2)5CH3

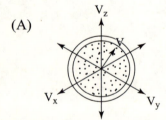

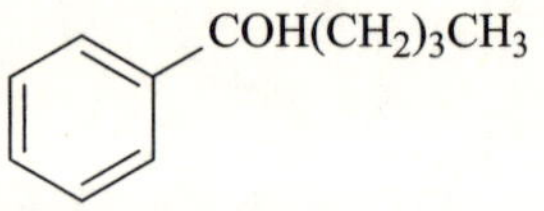

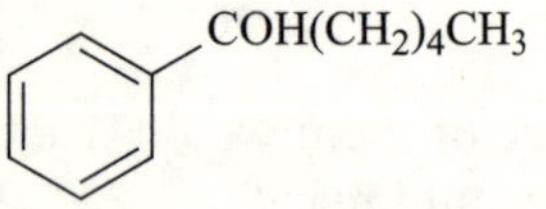

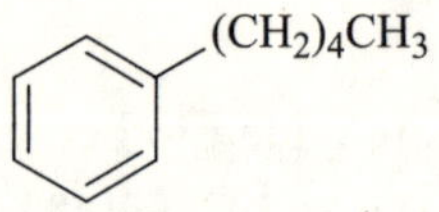

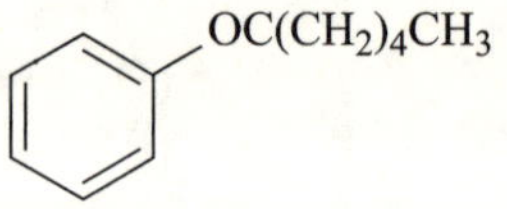

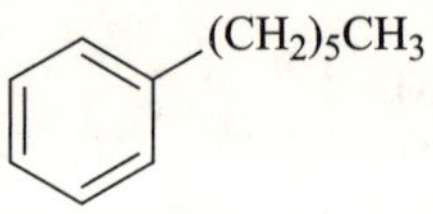

23. The reaction shown in question 22 is known as:

(A) Wolff-Kishner reduction.
(B) Clemmensen reduction.
(C) Friedel-Crafts reaction.
(D) Baeyer-Villiger oxidation.
(E) Rosenmund reduction.

24. The Maxwell distribution of molecular velocities is best represented by which of the following diagrams?

(A)
Vz
V
Vx
Vy

(B)
Vz
V
Vx
Vy

(C)
Vz
V
Vx
Vy

(D)
Vz
V
Vx
Vy

(E) None of the above

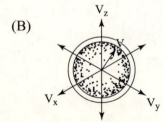

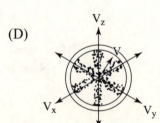

25. According to Le Châtelier's Principle, the addition of heat to the following reaction

$$CO_2(g) + 2H_2O(g) \rightarrow CH_4(g) + 2O_2(g)$$

will cause it to shift to the right. This reaction can therefore be described as

(A) spontaneous.
(B) endothermic.
(C) unimolecular.
(D) exothermic.
(E) adiabatic.

26. The rate constant of a chemical reaction is characterized by all of the following *except*:

(A) it is always dependent upon the composition of the reaction mixture.
(B) it depends exponentially upon the temperature.
(C) it is proportional to $e^{-Ea/Rt}$ (where E is the reaction's activation energy).
(D) the Eurim equation can be used to calculate it.
(E) it often follows the Arrhenius rate law.

27. The distribution of molecular speeds is dependent upon the molecular mass. Above, the speeds of H_2O, H_2, O_2 and CO_2 (versus the probability of the speed occurring) are shown. Select the answer that matches each molecule with its corresponding speed distribution curve.

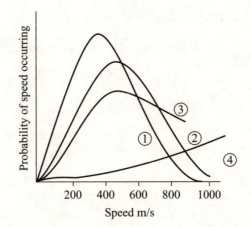

(A) ①—H_2O; ②—O_2; ③—CO_2; ④—H_2
(B) ①—H_2; ②—H_2O; ③—CO_2; ④—O_2
(C) ①—O_2; ②—CO_2; ③—H_2O; ④—H_2
(D) ①—CO_2; ②—H_2; ③—O_2; ④—H_2O
(E) ①—H_2O; ②—CO_2; ③—H_2; ④—O_2

28. $\frac{1}{2}Hg_2Cl_2(s) + \frac{1}{2}H_2(g) \rightarrow Hg(l) + HCl(aq)$ (not balanced). For this reaction

$$\Delta S_m^{\theta} = -31.0 \text{ J/k mole}$$

$$\Delta G_m^{\theta} = -25.82 \text{ kJ/mole}$$

$$T = 298 \text{ k}$$

$$\Delta E_m^{\theta} = -27.61 \text{ kJ/mole}$$

Using the appropriate information, calculate the enthalpy of the reaction.

(A) −38.69 kJ/mole   (D) −21.76 kJ/mole

(B) −35.06 kJ/mole   (E) 0 kJ/mole

(C) −16.58 kJ/mole

29. Transmetallation of an aryl bromide (or iodide) with an alkyllithium results in the production of a reagent that is capable of undergoing the same reactions as the Grignard reagents; this reagent is

(A) arylmetal.   (D) arylhalide.

(B) aryllithium.   (E) alkyllithium-bromide.

(C) alkylbromide (or iodide).

30. All of the following tests are used to identify aldehydes *except*:

    I.   Tollens' test   IV.   the ammonia test

    II. Fehling's test   V.   Benedict's test

    III. Baeyer's test

(A) I, II, and V   (D) II and IV

(B) III and IV   (E) III only

(C) IV only

31. For a second-order reaction, all of the following are true *except*:

(A) the half-life is not independent of the initial concentration.

(B) the rate can have a first-order dependence on each of the two reagents.

(C) no expression for the variation in the concentrations of the two reagents can be derived.

(D) a plot of $1/[A]_t$ against t is linear.

(E) the concentration of the reactant does not decrease by factors of $\frac{1}{2}$ in a series of regularly spaced time intervals.

32. The amount of chloride in a water supply is determined by titrating the sample against $AgNO_3$, as follows:

$$AgNO_3(aq) + Cl^-(aq) \rightarrow AgCl(s) + NO_3^-(aq)$$

What percentage of chloride is present in the water if 26.7 ml of 0.30M $AgNO_3$ is necessary to react with all of the chloride in a 14.0g sample? (Atomic weight Cl = 35.5.)

(A) $\dfrac{26.7(3)(1000)}{35.5(14)}$

(B) $\dfrac{26.7(3)(35.5)(100)}{1000(14)}$

(C) $\dfrac{26.7(3)(35.5)}{.3(1000)(14)}$

(D) $\dfrac{26.7(14)(.3)}{(1000)(35.5)}$

(E) $\dfrac{26.7(14)}{(.3)(1000)(35.5)}$

33. The boiling point of a substance is indicative of the intermolecular attractive forces present. With this in mind, list the following substances (Ne, HF, $BaCl_2$, H_2 and CO) in order of decreasing boiling points and then select the correct answer.

(A) $HF > CO > BaCl_2 > H_2 > Ne$
(B) $BaCl_2 > HF > CO > Ne > H_2$
(C) $HF > BaCl_2 > Ne > H_2 > CO$

(D) $H_2 > HF > BaCl_2 > CO > Ne$
(E) $BaCl_2 > CO > HF > H_2 > Ne$

34. Argon at 35°C and 1 atm. pressure in a container of volume $400cm^3$ is allowed to expand to $800cm^3$ and is simultaneously heated to a temperature of 115°C. The entropy change that would result could be obtained by solving which of the following equations?

(A) $nR\ln(115°C/35°C) + nC_{v,m}\ln(800cm^3/400cm^3)$
(B) $nR\ln[(388k/308k) + (800cm^3/400cm^3)]$
(C) $nR(800cm^3/400cm^3) + nC_{v,m}(388k/308k)$
(D) $nC_{v,m}\ln[(800cm^3/400cm^3) - (115°C/35°C)]$
(E) $nR\ln(800cm^3/400cm^3) + nC_{v,m}\ln(388k/308k)$

35. Detectors are often used in conjunction with chromatographic columns. They measure the separated solutes as they emerge. All of the features listed below are used in evaluating a detector *except* for

(A) stability.
(B) mass flow rate.
(C) linearity.

(D) noise level.
(E) response time.

36. The Aufbau principle is one that governs

(A) Coulomb potential.
(B) vapor pressure.
(C) critical molar volume.

(D) electronic configuration.
(E) the entropy.

37. Suppose that a sample has been analyzed by two different methods yielding standard deviations s_1 and s_2. Before t can be calculated, s_1 and s_2 have to be examined to determine whether or not the difference between them is significant. Given the following information and the table below, calculate the variance-ratio (v/r) and determine if s_1 and s_2 differ significantly.

Method 1	Method 2
$\overline{X}_1 = 41.24$	$\overline{X}_2 = 42.34$
$s_1 = 0.11$	$s_2 = 0.13$
$n_1 = 4$	$n_2 = 5$

F Values at the 95% Probability Level

$n - 1$ for smaller s^2	\multicolumn{6}{c}{$n - 1$ for larger s^2}
	3	4	5	6	10	20
3	9.28	9.12	9.01	8.94	8.79	8.66
4	6.59	6.39	6.26	6.16	5.96	5.80
5	5.41	5.19	5.05	4.95	4.74	4.56
6	4.76	4.53	4.39	4.28	4.06	3.87
10	3.71	3.48	3.33	3.22	2.98	2.77
20	3.10	2.87	2.71	2.60	2.35	2.12

(A) v/r = 1.40, no significant difference
(B) v/r = 0.72, no significant difference
(C) v/r = 7.34, the difference is significant
(D) v/r = 4.66, the difference is significant
(E) None of the above

38. To convert bromobenzene into methyl benzoate, a certain sequence of steps is required. These steps are listed below. Arrange them in the appropriate order and then choose the corresponding response.

Note: Each one of the steps may be used once, more than once, or not at all.

I. dry ether

II. excess methanol

III. carbon dioxide

IV. mineral acid catalyst

V. magnesium

VI. HBr

VII. sodium bicarbonate

(A) 6,1,5,3,5,7,2
(B) 1,5,6,6,3,2,4
(C) 5,1,6,3,7,2,7

(D) 6,5,1,3,2,7,4
(E) 5,1,3,6,2,4,4

39. The name of the compound pictured below is:

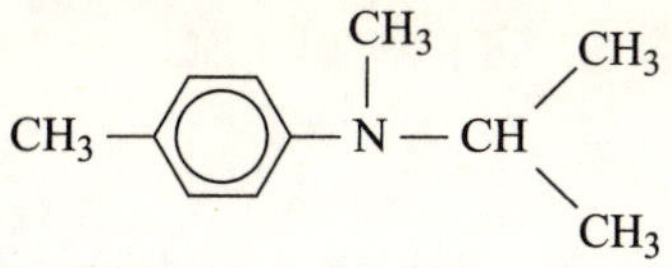

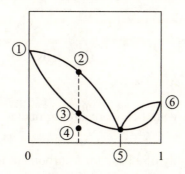

   (A) N,N-methylisopropyl-p-methyl aniline
   (B) p-isopropyl-p-methylaminotoluene
   (C) N,N-dimethyl-p-methylaminotoluene
   (D) p-methylisopropylamine-phenyl methane
   (E) N-methyl isopropyl-aminotoluene

40. In an isolated system, this reaction

$$Zn(s) + 2H^+(aq) \rightleftharpoons H_2(g) + Zn^{2+}(aq)$$

   is much more likely to take place than this reaction

$$Zn(s) + Cu^{2+}(aq) \rightleftharpoons Cu(s) + Zn^{2+}(aq).$$

   Which one of the following makes it possible to conclude this?

   (A) Third Law of Thermodynamics   (D) Dulong and Petit's Law
   (B) First Law of Thermodynamics   (E) Second Law of Thermodynamics
   (C) Einstein-Stark Law

41. In this low boiling azeotrope diagram, select the point where the azeotrope occurs.

   (A) ①   (C) ④   (E) ⑥
   (B) ②   (D) ⑤

42. Elements not found in nature, synthesized in nuclear reactions, and involving completion of the 5f electronic orbitals are known as the

   (A) lanthanides.   (C) actinides.   (E) rare gases.
   (B) halogens.   (D) transition metals.

43. Which of the following bonds ($\cdots$) is the least polar?

    (A) B $\cdots$ Cl   (D) C $\cdots$ Cl
    (B) H $\cdots$ I   (E) C $\cdots$ I
    (C) P $\cdots$ Br

44. The evolution of nitrogen gas upon the addition of sodium nitrite in mineral acid solution identifies the presence of a(n)

    (A) aromatic secondary amine.
    (B) tertiary amine.
    (C) aliphatic primary amine.
    (D) aromatic primary amine.
    (E) aliphatic tertiary amine.

45. A certain spectroscopic tool used for structure determination must be applied in the vapor phase. Its use is restricted to small molecules. In addition, it makes its determinations based on the energy differences between molecular rotational states. This technique is known as

    (A) infrared spectroscopy.   (D) mass spectroscopy.
    (B) n.m.r. spectroscopy.   (E) microwave spectroscopy.
    (C) ultraviolet spectroscopy.

46. The stability of a molecule is related to the strength of its covalent bonds. Based on this, select the most stable molecule.

    (A) O_2 (D) Cl_2
    (B) CH_4 (E) HF
    (C) H_2O

47. An isotope $^{242}_{94}Pu$ disintegrates by emitting 5α and 2β particles. The new isotope formed by this process is

    (A) $^{237}_{87}Cm$ (D) $^{237}_{89}Pu$
    (B) $^{222}_{82}Fr$ (E) $^{222}_{86}Rn$
    (C) $^{232}_{92}Am$

48. Indicate which one of the statements below, regarding nucleophilicity in a polar protic solvent, is *incorrect*.

    (A) Nucleophilicity is the affinity of a base for a carbon atom.
    (B) F^- is more reactive toward methyl iodide than Cl^-.
    (C) Second-row elements are invariably more nucleophilic than first-row elements of comparable basicity.
    (D) The rate of an S_N2 reaction may be markedly affected by the nucleophilicity of the attacking group.
    (E) The more basic electron pairs tend to be more nucleophilic.

49. Reactant formation in an endothermic reaction would be favored by which of the following?

    (A) an increase in temperature
    (B) a decrease in temperature
    (C) no change in temperature
    (D) first an increse and then a decrease in temperature
    (E) None of the above

50. A mixture of ethyl acetate and alcohol-free sodium ethoxide is heated at 78°C for eight hours. The mixture is then cooled to 10° and a small quantity of 33% aqueous aceticacid is slowly added. The aqueous layer is washed with ether and the combined organic layers are dried and distilled. Which of the compounds below is the chief product of the reaction?

    (A) ethyl acetoacetate
    (B) ethyl isobutyrate
    (C) dimethyl adipic acid
    (D) diethyl malonate
    (E) ethyl malonic acid

51. What is the principal product of the following reaction?

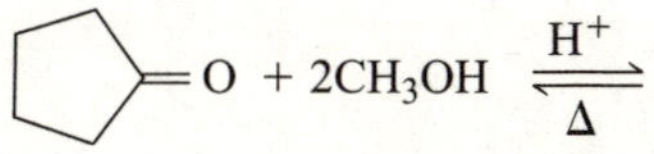

    (A) 5,5-dimethyl pentanal
    (B) cyclopentanone dimethyl ketal
    (C) 3-methyl-1,5-pentanedione
    (D) 2-methyl cyclopentanone
    (E) cyclopentane dimethyl acetal

52. A cell that is described as being "without a liquid junction"

    (A) cannot exist.
    (B) has only one electrode.
    (C) has two electrodes in the same electrolyte.
    (D) has a flowing junction modification.
    (E) has one electrode in two electrolytes.

53. If an aromatic or aryl halide is reacted with a strong base such as sodium amide ($NaNH_2$), and elimination takes place, all of the following may result *except*:

    (A)    (C) 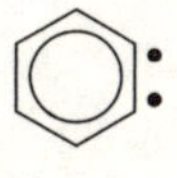   (E)

    (B)   (D)

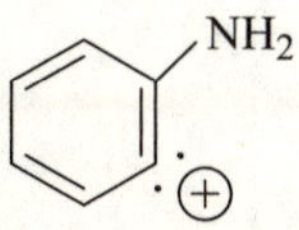

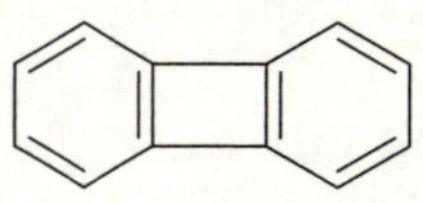

54. The heat flow of a system under isochoric conditions is a direct measurement of

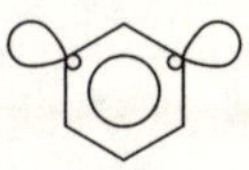

    (A) work.
    (B) ΔE.
    (C) ΔH.
    (D) ΔG.
    (E) entropy.

85

55. Select the graph that is typical of the height equivalent of a theoretical plate (HETP) versus mobile phase velocity for gas-liquid and liquid chromatography (GLC and LC, respectively).

(A)

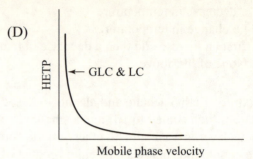

(D)

(B)

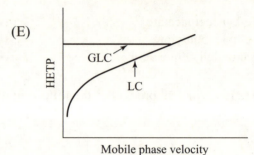

(E)

(C)

56. The stability of most cycloalkanes (which is indicated by their higher boiling and melting points), as well as their nonplanar structure, is not dependent upon:

(A) Baeyer strain.   (D) Strecker strain.

(B) Pitzer strain.   (E) nonbonded interactions.

(C) dipole-dipole interactions.

57. The nmr spectra for an isomer of $C_4H_8Br_2$ is shown below:

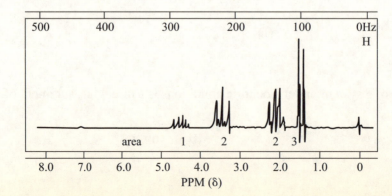

Based on this spectra, the name of the isomer is

(A) 1,1-dibromobutane.
(B) 1,3-dibromobutane.
(C) 1-bromo-2-bromomethyl propane.
(D) 1,2-cis-dibromobutane.
(E) 1,3-dibromo-2-methyl propane.

58. For the reaction below

$$2HN_3 + 2NO \rightarrow H_2O_2 + 4N_2$$

with the following molar enthalpies (at 25°C)

$$HN_3 - H_m^\theta = +264,\text{o kJ/mole}$$

$$N_2 - H_m^\theta = 0 \text{ kJ/mole}$$

$$H_2O_2 - H_m^\theta = -187.8 \text{ kJ/mole}$$

$$NO - H_m^\theta = +90.25 \text{ kJ/mole}$$

the change in the standard enthalpy for the reaction is

(A) −896.3 kJ.
(B) +937.4 kJ.
(C) −309.5 kJ
(D) +742.6 kJ.
(E) none of the above

59. Calculate the pOH of a solution made by mixing 70 ml of 0.10M NH_3 and 60 ml of 0.05M HCl. The reaction is $NH_3 + H_3O^+ \rightarrow NH_4^+ + H_2O$ with $k_{b\ NH_3} = 1.8 \times 10^{-3}$.

(A) $-\log(1.8 \times 10^{-3}) - \log\left(\dfrac{0.007}{0.003}\right)$

(B) $-\log(1.8 \times 10^{-3}) - \log\left(\dfrac{0.03}{0.04}\right)$

(C) $-\log(1.8 \times 10^{-3}) + \log\left(\dfrac{4.0}{3.0}\right)$

(D) $-\log(1.8 \times 10^{-3}) + \log\left(\dfrac{0.004}{0.003}\right)$

(E) $-\log(1.8 \times 10^{-3}) - \log\left(\dfrac{0.004}{0.003}\right)$

60. When compared to metals, nonmetals

(A) are less electronegative and have smaller atomic radii.
(B) have greater ionization energies and larger atomic radii.
(C) are more electronegative and have smaller atomic radii.
(D) have larger atomic radii and are more electronegative.
(E) have smaller atomic radii and lower ionization energies.

61. Which one of the following reactions is not usually stereospecific?

(A) Free-radical substitution
(B) S_N2
(C) E2
(D) Hydrogenation with Pd/H_2
(E) Addition of halogens to olefins

62. Catechol is treated with four reagents, as follows:

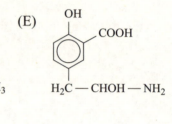

catechol $\xrightarrow[-HCl]{}$ A $\xrightarrow{POCl_3}$ B $\xrightarrow[-HCl]{^+CH_3NH_2}$ C $\xrightarrow{H_2 / Pd}$ D

What is the structure of D?

(A)
OH, OH
$H_2C-CH_2-CH_3$

(B)
OH, COOH
$H-C-CH_2-CH_3$
$\quad\ \ |$
$\quad\ OH$

(C)
OH, OH
$H-C-CH_2-NH-CH_3$
$\quad\ |$
$\quad OH$

(D)
OH, CHO
$O=C-NH-CH_3$

(E)
OH, COOH
$H_2C-CHOH-NH_2$

63. In the presence of Niewland catalyst (NH_4Cl, CuCl), acetylene dimerizes to form _____, which upon hydrogenation yields _____. The two blanks are best completed by which two substances, respectively?

   I. allylacetylene   III. 1,3-butadiene

   II. 2-butene   IV. vinylacetylene

(A) I and III   (C) II and IV   (E) None of the above pairs
(B) II and I   (D) IV and III

64. The best way to distinguish the presence of two enantiomers would be to

(A) compare their melting points.
(B) place one of them into solution and pass polarized light through it.
(C) dissolve each one (individually) in a particular solvent and then compare their respective solubilities.
(D) examine them for color differences.
(E) compare their respective abilities.

65. Which of the following expressions represent(s) a measure of the distribution of energy?

   I. The temperature   III. S (entropy)

   II. E (internal energy)   IV. The partition function

(A) I and IV   (C) I, II, and III   (E) III and IV
(B) II, III, and IV   (D) I only

66. Arrange the following acids in order of increasing strength: H_3O^+, H_2O, H_2, CCl_3CO_2H, HCO_4^- and HF.

    (A) $H_2O < HF < H_2 < H_3O^+ < HSO_4^- < CCl_3CO_2H$
    (B) $HF < H_2O < H_2 < HSO_4^- < CCl_3CO_2H < H_3O^+$
    (C) $H_2 < HF < H_2O < CCl_3CO_2H < H_3O^+ < HSO_4^-$
    (D) $H_2 < H_2O < HF < HSO_4^-CCl_3CO_2H < H_3O^+$
    (E) $H_2O < H_2 < H_3O^+ < HF < HSO_4^- < CCl_3CO_2H$

67. Calculate the number of carbon atoms in 27.3g of trichloroacetic acid. (Atomic weights: $C = 12.0$, $Cl = 35.5$, $O = 16.0$, $H = 1.0$.)

    (A) $27.3(2)(6.02 \times 10^{23})/163.5$

    (D) $\dfrac{27.3(6.02 \times 10^{23})(163.5)}{2(12.0)}$

    (B) $\dfrac{27.3(2)}{163.5}$

    (E) $\dfrac{27.3}{163.5}(6.02 \times 10^{23})$

    (C) $\dfrac{163.5(27.3)}{2(6.02 \times 10^{23})}$

68.

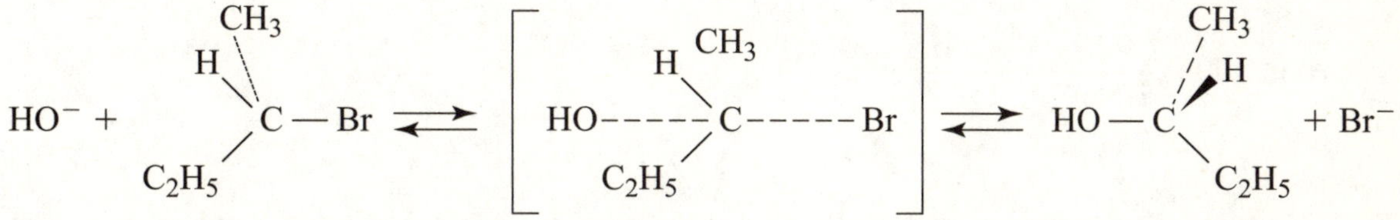

    The above reaction could best be described as a:

    (A) Markovnikov addition.
    (B) Cannizzaro reaction.
    (C) Wurtz inversion.
    (D) McLafferty rearrangement.
    (E) Walden inversion.

69. For the following reaction (carried out at 298 k) $\Delta u = -2180$ kJ/mol, $\Delta s = 182.4$ J/mol, and $\Delta H = -1630$ kJ/mol.

    Reaction: glucose $+ CO_2 \rightarrow 6CO_2 + 6H_2O$

    At constant volume, how much of this energy change can be extracted as work?

    (A) $[(-2810)] - [(298)(.1824)]$
    (B) $-2810 - 298/.1824$
    (C) $-2810 + 298(.1824)$
    (D) $-2810 - 298(182.4)$
    (E) $-2810 + 298(182.4)$

70. The molecules below are all nonaromatic *except* for:

(A)

(C)

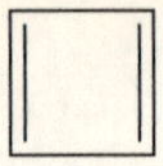

(E)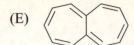

(B)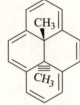

(D)

71. A 0.56g sample of iron ore is dissolved in acid; the iron is oxidized to the $+3$ state and then precipitated as $Fe_2O_3 \cdot xH_2O$. This precipitate is filtered, washed, and ignited to Fe_2O_3. The Fe_2O_3 weighs 0.29g. The reaction is: $2Fe^{3+} \rightarrow Fe_2O_3(s)$, and the atomic weights of iron and oxygen are 55.9 and 16.0, respectively. The percentage of iron in the sample would be equal to

(A) $100 \times \dfrac{0.56}{0.29} \times \dfrac{(55.9)^2}{159.8}$

(D) $100 \times \dfrac{55.9[(2 \times 159.8)/0.29]}{0.56}$

(B) $100 \times \dfrac{0.29[(2 \times 55.9)/159.8]}{0.56}$

(E) $100 \times \dfrac{[(2 \times 159.8)/0.56]0.29}{55.9}$

(C) $100 \times \dfrac{0.29}{2(55.9)} \times \dfrac{0.56}{159.8}$

72. One method of reducing carboxylic acid derivatives to aldehydes is the Stephen reduction. The reaction involves an intermediate that is readily hydrolyzed to the aldehyde. If the original carboxylic acid derivative is a nitrile 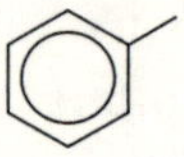 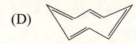 CN and the resulting aldehyde is 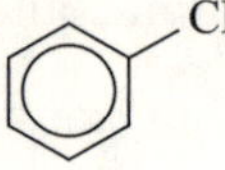 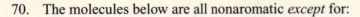 CHO, the intermediate is of the form

(A)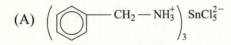

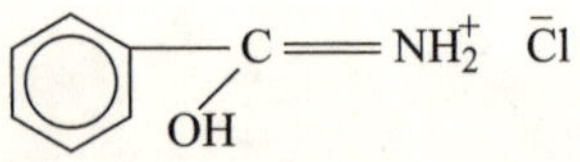

(D)

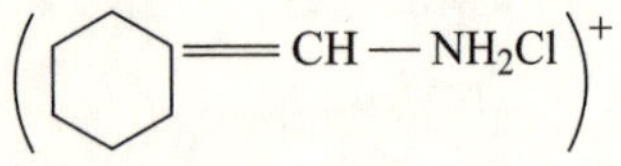

(B)

(E)

(C)

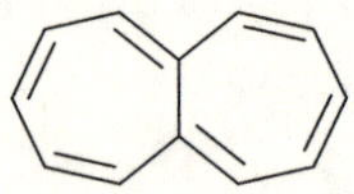

73. The graphs below show the behavior of various gases. Which of these gases exhibits behavior that deviates most significantly from that expected for an ideal gas?

(A)
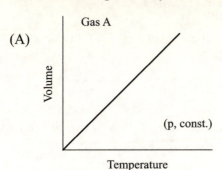

(D)
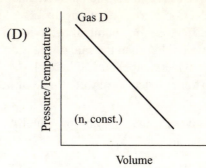

(B)
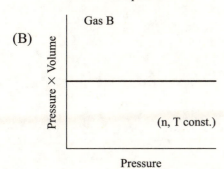

(E)
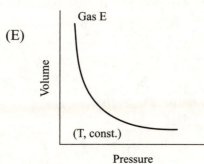

(C)
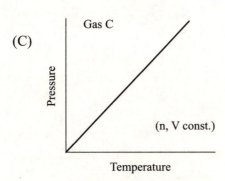

74. Which of the statements below about carbonate error is *not* true?

   (A) If methyl orange is used as the indicator, this type of error will be maximized.
   (B) It will be minimized if barium hydroxide is used as the titrant.
   (C) Sodium hydroxide can be prepared and then protected to avoid this type of error.
   (D) If the titrant is stored in a bottle equipped with a tube containing Ascarite, this error will be diminished.
   (E) A solution that has sodium carbonate at the bottom of its container has minimal error of this kind.

75. Which of the following statements is *true* of isotopes?

    (A) They have different atomic numbers and the same atomic masses.
    (B) Their electronic configurations differ.
    (C) Slight differences in chemical behavior of isotopes (called isotope effects) influence the kind of reaction rather than the rate of reaction itself.
    (D) They have identical chemical behaviors.
    (E) The first ones discovered were those of neon.

76. If an alkene gives 2-butanone and propanal when treated with ozone followed by zinc and water, what is its structure?

    (A) 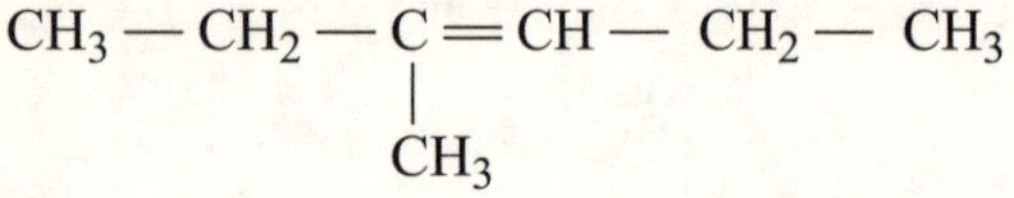
    $$CH_3 - CH_2 - \overset{\displaystyle |}{\underset{\displaystyle CH_3}{C}} = CH - CH_2 - CH_3$$

    (B)
    $$CH_3 - CH_2 - CH = CH - \overset{\displaystyle CH_3}{\underset{\displaystyle |}{CH}} - CH_3$$

    (C)
    $$CH_3 - CH_2 - CH_2 - \underset{\displaystyle |}{\overset{}{CH}} \;\|\; CH - CH_3$$
    $$CH_3 - CH_2 - CH_2$$
    $$|$$
    $$CH$$
    $$\|$$
    $$CH$$
    $$|$$
    $$CH_3$$

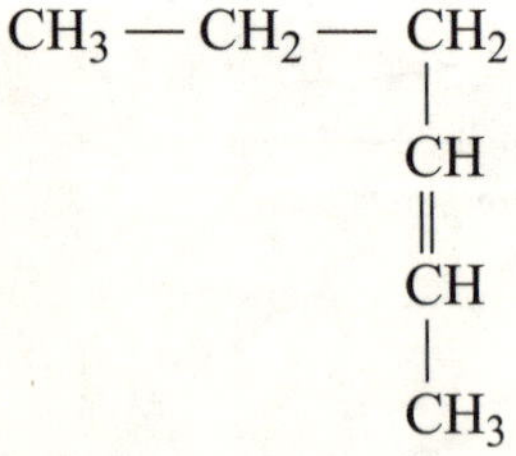

    (D) 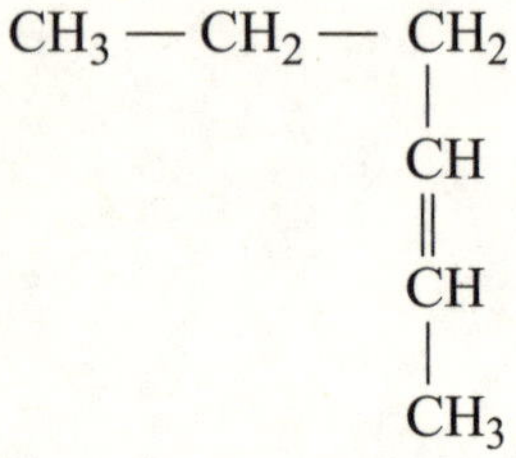
    $$CH_3 - CH_2 - CH_2$$
    $$|$$
    $$CH$$
    $$\|$$
    $$CH$$
    $$|$$
    $$CH_3$$

    (E) 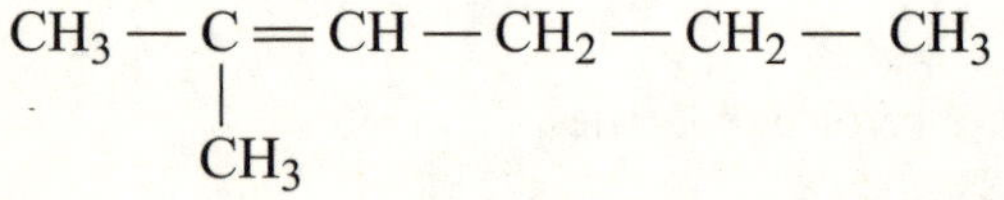
    $$CH_3 - \overset{\displaystyle |}{\underset{\displaystyle CH_3}{C}} = CH - CH_2 - CH_2 - CH_3$$

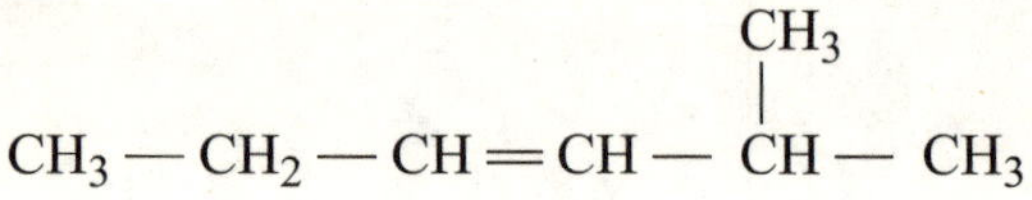

77. The two missing structures A and B are, respectively:

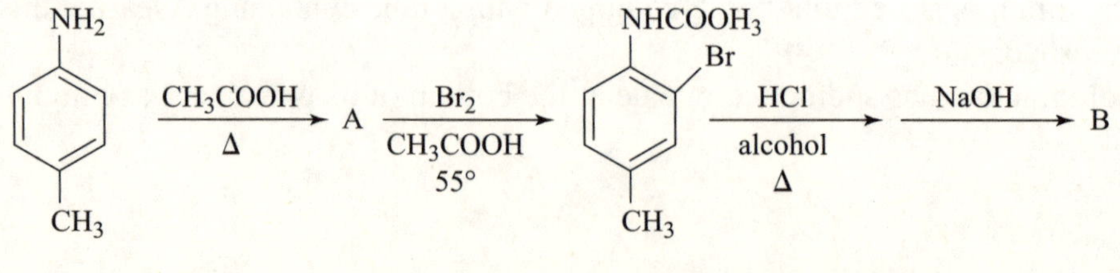

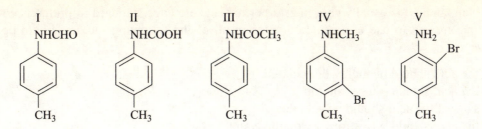

I	II	III	IV	V
NHCHO	NHCOOH	NHCOCH₃	NHCH₃	NH₂

(A) I and II   (C) III and V   (E) I and III
(B) III and IV   (D) II and IV

78. An atom containing two electrons that possess the following quantum numbers

$$n = 3, i = 1, m_1 = 1, M_s = -\frac{1}{2} \text{ and } l = 1, n = 3, m_s = -\frac{1}{2}, m_1 = 1$$

may not exist based on

(A) Hund's Rule.   (D) Heisenberg's Uncertainty Principle.
(B) Pauli's Exclusion Principle.   (E) Bohr's Model.
(C) Lewis's Law.

79. According to Henry's Law, at a fixed temperature, the amount of gas dissolved in a given quantity of solvent is proportional to the

(A) partial pressure of the solvent.
(B) total pressure of the solution.
(C) partial pressure of the gas in the solution.
(D) partial pressure of the gas above the solution.
(E) None of the above

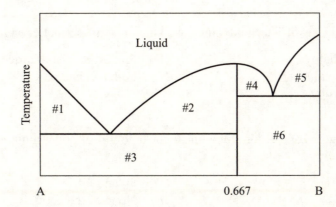

80. In the above phase diagram, numbers are assigned to specific areas. Select the answer that correctly describes the phases present in a given area.

(A) #3—solid A and solid A₂B   (D) #5—solid B and liquid AB₂
(B) #1—liquid A   (E) #2—liquid A₂B
(C) #6—solid B and solid AB₂

81. In the lab, an acid is usually chosen as a permanent reference standard in preference to a base. In selecting an acid to use in a standard solution all of the following factors should be considered *except*:

(A) the acid should be highly dissociated.
(B) the acid should not be volatile.
(C) salts of the acid should be soluble.
(D) the acid should be a strong oxidizing agent.
(E) a solution of the acid should be stable.

82. According to Gibbs phase rule, the number of degrees of freedom for a four-component system of one phase is:

(A) 5.   (D) 2.
(B) 3.   (E) 7.
(C) 4.

83.

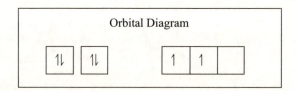

The above arrangement of electrons in the orbitals of a carbon atom is based on

(A) Heisenberg's Uncertainty Principle.
(B) Lewis's Law.
(C) Bohr's Model.
(D) Hund's Rule.
(E) Pauli's Exclusion Principle.

84. Based on the Third Law of Thermodyanics, we know that all perfect crystals at absolute zero have

(A) the same enthalpy.   (D) the same crystal lattices.
(B) differing ΔA values.   (E) both (A) and (C).
(C) the same entropy.

85. The vibrational degrees of freedom for a linear and a nonlinear polyatomic molecule of seven atoms each are, respectively:

(A) 30 and 32.   (D) 30 and 29.
(B) 29 and 30.   (E) None of the above
(C) 28 and 29.

86. Which of the following graphs best represents the Maxwell distribution of molecular speeds and its dependence on temperature?

(A)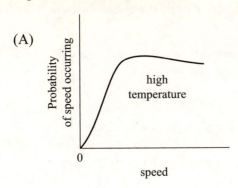

(D)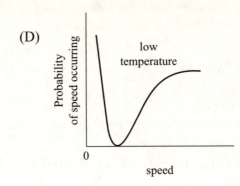

(B)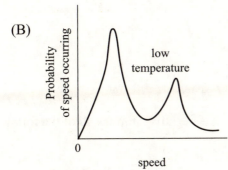

(E)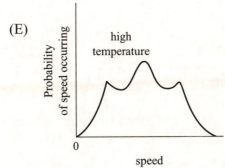

(C)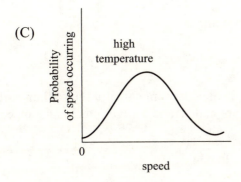

87. Based on the concept of nuclear stability, choose the correct statement from among the following.

(A) Heavier, more stable nuclei have somewhat larger numbers of protons than neutrons.
(B) A stable nucleus cannot have its configuration transformed even with the addition of energy from the outside.
(C) Unstable nuclei do not spontaneously change to nuclei with stable configurations.
(D) Usually, lighter stable nuclei have equal numbers of neutrons and protons.
(E) Nuclei can never have an equal number of protons and neutrons.

88. The energy of a molecule between two phases is intermediate between that of the free molecule and that of the molecule in the bulk. Its potential energy would be reduced if it is moved into the bulk. Thus, molecules are under the influence of a force that tends to draw them into the bulk. This force is called the

(A) flux
(B) adhesive force
(C) fugacity
(D) surface tension
(E) None of the above

89. The formula below represents a member of the class of compounds that are known as:

$$CH_3CH_2CH_2CH_2CH_2CH_2CH_2CH_2CH_2CH_2CH_2CH_2CH_2CH_2CH_2CH_2CH_2C \underset{\underset{O}{\|}}{} O^-Na^+$$

(A) steroids
(B) carbohydrates
(C) vitamins
(D) soaps
(E) acids

90. The expression for W, in the First Law of Thermodynamics, if negative, implies all of the following *except*:

(A) work has been done by the system.
(B) the total internal energy has decreased.
(C) a negative amount of work has been done on the system.
(D) the system has lost heat.
(E) work has been done on the outside world.

91. A small sample of some compound is heated with a piece of sodium metal until the sodium melts. Alcohol, aqueous acid, and later silver nitrate solution are added, and a silver precipitate appears. The original compound must contain a(n):

(A) epoxide.
(B) aldehyde.
(C) halogen.
(D) alkali metal.
(E) phenol.

92. A real gas, due to its intermolecular interactions, does not obey the ideal gas law. Instead its behavior is described by the Van der Waals equation of state. Choose the letter that correctly shows this equation.

(A) $p = (V - nb)/(nRT) - an^2/v^2$

(B) $\left(p + \dfrac{an^2}{V^2}\right)(V - nb) = nRT$

(C) $(p - b)\left(V - \dfrac{an^2}{V^2}\right) = nRT$

(D) $p = nRT/(an^2) - V + nb$
(E) $pV = (nRT - b)/an^2$

93. Which of the following pairs are anomeric?

I.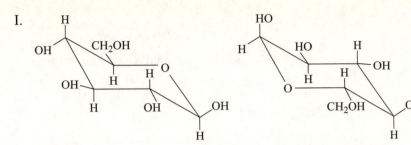

II.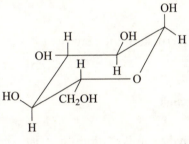

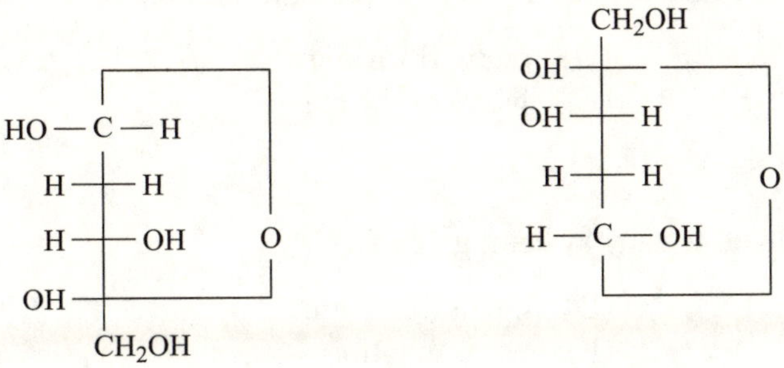

III.

IV.

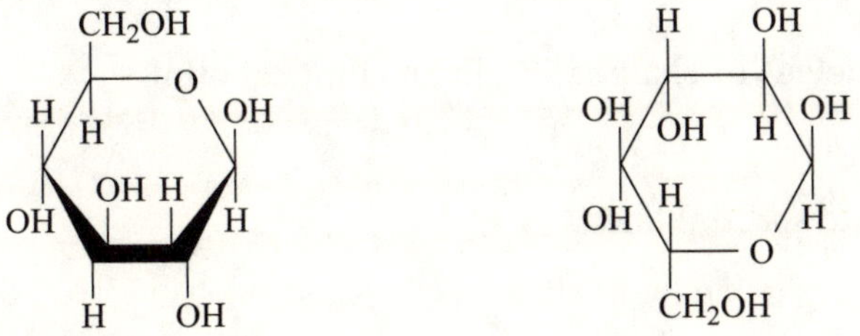

(A) I, III, and IV
(B) II only
(C) I only

(D) I and IV
(E) I and III

94. For the reaction below:

$$CaCO_3(g) \rightarrow CaO_{(s)} + CO_2(g)$$

(A) $\Delta H < 0$, $\Delta G \geq 0$ and $\Delta S > 0$
(B) $\Delta H \leq 0$, $\Delta G < 0$ and $\Delta S < 0$
(C) $\Delta S > 0$, $\Delta G < 0$ and $\Delta H > 0$
(D) $\Delta G \geq 0$, $\Delta H \geq 0$ and $\Delta S > 0$
(E) $\Delta S < 0$, $\Delta H > 0$ and $\Delta G < 0$

95. Nuclear magnetic resonance (nmr) spectroscopy is characterized by which of the following features?

    I.   chemical shift

    II. Rayleigh scattering

    III. minimal sensitivity to water

    IV. the ability to analyze caffeine samples

    (A) I only
    (B) II and III
    (C) I, II, and IV
    (D) I, II, III, and IV
    (E) I and IV

96. The separation factor (s or α) for a specific column is equal to the ratio of the:

    (A) retention times.
    (B) distributions coefficients.
    (C) resolutions.
    (D) eddy diffusions.
    (E) None of the above

97. The Schrödinger equation, when solved for any system, gives the

    (A) polarizability.
    (B) energy fluctuation.
    (C) magnetogyric ratio.
    (D) mean free path.
    (E) wave function.

98. Relaxation methods are crucial for the study of

    (A) reaction kinetics.
    (B) fast reactions.
    (C) equilibrium constants.
    (D) slow reactions.
    (E) rate theory.

99. The Bohr theory for "hydrogenlike" atoms consists (in part) of which of the following postulates?

    I.   The electron moves around the nucleus of charge $+Ze$ in an elliptical orbit.

    II. The orbit has constant energy.

    III. Transitions between orbits generate spectral lines.

    IV. The frequency of the spectral lines is given by $h/\Delta E$.

    (A) I, II, and III
    (B) I and IV
    (C) II and III
    (D) II only
    (E) IV only

100. Aldehydes and ketones exist in solution as an equilibrium mixture of two isomeric forms. These two forms are

    I.   keto form

    II. aldol form

    III. enol form

    IV. iso form

    (A) I and IV
    (B) II and III
    (C) II and IV
    (D) I and III
    (E) none of the preceeding combinations

101. Displacement reactions that proceed by the S_N2 mechanism are most successful with compounds that are

    (A) secondary halides with branches at C-2.
    (B) neopentyl system.
    (C) primary compounds with no branches at the β-carbon.
    (D) tertiary compounds with no branches at the β-carbon.
    (E) primary halides with branches at the α-carbon.

102. The alkylation of malonic esters with α, ω-dibromides is a general method for the synthesis of

    (A) acetoacetic esters   (D) five-carbon rings
    (B) straight-chain carboxylic acids   (E) diols
    (C) ketones

103. For a homologous series (n-hexane, n-heptane, n-octane, and n-nonane), select the graph that appropriately represents the relationship between the number of carbon atoms and the logarithm of the retention volume (V_R).

(A)
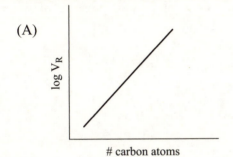

(D)
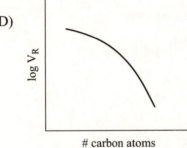

(B) 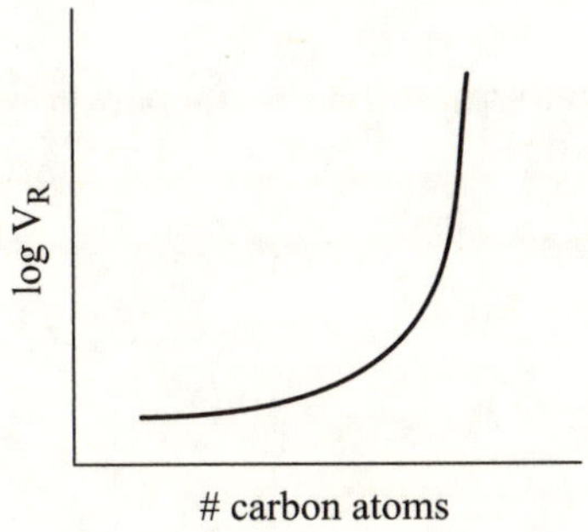
(E)
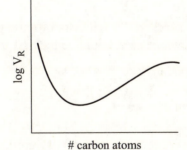

(C)

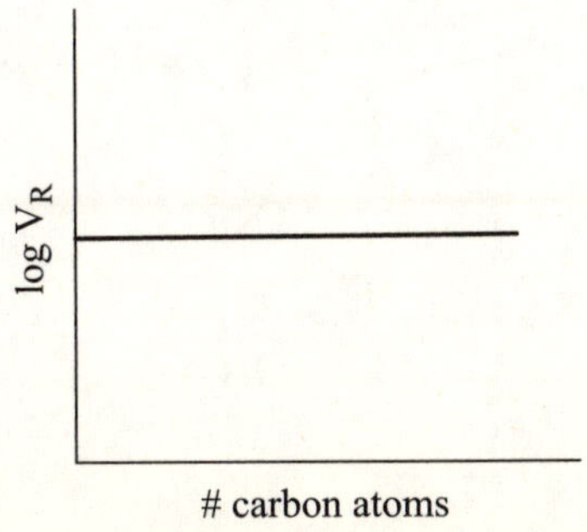

104. A sample of ammonium nitrite weighing 5.36g is heated in a test tube as shown below.

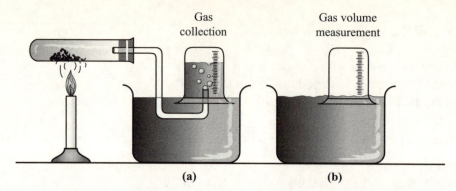

(a) Collection of a gas over water. (b) When the gas has been collected, the bottle is raised or lowered to equalize pressures inside and outside before measuring volume of gas collected.

The ammonium nitrite decomposes according to the following reaction: $NH_4NO_2(s) \rightarrow N_2(g) + 2H_2O(g)$. What total volume of N_2 will be collected in the beaker? (Barometric pressure is 750mm Hg, water and gas temperature are 26°C, $MW_{NH_4NO_2} = 64.0$, and vapor pressure of water at 26°C = 25mm Hg.)

(A) $\dfrac{5.36(750)}{64.0}(299)$

(D) $\dfrac{5.36}{64.0}\dfrac{(760)}{(750-25)}(299)(0.821)$

(B) $\dfrac{5.36(725)}{(0.0821)(64.0)}(299)$

(E) $\left(\dfrac{5.36}{64.0}\right)\left(\dfrac{760}{725}\right)\left(\dfrac{299}{0.0821}\right)$

(C) $\dfrac{5.36(750-25)}{64.0(299)(0.0821)}$

105. In order to successfully achieve a difficult gas-liquid chromatographic (GLC) separation, which one of the following gases would be the best to use as a carrier gas?

(A) hydrogen
(B) helium
(C) carbon dioxide

(D) nitrogen
(E) argon

106. Arrange the following compounds in order of decreasing boiling points.

(A) 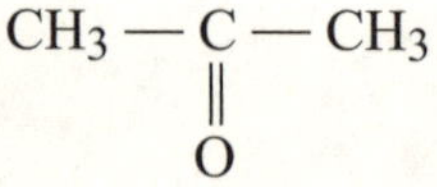
$$CH_3 - \underset{\underset{O}{\|}}{C} - CH_3$$

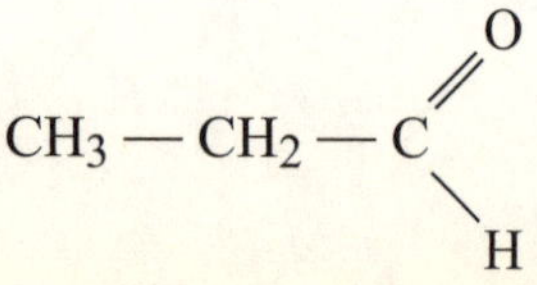

(D) 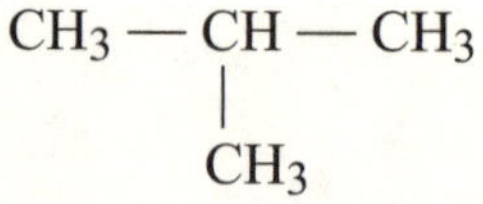
$$CH_3 - \underset{\underset{CH_3}{|}}{CH} - CH_3$$

(B)
$$CH_3 - \underset{\underset{OH}{|}}{CH} - CH_3$$

(E) 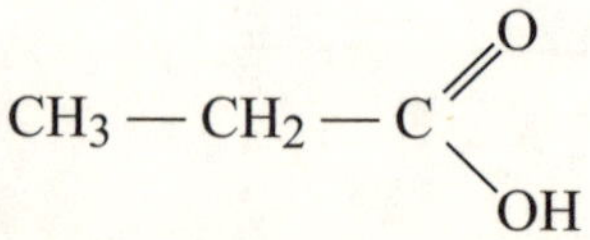
$$CH_3 - CH_2 - C\overset{\displaystyle O}{\underset{\displaystyle OH}{\diagdown}}$$

(C)
$$CH_3 - CH_2 - C\overset{\displaystyle O}{\underset{\displaystyle H}{\diagdown}}$$

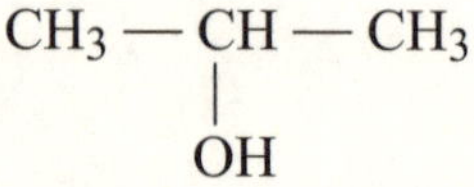

(F) $CH_3 - O - CH_3$

(A) B > E > A > C > F > D
(B) E > B > A > C > D > F
(C) A > B > E > F > C > D
(D) E > A > B > C > F > D
(E) B > A > C > E > D > F

107. If one measures the gradient of the E.M.F. of a cell with respect to temperature, the end result will be a value for

   (A) ΔH of the cell reaction.
   (B) ΔS of the cell reaction.
   (C) Q of the cell.
   (D) the heat of the cell reaction.
   (E) ΔG of the cell reaction.

108. The kinetic theory of gases is based on all of the following assumptions *except*:

   (A) a gas consists of many particles of mass m, in continual motion.
   (B) gas particles have negligible size.
   (C) at high pressures, gas particles are difficult to compress.
   (D) gas particles interact only by undergoing elastic collisions.
   (E) None of the above

109. What type of orbital hybridization and geometry is used by the central atom of NH_2^-?

   (A) sp^2 hybridization and trigonal planar.
   (B) sp^2 hybridization and tetrahedral geometry.
   (C) sp^3 hybridization and trigonal planar.
   (D) sp hybridization and linear geometry.
   (E) sp^3 hybridization and tetrahedral geometry.

110. The possible number of infrared absorption bands is very large for polyatomic molecules. Many of these vibrations are degenerate, that is, they

   (A) occur as overtones.
   (B) occur at the same frequency.
   (C) decrease over time.
   (D) fluctuate periodically.
   (E) occur at $\frac{1}{2}$ the wavelength of the fundamental node.

111. The number of stereoisomers that D-glucose (a six-carbon sugar) has is

   (A) 26
   (B) 24
   (C) 12
   (D) 16
   (E) 8

112.

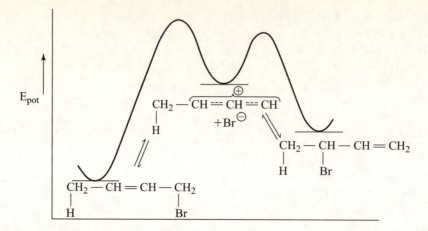

Based on the above diagram, one can conclude that

(A) 1,2 addition is most likely to occur at a low temperature.
(B) 1,4 addition is most likely to take place at a low temperature.
(C) 1,2 addition is favored by a high temperature.
(D) 1,2 addition and 1,4 addition are equally likely to occur at any given temperature.
(E) None of the above

113. A perpetual motion machine capable of generating increasing amounts of energy without interacting with its surroundings cannot exist. This is best explained by the

(A) First Law of Thermodynamics.   (D) Gibbs-Helmholtz equation.
(B) Third Law of Thermodynamics.   (E) Second Law of Thermodynamics.
(C) Energy Conservation Principle.

114. In the diagram shown, the reversible isothermal work of expansion done on the system is represented by which area(s)?

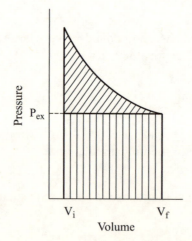

(A) ⧄ area only   (C) No work is done   (E) None of the above

(B) ‖‖‖ area only   (D) ⧄ and ‖‖‖ areas

115. Which one of the following represents the behavior of Helmholtz free energy (A), under constant volume and temperature conditions, for spontaneous, nonspontaneous, or equilibrium situations?

	Spontaneous Process	Equilibrium	Nonspontaneous Process
(A)	+	+	−
(B)	−	0	+
(C)	0	−	−
(D)	0	+	0
(E)	+	0	−

116. The height equivalent of a theoretical plate (HETP) has all of the following characteristics *except*

   (A) it is defined by the van Deemter equation.
   (B) it describes a certain length of chromatographic column.
   (C) the smaller this value is, the better the separation attainable.
   (D) the inverse of this quantity times the total column length is equal to the number of theoretical plates in the column.
   (E) equilibrium is attained at each height equivalent.

117. The basic data of chemical kinetics are the concentrations of the reactants and products as a function of time. There are several methods available for monitoring the concentrations of reactants and products. Of the methods listed below, select the one that is *not* used.

   (A) Thermal analysis
   (B) Recording of the pressure as a function of time
   (C) Measurement of the angle of optical rotation
   (D) Periodic bleeding of the reaction mixture for chromatographic analysis
   (E) Monitoring of the conductivity of a solution

118. Liquid-membrane electrodes contain a liquid exchanger that is held between two porous glass (or plastic) membranes. It serves to separate the test solution from the internal solution and has a greater tendency to bond calcium than any other ion. At each interface, the following reaction occurs:

$$Ca^{2+}(aq) + Ex^{2-} \rightleftharpoons CaEx$$

As it proceeds, a potential develops. This potential is equal to

   (A) $E_{Ext} = k_1 - \dfrac{0.059}{1} \log \dfrac{(a_2)_{aq}}{(a_1)_{Ext}}$

   (D) $E_{Ext} = k_1 + \dfrac{0.059}{2} \log \dfrac{(a_1)_{aq}}{(a_1)_{Ext}}$

   (B) $E_{Ext} = k_2 + \dfrac{0.059}{2} \log \dfrac{(a_1)_{Ext}}{(a_2)_{Ext}}$

   (E) $E_{Ext} = k_2 + \dfrac{0.059}{2} \log \dfrac{(a_1)_{aq}}{(a_2)_{Ext}}$

   (C) $E_{Ext} = k_2 + \dfrac{0.059}{1} \log \dfrac{(a_1)_{Ext}}{(a_1)_{aq}}$

119. $\Delta H_{formation}$ of NOCl(g) from the gaseous elements

$$\frac{1}{2}N_2(g) + \frac{1}{2}O_2(g) + \frac{1}{2}Cl_2(g) = NOCl(g)$$

is equal to 12.6 kcal/mole at 25°C. Assuming the gases are ideal, ΔE would equal which one of the following (1 kcal = 4.184 kJ)?

(A) 12.6 kJ   (D) 74,220 J

(B) 46,300 J   (E) insufficient information given

(C) 53.8 kJ   to find ΔE

120. Assuming that the energy of an electron is quantized, which of the following statements is *not* true?

(A) The centrifugal force created by the electron's motion about the nucleus is counterbalanced by the electrostatic attraction between the nucleus and the electron.

(B) The radius (R) of an electron's orbit about the nucleus is equal to $R = n^2 a_0 / z$, (where z = atomic number, a_0 = size of the orbit, and n = quantum number).

(C) If the principal quantum number (n) of an electron is known, only the size of its orbit and the energy of the electron can be calculated.

(D) As the principal quantum number increases, the difference in energy between the levels decreases.

(E) The energy (E) of an electron in a hydrogenlike ion is equal to $E = -kz^2/n^2$ (z = atomic number, k = a constant, and n = quantum number).

121. All of the following assumptions would be in agreement with the existence of ideal gases, *except* one, which is

(A) the particles of such a gas are in random motion.

(B) collisions between the gas particles are elastic.

(C) there are no mutual interactions between the particles of such a gas.

(D) the average translational kinetic energy of the particles is proportional to the absolute temperature.

(E) the gas particles have zero volume.

122. A sample of iron ore from the Bureau of Standards was analyzed by a chemist and the following results were obtained:

$$\bar{x} = 10.53 \ (\% \ iron), \ s = 0.05, \ n = 10.$$

The bureau's value for this sample is 10.61% iron. How do these results differ at a 95% probability level? (Use the table below as needed.)

Some Values of Student's t

Number of observations, n	Number of degrees of freedom, n − 1	Probability levels			
		50%	90%	95%	99%
2	1	1.000	6.314	12.706	63.66
3	2	0.816	2.920	4.303	9.925
4	3	0.765	2.353	3.182	5.841
5	4	0.741	2.132	2.776	4.604
6	5	0.727	2.015	2.571	4.032
7	6	0.718	1.943	2.447	3.707
8	7	0.711	1.895	2.365	3.500
9	8	0.706	1.860	2.306	3.355
10	9	0.703	1.833	2.262	3.250
11	10	0.700	1.812	2.228	3.169
21	20	0.687	1.725	2.086	2.845
∞	∞	0.674	1.645	1.960	2.576

(A) Not by much
(B) Significantly
(C) Can't be determined
(D) Not by much but still can't be used
(E) Results vary but are still within the range of use

123. 2.4 liter of HNO_3 solution reacts with 63 ml of 1.9N $Ba(OH)_2$ to produce a neutral solution. What is the molarity (M) of the original HNO_3 solution?

(A) $\dfrac{63(1.9)}{1000(2.4)}M$ (D) $\dfrac{(63)(1.9)}{1000(2)(2.4)}M$

(B) $\dfrac{63(1.9)}{1000}M$ (E) $\dfrac{(63)(1.9)}{100(2.4)}M$

(C) $\dfrac{2(63)(1.9)}{1000}M$

124. Kirchhoff's Law is applicable to a system when

(A) the temperature is a constant.
(B) all the heat capacities are known in the range of being examined.
(C) the heat capacity is measured at constant volume.
(D) only certain specific species are present.
(E) one assumes that all the heat capacity values are independent of temperature.

125. The charge on an electron was determined by measurement of the effect of an electric field on the rate at which charged oil droplets fell under the influence of gravity. This discovery was made by

    (A) J. J. Thomson.
    (B) E. Rutherford.
    (C) R. Millikan.
    (D) H. Becquerel.
    (E) W. C. Roentgen.

126. The van der Waals equation of state has two constant terms (a and b) that are not present in the combined gas law. The following is *true* of the terms a and b:

    (A) b corrects for the intermolecular forces of interaction and 'a' for the included volume of the molecules.
    (B) a corrects for the external pressure of the gas and 'b' for the internal pressure of the gas.
    (C) a corrects for the force of intermolecular interaction and 'b' for the excluded volume of the molecules.
    (D) b corrects for the free volume and 'a' for the intermolecular repulsion between molecules.
    (E) None of the above

127. Which of the following elements is *not* a component of Wood's metal?

    (A) Bismuth
    (B) Lead
    (C) Tin
    (D) Titanium
    (E) Cadmium

128. All of the following statements about ΔS are true *except*

    (A) it is a measure of the energy dispersal.
    (B) the natural tendency is for it to increase.
    (C) it is not a state function.
    (D) it can be defined both thermodynamically and statistically.
    (E) $\Delta S = O$ for a reversible process.

129. Volumetric glassware needs to be calibrated periodically in order to maintain its precision and accuracy. All of the methods listed below are ways of calibrating this glassware *except*

    (A) direct, absolute calibration
    (B) relative calibration
    (C) complex calibration
    (D) calibration by comparison
    (E) None of the above

130. The nucleophilic aromatic substitution that can occur on a benzene ring is affected by the substituent group(s) present. Which one of the following statements correctly describes such a substituent group and its effects?

    (A) $-CN$, electron withdrawing, destabilizes carbanion
    (B) $-COOH$, electron releasing, activates the ring
    (C) $-NO_2$, stabilizes carbanion, activates the ring
    (D) $-R$, destabilizes carbanion, electron withdrawing
    (E) $-CHO$, deactivates the ring, destabilizes carbanion

131. The strongly repulsive interaction that takes place when an α particle closely approaches a gold nucleus is best explained by

    (A) Dalton's theory.   (D) Gauss's law.
    (B) Marsden's rule.   (E) Coulomb's law.
    (C) Thomson's model.

132. All of the following equations are Maxwell's relations, with one exception. Indicate the letter of the equation that does not designate a correct Maxwell reaction.

    (A) $(\partial T/\partial V)_S = -(\partial P/\partial S)_V$ (D) $(\partial T/\partial P)_S = (\partial V/\partial S)_P$
    (B) $(\partial P/\partial T)_V = (\partial S/\partial V)_T$ (E) $(\partial S/\partial P)_V = -(\partial T/\partial V)_P$
    (C) $(\partial V/\partial T)_P = -(\partial S/\partial P)_T$

133. For a sodium ion selective electrode, all of the following statements are *true* except the

    (A) boundary potential depends upon the activities of both sodium and hydrogen ions.
    (B) electrode is specific for sodium ions.
    (C) potential is largely a function of the sodium ion activity.
    (D) selectivity of the glass electrode is related to the cation-exchange selectivity of the glass surface.
    (E) sodium ions can penetrate the gel and influence the diffusion potential.

134. What is the right configuration of an element with 24 electrons?

    (A) $1s^2 2s^2 2p^6 3s^2 3p^6 3d^6$ (D) $1s^2 2s^2 2p^6 3s^2 3p^6 4s^1 3d^5$
    (B) $1s^2 2s^2 2p^6 3s^2 3p^6 4s^2 3d^4$ (E) $1s^2 2s^2 3s^2 2p^6 3p^6 4s^2 3d^4$
    (C) $1s^2 2s^2 3s^2 2p^6 3p^6 4s^1 4p^5$

135. The Clapeyron equation applies to a phase change involving only condensed phases. However, the Clausius-Claypeyron equation applies to phase transitions between

    (A) two condensed phases at different temperatures only.
    (B) two condensed phases at different pressures only.
    (C) a liquid phase and a gas phase.
    (D) a gas phase and any condensed phase.
    (E) None of the above

136. Of the many chemical reactions known, only a few meet the necessary requirements in order to be used in titration processes. Which one of the requirements listed below is not necessary for a reaction to be used in titrimetric analysis?

    (A) The reaction can have no side reactions.
    (B) The equilibrium constant of the reaction must be very large.
    (C) The reaction should proceed according to a definite chemical equation.
    (D) The reaction should proceed very slowly so that the endpoint is readily observable.
    (E) Some instrumental method should be available to tell the analyst when to stop the addition of titrant.

Answer Key

1. D	24. C	47. E	70. B	93. D	116. E
2. E	25. B	48. B	71. B	94. C	117. A
3. A	26. D	49. B	72. E	95. E	118. D
4. C	27. D	50. A	73. D	96. E	119. C
5. E	28. B	51. B	74. A	97. E	120. C
6. E	29. B	52. C	75. E	98. B	121. E
7. E	30. E	53. B	76. A	99. C	122. B
8. E	31. C	54. B	77. C	100. D	123. A
9. D	32. B	55. A	78. B	101. C	124. B
10. E	33. B	56. D	79. D	102. D	125. C
11. B	34. E	57. B	80. C	103. A	126. C
12. D	35. B	58. A	81. D	104. D	127. D
13. A	36. D	59. E	82. A	105. D	128. C
14. B	37. A	60. C	83. D	106. B	129. C
15. D	38. E	61. A	84. C	107. B	130. C
16. D	39. A	62. C	85. E	108. C	131. E
17. B	40. E	63. D	86. C	109. E	132. E
18. A	41. D	64. B	87. D	110. B	133. B
19. D	42. C	65. E	88. D	111. D	134. D
20. B	43. E	66. D	89. D	112. A	135. D
21. C	44. C	67. A	90. D	113. A	136. D
22. E	45. E	68. E	91. C	114. D	
23. A	46. B	69. A	92. B	115. B	

Practice Exam 2

Detailed Explanations of Answers

1. **(D)**

   For an ideal solution

   $$\Delta H_{mixing} = 0, P_{solution} = \sum_{i}^{components} P_i$$

   $$\Delta S_{mixing} = -R\sum_{i}^{components} n_i \ln x_i$$

   and

   $$\Delta G_{mixing} = RT \sum_{i}^{components} n_i \ln x_i$$

2. **(E)**

   Aromatic amines are extremely activated toward substitution in the ring by electrophilic reagents. Hence, reaction of these amines usually occurs under relatively mild conditions. For this reason, halogenation readily occurs at all unsubstituted ortho and para positions, as shown:

3. **(A)**

   For a nonlinear molecule containing n atoms, there are $3n - 6$ fundamental vibrational modes. Nitryl chloride (NO_2Cl) is nonlinear and it has 4 atoms. Therefore, its number of fundamental modes is $3(4) - 6 = 6$.

4. **(C)**

   Hydrogen bonding is the electrostatic interaction between the X—H bond dipole of one molecule and the unshared electron pair of another molecule (Y). Consequently, the strength of a hydrogen bond increases as the X—H bond dipole increases. The unshared electron pair serves to attract the positive end of the X—H dipole; therefore, the pair cannot be too diffuse in space or occupy too large a volume because, in both cases, the dipole would not be as strongly and directly attracted. For this reason the strongest hydrogen bonding occurs when Y is one of the smaller atoms (N, O and F). O—H . . . Cl is the weakest hydrogen bond interaction because chlorine is a large atom and thus not a good electron pair donor. F—H . . . O is the strongest bond due to the large F—H bond dipole; however, the strength of the O—H . . . N hydrogen bond is close to that of the F—H . . . O hydrogen bond because nitrogen is a better donor than oxygen. Both F—H . . . O and O—H . . . N are stronger than N—H . . . O because of the smaller bond dipole of the N—H bond.

5.   (E)

Lattice energy is a measure of how much stabilization results from the packing together of oppositely charged ions in an ionic compound. MgO has the greatest lattice energy of the choices presented because the attraction between oppositely charged ions increases with the charge on the ion. MgO is the only substance of those listed with charges of positive two ($+2$) and negative two (-2).

6.   (E)

The correct answer to this question could have been determined in one of the following two ways. The reaction could have been "worked out" as follows:

$$CH_3CH_2 + Mg \xrightarrow{\text{ether}} CH_3CH_2 \xrightarrow{CO_2} CH_3CH_2$$
$$\hspace{1cm} | \hspace{4cm} | \hspace{4cm} |$$
$$\hspace{0.5cm} Cl \hspace{3.5cm} MgCl \hspace{2.5cm} CO_2^- {}^+MgCl$$

$$\xrightarrow[H_2SO_4]{H_2O} CH_3CH_2CO_2H$$

thus arriving at the solution to this problem, which is propionic acid. Or the spectra could have been "read," as shown.

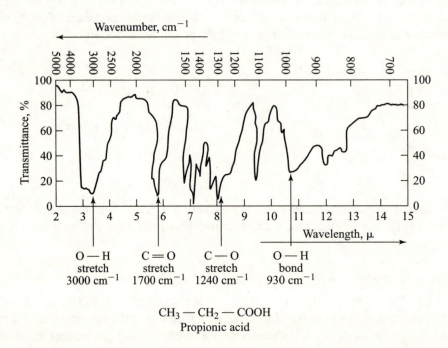

O—H stretch 3000 cm^{-1} C=O stretch 1700 cm^{-1} C—O stretch 1240 cm^{-1} O—H bond 930 cm^{-1}

$$CH_3 - CH_2 - COOH$$
Propionic acid

7.   (E)

There are essentially two types of detectors commonly used for GL chromatography: integral and differential. An integral detector provides, at any point in time, a measure of the total quantity of the solute that has passed through the detector up until that specific time. Differential detectors characteristically yield chromatograms consisting of peaks rather than steps. There are two types: those that measure the concentration of a solute and those that measure its mass flow rate.

8.   (E)

The vapor pressure of a solution containing a volatile solvent and a nonvolatile solute is given by

$$P_{solution} = P_1^0(1 - x_2)$$

So $P_{solution}$ = (23.76 torr)(1 − 0.250) = 17.8 torr

9.   (D)

Ionic substances have electrostatic bonds that are stronger than the Van der Waals forces found in atomic and molecular substances. Therefore, they have all the properties listed except for "deform when struck." When struck, ionic substances fracture due to the stronger bonds present.

10.   (E)

Hexanedione is a diketone and it is therefore characterized by the presence of two carbonyl groups, as shown:

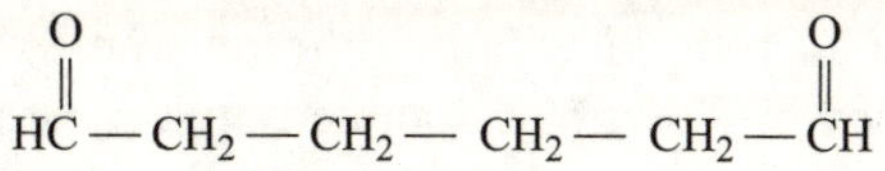

1, 6 hexanedione

To transform cyclohexanone into 1,6 hexadione, the following steps are required:

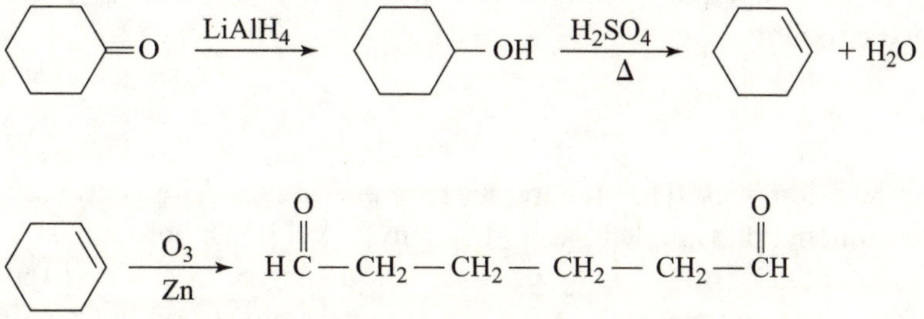

LiAlH$_4$ serves to reduce the carbonyl group, thus changing the cyclic ketone to a cyclic alcohol. This cyclic alcohol is dehydrated by H$_2$SO$_4$ and heat to form a cyclic alkene and water. O$_3$/Zn are the ozonolysis reagents; they cause the double bond of the cyclic alkene to break and two carbon-oxygen bonds to subsequently form (replacing the original carbon-carbon double bond, which was cleaved).

11.   (B)

An adiabatic system is one that has zero heat flow (in or out). If work is done, the temperature must decrease because internal energy is transformed into work.

12. (D)

The Perkin reaction is a typical base-catalyzed condensation in which the enolate ion of the acid anyhydride is an intermediate.

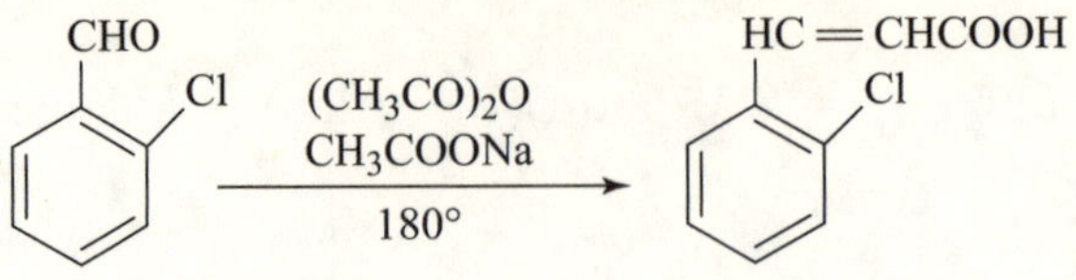

13. (A)

Many spectroscopic methods require a continuously varied wavelength of radiation over a wide range. Monochromators fulfill this requirement. The quality of any specific monochromator depends upon the radiant output purity, its spectral bandwidth, its wavelength resolving abilities, and its light-gathering power. A high signal-to-noise ratio is not required for effectiveness in a monochromator.

14. (B)

Λ_m° stands for the molar conductivity at infinite dilution where $\Lambda_m^\circ = \Lambda_m + Kc^{\frac{1}{2}}$, corresponding to the Z intercept of the graph shown. The molar conductivity Λ_m is a quantity that is dependent upon the number of ions present in a given solution where $\Lambda_m = \kappa/C$ and C = concentration and κ = conductivity.

Rho (ρ) represents a proportionality coefficient called the resistivity. It is equal to RA/l where A = cross sectional area, R = resistance, and l = length. The slope of the plot is qual to the Kohlrausch coefficient (K), which here is equal to −79.14. This constant depends more upon the nature of the salt in solution than its specific identity.

15. (D)

The Sandmeyer reaction is used to prepare benzene derivatives. The Wittig reaction is the reaction of alkyl halides with triphenyl phosphine to yield triphenyl alkyl phosphonium salts. The Ninhydrin test is used to identify amino acids. Tollen's reagent is used in the silver mirror test for an aldehyde. In the Lucas test, an alcohol is dissolved in a solution of zinc chloride and strong hydrochloric acid. Its time of reaction is then observed in order to determine the type of alcohol present.

16. (D)

Chlorine is used in the manufacture of plastics and insecticides. Bromine in the form of bromo-ethane is used as a gasoline additive. Fluorine is used to prepare fluorocarbons, which are in turn used as propellants. The above elements are all members of the halogen group.

17. (B)

The coordination number is the number of equally spaced donor atoms that are bonded to the central atom of a complex. $[Co(H_2NCH_2CH_2NH_2)_3]^{3+}$ (or $[Co(en)_3]^{3+}$) contains only 3 ligands; however, 6 donor atoms are bonded to the central atom cobalt. $H_2NCH_2CH_2NH_2$ (ethylenediamine) is a bidentate ligand because it grasps the central metal atom between 2 donor atoms.

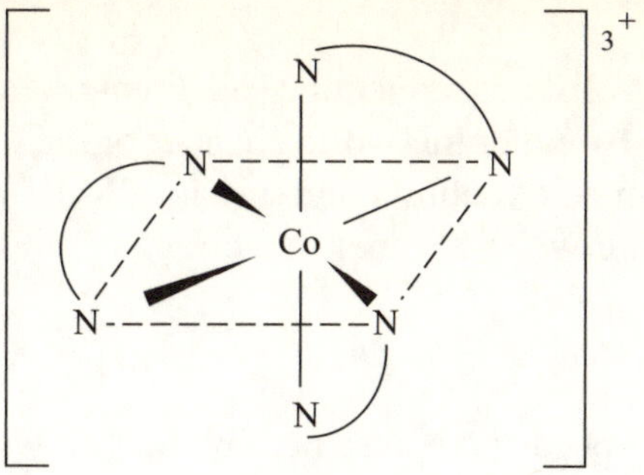

$Co\ (en)_3^{3+}$

The ethylenediamine has been written in shorthand notation as two nitrogen atoms connected by a line.

18. (A)

The unsaturated conjugated ring system of benzene exhibits a high stability toward chemical reagents. When benzene reacts, it has a greater tendency to undergo substitution rather than addition reactions. Upon combination with $O_3/Zn,H^+$, benzene produces glyoxal.

19. (D)

Fluorescence and phosphorescence methods are inherently applicable to lower concentration ranges than spectrophotometric determinations. This is because of the fact that the concentration-related parameter for fluorometry and phosphorimetry can be measured independently of the power source. Therefore, fluorometric methods are generally one to three times more sensitive than the corresponding spectrophotometric procedures. Conversely, the precision and accuracy of photoluminescence methods is generally two to five times poorer than spectrophotometric procedures.

20. (B)

By definition, the electrode where reduction takes place is the cathode, and the oxidation takes place at the anode. The reaction shown here is an oxidation, so (B) is the right answer.

21. (C)

Basic reagents such as sodium hydroxide do not usually react with double (or triple) bonds. Proton acids such as HCl and H_2SO_4, or Lewis acids like Br_2, add across the π bond of ethylene rapidly—even in the absence of a catalyst—due to their electron-seeking nature.

22. (E)

The reaction proceeds as follows:

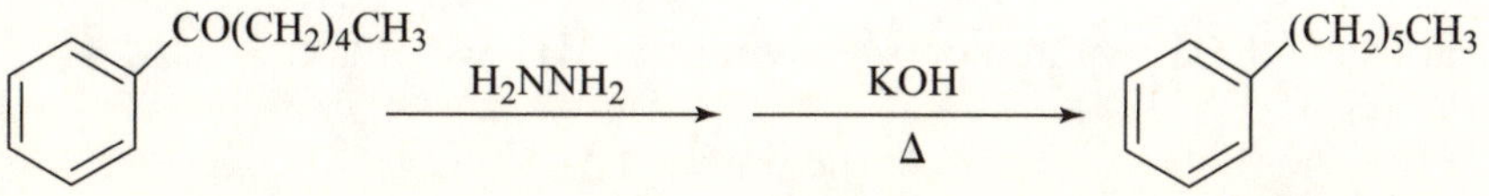

23. (A)

The above reaction is a Wolff-Kishner reduction. The direct reduction of carbonyl groups to hydrocarbons can be accomplished only by either the Wolff-Kishner or the Clemmensen reduction. The Clemmensen reduction takes place in an acid medium and, because KOH is a strong base, the only possible correct answer to this question is the Wolff-Kishner reduction.

24. (C)

The Maxwell distribution of speeds is represented by the following expression:

$$dF(v) = 4\pi(m/2\pi kT)^{\frac{3}{2}} v^2 \exp(-mv^2/2kT)dv$$

It is the probability that the speed lies in the range of v to v + dv regardless of the direction of motion.

25. (B)

Le Châtelier's principle states: If a system at equilibrium is disturbed by a change in temperature, pressure, or the concentration of one of the components, the system will shift its equilibrium position to counteract the effect of the disturbance. If the addition of heat caused the reaction to shift to the right (i.e., away from the reactants), this implies that heat is required for the reaction to go. This is indicative of an endothermic reaction.

26. (D)

The rate of a reaction is correctly described by choices A, B, C, and E. Choice D, however, is incorrect. There is no such equation as the Eurim equation. The Eyring equation is used at times to calculate the rate of a reaction. Whether or not it is applicable is determined by the partition function of the species involved.

27. (D)

Lighter molecules, on average, move much faster than heavier ones. In the figure for this question, the fastest molecule is, therefore, the H_2(②) and the slowest is the CO_2(①). the other two fall somewhere between these two extremes. Although carbon dioxide represents the slowest molecule in the distribution diagram, it is interesting to note that its molecules travel at about 700 mph.

28. (B)

In order to solve this problem, a noncalorimetric means of determining the enthalpy of a reaction is required.

$$\Delta G_m^\theta = \Delta H_m^\theta - T\Delta S_m^\theta$$

is the equation that meets these requirements. Solving for ΔH_m^θ we obtain:

$$\Delta H_m^\theta = \Delta G_m^\theta + T\Delta S_m^\theta$$

After changing the ΔS_m^θ from J/K mole to kJ/K mole, we can simply substitute and solve to find the enthalpy.

$$\Delta H_m^\theta = -25.82 \text{ kJ/mole} + (298K)(-0.032 \text{ kJ/Kmole})$$

$$\Delta H_m^\theta = -35.06 \text{ kJ/mole}$$

29. (B)

Transmetallation is an alternate method of preparing aryllithiums. The reaction is rapid, even at low temperatures. It is a displacement reaction on a halogen to form the lithium salt of a more stable anion.

(85%)

30. (E)

Tollens's test is characterized by a silver ion converting aldehydes to carboxylic acids. The ion is reduced to the metal slowly, and a bright silver metal forms on the walls of the vessel. In both Fehling's and Benedict's tests, aldehydes are oxidized; in the process, cupric ion complexed with tartrate or cupric ion alone is reduced to cuprous ions. The ammonia test involves the reaction of an ammonia derivative with an aldehyde (or ketone), resulting in the production of an easily idenfiable solid derivative. Baeyer's test is used to confirm the presence of conjugated dienes.

31. (C)

If a reaction is second-order by virtue of a first-order rate dependence on each of two reagents where rate $= k[A][B]$, it is possible to derive an expression for the variation in concentrations of A and B with time.

32. (B)

$$(26.7\text{ml AgNO}_3 \text{ solution})\left(\frac{1 \text{ liter}}{1000 \text{ ml}}\right)\left(\frac{0.3 \text{ moles AgNO}_3}{1 \text{ liter solution}}\right)$$

$$= 8.0 \times 10^{-3} \text{moles AgNO}_3$$

$$8.0 \times 10^{-3} \text{moles AgNO}_3 \left(\frac{1 \text{ mole CL}^-}{1 \text{ mole AgNO}_3}\right)\left(\frac{35.5\text{g CL}^-}{1 \text{ mole CL}^-}\right)$$

$$= 2.84 \times 10-1\text{g CL}^-$$

$$\frac{2.8 \times 10-1\text{g CL}^-}{14.0\text{g sample of H}_2\text{O}} \times 100 = 2.0\% \times \text{CL}^- \text{ in H}_2\text{O}$$

33. (B)

The boiling point of a liquid is that temperature at which its vapor pressure becomes equal to the atmospheric pressure. Differences in the forces of attraction between molecules of the liquids cause differences in their respective boiling points. Liquids composed of discrete molecules without permanent dipole moments (H_2, Ne, etc.) have low boiling points relative to their molecular weights because only the weak London forces need to be overcome during vaporization. On the other hand, molecules with permanent dipole moments (HF,CO) due to electronegativity differences have higher boiling points than non-polar molecules of similar molecular weights because the dipole-dipole attraction represents an additional force to be overcome during vaporization.

34. (E)

The initial state is ($400 cm^3$, 308 K) and the final state is ($800 cm^3$, 388k). The sample passes from the initial to the final state in two steps. The first involves an isothermal expansion from V_i to V_f, and the second involves heating from T_i to T_f at constant volume. The entropy change for the first step is

$$\Delta S = nR\ln(800cm^3/400cm^3)$$

and for the second, it is

$$\Delta S = nC_{v,m}\ln \left(\frac{388 \text{ K}}{308 \text{ K}} \right)$$

where $n = P_i V_i/RT_i$

Hence, the total entropy change for this reaction is

$$\Delta S_{total} = nR\ln(800cm^3/400cm^3) + nC_{v,m}\ln \left(\frac{388 \text{ K}}{308 \text{ K}} \right)$$

35. (B)

The stability of a detector is a measure of the amount of random, short-term fluctuations that occur in the chromatogram baseline. The fewer there are, the better and thus more stable the detector. Ideally, a detector response should be linear with respect to the quantity measured. **Noise** is an expression that denotes the random chromatographic fluctuations that may occur; it may originate in various instrumental components (i.e., amplifiers, recorders, etc.). The response time is the time it takes the detector to respond to the presence of a given solute; the shorter it is, the better the detector. Mass flow rate is not one of the detector's characteristics; rather it is a feature of the solute.

36. (D)

The Coulomb potential is defined as the potential due to an isolated ion in a vacuum. At a distance r from an ion of charge $z_i e$, it is:

$$\phi_1(r) = (z_i e/4\pi\varepsilon_0)(1/r)$$

Vapor pressure is the pressure exerted by a vapor in equilibrium with its liquid at a given temperature. The critical molar volume is the molar volume at the critical point, i.e., the state at which the gas and liquid merge.

The electronic configuration is the way in which the electrons are distributed to the atomic orbitals. And the entropy is a thermodynamic function that measures how the energy dispersal changes from one state to another. The **Aufbau** (German for "building up") principle governs the electronic configuration of any atom. It describes the sequence in which electrons feed into the orbitals in order, from lowest to highest energy.

37. (A)

To determine whether or not S_1 and S_2 differ significantly, the variance-ratio or F-test is required. $F = \dfrac{S_2^2}{S_1^2}$, so in this case, $F = (0.13)^2/(0.11)^2 = 1.40$.

On the table given under column $n - 1 = 4$, because $(S_2 > S_1)$ and row $n - 1 = 3$, we find $F = 9.12$. Because $9.12 > 1.40$, we can assume that the two standard deviations do not differ significantly.

38. (E)

The conversion proceeds as follows:

Bromobenzene

methyl benzoate

Hence, the correct sequence is magnesium, dry ether, carbon dioxide, HBr, excess methanol, and sulfuric acid (twice).

39. (A)

The primary functional group of this compound is nitrogen. Thus, this compound is a member of the aniline family. The ring substituents are named according to their position relative to the functional group. The methyl group is directly opposite the amine group, and this is indicated by the p (for para). Both the isopropyl and methyl groups are attached to the functional group of the compound, and this is indicated by the N,N prefix.

40. (E)

The Second Law of Thermodynamics states that in an isolated system, spontaneous processes occur in the direction of increasing entropy. The substances that react in the first reaction both show an increase in entropy: from solid to liquid and from liquid to gas. However, in the second reaction, the net entropy remains the same because one substance changes from a solid to a liquid and the other changes from a liquid to a solid. Hence, the total "randomness" of the system remains the same.

41. (D)

An azeotrope is said to exist when a mixture has reached the point where it boils without any charge in its composition. At this point, distillation can no longer occur because the condensate retains the composition of the liquid.

42. (C)

Lanthanides involve completion of the 4f orbitals. Halogens are found in nature. Transition metals involve completion of the 3d orbitals, and rare gases have all their orbitals completely filled. Thus, the only feasible correct answer to this question would be the actinides.

43. (E)

The polarity of any bond is proportionally related to the difference in the electronegativities of the 2 bound elements. The compound possessing the smallest electronegativity difference between its elements will therefore be the one with the least polar bond. Here the least polar bond is C . . . I because the electronegativity difference between carbon and iodine is only 0.2. Periodic trends in electronegativity, increasing from left to right and decreasing as you move down a group, are the key to finding the correct answer.

44. (C)

Primary aliphatic amines are converted into diazonium salts by sodium nitrite in mineral acid solution (or nitrous acid). Alkyl diazonium salts decompose spontaneously after generation, evolving nitrogen in addition to a mixture of other alcohols and alkenes.

45. (E)

Spectroscopy is a process in which the energy differences between allowed states of a system are measured by determining the frequencies of the corresponding light absorbed. The energy differences depend upon the type of motion involved in any particular quantum state. Therefore, the wavelength of light necessary to bring about an energy transition differs for each specific kind of motion. For each type of motion, light is absorbed in a different region of the spectrum. Infrared spectroscopy is primarily used to determine which functional groups are present in a compound. In nuclear magnetic resonance (nmr) spectroscopy, the energy differences in the states examined are created by a magnetic field and the structures of various compounds can be deduced. Ultraviolet spectroscopy is particularly important in organic chemistry for the determination of conjugated systems. In mass spectroscopy, organic molecules are vaporized, bombarded with an electron beam, and then converted to ions. These molecular ions fragment, the fragments are focused on an ion collector, and the exact mass of the fragments is determined. Hence, the only type of spectroscopy that could fulfill the specifications as stated in the question is microwave spectroscopy.

46. (B)

Bond strength increases as the number of pairs of electrons shared between atoms increases. The central atom of methane (carbon) is bound to four hydrogen atoms and therefore has four shared electron pairs. This is more than any of the other choices; hence, it has the strongest bonds and is the most stable molecule present.

47. (E)

An α particle is a helium nuclei ($^4_2$He). If 5 of them are emitted, the atomic mass number is reduced by 20 and the atomic number by 10. A β particle is simply an electron; when 2 are emitted, the atomic number increases by 2.

So,

$$^{242}_{94}\text{Pu} \rightarrow 5\,^{4}_{2}\text{He} + \,^{222}_{44}\text{X}$$

$$^{222}_{44}\text{X} \rightarrow 2\,^{0}_{-i}\text{e} + \,^{222}_{86}\text{Rn}$$

48. (B)

Choice (B) here is the incorrect statement. Second-row elements are invariably more nucleophilic than first-row elements of comparable basicities. Since fluorine is in the first row of the periodic table and chlorine is in the second row, we would expect Cl^- to be the more reactive toward methyl iodide. All the other given statements are correct.

49. (B)

An endothermic reaction is one with a positive heat of reaction. The positive value represents a heat transfer from the surroundings to the system. An example of an endothermic reaction is as follows:

$$\text{A} + \text{B} + \text{heat} \rightleftharpoons \text{C} + \text{D}$$

reactants   products

To favor the formation of reactants there should be a decrease in temperature that would cause the heat necessary to make the reaction go unavailable, and therefore there would be no choice to the reaction but to work in reverse, favoring reactant formation.

50. (A)

The reaction described is an example of a Claisen condensation. Many different 1,3-dicarbonyl compounds can be formed by this reaction. In this particular problem, ethyl acetoacetate is formed by the self-condensation of ethyl acetate upon treating the ester with sodium ethoxide in refluxing ethanol. The actual reaction that occurs is

$$2CH_3\overset{\overset{\displaystyle O}{\|}}{C}OC_2H_5 \xrightarrow[\;C_2H_5OH\;]{NaOC_2H_5} \xrightarrow{H_3O^+} CH_3\overset{\overset{\displaystyle O}{\|}}{C}CH_2\overset{\overset{\displaystyle O}{\|}}{C}OC_2H_5$$

51. (B)

The reaction proceeds as follows:

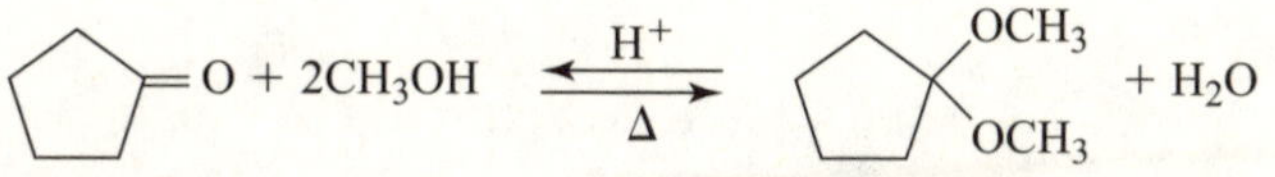

cyclopentanone   cyclopentanone
                                   dimethyl ketal

The addition of two moles of an alcohol to the carbonyl group of a ketone leads to formation of one mole of water and a ketal. The reaction conditions are not sufficiently vigorous to cause the ring to open. Instead, only the carbonyl group reacts, with the consequent formation of 1 mole of the product shown above.

52. (C)

An electrochemical cell consists of two electrodes dipped into an electrolyte. If both of the electrodes are dipped into the same electrolyte, the solution potential $\phi(s)$ is common to both electrodes and the arrangement is called a cell without a liquid junction. See the figure below.

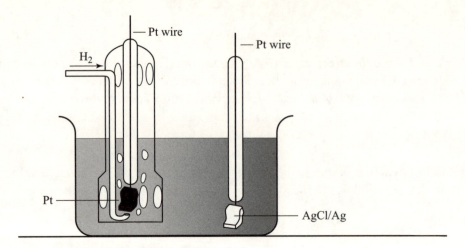

A simple electrochemical cell without a liquid junction.

53. (B)

This is the reaction described:

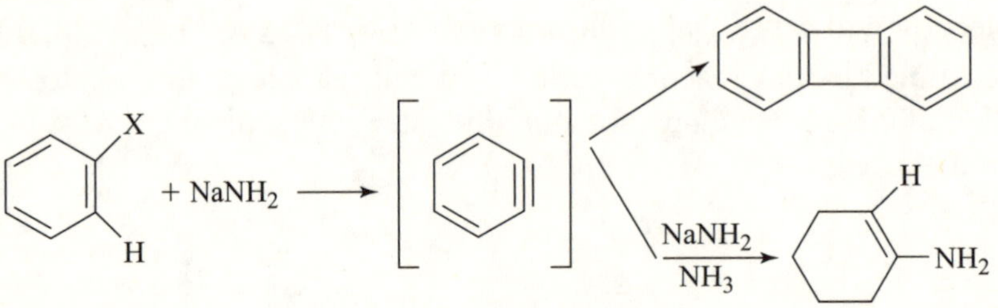

The intermediate reaction (in square brackets) is benzyne; it cannot be isolated because it reacts readily with either excess amide or with another benzyne to form a dimer. Choices (A), (C), and (D) are all structures that represent benzyne. Choice (E) is the benzyne dimer—biphenylene. (A), (C), (D), and (E) all exist at some phase of this reaction; however, (B) is an incorrect structure (see below) and therefore does not occur at any point during the above reaction.

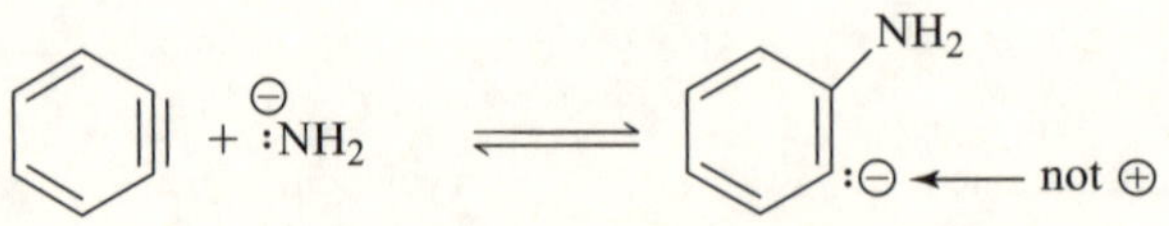

54. (B)

Isochoric conditions are constant volume conditions: under such conditions; $dV = 0$. If $dV = 0$, then it follows that work $(w) = 0$. Because $w = P \int_{2}^{1} dV$ or $-nRT\ln \frac{V_f}{V_i}$.

According to the First Law of Thermodynamics, $\Delta E = q - w$ if $w = 0$, then ΔE must be equal to q, the heat flow.

55. (A)

Unlike GLC, for LC longitudinal diffusion does not present a problem at low velocities. At a fast flow rate, no effects of longitudinal diffusion are seen for either GLC or LC; hence, the curve almost levels off. This is most likely related to the occurrence of turbulent flow.

56. (D)

Baeyer strain is the angle strain of the cycloalkanes due to their deviations from the normal tetrahedral angle. Pitzer strain is the torsional strain due to deviations from the staggered conformations. Dipole-dipole interactions result from the attraction or repulsion of groups by dipole forces. Nonbonded interactions are due to the steric strain introduced by repelling or attracting atoms. There is no such effect as Strecker strain. Strecker refers to a method of synthesizing α-amino acids.

57. (B)

Nuclear magnetic resonance spectroscopy results from the absorption of energy by the nuclei of the atoms of a molecule. The electronic environment around a hydrogen atom (as determined by the adjacent groups in the molecule) will cause that hydrogen atom to absorb radiation of slightly different energy values from the remaining hydrogen atoms in the molecule. Thus, different kinds of hydrogen atoms are easily distinguishable by this technique.

The area under each peak is proportional to the number of hydrogens represented by that peak. The number of smaller peaks is always one more than the number of adjacent hydrogens. Using the above information, the correct structure, which is 1,3-dibromobutane, can be readily deduced.

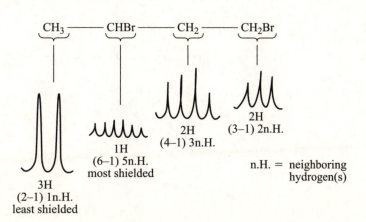

58. (A)

Hess's Law (of constant heat summation) states that the enthalpy change of any reaction is equal to the sum of the enthalpy changes of a series of reactions into which the overall reaction may be divided. This law is based on the fact that enthalpy is a state function and therefore dependent only on the initial and final states themselves and not on the path connecting them.

$$\Delta H^{\theta} = [H^{\theta}_{m_{H_2O_2}} + 4(H^{\theta}_{m_{N_2}})] - [2(H^{\theta}_{m_{NH_3}}) + 2(H^{\theta}_{m_{NO}})]$$

$$= [(-187.8 \text{ kJ}) + 4(0)] - [2(264.0 \text{ kJ}) + 2(90.25 \text{ kJ})]$$

$$= -896.3 \text{ kJ}$$

59. (E)

In order to solve this problem, the Henderson-Hasselbach equation is required. The reaction is

$$pH = pk_a - \log \frac{[HOA]}{[OA^-]} \text{ or } pOH = pk_b - \log \frac{[B]}{[HB^+]}$$

Here,

$$pOH = (-\log k_b) - \log \frac{[NH_3]}{[NH_4^+]}$$

The reaction is

	NH$_3$	+	H$_3$O$^+$	$\longrightarrow$	NH$_4^+$	+	H$_2$O
original mmol.	7.0		3.0		—		
change	−3.0		−3.0		+3.0		
mmol. at equilibrium	4.0 = 0.004 moles		0.0		+3.0 = 0.003 moles		

The concentrations are

$$[NH_3] = 0.004 - [OH^-] \cong 0.004$$

$$[NH_4^+] = 0.003 + [OH^-] \cong 0.003$$

$$pOH = 4.74 - \log \frac{0.004}{0.003}$$

$$pOH = 3.41 \text{ (pH} = 10.59)$$

60. (C)

Knowledge of the periodic trends make the answer to this question clear.

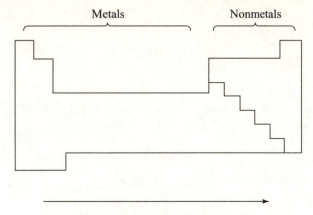

• Increasing ionization energy
• Decreasing atomic radius
• Increasing electronegativity

61. (A)

Sterospecific reactions are those that convert nonasymmetric molecules to one, two, or more stereoi-somers. S_N2 addition of halogens to olefins, hydrogenation with Pd/H_2 and E2 are all stereospecific reactions because their products are stereoisomers; this is not the case for free radical substitution reactions.

62. (C)

In this reaction sequence, an adrenal hormone is the final product. The first 2 steps constitute an acylation. Fries rearrangement and the next steps were used by Stolz to synthesize the adrenal hormone, adrenaline. It proceeds as follows:

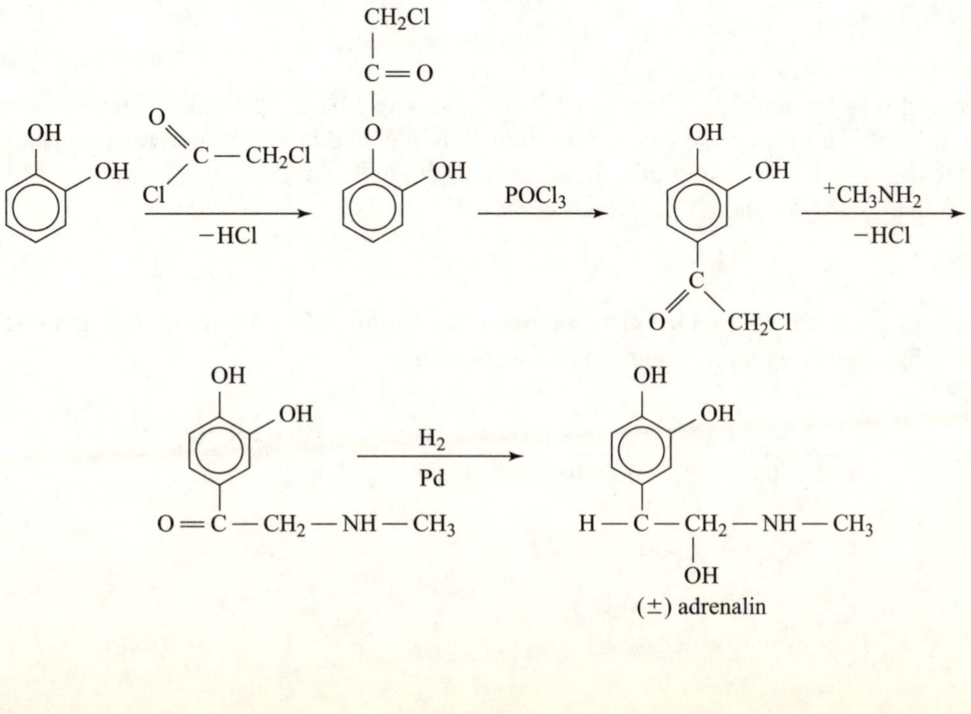

63. (D)

The reaction proceeds in the following manner.

$$2H-C \equiv C-H \xrightarrow[\text{CuCl}]{\text{NH}_4\text{Cl}} HC \equiv C-CH=CH_2 \xrightarrow{\text{2H}} CH_2=CH-CH=CH_2$$

Acetylene   Vinylacetylene   1, 3-butadiene

64. (B)

Enantiomers are configurational isomers that are mirror images of each other. An example of a pair of enantiomers is

They have exactly the same values for most of their physical properties such as melting point, solubility, color, etc. The most important way to distinguish them is to observe their rotation of polarized light. A pair of enantiomers will rotate the plane of polarized light in opposite directions and therefore be readily discernible.

65. (E)

Temperature is a parameter proportional to the average kinetic energy of the molecules of a particular substance. The internal energy (E or U) is the energy in a system; it is stored as either the kinetic energy of motion (of the molecules) or as potential energy, as in a chemical bond. The entropy (S) measures the change in energy dispersal of a particular system as it undergoes a phase change, and the partition function is also a measure of the energy distribution of a particular system. Hence the correct answer is (E).

66. (D)

The strength of an acid is a measure of its tendency to liberate protons. Thus, the strength of an acid increases as this tendency increases. For nonmetals the acid strength increases as you move down a group. Across a row, the acid strength increases with the increasing electronegativity of the nonmetal atom even as the polarity of the H—A bond increases.

67. (A)

Trichloroacetic acid (CCl_3CO_2H) has a molecular weight of 163.5 g/mole. In one mole of trichloroacetic acid, there are two moles of carbon atoms. Solving

$$\left(\frac{27.3\text{g}}{163.5\text{g/mole}}\right) \left(\frac{2 \text{ moles C}}{1 \text{ mole trichloroacetic acid}}\right) \left(\frac{6.02 \times 10^{23} \text{ atoms}}{1 \text{ mole}}\right)$$

68. (E)

Markovnikov addition is the electrophilic addition of an alkyl halide to an alkene. The Cannizzaro reaction is one in which aldehydes are treated with concentrated aqueous base and a disproportionation reaction results. The Wurtz inversion is used to prepare symmetric alkanes. The McLafferty rearrangement is a fragmentation reaction. The only remaining choice is the Walden inversion, a reaction in which the molecule is literally turned inside out.

69. (A)

The amount of this energy change that can be extracted as work at constant volume is given by ΔA (the Helmholtz function). If it were to take place at constant pressure, the work extracted would be equal to the Gibbs function (G).

$$\Delta A = \Delta U - T\Delta S \qquad \text{Therefore,}$$

$$\Delta A = (-2810 \text{ kJ/mole}) - (298K)(182.4 \text{ J/Kmole})$$
$$\parallel$$
$$= -2864 \text{ kJ/mole} \qquad\qquad 0.1824 \text{ kJ/mole}$$

The value of ΔH given is not necessary to solve the problem.

70. (B)

An aromatic molecule is a planar monocyclic molecule that has a particular even number of π electrons. That particular number (N) is given by Huckel's rule, where $N = 4n + 2$ when n is any positive integer, including zero. Monocyclic π systems with this specific number of electrons show relative stability when compared to their analogous acyclic compounds. If the number of π electrons is determined for each of the molecules, it will be discovered that only the second choice satisfies Huckels rule and is therefore aromatic.

71. (B)

The percentage of iron in the sample will be equal to the weight of iron in the sample divided by the weight of the sample itself times 100.

Grams iron (g) is equal to:

$$g = 0.286 \times \frac{2*(55.85)}{159.07}$$

$$(*\text{moles iron} = 2 \times \text{moles Fe}_2\text{O}_3)$$

$$\% \text{ iron} = \frac{g}{0.563} \times 100$$

$$\% \text{ iron} = \frac{0.286[(2(55.85))/159.7]}{0.563} \times 100$$

72. (E)

The Stephen reduction of nitriles is applied primarily to aromatic systems; it involves treatment with stannous chloride and hydrogen chloride in an inert solvent. In the reaction the acid derivative is reduced to an intermediate immonium salt, which is quickly hydrolyzed, as shown below.

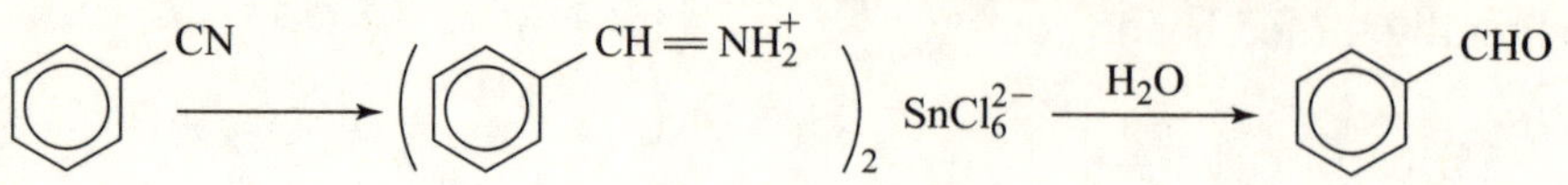

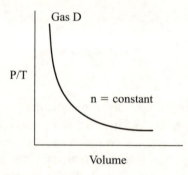

73. (D)

Graphs (A) and (E) illustrate Charles's Law ($V \alpha T$) and Boyle's law ($V \alpha 1/p$), respectively. Graphs (B) and (C) are both in accordance with the ideal gas law ($PV = nRT$). Graph (D) is the only one that diverges significantly from this law. If n is constant, pressure/temperature will vary inversely with the volume: $P/T \alpha 1/V$. Therefore, the curve should approach both axis asymptotically.

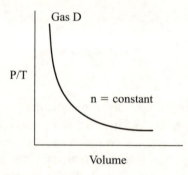

74. (A)

Carbonate error is introduced when sodium hydroxide absorbs CO_2, and sodium carbonate is formed as follows:

$$CO_2 + 2OH^- \longrightarrow CO_3^{2-} + H_2O$$

Carbonate ion is a base, but it combines with hydrogen ion in two steps:

$$CO_3^{2-} + H_3O^+ \longrightarrow HCO_3^- + H_2O$$

$$HCO_3^- + H_3O^+ \longrightarrow H_2CO_3 + H_2O$$

If phenolphthalein is the indicator used, the color change occurs when only the first reaction is complete and therefore an error is introduced because the carbonate ion has reacted with only one H_3O^+. However, OH^- ions were used in the formation of CO_3^{2-}. Conversely if methyl orange is the indicator used, the color change occurs when the second reaction is complete and no error results because each CO_3^{2-} ion combines with two H_3O^+ ions.

75. (E)

Isotopes of a particular element are characterized by the same atomic number and different atomic masses. The only difference in composition between them is in the number of neutrons in the nucleus. Thomson and Aston in 1912–1913, discovered the first isotopes (neon). All the other choices are inaccurate and therefore should be ruled out.

76. (A)

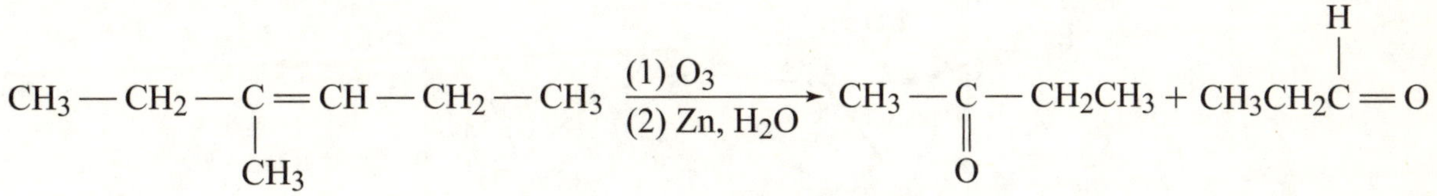

$$CH_3-CH_2-\underset{\underset{CH_3}{|}}{C}=CH-CH_2-CH_3 \xrightarrow[\text{(2) Zn, H}_2\text{O}]{\text{(1) O}_3} CH_3-\underset{\underset{O}{\|}}{C}-CH_2CH_3 + CH_3CH_2\overset{\overset{H}{|}}{C}=O$$

This is an ozonolysis reaction. It is used in locating carbon-carbon double bonds because the position of the carbonyl bonds in the products defines that of the original double bond in the original alkene.

77. (C)

The completed reactions are as follows:

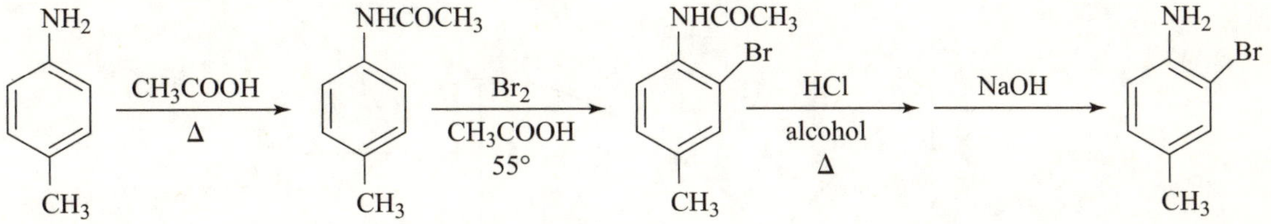

78. (B)

The Pauli Exclusion Principle states that no two electrons in an atom can have the same set of four quantum numbers, n, l, m_l, and m_s. Hund's Rule states: electrons occupy degenerate orbitals singly to the maximum extent possible with their parallel spins. There is no such law as Lewis's law. Heisenberg's Uncertainty Principle states: it is impossible to know both the exact momentum and the location of an electron in space simultaneously. Bohr's model describes the allowed energy states of a given electron.

79. (D)

Raoult's Law ($p_A = x_A p_A^*$) is obeyed for ideal solutions. However, for nonideal (or ideal dilute) solutions, Henry's Law is applicable. (See diagram below)

$$p_B = x_B K_B$$

where x_B is the mole fraction of solute
   K_B is some constant (with the dimensions of pressure)
   p_B is the solute's vapor pressure.

Or stated in another way, the amount of gas dissolved in a given quantity of solvent at a fixed temperature is proportional to the partial pressure of the gas above the solution.

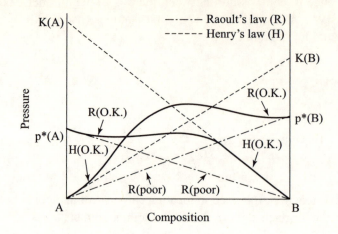

80. (C)

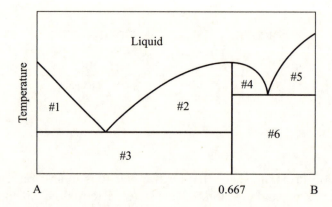

A congruent-melting compound is formed at $x_B = 0.667$. This means that there are two moles of B for every mole of A present; thus, the empirical formula of the compound is AB_2. Horizontal "tie lines" indicate the following compositions for each area:

#1—solid and liquid A in equilibrium

#2 and #4—liquid and solid AB_2

#3—solid A and solid AB_2

#5—solid and liquid B

#6—solid B and solid AB_2

81. (D)

If the acid used as a standard is a strong oxidizing agent, it will destroy the organic compounds used as indicators during titration. Hence, as a standard it will be useless because no endpoints will be able to be determined conclusively.

82. (A)

Gibbs phase rule is $f = C - P + 2$

where   f is the degrees of freedom
               P is the number of phases present
and   C is the number of components in the system.

So in this case, $f = 4 - 1 + 2 = 5$ degrees of freedom.

83. (D)

As seen in question 78, the Pauli Exclusion Principle states that no two electrons in an atom can have the same set of four quantum numbers, n, l, m_l, and m_s. Hund's Rule states: electrons occupy degenerate orbitals singly to the maximum extent possible with their parallel spins. There is no such law as Lewis's law. Heisenberg's Uncertainty Principle states: it is impossible to know both the exact momentum and the location of an electron in space simultaneously. Bohr's model describes the allowed energy states of a given electron.

84. (C)

The phrase that is key to answering this question correctly is "based on the Third Law of Thermodynamics." The Third Law states: All perfect crystals have the same entropy at absolute zero.

85. (E)

A linear polyatomic molecule that contains N atoms will have $3N - 5$ vibrational degrees of freedom. A nonlinear polyatomic molecule will have $3N - 6$ degrees. In this case, N = 7, so the linear and nonlinear molecules will have 16 and 15 degrees of freedom, respectively.

86. (C)

The figure below shows the distribution of molecular speeds at two widely different temperatures. Of particular interest is the fact that the tail toward high speeds is much larger at the higher temperature.

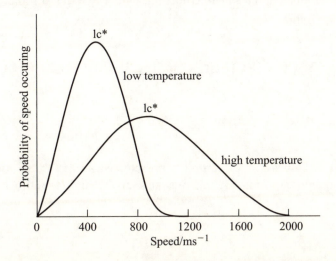

The Maxwell distribution of speeds and its dependence on the temperature.

Graph (B) is an X-p.e.s. spectrum of the azide ion; Graph (D) is the Morse potential energy curve; and Graph (E) is the nmr spectrum of nitric acid monohydrate.

87. (D)

The nuclear stability curve below indicates the correct answer. (The straight line represents equal numbers of protons and neutrons, for comparison.)

A plot of N versus Z for stable, naturally occuring nuclei. Broken portion of the curve represents elements with atomic number above 83.

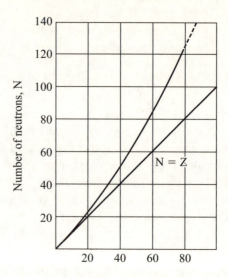

88. (D)

A measure of the rate of flow if energy, matter, charge, or momenum is being transported from one region of a system to another is the flux. An adhesive force is the force present between unlike substances such as glass and water. Fugacity is a type of equivalent pressure. The surface tension is the attractive force described in this question.

89. (D)

When an oil or a fat is boiled with sodium hydroxide, glycerol and a sodium carboxylate (or sodium soap) result. The cleansing action of a soap is dependent upon the two portions it is comprised of: a long alkyl chain, which is oil-soluble, and a salt-like portion, which is water-soluble.

Sodium Stearate

$$CH_3CH_2CH_2CH_2CH_2CH_2CH_2CH_2CH_2CH_2CH_2CH_2CH_2CH_2CH_2CH_2CH_2C \overset{\displaystyle \parallel}{\underset{\displaystyle O}{}} \!\!\!\!\! — O^-Na^+$$

oil-soluble portion   water-soluble portion

The oil-soluble portion dissolves any oil droplets present, while the water-soluble portion keeps the whole combination in aqueous solution. By this means, soaps are able to remove greasy substances from cloth or other surfaces.

90. (D)

The First Law of Thermodynamics is $U = Q + W$.

If W is negative, work has been done by the system on the outside world and this has caused a decrease in the internal energy of the system. Nothing can be said about the heat of the system unless more information is given about U and Q.

91. (C)

The steps described in this question constitute the sodium fusion test. It is frequently used to determine the presence of a halogen in an organic compound.

92. (B)

The Van der Waals equation of state can be represented in one of two ways:

$$p = (nRT/(V - nb)) - (an^2/V^2) \text{ or}$$

$$nRT = \left(p + \frac{an^2}{V^2}\right)(V - nb)$$

where a is a constant added in order to correct for the force of interaction between molecules, and b corrects for the excluded volume of the molecules. These factors are necessary because a real gas, unlike an ideal gas, has a nonzero volume as well as attractive and repulsive forces between its molecules.

93. (D)

Anomers are by definition cyclic isomers of glucose that differ only in their stereochemistry at C-1, the acetal carbon. The pairs in I and IV are, according to this definition, anomers. The structures in pair II are not six carbon sugars; hence, it is impossible for them to be glucose isomers of any kind. Pair III is composed of two structures, both of which are the same molecule (α-D-glucose).

94. (C)

At high temperatures this reaction becomes spontaneous. ΔS is positive because the products are disordered to a greater extent than the reactions, ΔH is positive because the products have a greater heat content than the reactants, and ΔG is negative because this reaction is spontaneous.

95. (E)

Nmr spectroscopy is a technique based upon the measurement of absorption of electromagnetic radiation in the radio frequency range of 4 to 600 MHz. In contrast to the other types of absorption, nuclei of atoms, instead of outer electrons, are involved in the absorption process.

Chemical shifts arise from the secondary magnetic fields produced by the circulation of electrons in the molecule. This movement of electrons creates a small magnetic field that ordinarily opposes the applied field of the NMR. Rayleigh scattering is a result of incomplete interference that occurs in Raman spectroscopy. Minimal sensitivity to water is another property of Raman spectroscopy. The quantitative determination of an absorbing species, even in a multicomponent mixture, is possible with nmr spectroscopy; thus, aspirin, caffeine, and phenacetin are often determined by this method.

96. (E)

The separation factor, α, is equal to the ratio of the retention times, which is, in most cases, the same as the ratio of the distribution coefficients (k) for two given solutes:

$$\alpha = \frac{t_{R_2}}{t_{R_1}} \cong \frac{k_2}{k_1}$$

The resolution R is a different parameter. It is defined as follows:

$$R = \frac{2(t_{R_2} - t_{R_1})}{W_{b_1} + W_{b_2}}$$

R, unlike α, gives an indication of how effectively a given column can separate two solutes. Eddy diffusion is a component of the van Deemeter equation and it is usually a constant, independent of the velocity.

97. (E)

The Schrodinger equation:

$$(-h^2/2m)(d^2\psi/dx^2)\psi(x) + V(x)\psi(x) = E\psi(x)$$

is central to quantum mechanics. When solved it gives the wavefunction for any system. Classically, particles were thought to be localized. This idea was later replaced by the notion that a particle's position is distributed, like the amplitude of a wave—this is the basis of the wave-function concept.

98. (B)

Relaxation methods permit the study of fast reactions. A reaction mixture at equilibrium is interrupted by a shock (pressure, thermal, or electric); it is then permitted to return to equilibrium. For small displacements from equilibrium, the restoration is always first-order giving $\Delta C_i = \Delta C_{i,o} e^{-t/\tau}$, where ΔC_i is the displacement from equilibrium at time t, $\Delta C_{i,o}$ is the initial displacement from equilibrium, and τ is the relaxation time.

99. (D)

The Bohr theory for hydrogen-like atoms consists of 3 basic postulates:

1) The electron moves around the nucleus of charge $+Ze$ in a circular orbit of constant energy.

2) The only orbits allowed are those in which the electron has an angular momentum equal to nn (n = an integer).

3) The transitions that take place between orbits generate spectral lines, with the frequency of a line being equal to $(\Delta E)h$ (ΔE = the energy difference between the initial and final orbits).

100. (D)

$$CH_3 - \overset{\overset{\displaystyle O}{\|}}{C} - CH_2CH_3 \rightleftharpoons CH_3 - \overset{\overset{\displaystyle OH}{|}}{C} = CH - CH_3$$

keto   enol

The two forms of the ketone shown are isomers that differ only by the placement of a proton, or tautomers. The keto form is the ketone and the enol form (from -ene + -ol) is the unsaturated alcohol form.

101. (C)

The ease of reaction by the S_N2 mechanism depends significantly upon the structure of the alkyl group to which the halogen is attached. Branching of the chain next to the carbon where the substitution occurs has a significant effect on the rate of reaction. Also, let's suppose hydrogens of the methyl group are replaced (by more methyl groups); the area in the rear of the leaving group becomes more encumbered. Nucleophilic attack is hindered (steric hindrance) and the reaction rate decreases. Because branching and bulkier substitutes (on the methyl group) hinders the reaction rate, we would expect (by elimination) (C) to be the correct choice.

102. (D)

Through a nucleophilic displacement reaction, three- to six-carbon rings are formed by the alkylation of malonic esters with α,ω-dibromides. During the synthesis of the cyclic group (i.e., not straight chain), carboxylic acids are formed. The other choices have nothing whatsoever to do with this reaction.

103. (A)

Within a homologous series, the logarithm of the retention volume is a linear function of the number of carbon atoms once the experiment is performed meticulously.

104. (D)

According to the ideal gas equation, $pV = nRT$; hence

$$V = \frac{nRT}{P}$$

We find n, the number of moles of ammonium nitrite (NH_4NO_2), as shown.

$$n = 5.36g\ NH_4NO_2 \left(\frac{1\ mole\ NH_4NO_2}{64.0g\ NH_4NO_2} \right) = 0.084\ moles$$

Then to find the pressure (p) of nitrogen gas in the flask when the water levels inside and out are equalized, we subtract $750 - 25 = 725$ mmHg and convert to atmospheres:

$$725mm\ Hg \left(\frac{1\ atm}{760mm\ Hg} \right) = 0.95atm. \cong 1.0\ atm.$$

Therefore,

$$V = \frac{(0.084\ moles)(0.0821\ L - atm/K - mole)(299\ k)}{1.0\ atm.}$$

$$= 2.06 \cong 2.01$$

105. (D)

Quite a variety of gases have been used in GLC. The lighter gases (such as hydrogen and helium) allow more longitudinal diffusion of solutes, which tends to decrease the column efficiency, especially at lower flow rates. The best carrier gas for a difficult separation is therefore nitrogen, which, in addition to being more effective, is cheaper than helium and safer to use than hydrogen.

106. (B)

Carboxylic acids have the highest boiling point of the groups shown. Both oxygens of their carboxyl group can be hydrogen bonded; thus the attractions between carboxylic acid molecules are very large. The next highest boiling point is that of the alcohols; they, too, have significant intermolecular attractions due to their hydrogen bonding capabilities. However, unlike carboxylic acids, it has only one oxygen for hydrogen bonding and therefore its intermolecular attractive forces are not as great as those found in a carboxylic acid. Aldehydes and ketones have a polar carbonyl group and therefore they exhibit a relatively strong dipole-dipole interaction. Thus, their boiling points are higher than nonpolar compounds of comparable molecular size; however, they cannot form intermolecular hydrogen bonds and thus have lower boiling points than alcohols and carboxylic acids of comparable molecular weight. Acetone is more polar than propanal, resulting in a higher boiling point. The carbon-oxygen bond of ethers is polar; nevertheless, the charges on adjacent molecules are prevented from interacting by the presence of the alkyl group. Thus, only weak intermolecular attractions are evidenced. Hydrogen bonding is impossible because no hydrogens are bound to the oxygen atom. Ethers have boiling points similar to those of the alkanes with comparable molecular weights. Isobutane has a molecular weight (58 g/mole), which is higher than that of ethyl ether (46 g/mole), and therefore isobutane has a higher boiling point.

107. (B)

Measurement of the cell E.M.F.s are a source of information on the ΔS, ΔG, and ΔH of a given reaction.

$$\Delta G_m = -FE \text{ and } (\partial \Delta G/\partial T)_P = -\Delta S$$

Therefore, the variation of the cell e.m.f. with temperature is

$$(\partial E/\partial T)_P = \Delta S_m/F$$

Thus, the measure of the gradient of the E.M.F. of a cell with respect to temperature gives the value of the entropy change of the cell reaction (as demonstrated by the above equation).

108. (C)

The kinetic theory of gases is based on essentially three assumptions, as follows:

1) Gas consists of several particles of mass m in continual random motion.

2) The particles have negligible size because their diameters are much smaller than the average distance between them.

3) The particles interact only by elastic collisions.

Choices (A), (B), and (D) are all mentioned in the theory's assumptions; however, choice (C) is not. In fact, it describes one characteristic of real gas.

109. (E)

The Lewis structure for NH_2^- is $[H\!:\!\overset{\displaystyle ..}{\underset{\displaystyle ..}{N}}\!:\!H]^-$. According to the valence-shell electron pair repulsion (VSEPR) model, the four electron pairs around nitrogen should be arranged in a tetrahedral fashion. Such a tetrahedral arrangement is characteristic of sp^3 hybridization.

110. (B)

By definition, vibrations that are degenerate occur at the same frequency.

111. (D)

Stereoisomers are compounds that have the same sequence of covalent bonds but differ in the relative disposition of their atoms in space. D-glucose has 4 asymmetric carbons (carbons with four different groups attached to them). The number of stereoisomers that a compound has is equal to 2^n, where n is the number of asymmetric carbons. In this case $2^4 = 16$ stereoisomers for D-glucose exist. An alternative method of answering this question would be to start with D-glucose and draw all the possible stereoisomers, as shown:

D-allose

D-altrose

D-glucose

D-mannose

D-gulose

D-idose

D-galactose

D-talose

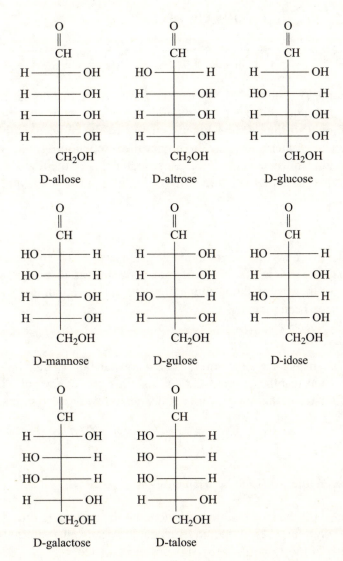

Each of the above structures has its own enantiomer (the L-isomer). Thus, altogether, D-glucose has sixteen stereoisomers.

112. (A)

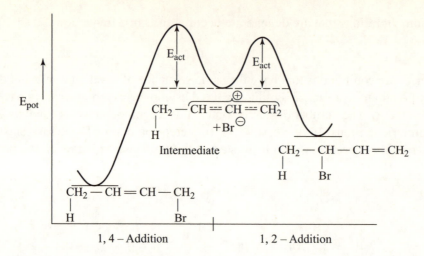

The activation energy (E_{act}) is the energy barrier that must be overcome for a reaction to go from reactants to products. The higher this barrier is, the more energy is required for the reaction to proceed. Temperature is proportional to the average kinetic energy of the molecules that constitute a specific object or environment. The greater an E_{act} is, the higher the temperature (hence energy level) will have to be for the reaction to go. Conversely, the lower a particular E_{act} is, the lower the temperature that will favor the occurrence of that particular reaction. Thus, 1,2-addition is most favored by a low temperature and 1,4-addition by a high one.

113. (A)

According to the First Law of Thermodynamics, the energy of an isolated system is constant. Only by work or heat passing through the walls of such a system can its energy be changed. The energy of a closed system cannot increase without interacting with its surroundings, and therefore a perpetual motion machine as described cannot exist.

114. (D)

In an isothermal expansion, the temperature is held constant and is thus independent of the volume (V). Also, reversibility means that the external and internal pressures at any point in time differ only by an infinitesimal amount (dP), so a definition of work applicable to reversible systems can be derived, thus:

$$w = -p_{in} \int_{V_i}^{V_f} dV \text{ and } p = \frac{nRT}{V},$$

therefore, isothermal reversible work can be defined as $W = -nRT \ln V_f/V_i$.

The ⦀ area represents the irreversible work done on the system against constant pressure. More work is extracted from a system when it operates reversible because the internal and external pressures are matched; hence, none of the system's "pushing" power is wasted.

115. (B)

Helmholtz free energy, (A), is defined as $\Delta A = \Delta E - T\Delta S$. A system spontaneously tends to go toward a state of lower internal energy and higher entropy. Thus, a spontaneous process would have a negative ΔA value, and conversely a nonspontaneous process would have a positive ΔA value. At equilibrium there is no change in entropy (S) or in the internal energy (E); hence, ΔA is equal to zero.

116. (E)

Choices (A) through (D) are all true of the HETP. Choice (E), however, is false because equilibrium is not attained at any point in the column. Rather, the HETP represents a specific length of column; once a mixture has passed through it, it would have been subjected to the same degree of fractionation as would have been attained in one equilibrium step.

117. (A)

Thermal analysis is a technique used to detect a phase change. It makes use of the effect of the enthalpy change during first-order reactions. It has no application to the determination of a reaction rate.

118. (D)

Two potentials are developed, an external one and an internal one, where

$$E_{ext} = k_1 + \frac{0.059}{2} \log \frac{(a_1)_{aq.}}{(a_1)_{ext.}}$$

and

$$E_{int} = k_2 + \frac{0.059}{2} \log \frac{(a_2)_{aq.}}{(a_2)_{ext.}}$$

119. (C)

$$\Delta E = \Delta H - \Delta(PV)$$

However, for gases $PV = nRT$, so

$$\Delta PV = RT\Delta n_{gas}$$

$$\Delta n_{gas} = n_{NOCl} - \tfrac{1}{2}nN_2 - \tfrac{1}{2}nO_2 - \tfrac{1}{2}nCl_2$$

$$-1 - \tfrac{1}{2}(1) - \tfrac{1}{2}(1) - \tfrac{1}{2}(1) = -\tfrac{1}{2} \text{ mole}$$

Hence, $\Delta E = \Delta H - \Delta(pV)$

$$= [(12.57\text{kcal})(4.184\text{kJ/kcal})] - [(8.314 \times 10^{-3} \text{ kJ/moleK})(298\text{K})(-\tfrac{1}{2}\text{mole})]$$

120. (C)

The energy of an electron in an atom cannot vary continuously, rather it is limited to a specific number of discrete values; thus, the electron's energy is said to be quantized. If the principal quantum number n is known, the energy, the size of orbit, and angular momentum of the electron can be determined.

121. (E)

The volumes of the particles of an ideal gas are negligible compared to the volume of the space enclosing the gas. However, the particles could not have zero volume. If they did, there could be no collisions (elastic or otherwise); hence, there would be nothing to impede the flow of the gas particles from one place to another at rates proportional to their speeds.

122. (B)

To calculate t, the following equation is used

$$\mu = \bar{x} \pm \frac{ts}{\sqrt{1}}$$

Substituting: $10.61 = 10.53 \pm \dfrac{t(0.05)}{\sqrt{10}}$

so $t = 5.06 \cong 5.1$

In the given table, at 9 degrees of freedom (n − 1) and 95% probability level, t = 2.62. Because 5.1 > 2.62, we know that the chemists' results do differ significantly from those of the bureau.

123. (A)

Molarity is, by definition, the number of moles of solute divided by the liters of solution. HNO_3 reacts with OH^- on a one-to-one molar basis. The moles of OH^- are equal to

$$63ml \times \frac{1 \text{ liter}}{1000ml} \times \frac{1.9 \text{ moles}}{1 \text{ liter}} = 0.12 \text{ moles}$$

The original HNO_3 solution had to contain 0.12 moles of HNO_3 in 2.4 liters of solution. Thus, its molarity is

$$\frac{0.12 \text{ moles } H^+}{2.4 \text{ liters}} = 0.05M$$

124. (B)

Kirchoff's Law:

$$\Delta H(T_f) = \Delta H(T_i) + \int_{T_i}^{T_f} \Delta C_p(T)dt$$

where $\Delta C_p(T)$ is the difference of the heat capacities of the product and reactant mixtures at the temperature T. The temperature could not be a constant because the integration is with respect to T. The heat capacity is measured at constant pressure (not volume), as indicated by the "p" subscript. This expression is applicable to every specie present in the system, and if all of the heat capacities were temperature independent, then Kirchhoff's Law would be unnecessary. Therefore the only remaining choice, (B), has to be the correct one.

125. (C)

J.J. Thomson measured the ratio of electrical charge to mass of the electron using a cathode ray tube. Rutherford used scattered α particles to determine the atom's structure. Becquerel discovered radioactivity and Roentgen discovered X-rays; thus, the only possible answer is Millikan.

126. (C)

See the answer to question 92.

127. (D)

Wood's metal is a very useful alloy composed of bismuth (50%), lead (25%), tin (12.5%), and cadmium (12.5%).

128. (C)

A state function is one that is a property of the present state of the system; its value is completely independent of the way in which the state was attained. The entropy (ΔS) is a state function.

129. (C)

In direct, absolute calibration, the volume delivered by a volumetric piece of glassware is obtained from the weight of the sample and its density. Relative calibration involves discharging the glassware several times into a flask and marking the level of the meniscus on the flask calibration by comparison. Indirect, absolute calibration consists of calibrating a piece of glassware by comparing it with another vessel that had been directly calibrated. There is no such procedure as complex calibration.

130. (C)

A substitutent group can be classified as either electron donating or electron withdrawing. A group that withdraws electrons tends to neutralize the negative charge of the ring and hence becomes more negative itself; this dispersal of the charge stabilizes both the carbanion and the transition state and thus speeds up the reaction. An electron-donating group releases electrons, intensifies the negative charge, destabilizes the carbanion and the transition state, and thereby slows down the reaction. If the carbanion is stabilized, the ring becomes activated. Conversely, if the carbanion is destabilized, the ring becomes deactivated.

131. (E)

Coulomb's Law states that like charges repel each other. An α particle has a 2+ charge; therefore, when it approaches a gold nuclei with a 79+ charge, repulsion occurs.

132. (E)

The Maxwell relations apply to closed reversible systems in which only PV-work is considered. There are several of these relations due to the number of ways in which the four variables (T, S, p, and V) can be combined in the following format: $(\partial W/\partial X)_Z = \pm(\partial Y/\partial Z)_X$.

Relations are valid only if the cross products XY and WZ are work terms (i.e., pV and ST). Keeping this rule in mind, the only incorrect Maxwell relation shown is

$$(\partial S/\partial p)_V = -(\partial T/\partial V)_p$$

(with cross products Tp and SV).

133. (B)

Ion selective electrodes are not specific for a given ion but rather they possess a certain selectivity for a particular ion. For that reason, they are called ion selective electrodes.

134. (D)

The 4s orbital is lower in energy than the 3d orbital. Therefore, electrons will tend to fill the 4s orbital before the 3d orbital. The $4s^1 3d^5$ configuration occurs rather than the $4s^2 3d^4$ configuration because of the special stability associated with precisely half-filled sets of degenerate orbitals. There is just enough gain in stability with this arrangement to cause an electron to move from a 4s to a 3d orbital.

135. (D)

The Clapeyron equation is $\frac{dP}{dT} = \frac{\Delta H}{T \Delta V}$ where ΔH is the enthalpy change for the phase transition and ΔV is the corresponding volume change. In the Clausius-Clapeyron equation, RT/P is substituted for ΔV because ΔV is assumed to be essentially equal to V_{gas}. The equation, then, is

$$\frac{dP}{dT} = (\Delta H) \frac{P}{RT^2}$$

This equation is applicable to a phase transition between a gas and any condensed phase (liquid or solid).

136. (D)

For a reaction to be used in titrimetric analysis, it is most desirable for the reaction to be a rapid rather than a slow one. The titration could be completed in a few minutes rather than over an extended period of time. The endpoint of any reaction, whether slow or fast, is the difference of one drop. Hence, the speed with which a reaction proceeds cannot influence the accuracy with which the endpoint can be determined.

Practice Exam 3

Answer Sheet: Practice Exam 3

1. Ⓐ Ⓑ Ⓒ Ⓓ Ⓔ
2. Ⓐ Ⓑ Ⓒ Ⓓ Ⓔ
3. Ⓐ Ⓑ Ⓒ Ⓓ Ⓔ
4. Ⓐ Ⓑ Ⓒ Ⓓ Ⓔ
5. Ⓐ Ⓑ Ⓒ Ⓓ Ⓔ
6. Ⓐ Ⓑ Ⓒ Ⓓ Ⓔ
7. Ⓐ Ⓑ Ⓒ Ⓓ Ⓔ
8. Ⓐ Ⓑ Ⓒ Ⓓ Ⓔ
9. Ⓐ Ⓑ Ⓒ Ⓓ Ⓔ
10. Ⓐ Ⓑ Ⓒ Ⓓ Ⓔ
11. Ⓐ Ⓑ Ⓒ Ⓓ Ⓔ
12. Ⓐ Ⓑ Ⓒ Ⓓ Ⓔ
13. Ⓐ Ⓑ Ⓒ Ⓓ Ⓔ
14. Ⓐ Ⓑ Ⓒ Ⓓ Ⓔ
15. Ⓐ Ⓑ Ⓒ Ⓓ Ⓔ
16. Ⓐ Ⓑ Ⓒ Ⓓ Ⓔ
17. Ⓐ Ⓑ Ⓒ Ⓓ Ⓔ
18. Ⓐ Ⓑ Ⓒ Ⓓ Ⓔ
19. Ⓐ Ⓑ Ⓒ Ⓓ Ⓔ
20. Ⓐ Ⓑ Ⓒ Ⓓ Ⓔ
21. Ⓐ Ⓑ Ⓒ Ⓓ Ⓔ
22. Ⓐ Ⓑ Ⓒ Ⓓ Ⓔ
23. Ⓐ Ⓑ Ⓒ Ⓓ Ⓔ
24. Ⓐ Ⓑ Ⓒ Ⓓ Ⓔ
25. Ⓐ Ⓑ Ⓒ Ⓓ Ⓔ
26. Ⓐ Ⓑ Ⓒ Ⓓ Ⓔ
27. Ⓐ Ⓑ Ⓒ Ⓓ Ⓔ
28. Ⓐ Ⓑ Ⓒ Ⓓ Ⓔ
29. Ⓐ Ⓑ Ⓒ Ⓓ Ⓔ
30. Ⓐ Ⓑ Ⓒ Ⓓ Ⓔ
31. Ⓐ Ⓑ Ⓒ Ⓓ Ⓔ
32. Ⓐ Ⓑ Ⓒ Ⓓ Ⓔ
33. Ⓐ Ⓑ Ⓒ Ⓓ Ⓔ

34. Ⓐ Ⓑ Ⓒ Ⓓ Ⓔ
35. Ⓐ Ⓑ Ⓒ Ⓓ Ⓔ
36. Ⓐ Ⓑ Ⓒ Ⓓ Ⓔ
37. Ⓐ Ⓑ Ⓒ Ⓓ Ⓔ
38. Ⓐ Ⓑ Ⓒ Ⓓ Ⓔ
39. Ⓐ Ⓑ Ⓒ Ⓓ Ⓔ
40. Ⓐ Ⓑ Ⓒ Ⓓ Ⓔ
41. Ⓐ Ⓑ Ⓒ Ⓓ Ⓔ
42. Ⓐ Ⓑ Ⓒ Ⓓ Ⓔ
43. Ⓐ Ⓑ Ⓒ Ⓓ Ⓔ
44. Ⓐ Ⓑ Ⓒ Ⓓ Ⓔ
45. Ⓐ Ⓑ Ⓒ Ⓓ Ⓔ
46. Ⓐ Ⓑ Ⓒ Ⓓ Ⓔ
47. Ⓐ Ⓑ Ⓒ Ⓓ Ⓔ
48. Ⓐ Ⓑ Ⓒ Ⓓ Ⓔ
49. Ⓐ Ⓑ Ⓒ Ⓓ Ⓔ
50. Ⓐ Ⓑ Ⓒ Ⓓ Ⓔ
51. Ⓐ Ⓑ Ⓒ Ⓓ Ⓔ
52. Ⓐ Ⓑ Ⓒ Ⓓ Ⓔ
53. Ⓐ Ⓑ Ⓒ Ⓓ Ⓔ
54. Ⓐ Ⓑ Ⓒ Ⓓ Ⓔ
55. Ⓐ Ⓑ Ⓒ Ⓓ Ⓔ
56. Ⓐ Ⓑ Ⓒ Ⓓ Ⓔ
57. Ⓐ Ⓑ Ⓒ Ⓓ Ⓔ
58. Ⓐ Ⓑ Ⓒ Ⓓ Ⓔ
59. Ⓐ Ⓑ Ⓒ Ⓓ Ⓔ
60. Ⓐ Ⓑ Ⓒ Ⓓ Ⓔ
61. Ⓐ Ⓑ Ⓒ Ⓓ Ⓔ
62. Ⓐ Ⓑ Ⓒ Ⓓ Ⓔ
63. Ⓐ Ⓑ Ⓒ Ⓓ Ⓔ
64. Ⓐ Ⓑ Ⓒ Ⓓ Ⓔ
65. Ⓐ Ⓑ Ⓒ Ⓓ Ⓔ
66. Ⓐ Ⓑ Ⓒ Ⓓ Ⓔ

67. Ⓐ Ⓑ Ⓒ Ⓓ Ⓔ
68. Ⓐ Ⓑ Ⓒ Ⓓ Ⓔ
69. Ⓐ Ⓑ Ⓒ Ⓓ Ⓔ
70. Ⓐ Ⓑ Ⓒ Ⓓ Ⓔ
71. Ⓐ Ⓑ Ⓒ Ⓓ Ⓔ
72. Ⓐ Ⓑ Ⓒ Ⓓ Ⓔ
73. Ⓐ Ⓑ Ⓒ Ⓓ Ⓔ
74. Ⓐ Ⓑ Ⓒ Ⓓ Ⓔ
75. Ⓐ Ⓑ Ⓒ Ⓓ Ⓔ
76. Ⓐ Ⓑ Ⓒ Ⓓ Ⓔ
77. Ⓐ Ⓑ Ⓒ Ⓓ Ⓔ
78. Ⓐ Ⓑ Ⓒ Ⓓ Ⓔ
79. Ⓐ Ⓑ Ⓒ Ⓓ Ⓔ
80. Ⓐ Ⓑ Ⓒ Ⓓ Ⓔ
81. Ⓐ Ⓑ Ⓒ Ⓓ Ⓔ
82. Ⓐ Ⓑ Ⓒ Ⓓ Ⓔ
83. Ⓐ Ⓑ Ⓒ Ⓓ Ⓔ
84. Ⓐ Ⓑ Ⓒ Ⓓ Ⓔ
85. Ⓐ Ⓑ Ⓒ Ⓓ Ⓔ
86. Ⓐ Ⓑ Ⓒ Ⓓ Ⓔ
87. Ⓐ Ⓑ Ⓒ Ⓓ Ⓔ
88. Ⓐ Ⓑ Ⓒ Ⓓ Ⓔ
89. Ⓐ Ⓑ Ⓒ Ⓓ Ⓔ
90. Ⓐ Ⓑ Ⓒ Ⓓ Ⓔ
91. Ⓐ Ⓑ Ⓒ Ⓓ Ⓔ
92. Ⓐ Ⓑ Ⓒ Ⓓ Ⓔ
93. Ⓐ Ⓑ Ⓒ Ⓓ Ⓔ
94. Ⓐ Ⓑ Ⓒ Ⓓ Ⓔ
95. Ⓐ Ⓑ Ⓒ Ⓓ Ⓔ
96. Ⓐ Ⓑ Ⓒ Ⓓ Ⓔ
97. Ⓐ Ⓑ Ⓒ Ⓓ Ⓔ
98. Ⓐ Ⓑ Ⓒ Ⓓ Ⓔ
99. Ⓐ Ⓑ Ⓒ Ⓓ Ⓔ

Continued

100. Ⓐ Ⓑ Ⓒ Ⓓ Ⓔ
101. Ⓐ Ⓑ Ⓒ Ⓓ Ⓔ
102. Ⓐ Ⓑ Ⓒ Ⓓ Ⓔ
103. Ⓐ Ⓑ Ⓒ Ⓓ Ⓔ
104. Ⓐ Ⓑ Ⓒ Ⓓ Ⓔ
105. Ⓐ Ⓑ Ⓒ Ⓓ Ⓔ
106. Ⓐ Ⓑ Ⓒ Ⓓ Ⓔ
107. Ⓐ Ⓑ Ⓒ Ⓓ Ⓔ
108. Ⓐ Ⓑ Ⓒ Ⓓ Ⓔ
109. Ⓐ Ⓑ Ⓒ Ⓓ Ⓔ
110. Ⓐ Ⓑ Ⓒ Ⓓ Ⓔ
111. Ⓐ Ⓑ Ⓒ Ⓓ Ⓔ
112. Ⓐ Ⓑ Ⓒ Ⓓ Ⓔ

113. Ⓐ Ⓑ Ⓒ Ⓓ Ⓔ
114. Ⓐ Ⓑ Ⓒ Ⓓ Ⓔ
115. Ⓐ Ⓑ Ⓒ Ⓓ Ⓔ
116. Ⓐ Ⓑ Ⓒ Ⓓ Ⓔ
117. Ⓐ Ⓑ Ⓒ Ⓓ Ⓔ
118. Ⓐ Ⓑ Ⓒ Ⓓ Ⓔ
119. Ⓐ Ⓑ Ⓒ Ⓓ Ⓔ
120. Ⓐ Ⓑ Ⓒ Ⓓ Ⓔ
121. Ⓐ Ⓑ Ⓒ Ⓓ Ⓔ
122. Ⓐ Ⓑ Ⓒ Ⓓ Ⓔ
123. Ⓐ Ⓑ Ⓒ Ⓓ Ⓔ
124. Ⓐ Ⓑ Ⓒ Ⓓ Ⓔ
125. Ⓐ Ⓑ Ⓒ Ⓓ Ⓔ

126. Ⓐ Ⓑ Ⓒ Ⓓ Ⓔ
127. Ⓐ Ⓑ Ⓒ Ⓓ Ⓔ
128. Ⓐ Ⓑ Ⓒ Ⓓ Ⓔ
129. Ⓐ Ⓑ Ⓒ Ⓓ Ⓔ
130. Ⓐ Ⓑ Ⓒ Ⓓ Ⓔ
131. Ⓐ Ⓑ Ⓒ Ⓓ Ⓔ
132. Ⓐ Ⓑ Ⓒ Ⓓ Ⓔ
133. Ⓐ Ⓑ Ⓒ Ⓓ Ⓔ
134. Ⓐ Ⓑ Ⓒ Ⓓ Ⓔ
135. Ⓐ Ⓑ Ⓒ Ⓓ Ⓔ
136. Ⓐ Ⓑ Ⓒ Ⓓ Ⓔ

Practice Exam 3

Time: 170 Minutes
        136 Questions

Directions: *Choose the best answer for each question and mark the letter of your selection on the corresponding answer sheet.*

1. Which of the following compounds has most likely been formed by covalent bonding of atoms?

    (A) CaF_2 (D) MgO
    (B) SiH_4 (E) RbCl
    (C) NaCl

2. The halogens are best described by which of the following statements?

    (A) They are members of Group VIII in the periodic table.
    (B) Their outer electron shells are complete.
    (C) They are all oxidizing agents.
    (D) Most of them are colorless.
    (E) They are all gases at room temperature and pressure.

3. According to the Brønsted-Lowry concept, which of the following species cannot function as an acid?

    (A) $[Fe(H_2O)_6]^{3+}$ (D) H_3O^+
    (B) HSO_4^- (E) SO_4^{2-}
    (C) NH_4^+

4. Which of the compounds below has dipole moment zero?

    (A) CH_4 (D) NH_3
    (B) CH_3Cl (E) HF
    (C) H_2O

5. Identify the compound below that has bonds formed by an overlap of sp and p orbitals.

    (A) BF_3 (D) NH_3
    (B) $BeCl_2$ (E) H_2O
    (C) CH_4

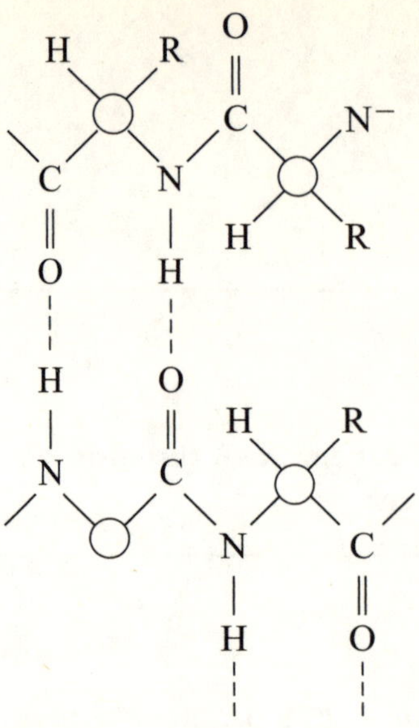

6. The above formula depicts a group of compounds known as

(A) napthenes. (D) carbohydrates.
(B) steroids.   (E) vitamins.
(C) proteins.

7. The permanganate ion, MnO_4^-, absorbs light in the visible region. A 3.52×10^{-4} M solution of $KMnO_4$ in a 1.00 cm cell has an absorbance, A, of 0.855 at 525 nm. Calculate the molar extinction coefficient, ε, for the MnO_4^- ion.

(A) $(0.855)(1.00)(3.52 \times 10^{-4})$
(B) $525/(1.00)(3.52 \times 10^{-4})$
(C) $0.855/(1.00)(3.52 \times 10^{-4})$
(D) $(3.52 \times 10^{-4})(1.00)/0.855$
(E) $0.855(525)/3.52 \times 10^{-4}$

8. Four determinations of a bromide solution in a sample yielded the following values: 43.28%, 43.19%, 43.62%, and 43.24%. The Q-test value for 4 measurements at the 90% confidence level is 0.76. What is the best average to report for these results?

(A) 43.24 (D) 43.28
(B) 43.33 (E) 43.25
(C) 43.19

9. A student would like to separate the various components of a sample of ink in the laboratory. Which of the following techniques would be most suitable for him to use?

(A) Filtration   (D) Distillation
(B) Titration   (E) Fractional crystallization
(C) Paper chromatography

10. Gravimetric analysis does not involve which of the following processes?

    (A) Titrating   (D) Precipitating
    (B) Filtering   (E) Digesting
    (C) Washing

11. The infrared spectra shown below is characteristic of a group of compounds known as

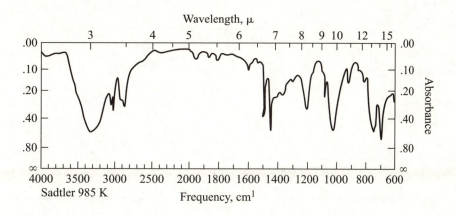

    (A) ethers.   (D) alcohols.
    (B) alkanes.   (E) aldehydes.
    (C) alkenes.

12. Which of the following statements concerning the pH meter is (are) correct?

    I. The pH meter may be used to measure the acidity (or alkalinity) of a solution.

    II. The pH meter must consist of at least a reference electrode, an indicating electrode, and a potential-measuring meter.

    III. The potential of a reference electrode of a pH meter depends largely upon the hydrogen ion concentration of the measured solution.

    (A) I only   (D) I and III only
    (B) I and II   (E) II and III only
    (C) III only

13. In a titration of Na_2CO_3 with HCl, which of the relations shown below would yield the molarity of HCl to the pH 4 end point?

$$2HCl + Na_2CO_3 \rightleftharpoons H_2CO_3 + 2NaCl$$

(A) $\dfrac{(gNa_2CO_3)(2)}{(\text{mol. wt. } Na_2CO_3)(\text{ml HCl}/1000)}$

(B) $\dfrac{(gNa_2CO_3)(\frac{1}{2})}{(\text{mol HCl}/1000)}$

(C) $\dfrac{(\text{moles } Na_2CO_3)(\frac{1}{2})}{(\text{ml HCl}/1000)}$

(D) $\dfrac{(\text{moles } Na_2CO_3)}{(\text{ml HCl}/1000)}$

(E) $\dfrac{(g \text{ HCl})(2)}{(\text{mol. wt. } Na_2CO_3)(\text{ml HCl}/1000)}$

14. We would like to calculate the momentum of an electron. Which of the formulas below would be most appropriate? (Note that m_e = mass of electron, v = velocity of the electron, h = Planck's constant.)

(A) $\dfrac{m_e v^2}{2}$

(B) hv

(C) $m_e v$

(D) hv^2

(E) $m_e v^2$

15. The symbol for an uranium atom is $^{238}_{92}U$. How many neutrons are present in this atom?

(A) 92

(B) 146

(C) 238

(D) 330

(E) Cannot determine

16. B_5H_9 ignites spontaneously in air according to the following reaction:

$$2B_5H_9(g) + 12\,O_2(g) \rightarrow 5B_2O_3(s) + 9H_2O(l)$$

What is the heat of reaction under standard conditions?

The tabulated standard heats of formation of reactants and products are

Substance	$\Delta H°_{298}$
$B_5H_9(g)$	$+60$ kJ mol^{-1}
$O_2(g)$	0.0 kJ mol^{-1}
$B_2O_3(s)$	-1260 kJmol^{-1}
$H_2O(l)$	-280 kJ mol^{-1}

(A) -8940 kJ   (D) $+8700$ kJ
(B) $+8940$ kJ   (E) $+8820$ kJ
(C) -8700 kJ

17. The free energy of a gas depends on its partial pressure according to the expression $G = G° + RT \ln(P/p°)$. Which of the following plots below shows agreement with this relationship?

(A)

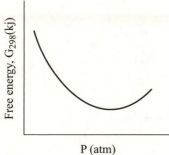

(D)

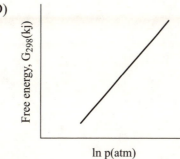

(B)

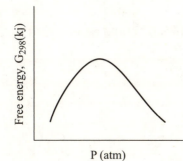

(E)

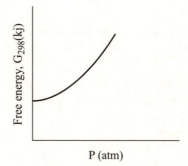

(C)

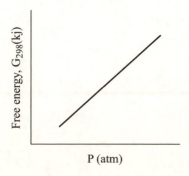

18. The following statements concern the amino acids. Which of the statements below is *not* true?

    (A) They are nonvolatile crystalline solids.
    (B) They are appreciably soluble in water, but insoluble in nonpolar solvents such as benzene.
    (C) Their aqueous solutions behave like solutions of high dipole moment.
    (D) Acidity and basicity constants are fairly high for —COOH and —NH_2 groups.
    (E) The acidic group of a simple amino acid is —NH_3^+ and the basic group is —COO^-.

19. Which of the following reagents may not be used for the oxidation of aldehydes and ketones to organic acids?

    (A) $Ag(NH_3)_2^+$ (D) KOCl and H_2SO_4
    (B) $KMnO_4$ (E) $LiAlH_4$
    (C) $K_2Cr_2O_7$

20. Which of the following compounds below exhibits three (3) signals in the nuclear magnetic resonance spectrum?

    (A) CH_3CH_2Cl (D) $CH_3CH_2CH_2Cl$

    (B) $CH_3CHClCH_3$ (E)

    (C)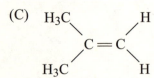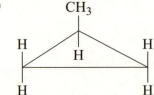

21. How much barium nitrate is required to prepare 250.0ml of a 0.1000M solution? (The molecular weight of barium nitrate is MW = 199.344.)

    (A) $\dfrac{(250)(199.344)}{(1000)(0.1000)}$

    (B) $\dfrac{(250)(0.1000)}{(199.344)(1000)}$

    (C) $\dfrac{(250)(0.1000)(199.344)}{1000}$

    (D) $\dfrac{(250)}{(0.100)(199.344)(1000)}$

    (E) None of the above

22. The five graphs shown below are titration curves. The pH of the solution in a flask is plotted against the ml of the solution added from a buret. A weak base is initially in the flask and a weak acid is added by the buret. Which graph below best represents the nature of the titration?

(A)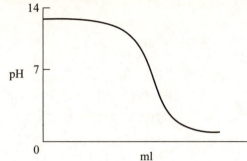

(D)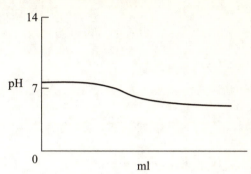

(B)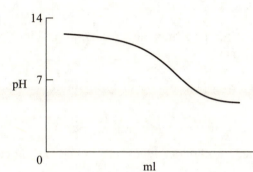

(E)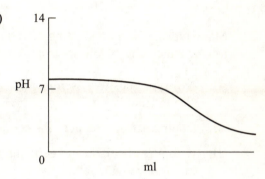

(C)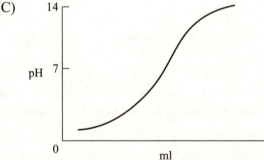

23. Which of the following statements about chemical equilibrium is accurate?

   I. Equilibrium is reached when ΔG (free energy change) equals zero.

   II. $\Delta G°$ (standard free energy change) $= -RT \ln K_{eq}$ (where T = temperature, R = gas constant, K_{eq} = equilibrium constant).

   III. $\Delta G°$ is independent of pressure.

   (A) I only
   (B) II and III
   (C) I and II

   (D) II only
   (E) I, II, and III

24. What is the equilibrium constant for the gaseous reaction shown below? (Note "a" represents activity.)

$$\tfrac{1}{2}N_2(g) + 3/2H_2(g) \rightleftharpoons NH_3(g)$$

(A) $K_{eq} = \dfrac{^aNH_3}{^aN_2\ ^aH_2}$

(D) $K_{eq} = \dfrac{^aNH_3}{\tfrac{1}{2}^aN_2\ \tfrac{3}{2}^aH_2}$

(B) $K_{eq} = \dfrac{a^{\frac{1}{2}}NH_3}{^aN_2\ ^aH_2}$

(E) $K_{eq} = \dfrac{\tfrac{1}{2}^aN_2\ ^aH_2}{^aNH_3}$

(C) $K_{eq} = \dfrac{^aNH_3}{a^{\frac{1}{2}}N_2\ a^{\frac{3}{2}}H_2}$

25. Many types of semiconducting materials exist, including silicon and germanium. Which of the following statements below are *true* of these elements?

 I. A p-type (positive) semiconductor is formed when silicon or germanium is doped with a Group III element.

 II. Doping actually reduces the conductivity of a silicon or germanium crystal.

 III. If doping of silicon and germanium produces nonbonded electrons, Si and Ge can be referred to as n-type conductors.

(A) I only
(B) I and II
(C) III only

(D) II only
(E) None of the above

26. Two moles of an ideal gas are isothermally and irreversibly expanded from 10 atm to 1 atm. The external pressure is constant at 1 atm and the temperature is 300 K. Calculate the work done. (Take "R," the gas constant, to be 8.3 Jmol^{-1} K^{-1}.)

(A) −4482J
(B) 44,820J
(C) −4980J

(D) 49,800J
(E) None of the above

27. Examine the structures below, then indicate which has the lowest boiling point.

(A) C—C—C—C—C

(D) C—C—C—C—C—C

(B)
```
C — C — C — C
        |
        C
```

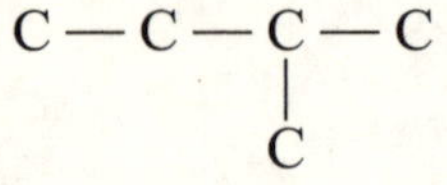

(E) 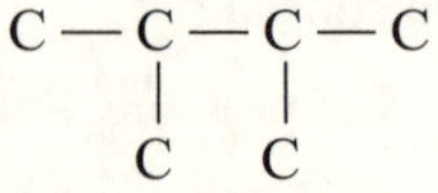
```
C — C — C — C
    |   |
    C   C
```

(C)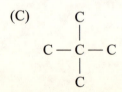

28. The name of the compound below is:

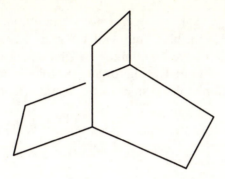

(A) Bicyclo[2.2.1] octane
(B) Bicyclo[2.2.1] nonane
(C) Norbornane

(D) Bicyclo[2.2.2] octane
(E) Tricyclo[2.2.1.0] heptane

29. Which of the groups below is considered to have a deactivating effect during aromatic substitution?

(A) —OH
(B) —NHCOCH$_3$
(C) —CH$_3$

(D) —NH$_2$
(E) —CN

30. Trimethylacetic acid [(CH$_3$)$_3$CCOOH] is converted to ethyl trimethylacetate [(CH$_3$)$_3$CCOOC$_3$H$_5$] by treating it with

(A) thionyl choride (SOCl$_2$) followed by ethanol (C$_2$H$_5$OH).
(B) a basic solution and ethanol.
(C) FeBr$_3$/Br$_2$ and ethanol.
(D) dry ethanol.
(E) pure ethanol followed by heating.

31. Which of the following below is *not* associated with chromatography?

(A) Liquid separation
(B) HPLC
(C) Ion exchange

(D) Selective adsorption
(E) Solid-solid separation

32. Raman spectroscopy may often be used to

(A) examine vibrations of molecules in the infrared region.
(B) identify compounds, especially in the ultraviolet region.
(C) identify the structural type of the compound under study.
(D) identify compounds, but only at conditions of low temperatures and high pressures.
(E) directly determine the mass of the compound under study.

33. Arrange the various regions of the electromagneic spectrum in the correct order, in terms of wavelengths.

    (A) Infrared > ultraviolet > visible > microwave > radio frequency
    (B) Microwave > infrared > visible > ultraviolet > radio frequency
    (C) Radio frequency > microwave > infrared > visible > ultraviolet
    (D) Ultraviolet > visible > infrared > microwave > radio frequency
    (E) Visible > infrared > ultraviolet > microwave > radio frequency

34. The diagram below represents the mass spectrometer. Which area represents the ionization chamber?

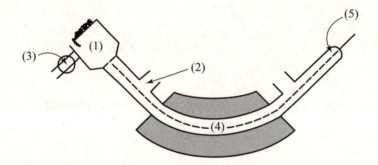

    (A) 1   (D) 4
    (B) 2   (E) 5
    (C) 3

35. Which of the following phenomena does not relate to optical spectroscopy?

    (A) Emission   (D) Doping
    (B) Absorption   (E) Scattering
    (C) Fluorescence

36. How many atoms are there in 0.65g of gold? (Atomic weight of gold = 196.9665.)

    (A) $196.965(0.65)$

    (B) $\dfrac{0.65}{196.9665}$

    (C) $196.9665(0.65)(6.02 \times 10^{23})$

    (D) $\dfrac{0.65}{196.9665(6.02 \times 10^{23})}$

    (E) $\dfrac{196.9665(0.65)}{6.02 \times 10^{33}}$

37. Which of the following is *not* a state function?

    (A) Enthalpy   (D) Free energy
    (B) Entropy   (E) Helmholtz energy
    (C) Work

38. The equation $\bar{v} = R_H \times \left(\dfrac{1}{4} - \dfrac{1}{n^2} \right)$ is referred to as the Rydberg equation. This equation gives the

    (A) velocity of electrons as they are moving within the spectral lines.
    (B) rate of absorption of hydrogen atoms in the ultraviolet region.
    (C) rate of emission of hydrogen atoms in the Lyman series.
    (D) rate of emission of heated hydrogen atoms.
    (E) wave numbers for the series of lines in the hydrogen spectrum.

39. Mercury weighs 201.6658 a.m.u. (atomic mass unit); however, the observed atomic mass is only 199.9683 a.m.u. What has happened to the 1.6975 a.m.u. of matter?

    (A) It has been converted to energy, which is given off.
    (B) This matter is used to form a compound.
    (C) Numerous side reactions utilize this matter.
    (D) It has been lost to the atmosphere.
    (E) We cannot tell; this is still being researched by scientists.

40. Who postulated the following equation for energy emission (ΔE), when an electron drops from state n_2 to n_1?

$$\Delta E = E_1 - E_2 = -k \left(\frac{1}{n_1^2} - \frac{1}{n_2^2} \right)$$

    (A) Einstein   (D) Rutherford
    (B) Planck   (E) Heisenberg
    (C) Bohr

41. Examine the model shown below. In which area would the chance of finding an electron be greater?

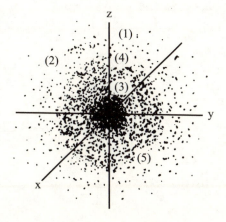

    (A) 1   (D) 4
    (B) 2   (E) 5
    (C) 3

42. The structure shown below, for NH_4^+ and SO_4^{2-}, is referred to as

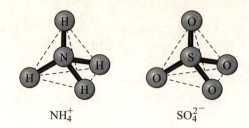

$$NH_4^+ \qquad SO_4^{2-}$$

(A) trigonal.
(B) trigonal planar.
(C) planar.
(D) tetrahedral.
(E) octahedral.

43. The compounds CH_3—⬡—OH is commonly referred to as

(A) toluene.
(B) methyl benzoalcohol.
(C) p-cresol
(D) p-phenol.
(E) o-phenol.

44. Which of the following reactions represents an aldol condensation?

(A)

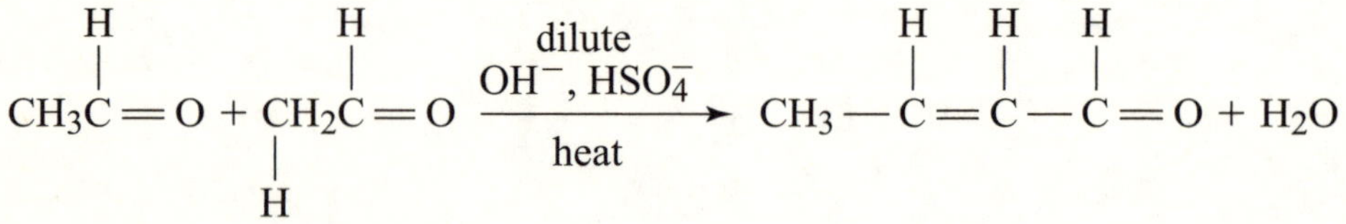

$$CH_3C{=}O + CH_2C{=}O \xrightarrow[\text{heat}]{\substack{\text{dilute}\\ OH^-,\ HSO_4^-}} CH_3-C{=}C-C{=}O + H_2O$$

(B)

⬡=O + Br_2 $\xrightarrow{H^+}$ ⬡=O (with Br) + HBr

(C)

$$HOCH_2-N(H)-C({=}O)-N(H)-CH_2OH \xrightarrow[\text{urea}]{HCHO}$$

～N—CH₂—N—C—N～
O=C ‖ ‖
     O CH₂
～N—CH₂—N—C—N～
          ‖
          O

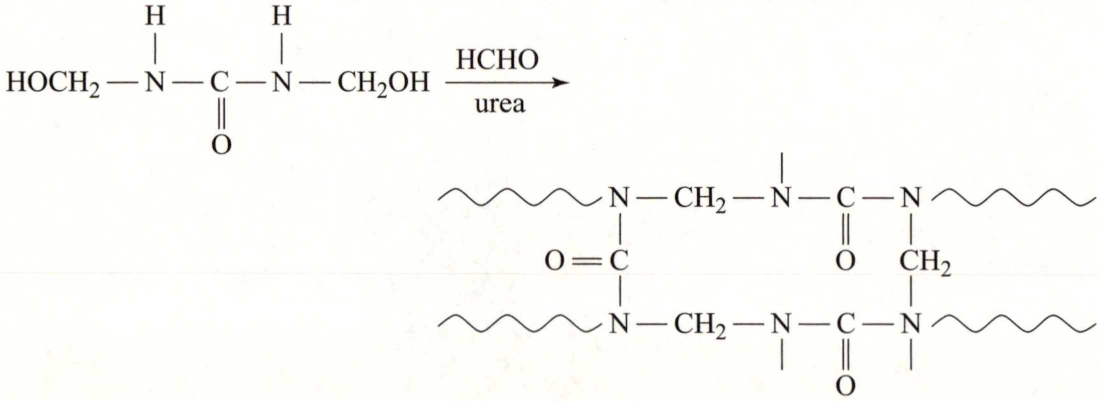

(D)

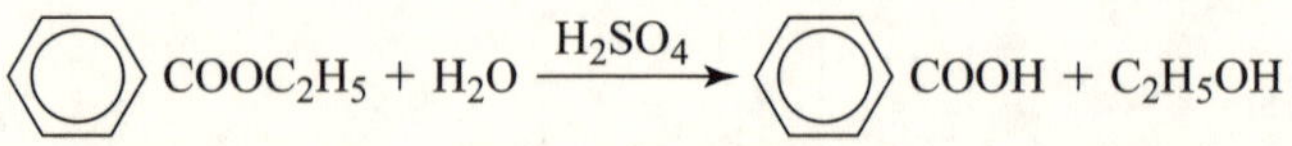

⬡COOC$_2$H$_5$ + H_2O $\xrightarrow{H_2SO_4}$ ⬡COOH + C_2H_5OH

(E)

$(CH_3CO)_2O$ + [trimethylbenzene] $\xrightarrow{AlCl_3}$ $CH_3-C({=}O)-$[trimethylphenyl]$-CH_3 + CH_3COOH$

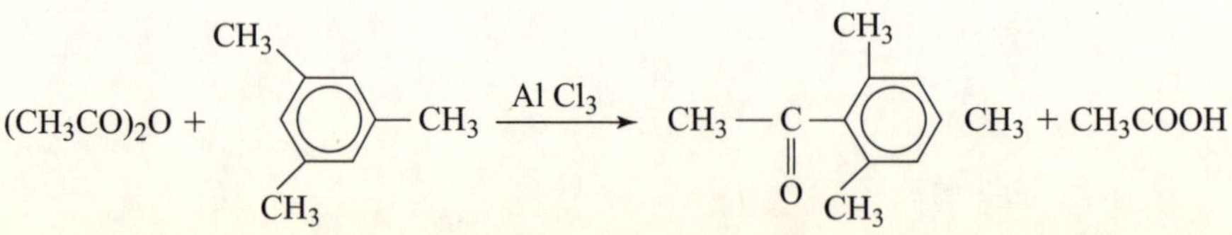

45. Arrange the following in order of reactivity toward CN^-.

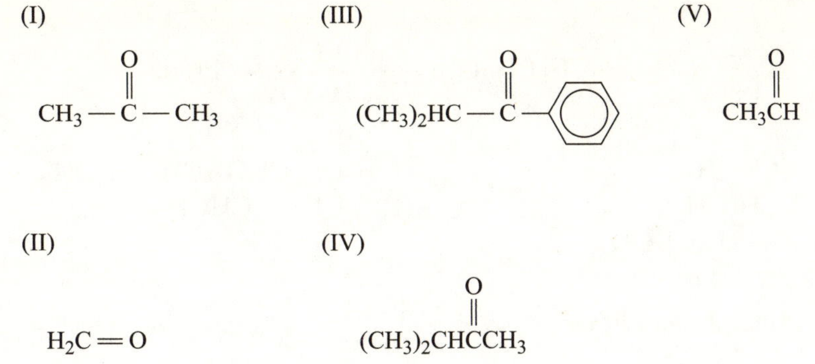

(I)

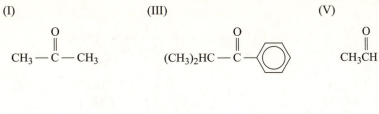

CH₃—C—CH₃

(III)

$(CH_3)_2HC—C$

(V)

CH_3CH

(II)

$H_2C=O$

(IV)

$(CH_3)_2CHCCH_3$

(A) III < IV < I < V < II
(B) IV < III < I < V < II
(C) II < V < I < IV < III

(D) I < III < IV < V < III
(E) V < II < I < IV < III

46. This question concerns the effect of substituents on the —COOH group of organic acids. Which of the following statements is *not* true?

(A) A substituent that is electron withdrawing tends to weaken the acid.
(B) Any factor that makes the anion less stable decreases the acidity.
(C) Electron releasing substitutents tend to intensify the negative charge on the anion.
(D) For the aromatic acids, acid-weakening groups activate the ring toward electrophilic substitution.
(E) In general, substituents that have the largest effect on the acid's reactivity would be expected to have the largest effect on acidity.

47. Heating of nitrobenzene, in iron and dilute hydrochloric acid, in the presence of a catalyst yields which of the following structures as the final product?

(A)  ⬡ NH₂

(B)  ⬡ NHCl

(C)  ⬡

(D) 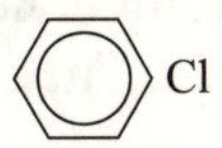 ⬡ Cl

(E) 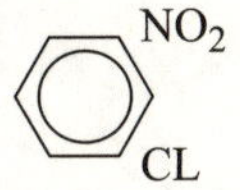 ⬡ NO₂
       CL

48. The reduction of 2-butyne to n-butane in the laboratory involves

(A) the use of an organo-metallic catalyst.
(B) the treatment of 2-butyne with hydrogen in the presence of a nickel catalyst.
(C) the use of an oxidizing agent such as $Cr_2O_4^{2-}$ in the presence of hydrogen.
(D) the use of a strong base such as KOH, along with sodamide ($NaNH_2$).
(E) heating 2-butyne, in the presence of the Al_2O_3 catalyst over a stream of hydrogen gas.

GRE CHEMISTRY

49. n-Butyl alcohol undergoes dehydration in the presence of 75% H_2SO_4 at 140°F. The chief product of this reaction is

$$CH_3CH_2CH_2CH_2OH \xrightarrow[\text{75% } H_2SO_4]{140°F} \text{Product}$$

(A) $CH_3CH{=}CHCH_3$
(B) $CH_2{=}CHCH_2CH_3$
(C) $CH2OHCH_2CH_2CH_2OH$

(D) $CH_3CHOHCH_2CH_2OH$
(E) $CH_2{=}CHCH{=}CH_2$

50. Le Châtelier's Principle states that

(A) reaction equilibrium is obtained only in certain conditions of temperature and pressure.
(B) increasing temperature, while reducing pressure at the same time, enhances equilibrium.
(C) neither temperature nor pressure have a major effect on chemical equilibrium.
(D) stress applied to a system at equilibrium shifts the system in such a way as to relieve the stress.
(E) equilibrium is eventually obtained, regardless of external factors on a system.

51. Which of the expressions below best represents the Boltzmann distribution law (concerning molecules "N")?

(A) $\dfrac{d\ln k}{dN} = \dfrac{\Delta H}{RT^2}$

(B) $\dfrac{dN/L}{du_x} = Ae^{\frac{1}{2}mu_x^2/kT}$

(C) $N_i = N_o\exp\left[\dfrac{-(\varepsilon_i - \varepsilon_o)}{kT}\right]$

(D) $E = mc^2\left[\dfrac{N}{N_o}\right]$

(E) Not given

52. Use Kohlrausch's Law to calculate the conductivity (λ_o) of NH_4OH. Use the fact that $\lambda_{o(NH_4CL)} = 150$, $\lambda_{o(NaOH)} = 248$, and $\lambda_{o(NaCl)} = 127$. The units of λ_o are Ohm^{-1} cm^2mol^{-1}.

(A) 525　　(C) 271　　(E) 121
(B) 29　　(D) 98

53. 0.585g of detergent was burned to destroy certain organics. The residue was washed in hot HCl, which converted the phosphorous (P) present to H_3PO_4. After further filtering and washing, the precipitate was converted to $Mg_2P_2O_7$ (MW = 222.6). This final residue weighed 0.432g. Calculate the percentage of P (MW = 30.97) in the sample of detergent.

(A) $\%P = \dfrac{0.432 \times 2 \times 30.97 \times 100}{(222.6)(0.585)}$

(B) $\%P = \dfrac{222.6(0.432)(2)(100)}{(0.585)(30.97)}$

(C) $\%P = \left(\dfrac{0.432}{30.97}\right)\left(\dfrac{0.585}{222.6}\right) \times \dfrac{1}{2} \times 100$

(D) $\%P = \left(\dfrac{0.432}{30.97}\right)\left(\dfrac{222.6}{0.585}\right)\dfrac{1}{2} \times 100$

(E) Not enough information given to determine the percentage of P.

54. The question below concerns the glass electrode. Which of the statements is (are) true?

    I.   The glass electrode is the most important indicator electrode for the hydrogen ion.

    II. Small glass electrodes may be used to detect the pH in a cavity of a tooth.

    III. The glass electrode may not be used to determine pH in viscous solutions.

    (A) I only   (C) III only   (E) II and III only
    (B) II only   (D) I and II only

55. During the electrolysis of a $CuCl_2$ solution, which of the following reactions is possible at the anode?

    (A) $2H_2O(l) = O_2(g) + 4H^+(aq) + 4e^-$ (D) $Cu(s) = Cu^{2+}(aq) + 2e^-$
    (B) $Cu^{2+}(aq) + 2e^- = Cu(s)$ (E) None of the above
    (C) $2H^+(aq) + 2e^- = H_2(g)$

56. Which of the following methods below does *not* represent a method of separating mixtures?

    (A) Filtration   (D) Fractional crystallization
    (B) Distillation   (E) Solvation
    (C) Gas-liquid chromatography

57. The question below refers to the Nuclear Magnetic Resonance Spectra (N.M.R.). Which of the following statement(s) below is (are) true?

    I.   The hydrogen nucleus (proton) is the most commonly investigated nucleus in N.M.R. spectroscopy.

    II. Nuclei with a spin (quantum) number of zero do not give signals in N.M.R. spectroscopy.

    III. Absorption of energy by the nuclei is crucial for the production of an N.M.R. signal.

    (A) I only   (C) I and II only   (E) I, II, and III
    (B) II only   (D) I and III only

58. Which of the following scientists made the following proposal? "Equal volumes of gases, under the same conditions of temperature and pressure, contain the same number of particles."

    (A) Gay-Lussac   (D) Curie
    (B) Dalton   (E) None of the above
    (C) Berzelius

59. Which formula below could be used to calculate the wavelength (λ) of an electron given its velocity (v) and its mass (m), and if h is a constant?

    (A) $\lambda = hmv$ (C) $\lambda = \dfrac{mv_2}{h}$ (E) $\frac{1}{2}mv^2(h)$

    (B) $\lambda = \dfrac{hv}{m}$ (D) $\lambda = \dfrac{h}{mv}$

60. Which statement below is *not* true for the reaction?

$$Fe^{3+} + e^- \rightarrow Fe^{2+}$$

(A) Fe^{3+} is being reduced.

(B) The oxidation state of Fe has changed.

(C) Fe^{3+} could be referred to as an oxidizing agent in this reaction.

(D) The above reaction is similar (in type) to that of an oxide losing oxygen.

(E) Both Fe^{3+} and Fe^{2+} are called anions.

61. What is the hydrogen ion H^+ concentration of a 0.0020M potassium hydroxide solution?

(A) $[H^+] = \dfrac{K_w}{0.0020}$

(B) $[H^+] = K_w[0.0020]$

(C) $[H^+] = \dfrac{0.0020}{K_w}$

(D) $[H^+] = -\log_{10}\left[\dfrac{K_w}{0.0020}\right]$

(E) None of the above

62. Identify the name of the coordination compound $K_4Fe(CN)_6$.

(A) Potassium hexacyanoferrate

(B) Potassium hexacyanoferrate (II)

(C) Potassium hexacyanoferrate (III)

(D) Potassium hexacyanoferrate (IV)

(E) Potassium cyanoferrate (IV)

63. Examine the plot below for particle amplitude (ψ) versus atomic radius (r), then indicate which of the following expressions best describes the graphical representation.

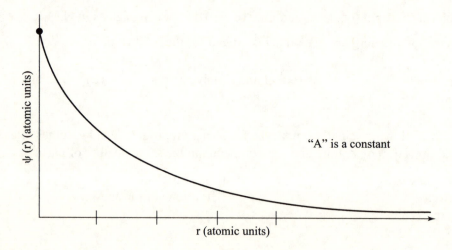

"A" is a constant

(A) $\psi(r) = Ar^2$

(B) $\psi(r) = Ae^{-r}$

(C) $r = \dfrac{A}{\psi(r)}$

(D) $\psi(r) = \dfrac{A}{r^2}$

(E) None of the above

64. Which of the statements below is *not* a property of ammonia?

   (A) Ammonia is a Brønsted base.
   (B) It has the ability to form complex molecules.
   (C) Ammonia may display acidic behavior.
   (D) The ammonia molecule is trigoral pyramidal in shape.
   (E) Ammonia cannot be easily liquefied by cooling and/or compressing.

65. The statements below concern trans-1,2-dimethylcyclohexane; indicate which of these statements is (are) correct.

   I. It is a nonsuperimposable molecule.

   II. Trans 1-2-dimethylcyclohexane can exist in two conformations, with the — CH_3 groups being on the opposite sides of the ring in each case.

   III. The preferred conformation of the molecule is a boat form, with methyl groups pointing away from the ring.

   (A) I only
   (B) II only
   (C) I and II only
   (D) I and III only
   (E) I, II, and III

66. An unknown compound is oxidized to a carboxylic acid in the presence of potassium permanganate. The same compound is oxidized to an aldehyde, losing an α-hydrogen in the presence of pyridinium chloro-chromate ($C_5H_5NH^+CrO_3Cl^-$). The compound is also known to exhibit mild acidic properties because it reacts with active metals (e.g., Na), liberating hydrogen gas. Based on these facts, this compound is most likely a

   (A) primary amine.
   (B) secondary ketone.
   (C) primary alcohol.
   (D) primary ketone.
   (E) tertiary ketone.

67. A perfect crystal at °K has

   (A) zero enthalpy.
   (B) zero entropy.
   (C) maximum entropy.
   (D) reached a state of equal entropy and enthalpy; pressure, however, must be constant.
   (E) reached a state where the entropy is positive, fixed, and unchangeable.

68. The equation below represents a form of the combined gas law known as the van der Waals equation. What is the significance of the $\dfrac{an^2}{V^2}$ term in the expression?

$$\text{Equation: } \left(P + \frac{an^2}{V^2}\right)(v - nb) = nRT$$

(A) an^2/V^2 represents the "excluded volume" (volume occupied by gas molecules), which simpler gas equations neglect.

(B) $\dfrac{an^2}{V^2}$ represents the pressure exerted on the wall of the container by the gas molecules.

(C) $\dfrac{an^2}{V^2}$ represents the molecular attraction between the gas molecules.

(D) $\dfrac{an^2}{V^2}$ accounts for the dissociation of the gas molecules.

(E) $\dfrac{an^2}{V^2}$ accounts for the energy of collision among molecules.

69. What is the oxidation number of chlorine in ClO_4^-?

(A) $+1$ (D) $+7$
(B) $+3$ (E) $+8$
(C) $+5$

70. The most electronegative of these group (I) elements is

(A) K   (D) Rb
(B) Li   (E) Cs
(C) Na

71. Which of the reactions below best represents the Haber process reaction for the production of ammonia?

(A) $NH_4^+(aq) + OH^-(aq) \rightarrow NH_3(g) + H_2O(l)$

(B) $Mg_3N_2 + 6H_2O \rightarrow 3Mg(OH)_2 + 2NH_3(g)$

(C) $N_2(g) + 3H_2(g) \overset{\text{catalyst}}{\rightleftarrows} 2NH_3(g)$

(D) $Li_3N + 3H_2O \rightarrow 3Li^+ + 3OH^- + NH_3(g)$

(E) $N_2H_2 + H_2O \overset{Na^+}{\rightleftarrows} NH_3(g) + NO(g) + NaH$

72. Which of the following statements below concerning carbon and its compounds is (are) *true*?

   I. Carbon monoxide is produced when carbon is burned with insufficient oxygen.

   II. Carbon dioxide may undergo sublimation.

   III. Carbonic acid may be referred to as a diprotic acid.

   (A) I and II only
   (B) I and III only
   (C) II and III only
   (D) III only
   (E) I, II, and III

73. The following statements below concern ion-exchange chromatography. Indicate which statement(s) is (are) correct.

   I. Ion-exchange material usually consists of a structure with electrically charged sites of one particular charge sign and mobile ions of the other charge sign.

   II. In a cation exchanger, the immobile molecular network is cationic.

   III. The ion exchange may be used to substitute one ion for another in a solution.

   (A) I only
   (B) I and II only
   (C) II and III only
   (D) III only
   (E) None of the above

74. The reaction below takes place by nucleophilic substitution. Which of the following is the product for this reaction?

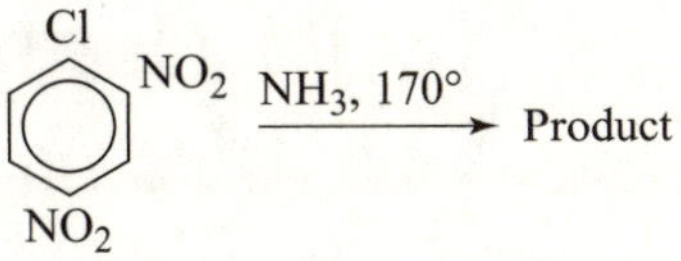

   (A)
   (C)
   (E)

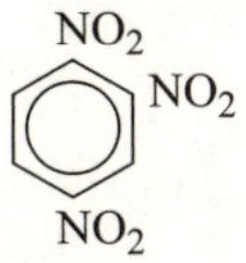

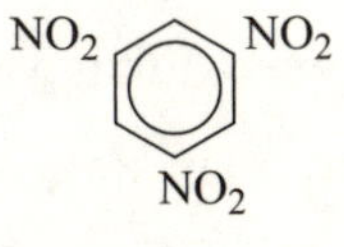

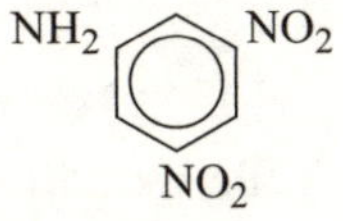

   (B)
   (D)

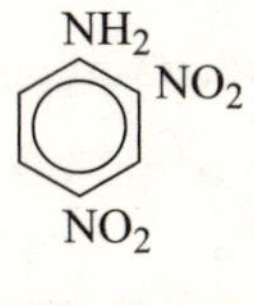

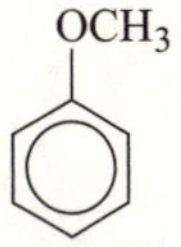

75. Which of the following compounds participate in hydrogen bonding?

   (A) CH_3Cl
   (B) CH_3OCH_3
   (C) CH_3NH_2
   (D) CH_3CH_2Cl
   (E)

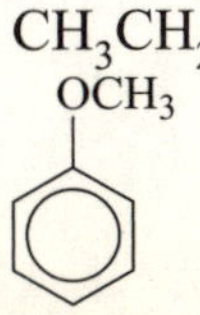

76. Which of the following reactions does *not* produce a high yield of alcohol?

(A) 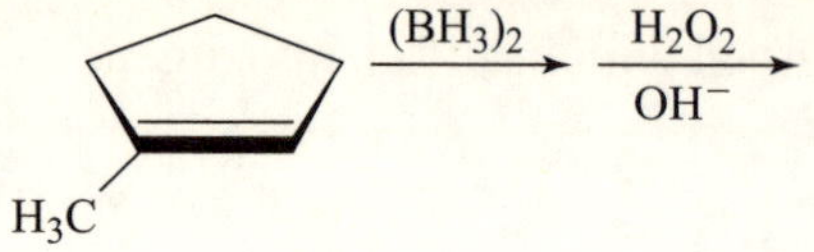 [structure: methylcyclopentadiene] $\xrightarrow[OH^-]{(BH_3)_2 \quad H_2O_2}$

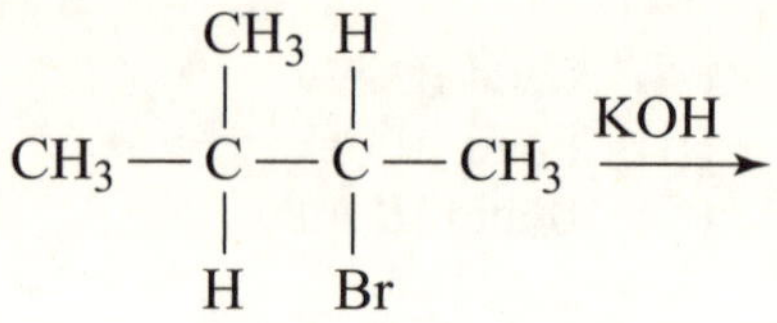

(D) 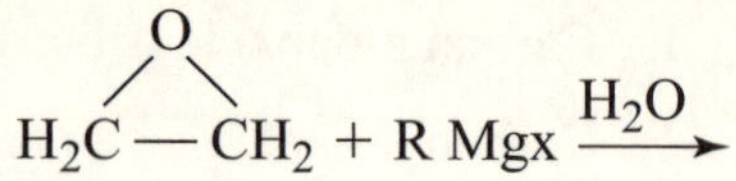 [epoxide structure] $H_2C \overset{O}{-} CH_2 + R\,Mgx \xrightarrow{H_2O}$

(B) 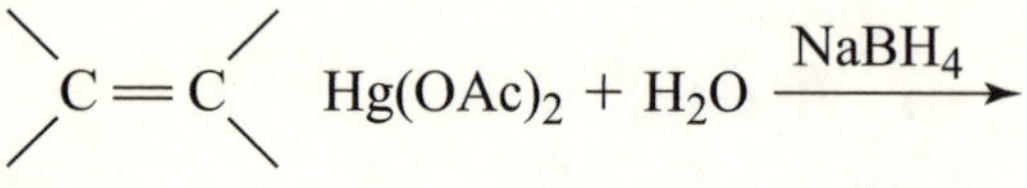 $>C = C< \quad Hg(OAc)_2 + H_2O \xrightarrow{NaBH_4}$

(E) $CH_3 - \overset{\overset{CH_3}{|}}{\underset{\underset{H}{|}}{C}} - \overset{\overset{H}{|}}{\underset{\underset{Br}{|}}{C}} - CH_3 \xrightarrow{KOH}$

(C) [benzene ring]$-CH_2Cl \xrightarrow{\text{aqueous NaOH}}$

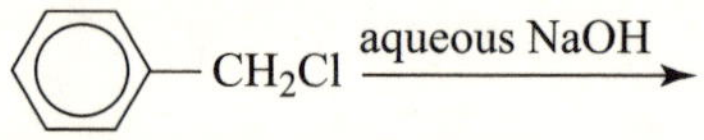

77. Propene is treated with potassium permanganate. What is the major product?

(A) 1,2 ethane-diol
(B) 1,2 propanediol
(C) Propanal

(D) Ethanal
(E) Propan-2-01

78. Which of the following is *not* true for the nucleophilic substitution referred to as the S_N2 reaction?

(A) This reaction is of second-order kinetics.
(B) There is complete stereochemical inversion.
(C) There's absence of rearrangement.
(D) Racemization is evident.
(E) $CH_3w > 1° > 2° > 3°$ (w refers to a substituent; 1°, 2°, 3° refer to the carbon atoms).

79. Which of the following reacts with hydrogen and nickel to form propane?

(A) $CH_3CH = CH_2$

(B) $CH_3CH_2CH_2OH$

(C) $CH_3\overset{\underset{|}{CH_3}}{CHCH_3}$

(D) $CH_3CH \overset{|}{\underset{OH}{}} CH_3$

(E) $CH_3CH_2CH = CH_2$

80. The following statements below concern the oxidation of aldehydes and ketones. Indicate which statement(s) is (are) correct.

I. The oxidation of an aldehyde may be accomplished by a mild silver ion oxidizing agent.

II. Oxidation of aldehydes to carboxylic acids take place more readily than the oxidation of ketones.

III. In order to oxidize aldehydes, we must generally use oxidizing agents that are stronger than those used to oxidize primary and secondary alcohols.

(A) I only
(B) I and II only
(C) II and III only

(D) III only
(E) I, II, and III

81. The diagram below represents the mass spectra of a hydrocarbon, where m/e is the compound's molecular weight. Which of the following statements below concerning the mass spectra is *incorrect*?

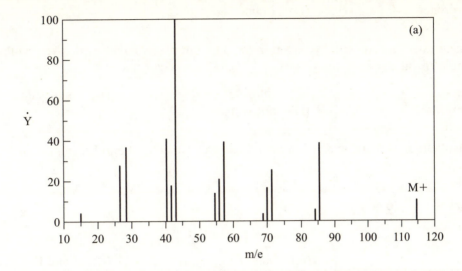

(A) The Y-axis represents the relative intensity of the compound(s).

(B) The mass spectra may be used to prove the identity of compounds.

(C) Mass spectral studies help to establish the structure of new compounds.

(D) M^+ (the molecular ion), once identified, gives the most accurate molecular weight attainable for any compound.

(E) M^+ is always referred to as the base peak.

82. Which of the following statements concerning the noble gases helium (He) and neon (Ne) is correct? (Atomic numbers are He = 2, Ne = 10.)

(A) The boiling point of He is greater than the boiling point of Ne.

(B) Both have their outer shells completed with 8 electrons.

(C) Both He and Ne solidify when enough cooling is applied to their liquid form.

(D) Both helium and neon have low (subzero°C) boiling points.

(E) Both are used for filling electric gas lamps.

83. Which of the oxides below exhibits amphoteric properties?

(A) Na_2O (C) Cl_2O_7 (E) P_2O_5
(B) MgO (D) ZnO

84. The equation below is referred to as

$$\frac{\delta^2\psi}{\psi x^2} + \frac{\delta^2\psi}{\delta y^2} + \frac{\delta^2\psi}{\delta z^2} + \frac{8\pi^2 m e}{h}\left(E - V_{(x,y,z)}\right)\psi_{(x,y,z)} = 0$$

(V = potential energy, m_e = mass of electron, ψ = particle's amplitude)

(A) The Schrödinger equation   (D) Bohr's atomic energy equation
(B) The Maxwell's equation   (E) The de Broglie wave relationship
(C) Planck's equation to explain the uncertainty principle

85. Which of the elements below is the most powerful oxidizing agent?

    (A) Fluorine   (C) Carbon   (E) Phosphorous
    (B) Hydrogen   (D) Iodine

86. An element mixes safely with hydrogen in the dark but reacts rather explosively with hydrogen in light. The element is

    (A) chlorine.   (C) fluorine.   (E) potassium.
    (B) phosphorous.   (D) nitrogen.

87. For the isothermal isobaric expansion of an ideal gas, which of the following is *true*?

    I. Energy change (ΔE) = 0

    II. Heat = work (q = w)

    III. $\Delta H \neq 0$

    (A) I only   (C) I and III   (E) I and II
    (B) II and III   (D) III only

88. 0.02N NaCl ($L = 0.15\Omega^{-1}m^{-1}$) was used to calibrate a conductivity cell. The measured resistance was 680 Ω. Find the cell constant.

    (A) $\dfrac{0.15}{680}$ (D) $680(0.02)$

    (B) $\dfrac{0.15(0.02)}{680}$ (E) $\dfrac{1}{(0.15)(680)}$

    (C) $(0.15)(680)$

89. Which of the following properties is (are) true for ideal solutions?

    I. $\Delta H(\text{mixing}) = 0$

    II. $V_{sol.} = {}_{i}\Sigma^{\text{components}} V_i$ (V = volume)

    III. $P_i = P_i^o x_i$ (P_i = Partial pressure of component i, P_i^o is the vapor pressure of the pure component i at that temperature, and x_i is the mole fraction.)

    (A) I only   (C) II and III   (E) I, II, and III
    (B) I and II   (D) III only

90. The log of the rate constant of a reaction is

    (A) directly proportional to temperature changes.
    (B) inversely proportional to temperature.
    (C) not affected by temperature changes.
    (D) only affected by the activation energy, not the temperature changes.
    (E) not dependent on the activation energy or the temperature.

91. The glyceride shown below undergoes esterification in an acid medium. Which of the following is a major organic product formed?

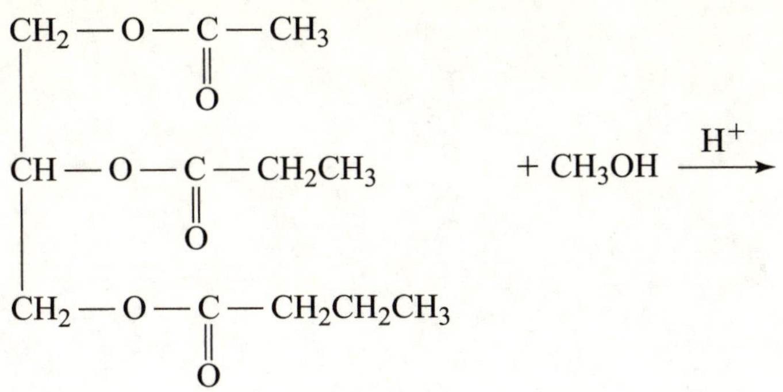

$$CH_2 - O - \underset{\underset{O}{\|}}{C} - CH_3$$
$$|$$
$$CH - O - \underset{\underset{O}{\|}}{C} - CH_2CH_3 \qquad + CH_3OH \xrightarrow{H^+}$$
$$|$$
$$CH_2 - O - \underset{\underset{O}{\|}}{C} - CH_2CH_2CH_3$$

(A) 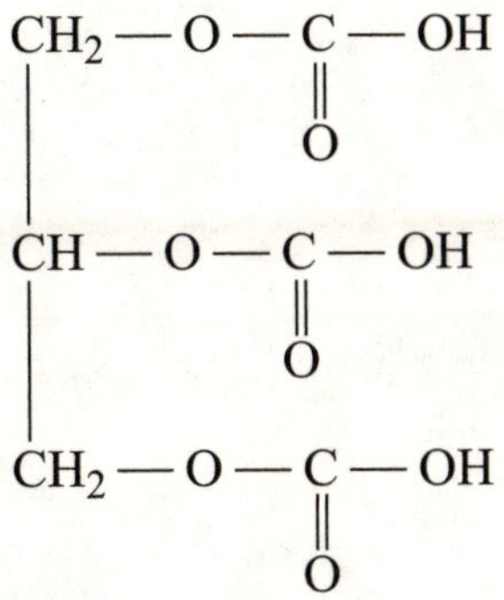
$$CH_2 - O - \underset{\underset{O}{\|}}{C} - OH$$
$$|$$
$$CH - O - \underset{\underset{O}{\|}}{C} - OH$$
$$|$$
$$CH_2 - O - \underset{\underset{O}{\|}}{C} - OH$$

(B) 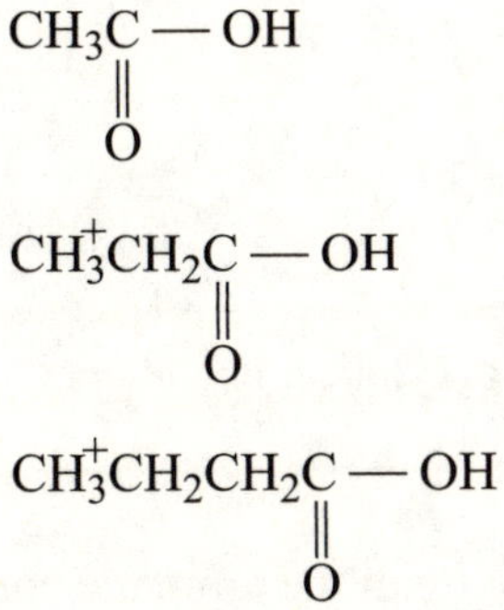
$$CH_3\underset{\underset{O}{\|}}{C} - OH$$

$$CH_3^+CH_2\underset{\underset{O}{\|}}{C} - OH$$

$$CH_3^+CH_2CH_2\underset{\underset{O}{\|}}{C} - OH$$

(C)
$$CH_3COOCH_3$$
$$+$$
$$CH_3CH_2COOCH_3$$
$$+$$
$$CH_3CH_2CH_2COOCH_3$$

(D) 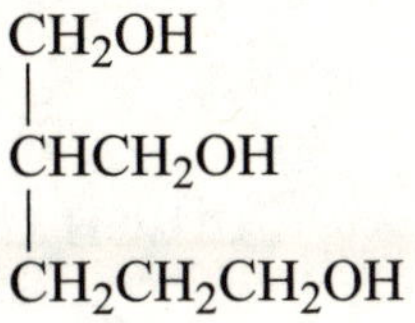
$$CH_2OH$$
$$|$$
$$CHCH_2OH$$
$$|$$
$$CH_2CH_2CH_2OH$$

(E) 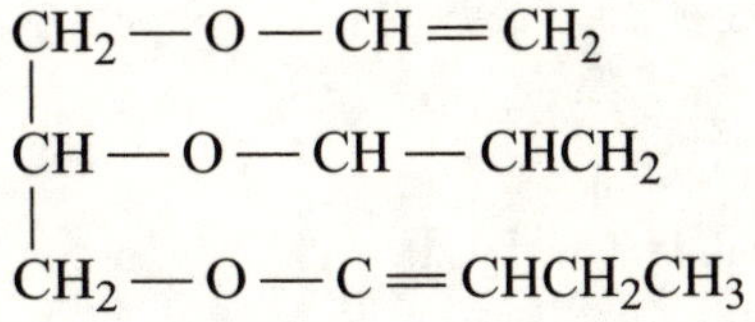
$$CH_2 - O - CH = CH_2$$
$$|$$
$$CH - O - CH - CHCH_2$$
$$|$$
$$CH_2 - O - C = CHCH_2CH_3$$

92. Which of the compounds below is the strongest acid?

(A)
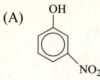

(B)

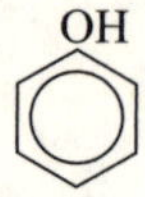

(C)

(D)

(E)

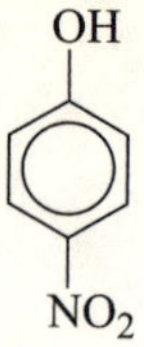

93. Consider the reaction below and indicate which of the following is (are) the major product(s) of this reaction.

$$CH_3CH_2CHCH_2OH \xrightarrow{KMnO_4}$$

with CH₃ branch

(A)   CH₃CH₂CHCHO   with CH₃ branch

(D)   Both (B) and (C)

(B)   CH₃CH₂CHCOOH   with CH₃ branch

(E)   Hard to tell from given information, but (A) and (B) are formed in large amounts.

(C)   CH₃CH₂CCH₂OH   with CH₂ double bond

94. Which of the following statements concerning the Friedel-Crafts alkylation is *correct*?

  I.   It involves the use of a Lewis acid.

  II. Both aryl and alkyl halides may be usd to initiate the reaction with the aromatic compound.

  III. The reaction is referred to as an electrophilic aromatic substitution.

(A)   I and II only
(B)   I and III only
(C)   II and III only
(D)   III only
(E)   I, II, and III

95. Below are statements about the chemical behavior of metallic elements. Indicate the incorrect statement.

(A)   Metals are reducing agents.
(B)   Metals form basic hydroxides.
(C)   Metals exhibit higher electronegativities than nonmetals.
(D)   Metals exhibit low ionization potentials.
(E)   Metals generally have one to five electrons in their outermost shell.

96. Which of the following compounds does *not* contain a covalent bond?

    (A) PH_3
    (B) $GeCl_4$
    (C) H_2S

    (D) CsF
    (E) CH_3Cl

97. Given that oxygen is in its ground state, which of the statements below concerning its electron shells is (are) *correct*? (Note that N, l, M, and s refer to quantum numbers.)

    I. The first (electron) shell of oxygen ($1s^2$) may be described (using quantum numbers) as 1, 0, 0, $+\frac{1}{2}$ and 1, 0, 0, $-\frac{1}{2}$.

    II. The second shell ($2s^2$) is described using quantum numbers as 2, 1, 1, $+\frac{1}{2}$ and 2, 1, 1, $-\frac{1}{2}$.

    III. The fourth quantum number, s, describes the ways in which an electron, e^-, may be aligned with a magnetic field.

    (A) I only
    (B) I and II only
    (C) I and III only

    (D) II and III only
    (E) I, II, and III

98. Which of the following is *not* true for a carbocation?

    (A) A carbocation may combine with a negative ion.
    (B) Rearrange to form a more stable carbocation.
    (C) Eliminate a hydrogen ion to form an alkene.
    (D) Alkylate an aromatic ring.
    (E) Not remove a hydride ion from an alkane.

99. Which of the following reactions do *not* require the presence of a base to proceed?

    (A) $CH_3CH_2OH + CH_3 - \langle \bigcirc \rangle - SO_2Cl \longrightarrow CH_3 - \langle \bigcirc \rangle - SO_2CH_2CH_3$

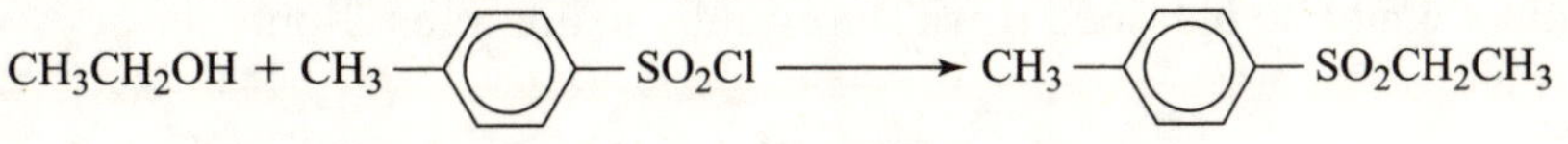

    (B) $CH_3 - CH - CH_2 \longrightarrow CH_3CH - CH_2$
    with OH, Cl below the first, and O bridging the second (epoxide)

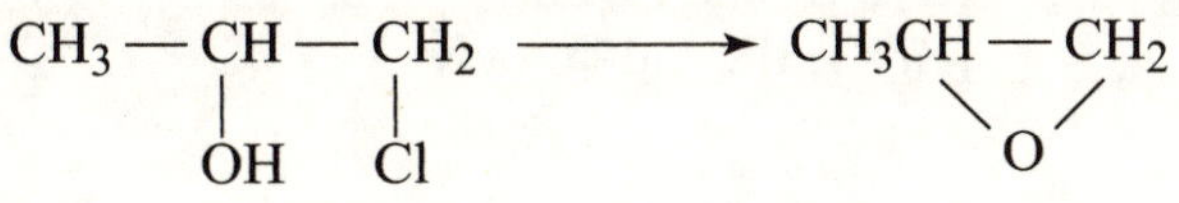

    (C)

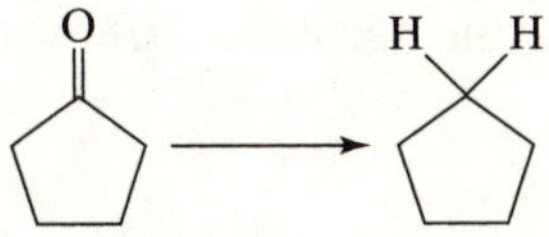

    (D) $+ HCHO \longrightarrow$ $+ HCOO^-$

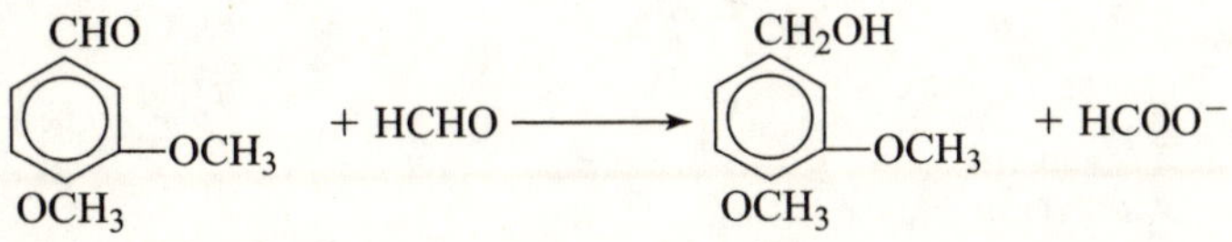

    (E) $CH_3 - \overset{H}{\underset{}{C}} = O + 2C_2H_5OH \rightleftharpoons CH_3 - \overset{H}{\underset{OC_2H_5}{C}} - OC_2H_5 + H_2O$

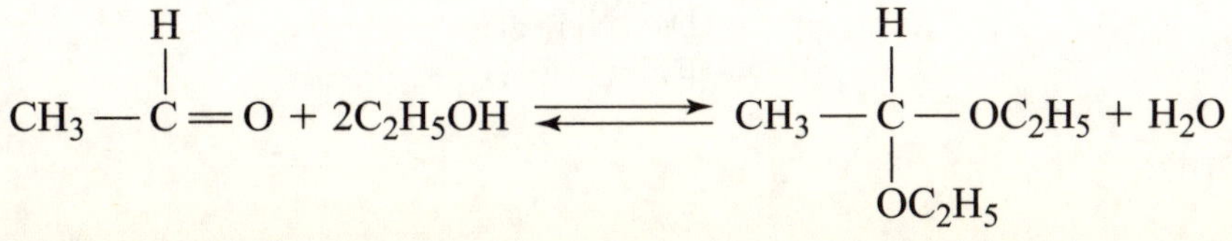

100. Examine the reaction of cis 2-butene shown below:

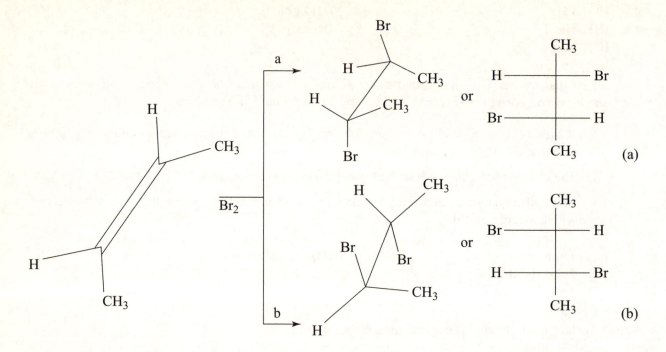

Which of the following statements concerning the above reaction is *true*?

I. (a) and (b) are enantiomers.

II. The products (a) and (b) are called the meso-product.

III. The reaction is referred to as anti-addition.

IV. The meso-product could be obtained if we start out by using trans-2-butene.

(A) I only
(B) I and III only
(C) I, II, and III only

(D) III and IV only
(E) I, III, and IV only

101. Assume that the compound francium astatine existed. Which of the formulas below would best represent this compound?

(A) FrAt
(B) Fr_2At
(C) $FrAt_2$

(D) Fr_2At_3
(E) Fr_3At_2

102. Which of the compounds below is a strong base?

(A) $Cu(OH)_2$
(B) $Fe(OH)_3$
(C) KOH

(D) NH_4OH
(E) $Cr(OH)_3$

103. Which of the salts below will produce an alkaline solution when dissolved in water?

    (A) NH_4Cl (C) Na_2CO_3 (E) $NaSO_4$
    (B) $NaCl$ (D) $NaNO_3$

104. Calculate C_p° for water at 373.1K given $C_V^\circ = 26.0$ $Jmol^{-1}K^{-1}$ and R = 8.3 $Jmol^{-1}K^{-1}$.

    (A) 17.7 $Jmol^{-1}K^{-1}$

    (B) $\dfrac{373.1}{26.0(8.3)}J^{-2}mol^2K$

    (C) $34.32mol^{-1}K^{-1}$

    (D) $\dfrac{26.0}{8.3}$

    (E) $\dfrac{8.3}{26.0}$

105. The kinetic energy for a molecule, k.e. $= \frac{1}{2}mu^2$ (m = mass and u^2 = average of the square of the velocity). It has been determined that $u^2 = \dfrac{3kT}{m}$; k is Boltzmann's constant. Find the ratio of the kinetic energies at 300°C and 200°C.

    (A) $\dfrac{573}{473}$

    (B) $\dfrac{573}{473}(u^2)$

    (C) $\dfrac{573}{473}\dfrac{1}{2}mu^2$

    (D) $\dfrac{573}{473}\left[\dfrac{mu^2\ 100°C}{mu^2\ 200°C}\right]$

    (E) Cannot be determined; not enough data given

106. Consider the reaction coordinate diagram for the consecutive reactions below:

$$B \xrightarrow{K_1} >, C \xrightarrow{K_2} > D$$

The overall reaction is $B \rightarrow D$ (for an exothermic reaction). Which of the following best describes how k_1 relates to k_2? (k_1 and k_2 represent rate constants?)

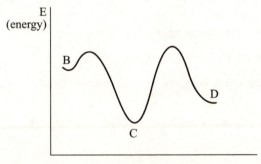

Reaction Coordinate

    (A) $k_1 < k_2$ (D) k_1 about equal to k_2
    (B) $k_1 < < k_2$ (E) Cannot tell
    (C) $k_1 > k_2$

107. Consider the following statements about the NMR spectrum. Then indicate which statement(s) is (are) correct.

   I. The number of NMR signals tells how many different types of protons are present in a molecule.

   II. The area under an NMR signal is directly related to the number of protons causing the signal.

   III. The position of an NMR signal tells us something about the electronic environment of each kind of proton.

   (A) I only
   (B) I and II only
   (C) I and III only
   (D) II and III only
   (E) I, II, and III

108. The diagram below represents the potential energy of the C—H bond as a function of the C—H bond distance. Study the diagram, then indicate which of the statements is (are) correct.

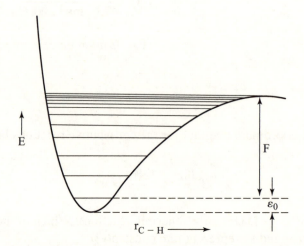

Schematic diagram of potential for a C—H bond in methane.

   I. ε_0 is referred to as the zero point energy of vibration.

   II. The value of F is the bond dissociation energy.

   III. Usually at a temperature of absolute zero, the atoms (of CH_4) cease to vibrate.

   (A) I only
   (B) I and II only
   (C) II and III only
   (D) I, II, and III
   (E) None of the above

109. The product of the Diels-Alder reaction between a diene and a dienophile is shown below:

(A) 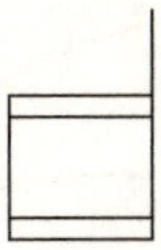 [square with horizontal lines]   (C)  [hexagon]   (E) $C{=}C{-}C{=}C$

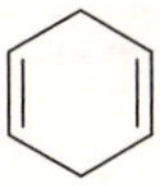

(B) [hexagon with double bond]   (D) [hexagon with inner hexagon]

110. Which of the following statements concerning Michael addition is *not* true?

   (A) The process involves nucleophilic addition.
   (B) Carbanions are added to α,β-unsaturated carbonyl compounds, forming carbon-carbon bonds.
   (C) A base is necessary to initiate the addition.
   (D) The carbanion is generally generated from a fairly acidic substance.
   (E) Compounds such as ammonia and primary and secondary amines often tend to inhibit Michael addition.

111. For the following set of reactions

$$P + Q \underset{k_2}{\overset{k_1}{\rightleftharpoons}} R \text{ and } R + S \xrightarrow{k_3} T, \text{ find } \frac{dC_R}{dt}$$

find $\dfrac{dC_R}{dt}$

   (A) $k_1[P][Q] - k_2[R]$ (D) $-k_2[R] - k_3[R][S]$
   (B) $-k_1[Q] + k_2[R]$ (E) $k_1[P][Q] - k_3[R][S]$
   (C) $k_1[P][Q] - k_2[R] - k_3[R][S]$

112. For a constant pressure system, which of the following equations is *true*? (Note P = pressure, ΔH = enthalpy change, ΔV = volume change, and ΔE = energy change.)

   (A) $P = \dfrac{\Delta H + \Delta E}{\Delta V}$ (D) $P = \dfrac{\Delta H - \Delta E}{\Delta V}$

   (B) $P = \dfrac{\Delta V}{\Delta H + \Delta E}$ (E) $\dfrac{\Delta E - \Delta V}{\Delta H}$

   (C) $P = \dfrac{\Delta H - \Delta V}{\Delta E}$

113. Which of the graphs below best represents the distribution of the blackbody radiation at several temperatures?

(A)

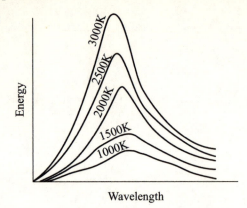

(D)

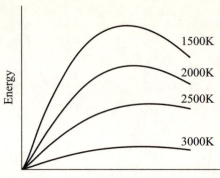

(B)

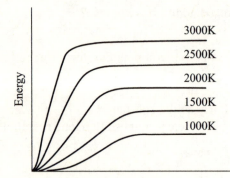

(E)

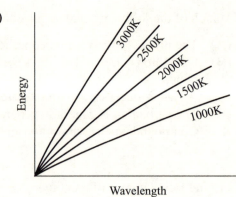

(C)

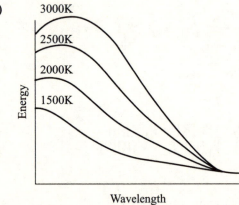

114. Examine the structure shown below. It shows a high degree of stereospecificity.

This structure most likely represents:

(A) a sex attractant.
(B) a pheromone.
(C) a cholesterol.
(D) a glucose.
(E) Both (A) and (B) are represented by the above structure.

115. Several types of organic compounds undergo elimination to form alkenes when heated to relatively high temperatures. Which of the compounds below does not exhibit this tendency?

(A) $R—\overset{\overset{\displaystyle O}{\|}}{C}—OCH_2CHR'_2$ (an ester)

(B) $R—S—\overset{\overset{\displaystyle S}{\|}}{C}—OCH_2CHR'_2$ (a xanthate)

(C)

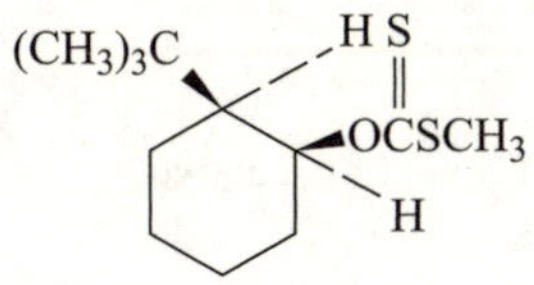

(D)

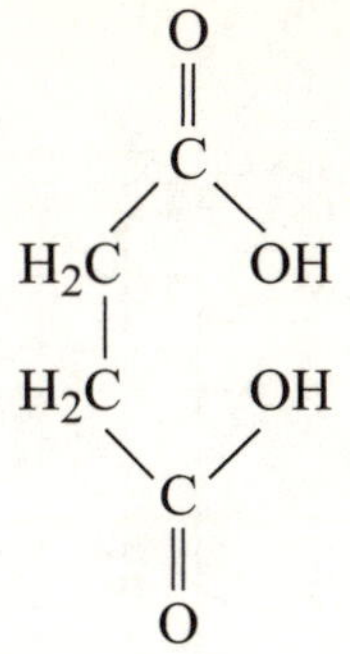

(E)

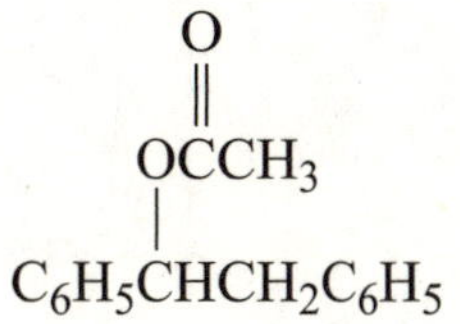

116. The reactions below represent a possible mechanism for the chlorination of methane. Indicate which of the statements below is (are) *true*.

Mechanism

(1) $Cl_2 \xrightarrow{\text{uv light}} 2Cl\cdot$

(2) $Cl\cdot + CH_4 \rightarrow HCl + \cdot CH_3$

(3) $CH_3\cdot + Cl_2 \rightarrow Cl\cdot + CH_3Cl$

(4) $Cl\cdot + Cl\cdot \rightarrow Cl_2$

(5) $CH_3\cdot + Cl\cdot \rightarrow CH_3Cl$

   I. Steps (2), (3), and (4) represent the chain-propagating steps.

  II. If we add oxygen to the reaction vessel, the series of reactions shown above would proceed more rapidly, and oxygen would catalyze the reaction.

 III. Step (4) is most likely the rate determinant step.

 IV. Step (5) represents a possible termination step for the reaction.

(A) I only

(B) II only

(C) IV only

(D) II and IV only

(E) None of the above statements is correct.

117. Which of the following spectral lines represent the Paschen series?

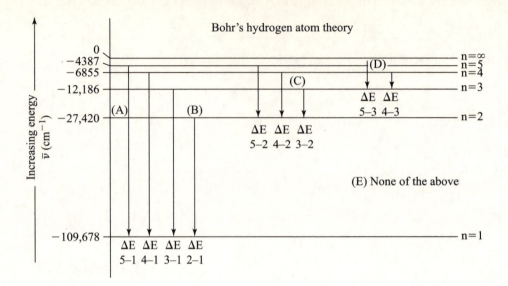

Bohr's hydrogen atom theory

118. What is the velocity of a 300g ball having a de Broglie wavelength of 0.06135×10^{-10} m (take h, Planck's constant, to be 6.6262×10^{-34} kg m²sec⁻²sec)?

(A) $6.6262(0.06135)(.300) \times 10^{-44}$

(B) $0.06135 \times 10^{-10}(0.300)/(6.6262 \times 10^{-34})$

(C) $\dfrac{6.6262 \times 10^{-34}}{(0.06135 \times 10^{-10})(0.300)}$

(D) $\dfrac{6.6262 \times 10^{-34}(0.300)}{(0.06135 \times 10^{-10})}$

(E) $\dfrac{(6.6262 \times 10^{-34})(0.300)}{(0.06135 \times 10^{-10})(1000)}$

119. How much heat is absorbed by 100g of water when its temperature decreases from 25°C to 5°C? (Take the specific heat of water to be 4.2 J/gK°.)

(A) 8,400J
(B) −8,400J
(C) 2000/4.2J
(D) −2000/4.2J
(E) −84/100J

120. Which of the following factors does *not* contribute to the energy (ε_α) of a system that has a large number of molecules (N)?

(A) Electronic
(B) Vibrational
(C) Rotational
(D) Nuclear
(E) Thermal

121. Which of the following equations below represents the Nernst equation for overall cell potentials?

(A) $\varepsilon = \varepsilon^{\circ} - \dfrac{RT}{nF}\ln Q$

(D) $\varepsilon = -nF\displaystyle\int_{T_1}^{T_2} \dfrac{\delta\varepsilon}{\delta T}\ln Q$

(B) $\varepsilon = \varepsilon^{\circ} - \dfrac{nF}{RT}\ln Q$

(E) Not given

(C) $\varepsilon = \displaystyle\int_{T_1}^{T_2} \dfrac{\delta\varepsilon}{\delta T}dT$

122. The infrared spectrum (I.R.) is frequently used for the analysis of organic compounds. Which of the statements below concerning I.R. spectroscopy is (are) correct?

   I. This technique (I.R. analysis) by itself yields more information about the compound's structure than any other technique.

   II. Absorption due to carbon-hydrogen stretching occurs at the lower frequency end of the I.R. spectrum.

   III. It is the absorption of infrared light that causes the changing vibrations of a molecule.

(A) I only
(B) I and II only
(C) II only

(D) II and III only
(E) None of the above

123. Consider the reaction below:

$$CH_3 - \underset{\underset{CH_3}{|}}{C} = CH - CH_3 + HI \longrightarrow CH_3 - \underset{\underset{I}{|}}{\overset{\overset{CH_3}{|}}{C}} - CH_2 - CH_3$$

2-Methyl-2-butene   2-Iodo-2-methylbutane

An acid is added to a carbon-carbon double bond of an alkene and the hydrogen of the acid attaches itself to the carbon holding the greater number of hydrogens. This phenomenon is referred to as

(A) the Saytzeff's rule
(B) Markovnikov's rule
(C) electrophillic addition to a carbon-carbon double bond involving a carbocation.
(D) nucleophilic attack by the acid on the ($-$C$=$C$-$) carbon-carbon double bond.
(E) Both (B) and (C) are correct.

124. Consider the two half-reactions

$$Ag \rightarrow Ag^+ + e^- \qquad E° = -0.80V$$
$$Zn^{2+} + 2e^- \rightarrow Zn \qquad E° = -0.76V$$

Which of the following statements is (are) *true*?

  I. The standard potential [E°] for the reaction (as it's written) is $+1.56V$.

 II. As written, the reaction is spontaneous.

III. The sign of the reaction potential indicates whether the reaction is spontaneous or not.

(A) I only
(B) I and II only
(C) III only
(D) II and III only
(E) I, II, and III

125. Consider the reaction

$$X + Y \rightarrow Z$$

The data below was obtained for the reaction after a kinetic study.

Run	[X]	[Y]	Rate (mole/liter-min)
1	2.0M	2.0M	1.5
2	6.0M	2.0M	4.5
3	2.0M	6.0M	1.5

Determine the rate expression for the reaction.

(A) Rate = k[X][Y]
(B) Rate = k[X]^2
(C) Rate = k[X]
(D) Rate = k[Y]
(E) The rate is independent of the concentrations of X and Y.

126. A crystal sublimes according to the reaction

$$X_2(s) \rightleftharpoons X_2(g).$$

Which of the following expressions represents the temperature at which solid crystal is in equilibrium with gaseous crystal? (ΔH = change in enthalpy, ΔG = change in free energy, ΔS = entropy change.)

(A) $T_{equib} = \dfrac{\Delta H}{\Delta S}$

(B) $T_{equib} = \dfrac{\Delta G - \Delta H}{\Delta S}$

(C) $T_{equib} = \dfrac{\Delta G + \Delta H}{\Delta S}$

(D) $T_{equib} = \dfrac{\Delta S}{\Delta H}$

(E) $T_{equib} > \dfrac{\Delta S}{\Delta H}$

127. The Joule-Thompson experiment is a constant-enthalpy process measuring $\left(\frac{\delta T}{\delta P}\right)_H$ as real gases undergo a(n):

    (A) isothermal compression.
    (B) isentropic expansion.
    (C) throttled adiabatic expansion.
    (D) adiabatic compression.
    (E) isothermal expansion.

128. The radioactive decay of plutonium-241 $^{241}_{94}Pu$ to neptunium (Np), takes place in two steps: first a beta emission followed by an alpha emission. The symbol of Np after the radioactive emissions should be

    (A) $^{236}_{93}Np$

    (B) $^{237}_{93}Np$

    (C) $^{241}_{95}Np$

    (D) $^{235}_{92}Np$

    (E) $^{236}_{92}Np$

129. A reaction mixture consists of N_2, H_2, and NH_3. At 298°K, what is ΔG for the following reaction (P = pressure)?

    Reaction: $N_2(g) + 3H_2(g) \rightarrow 2NH_3(g)$

    (A) $\Delta G = \Delta G° + 2.3RT \log \dfrac{P_{N_2} P^3_{H_2}}{P^2_{NH_3}}$

    (D) $\Delta G = \Delta G° + 2.3RT \left/ \left(\dfrac{P^2_{NH_3}}{P_{N_2} P^3_{H_2}}\right)\right.$

    (B) $\Delta G = 2.3RT \log \dfrac{P^2_{NH_3}}{P_{N_2} P^3_{H_2}}$

    (E) $\Delta G = \Delta G° + 2.3RT \left(\dfrac{P^2_{NH_3}}{P_{N_2} P^2_{H_2}}\right)$

    (C) $\Delta G = \Delta G° + 2.3RT \log \dfrac{P^2_{NH_3}}{P_{N_2} P^3_{H_2}}$

130. The maximum possible work from a spontaneous process at isothermal and isobaric conditions is equal to

    (A) the free energy change
    (B) $\Delta G° + 2.3RT$
    (C) $\Delta H° + T\Delta S°$

    (D) $\dfrac{\Delta G - \Delta H}{\Delta T}$

    (E) Expression (C), but the system must be adiabatic.

131. The least accurate of the volumetric measuring devices is the

    (A) pipet.
    (B) buret.
    (C) volumetric flask.

    (D) graduate cylinder.
    (E) (A), (B), (C), (D) are all accurate; none is more accurate than the other.

132. The diagram below represents an idealized NMR spectrum due to —CH—CH$_2$— grouping. Which of the following statement(s) concerning this spectrum is (are) *correct*?

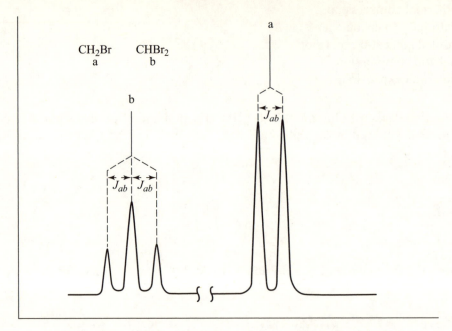

Spin-spin splitting. Signal a is split into a doublet by coupling with one proton; signal b is split into a triplet by two protons. Spacings in both sets represent the same (J_{ab}).

   I.   The total area under the doublet is twice the total area of the triplet.

  II.   The picture represents a 1:1:1 triplet and a 1:1 doublet.

 III.   The peak area in the picture reflects the number of absorbing protons.

(A) I only
(B) I and II only
(C) I and III only

(D) II and III only
(E) I, II, and III

133. For solids and liquids

$$C_p - C_v = \frac{\alpha^2 VT}{\beta},$$

C_p and C_v represent heat capacities at constant pressure (P) and volume (V), respectively. (Note T = temperature.) β is a constant called the

(A)   coefficient of thermal expansion.
(B)   viral coefficient.
(C)   Benedict-Webb-Rubin constant.
(D)   Van der Waals expansion factor.
(E)   isothermal compressibility factor.

134. Consider the plot below, which illustrates how ΔG° varies with the temperature (T). Which of the following statements is (are) *true*?

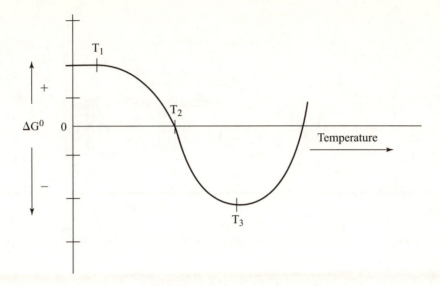

   I. ΔG° at T_1 is positive.

  II. $\left(\dfrac{\delta \Delta G^\circ}{\Delta T}\right)_P = 0$ at T_3

 III. ΔH° = positive value at T_2

(A) I only
(B) I and II only
(C) I and III only

(D) III only
(E) I, II, and III

135. The statements below are based on the molecular orbital theory. Indicate which one of them is incorrect.

(A) Valence electrons are influenced by all nuclei and electrons in the molecule.
(B) The combination of the number of atomic orbitals is the same as the number of molecular orbitals.
(C) Molecular orbitals with rotational symmetry about the bond axis are called π orbitals.
(D) Sigma bonds can be formed using p orbitals directed along the molecular axis.
(E) $\int (N\psi)^2 dT = 1$ represents the wave function for molecular orbitals. This equation indicates that the probability of finding the electron outside the nucleus is unity. (N represents the normalization constant.)

136. The apparatus below is used to measure the electrode potential of zinc. Indicate which of the statement(s) below is (are) true: (Note that the following half-reactions $Zn \rightarrow Zn^{+2} + 2e$; $2H^+ + 2e^- \rightarrow H_2$ take place in this system.)

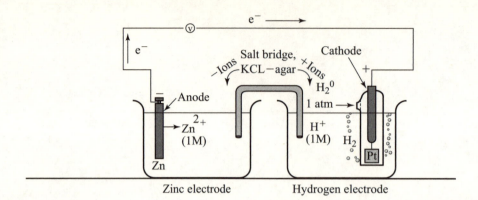

I. The two halves of the cell are connected by the salt bridge. It permits a current to flow and the two solutions to mix.

II. The hydrogen electrode serves as a reference electrode.

III. The reactions occurring at the zinc electrode as current flows are $Zn \rightarrow Zn^{+2} + 2e^-$ and $2H^+ + 2e^- \rightarrow H_2$.

(A) I only
(B) II only
(C) I and II only

(D) II and III only
(E) I, II, and III

Answer Key

1. B	24. C	47. A	70. B	93. B	116. C
2. C	25. E	48. B	71. C	94. B	117. D
3. E	26. A	49. A	72. E	95. C	118. C
4. A	27. C	50. D	73. E	96. D	119. B
5. B	28. D	51. C	74. D	97. C	120. E
6. C	29. E	52. C	75. C	98. E	121. A
7. C	30. A	53. A	76. E	99. E	122. E
8. A	31. E	54. D	77. B	100. E	123. E
9. C	32. A	55. A	78. D	101. A	124. C
10. A	33. C	56. E	79. A	102. C	125. C
11. D	34. A	57. E	80. B	103. C	126. A
12. B	35. D	58. E	81. E	104. C	127. C
13. A	36. D	59. D	82. D	105. A	128. B
14. C	37. C	60. E	83. D	106. C	129. C
15. B	38. E	61. A	84. A	107. E	130. A
16. A	39. A	62. B	85. A	108. B	131. D
17. D	40. C	63. B	86. A	109. C	132. C
18. D	41. C	64. E	87. A	110. E	133. E
19. E	42. D	65. C	88. C	111. C	134. E
20. D	43. C	66. C	89. E	112. D	135. C
21. C	44. A	67. B	90. B	113. A	136. B
22. D	45. A	68. C	91. C	114. E	
23. E	46. A	69. D	92. E	115. D	

Practice Exam 3

Detailed Explanations of Answers

1. **(B)**
   Keeping in mind that covalent bonds are generally formed between nonmetal elements, B is correct because the position of silicon and hydrogen in the periodic table indicate a tendency to form covalent bonding. All other compounds are electrovalently bonded, in which the electron needs of the anions are met by the cations (which have a willingness to donate one or two electrons from its outer shells).

2. **(C)**
   The willingness of the halogens to complete their outer shell by gaining an electron (oxidation) makes them very good oxidizing agents.

3. **(E)**
   A Brønsted-Lowry acid is defined as a substance that is able to donate a proton (i.e., a hydrogen ion, H^+) to some other substance. Because there is no proton present in SO_4^{2-}, SO_4^{2-} cannot function as a Brønsted-Lowry acid.

4. **(A)**
   Molecules that contain symmetrically opposing dipoles (positive and negative charges separated by a distance) have a net dipole moment of zero. Such is the case with methane.

$$\delta^- \qquad \delta^+$$
$$H—C$$

δ^-, δ^+—partial negative and positive charges (respectively)

$\rightarrow$ direction of pull

5. **(B)**
   $BeCl_2$ is a linear molecule; the $2\bar{s}$ and 2p atomic orbitals hybridize to form two sp hybrid orbitals. These sp orbitals overlap with p orbitals from the chlorine atoms to form hybrid bonds.

6. **(C)**
   Peptides are amides formed by interaction between amino groups and carboxyl groups of amino acids.

   Proteins are made up of polypeptide chains.

Suppose you have a peptide chain in which each chain is held by hydrogen bonds to the two neighboring chains. A hypothetical structure for a protein could be

7. **(C)**

A knowledge of Beer's law (for the absorption of light) is necessary to solve this problem.

Beer's law states that A, the absorbance, is equal to the product of the concentration C in mol liter^{-1}, the length l in cm, and the extinction coefficient ε. Hence

$$A = \varepsilon \, cl$$

$$\Rightarrow \quad \varepsilon = \frac{A}{lc} = \frac{0.855}{(1.00 \text{cu})(3.52 \times 10^{-4} \text{ mol liter}^{-1})}$$

8. **(A)**

The solution to this question requires knowledge of the Q-test technique for the evaluation of data.

$$Q_{exp} - \left[\frac{\text{Suspect value – Nearest value}}{\text{Largest value – Smallest value}} \right]$$

If Q_{exp} is greater than the Q-value at the 90% confidence level, then the suspect value (in this case 43.62%) would not be included in the average.

$$\text{Now} \quad Q_{exp} = \frac{43.62 - 43.28}{43.62 - 43.19} = 0.79$$

$$\Rightarrow \quad Q_{exp} > Q_{90\% \text{ confidence}}; \text{ i.e. } 0.79 > 0.76$$

Hence, we will discard 43.62%. Therefore, the best value to report would be

$$(43.28 + 43.19 + 43.24)/3 = 43.24$$

9. (C)

The different components of ink would move along the pores of the paper at different rates, thus making separation possible. All the other choices are incorrect.

10. (A)

Tritation is carried out in volumetric, not gravimetric, analysis.

11. (D)

A conspicuous feature is the strong, broad band in the 3200–3600 cm^{-1} region due to the O—H stretching; it is unique to the alcohols.

12. (B)

The reference electrode of a pH meter is one that has a potential that is independent of the hydrogen ion concentration of the measured solution. Note it is the indicating electrode, the one that is dependent upon the [H$^+$] ions in the measured solution.

13. (A)

Note that molarity of HCl is defined as

$$\frac{\text{moles HCl}}{\text{liter}} = \frac{(\text{moles Na}_2\text{CO3})(2)}{\text{ml HCl}/1000}$$

$$= \frac{(\text{g Na}_2\text{CO}_3)(2)}{(\text{mol. wt. Na}_2\text{CO}_3)(\text{ml HCl}/1000)}$$

The factor 2 is needed because each mole of Na$_2$CO$_3$ reacts with 2 moles HCl.

14. (C)

The momentum of any particle is the product of its mass and velocity.

15. (B)

Because electron mass is negligible, the number of neutrons = mass number − atomic number = 238 − 92 = 146.

16. (A)

The standard heat of reaction (ΔH°_{298}) is (the summation of the standard heats of formation of products) − (the summation of the standard heats of formation of reactants).

Therefore $\Delta H^\circ_{298} = 5(-1260) + 9(-280) - 2(60)$

$$= -8940 \text{ kJ.}$$

17. (D)

Note G versus ln p, should be in the form of a straight line. G = G$^\circ$ + RTln(P/p$^\circ$) is a linear function of the form y = mx + b. Note that (C) is incorrect. The p axis is expressed in the form of natural logarithms.

18.   (D)

The acidity and basicity constants are ridiculously low for —COOH and —NH_2 groups. Glycine, for instance, an amino acid, has a $K_a = 1.6 \times 10^{-10}$ and a $K_b = 2.5 \times 10^{-12}$. All the other statements listed about amino acids are true.

19.   (E)

$LiAlH_4$ may not be used to oxidize aldehydes and ketones to carbocyclic acids; actually $LiAlH_4$ reduces these compounds to alcohols.

20.   (D)

We have to look for equivalent protons, i.e., hydrogen atoms that are stereochemically equivalent; these protons will give identical signals in the N.M.R. spectrum. For example,

$$CH_3—CH_2—Cl$$
$$\quad a \qquad b$$

this compound will give 2 N.M.R. signals because there are two different sets of equivalent hydrogens designated a and b, respectively. Similarly, for $CH_3CHClCH_3$ and

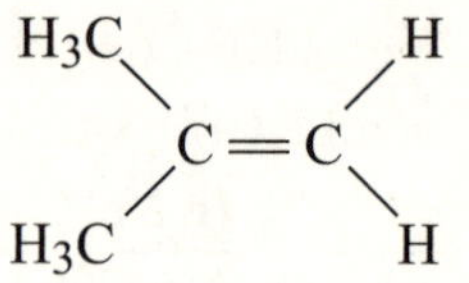

H$_3$C   H

C=C

H$_3$C   H

we have 2 N.M.R. signals.

$CH_3—CHCl—CH_3$;
  a   b   a

2 N.M.R. signals

a   b

H$_3$C   H

C=C

H$_3$C   H

a   b

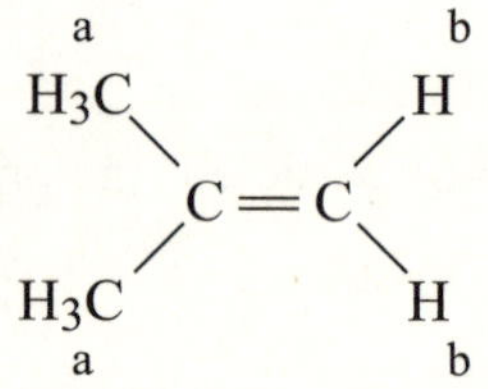

2 N.M.R. signals

Methylcyclopropane has 4 types of

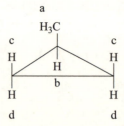

stereochemically equivalent hydrogens and will have 4 N.M.R. signals. Finally, on examination of n-propyl chloride

$$CH_3-CH_2-CH_2-CL$$
$$\quad\;\; a \qquad b \qquad c$$

we notice 3 sets of equivalent hydrogen atoms; hence the compound will exhibit 3 signals in the N.M.R. spectrum.

21. (C)

Grams of materials present = (moles)(MW)

$$\text{Moles} = \text{volume} \times \text{molarity} = 250\text{ml} \times \frac{0.1 \text{ mole}}{\text{liter}}$$

$$= 250\text{ml} \times \frac{0.1000 \text{ moles}}{1} \times \frac{11}{1000\text{ml}}$$

Grams Barium nitrate present $\quad = MWX \times \text{moles}$

$$= (199.344)(250)(0.1000)/(1000).$$

22. (D)

Because a weak basic solution was initially present, the pH must be slightly greater than 7 on the pH axis. As the weak acidic solution is added, the mixture should neutralize, then become slightly acidic. Graph (D) best represents this trend.

23. (E)

All three statements are accurate. Note that ΔG, not $\Delta G°$, is dependent on pressure.

24. (C)

The equilibrium constant can be expressed as the product of the activities of the products formed, divided by the product of the activities of the reactants. (Note that each chemical substance in the reacting vessel is raised to a power that is actually the number of moles of that substance from stoichiometry.)

25. (E)

Both statements I and III are correct. II is incorrect because doping enhances the conductivity of both silicon and germanium.

26. (A)

For isothermal expansion

$$q = -w \text{ (heat} = -\text{work)}$$

$$\Rightarrow \quad q = \int P dv = -P \int dv = -P(v_2 - v_1)$$

$$= nRT \left(1 - \frac{P_2}{P_1}\right) = 2(8.3)(300)(.9)$$

$$= -4482J$$

27. (C)

Branching lowers the boiling point. Notice that (D) and (E) have more carbons, meaning more bonds to break. This requires more energy; hence the boiling point would be relatively higher than (A), (B), and (C). Because (C) is the most branched of the 5 carbon compounds, it would be expected to have the lowest boiling point.

28. (D)

Octane because there 8 carbons; bicyclo because there are 2 rings; and [2,2,2] because the number of shared carbons between bridgeheads is two, two, and two (see below).

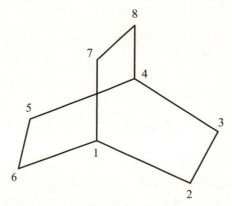

Bicyclo [2·2·2] octane

29. (E)

Only —CN is considered to be a destabilizer because this group destabilizes the carbocation by withdrawing electrons (from the ring).

30. (A)

Acids are frequently converted to esters via the acid chlorides. The equation for this reaction is as follows:

$$(CH_3)_3CCOOH \xrightarrow{\text{SOCl}_2} (CH_3)_3CCOCl \xrightarrow{\text{C}_2\text{H}_5\text{OH}} (CH_3)_3CCOOC_2H_5$$

Trimethylacetic acid   Ethyltrimethylacetate

31. (E)

Chromatography is not generally used for solid-solid separation. The technique (chromatography) is based upon selective adsorption, separating samples in liquid or gas phases. HPLC refers to "high performance liquid chromatography," and ion exchange chromatography is a special type of liquid phase chromatography.

32. (A)

Some (symmetrical) molecules such as ethylene (CH_2=CH_2) do not exhibit all their vibrations in infrared spectra. Raman spectroscopy helps by examining the vibrations of these molecules.

33. (C)

The wavelengths range from 1×10^{-7} m to 10m, from the ultraviolet to the radio frequency region.

34. (A)

(A) on the diagram represents the ionization chamber.

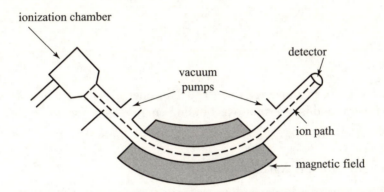

In a mass spectrometer, bombardment of a sample in a gas phase by high-energy electrons produces a positive ion charge, which fragments itself and forms other positive ion fragments. These fragments (mainly singly charged ions) are directed in the mass spectrometer, through a magnetic field.

By varying the magnetic field, ions with progressively higher masses strike the detector, so one can plot intensity of magnetic field (proportional to the number of ions of particular masses) $\times$ ratio of m/e.

35. (D)

All the other phenomena relate to optical spectroscopy, except doping, which relates to the creation of semiconductor types.

36. (D)

In 0.65g of gold there are

$$\frac{0.65\text{g}}{1.96.9665\text{g mol}^{-1}} = \frac{0.65}{196.9665}\text{mole}$$

Therefore, because there are 6.02×10^{23} atoms per mol of gold, then in 0.65g of gold, we have $\left(\dfrac{0.65}{196.9665}\right)(6.02 \times 10^{23})$ atoms of gold.

37. (C)

Work is not a state function. The amount of work done by a system is dependent on the path chosen.

38. (E)

Hydrogen lines were found in visible (Balmer series) ultraviolet (Lyman series) and then in the infrared (Paschen series) regions. The Rydberg equation summarizes the geometric regularities of each series

$$\bar{v} = R\left(\frac{1}{n_2^2} - \frac{1}{n_1^2}\right)$$

in which $\bar{v}$ is the reciprocal of the wavelength of the emitted light corresponding to a particular line and is called the wavenumber. In this case we used the Balmer series, in which $n_2 = 2$ and $n_1 = 3, 4, 5,$ ..., resulting in

$$\bar{v} = R_H\left(\frac{1}{4} - \frac{1}{n^2}\right)$$

39. (A)

The missing mass has been converted to energy. This energy is needed in order to prevent the splitting of the nucleus (fission) and is referred to as binding energy.

40. (C)

Bohr was responsible for this equation.

41. (C)

(C) is in the densest region. This is Bohr's model, which says that the probability of finding an electron is greater in the denser regions.

42. (D)

The four atoms at the corners (H and O) form a regular tetrahedron.

43. (C)

The common name of this compound is p-cresol.

44. (A)

Aldol condensation involves the reaction of 2 molecules of an aldehyde or a ketone in the presence of a dilute acid or base.

45. (A)

Here steric hindrance is an important factor. The bulkier the substitutent on the central carbon*, the slower and more difficult it is for the reaction to proceed.

* Refers to the carbon with the doubly bonded oxygen atom.

46. (A)

Electron-withdrawing substituents disperse the negative charge, stabilizing the anion. If there is an increase in the stability of the anion, the acidity should increase.

47. (A)

The reaction sequence is as follows:

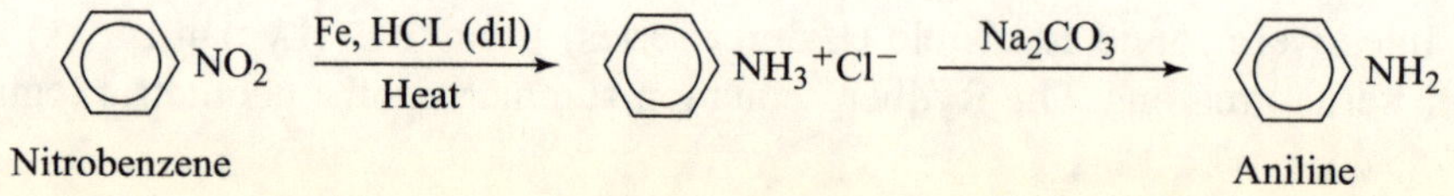

48. (B)

The laboratory process generally involves the use of nickel catalyst in the present of hydrogen.

$$CH_3-C\equiv-CH_3 \xrightarrow[ni]{2H} CH_3CH_2CH_2CH_3$$

2-Butyne   n-Butane

49. (A)

The acid present catalyzes the reaction, leading to H_2O elimination. After rearrangement of the carbocation to its most stable form, we get $CH_3CH\!=\!CHCH_3$ as the chief product.

50. (D)

Statement (D) best describes Le Châtellier's Principle (concerning equilibrium).

51. (C)

The law states that for N_o molecules in any state with energy ε_o, the number of molecules with ε_i is

$$N_i = N_o exp\left[\frac{-(\varepsilon_i - \varepsilon_o)}{kT}\right]$$

52. (C)

Applying Kohlransch's Law, we have:

$$\lambda_{O(NH_4 OH)} = \lambda_{O(NH_4Cl)} + \lambda_{O(NaOH)} - \lambda_{O(NaCl)}$$

$$= 150 + 248 - 127 = 271$$

53. (A)

This problem concerns gravimetric analysis. We have the following formula:

$$\%A = \frac{wt.\ participate \times \frac{a \times M.W.A.}{b \times M.W.\ Prec.} \times 100}{wt.\ sample}$$

In our case,

$$\%P = \frac{wt.\ Mg_2P_2O_7 \times \frac{a \times M.W.A.}{b \times M.W.\ Prec.} \times 100}{0.585}$$

where $\quad \dfrac{a}{b} = \dfrac{2}{1} \dfrac{moles\ P\ in\ Precip.}{moles\ P\ in\ sample}$

$$\%P = \frac{0.432 \times 2 \times 30.97 \times 100}{(0.585)(222.6)}$$

54. (D)

Both statements I and II are correct; the glass electrode is the most important indicator electrode for hydrogen ion. It is subject to few of the interferences that affect other pH-sensing electrodes. This electrode can be used without interference to measure the pH of viscous fluids, and the smaller version may even be employed to measure the pH in a cavity of a tooth.

55. (A)

During electrolysis, anions migrate toward the anode, and cations migrate to the cathode. Hence, in the electrolysis of $CuCl_2$, the following oxidation processes take place at the anode:

(1) $Cl^-(aq) = \frac{1}{2}Cl_2(g) + 1e^-$ and
(2) $2H_2O(l) = O_2(g) + 4H^+(aq) + 4e^-$

making (A) the only correct choice.

56. (E)

Solvation is not a means of separating a mixture, but rather represents the attraction of an ion to the oppositely charged end of a solvent molecule. All the other choices are techniques that may be used for separation of mixtures.

57. (E)

All three statements are correct. The proton is the most commonly investigated nucleus in N.M.R. spectroscopy; this method is often referred to as P.M.R. (proton magnetic resonance). Nuclei with spin numbers of zero (e.g., ^{13}C), do not produce N.M.R. signals because they exhibit no magnetic properties.

Like electrons, nuclei of certain atoms are considered to spin; this spinning generates a magnetic moment. Consider a proton; its moment can be aligned with or against the external field. Alignment with the field is more stable and energy must be absorbed to "flip" the proton over to the less stable alignment against the field.

Varying the magnetic field and maintaining constant the frequency of radiation at some value of the field, the necessary energy to flip the proton is achieved, and a signal is observed. Thus, an N.M.R. spectrum is produced.

58. (E)

Avogadro was responsible for this proposal. He used this theory to explain Gay-Lussac's observations concerning gases.

59. (D)

De Broglie developed this relation $\lambda = \frac{h}{mv}$ for the electron.

60. (E)

Fe^{3+} and Fe^{2+} are actually cations (positively charged ions), not anions. Note that (D) is true because the loss of oxygen is also referred to as reduction.

61. (A)

Because potassium hydroxide is a strong base, a large amount of OH^- ions will be present in solution enhancing this reaction (due to the common ion effect):

$$KOH \rightleftharpoons [K^+][OH^-]$$

$$0.002 \text{ m} \quad 0.002m \quad 0.002m$$

$$H^+ + OH^- \rightarrow H_2O \text{ [Mostly]}$$

Now
$$K_W = [H^+][OH^-]$$

Hence
$$[H^+] = \frac{K_w}{[OH^-]} = \frac{K_w}{0.0020}$$

62. (B)

$(CN)_6$ is referred to as hexacyano, and because the oxidation number of Fe is $+2$, the compound is referred to as ferrate (II).

63. (B)

The plot represents an exponential function, which fits the function $\psi(r) = Ae^{-r}$.

64. (E)

(E) is the only statement here not true for ammonia. Ammonia is easily liquefied by cooling and compression; liquid ammonia boils at $-33.43°C$, and the solid melts at $-77.76°C$.

65. (C)

The preferred conformation of trans-1,2,-Dimethylcyclohexane is a chair form, as shown below:

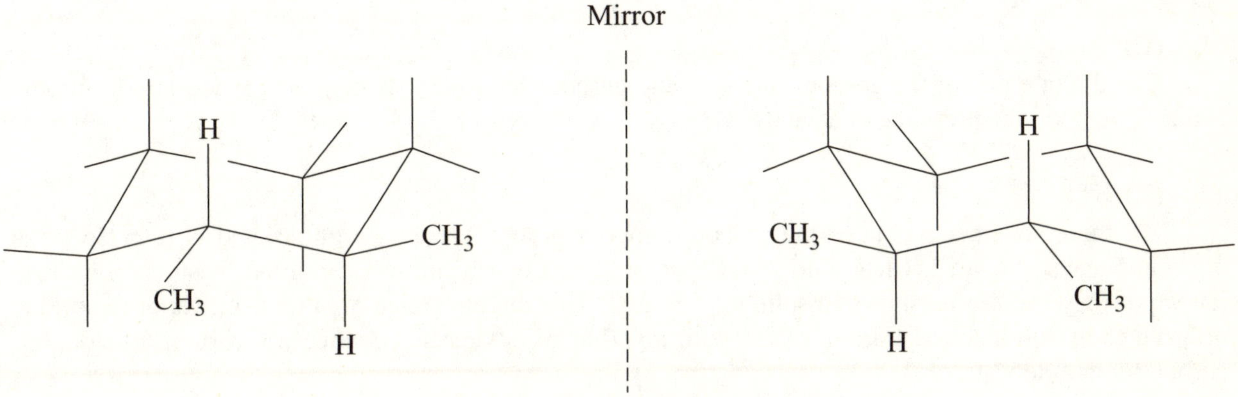

Nonsuperimposable
Trans–1, 2–Dimethylcyclohexane

As can be seen from the diagram, the compound is not superimposable. Also (not shown in diagram above) the CH_3 groups may exist in a diaxial form (opposite sides of the ring) or in the (Di) equatorial position.

66. (C)

A primary alcohol loses one α-hydrogen during oxidation (note that α-hydrogen is the one attached to the carbon bearing the —OH group).

$$\underset{\substack{\text{a } 1° \text{ alcohol}}}{R-\overset{\displaystyle -OH}{\underset{\displaystyle H \quad \alpha-\text{hydrogen}}{C}}-OH} \xrightarrow{C_5H_5NH^+CrO_3Cl^-} \underset{\text{an aldehyde}}{R-\overset{\displaystyle H}{C}=O}$$

Also, a primary alcohol is oxidized readily to a carboxylic acid in the presence of potassium permanganate. Under milder conditions—such as in $C_5H_5NHCrO_3Cl$ and CH_2Cl_2—the primary alcohol is oxidized to an aldehyde.

67. (B)

This is actually the third law of thermodynamics.

68. (C)

Van der Waals included the term $\dfrac{an^2}{V^2}$ to account for the intermolecular attraction among gas molecules.

69. (D)

Because oxygen has an oxidation number of -2, chlorine must have an oxidation number of $+7$ for the chlorate ion to have the sum of $1Cl(+7) + 40(-2) = -1$. Thus the oxidation number of Cl is $+7$.

70. (B)

Electronegativity decreases as we descend this group. The smaller atoms of Li would more readily accept an electron than the larger atoms of cesium.

71. (C)

The direct union of the gaseous nitrogen and gaseous hydrogen elements is carried out during the Haber process in the presence of a catalyst.

72. (E)

All three statements concerning carbon compounds are correct. Carbonic acid is referred to as diprotic because the acid reacts with water, releasing two hydrogen ions (protons). Also carbon dioxide vapor may freeze to a snowlike solid at $-56.2°C$. This direct change of state from vapor to solid is referred to as sublimation. Carbon reacts with insufficient oxygen to produce not carbon dioxide, but carbon monoxide.

73. (A)

Because only statements I and III are correct, statement II is incorrect because the immobile molecular network in a cation exchanger is anionic rather than cationic.

74. (D)

The reaction is

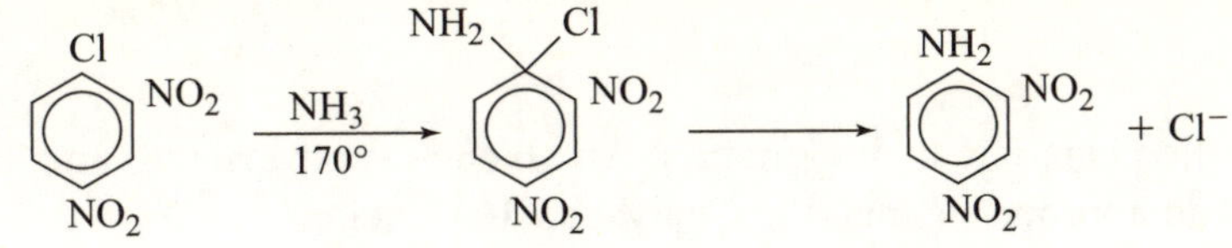

(Biomolecular displacement)

75. (C)

The very electronegative atoms, F, O, or N make hydrogen bonding possible. Because CH_3Cl and CH_3CH_2Cl do not contain any of these atoms, they cannot form hydrogen bonds. Although CH_3OCH_3 and 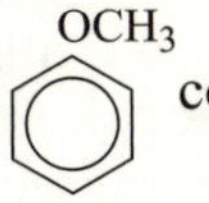 contain oxygen atoms, they are not directly bonded to hydrogen atoms, e.g.,

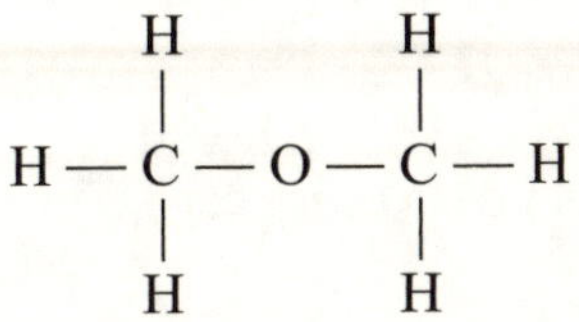

and therefore cannot form hydrogen bonds. Only CH_3NH_2 form hydrogen bonds due to the N—H bond present.

76. (E)

The major product here is an alkene. No alcohol is produced under these conditions.

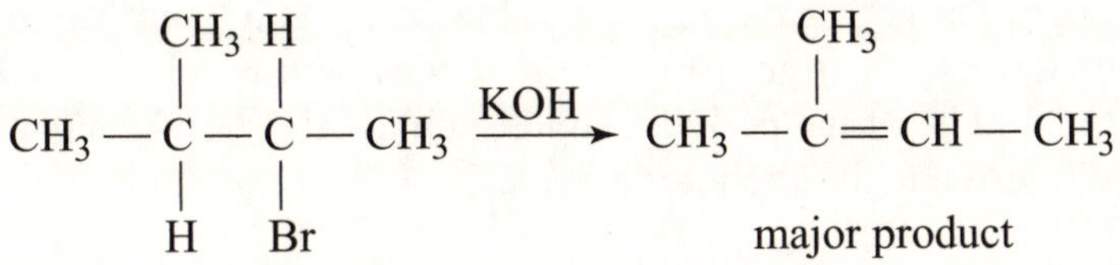

major product

77. (B)

The reaction is as follows:

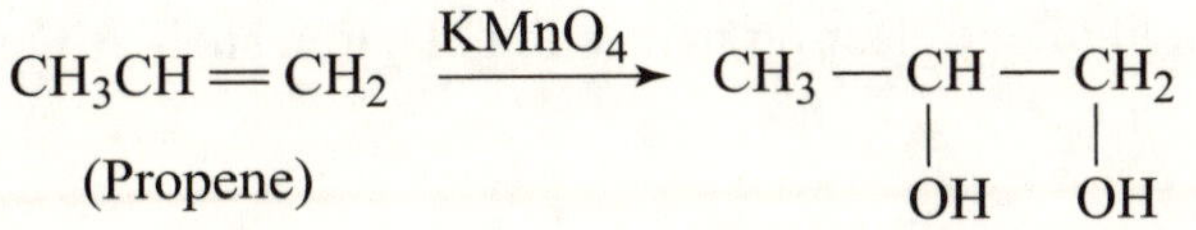

1, 2 Propane diol

78. (D)

Racemization is typical of S_N1 not S_N2 reactions. All the other statements are true for S_N2 reactions.

79. (A)

The process is called catalytic hydrogenation. An alkene is converted to an alkane in the presence of heat, hydrogen, and an appropriate metallic catalyst such as nickel.

80. (B)

The Tollens's reagent $[Ag(NH_3)_2^+]$ is used to oxidize aldehydes to carboxylic acids; this is a mild oxidizing agent.

The oxidation of aldehydes also takes place more readily then ketone oxidations; this is due largely to their structural differences. While an aldehyde has a hydrogen atom attached to the carbonyl carbon, a ketone has either an alkyl or aryl group—which, of course, makes oxidation in the latter case more difficult. The oxidizing agents used for the oxidation of primary and secondary alcohols can be used for oxidizing aldehydes, but even milder oxidizing agents, such as Tollens's reagent, can accomplish this.

81. (E)

M^+ is sometimes the base peak, but not in every case. The other statements are all true for the mass spectra.

82. (D)

Helium has only 2 electrons in its outermost shell. The boiling points of helium and neon are, respectively, $-268.9°C$ and $-246.1°C$. Note also that liquid helium cannot be solidified by cooling and is not used in gas lamps.

83. (D)

Oxides of elements at the left of the periodic table (e.g., Na_2O and MgO) generally form basic solutions in water, while those to the right form acidic oxides with water (e.g., Cl_2O_7 and P_2O_5). Some oxides of elements in the middle of the periodic table, such as Al_2O_3 and ZnO, exhibit both acidic and basic properties and are referred to as amphoteric oxides.

84. (A)

This equation is the Schrödinger wave equation for a particle in three dimensions.

85. (A)

Fluorine, having a deficit of one electron in its outer electron shell, is the strongest oxidizing agent of all the known elements.

86. (A)

Chlorine combines with hydrogen in the dark, but the same reaction in light is rather explosive—this reaction is a photochemical reaction. The light here acts as a catalyst, speeding up the reaction.

87. (A)

For an isothermal isobaric expansion of an ideal gas, T (temperature) and pressure (P) are constant.

$$\Delta E = \Delta H = C_p \Delta T° = 0$$

$$\Delta E = qtw$$

$$\text{as } \Delta E = 0$$

$$q = W = \int_{v_1}^{v_2} Pdv = P\Delta v$$

88. (C)

The cell constant is defined as

$$\frac{1}{A} = kR = (0.15)(680)$$

k = specific conductance, which in this case is given by L. L refers to conductance of the electrolytic solution.

89. (E)

All three of these statements are true for an ideal solution. Note that $P_i = P_i°x_i$ is Raoult's Law, which is true for all ideal solutions.

90. (B)

The equation relating the rate constant k to the temperature (T) is

$$\ln k = \ln A - \left(\frac{\Delta E}{R}\right)\frac{1}{T}$$

where ΔE is the activation energy. From the equation, we notice that ln k is directly proportional to ΔE and inversely proportional to T.

91. (C)

Transesterification (cleavage by an alcohol) takes place. A possible mechanism describing this type of reaction is shown below. (A simple representation is used for clarity.)

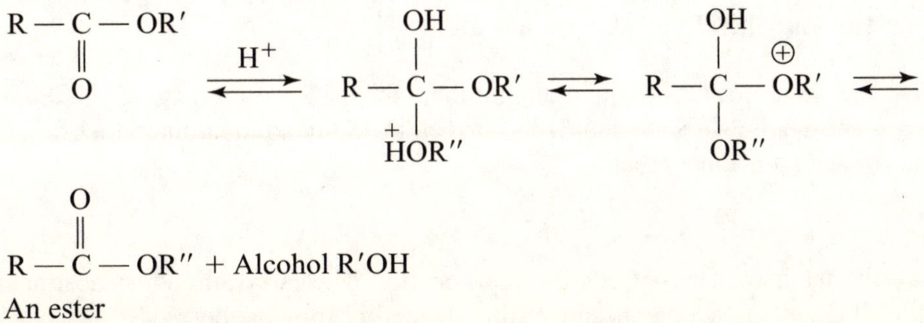

An ester

This is the mechanism whereby (C) is formed.

92. (E)

Phenols are generally stronger than alcohols (due to structure); the former has a K_a of about 10^{-10}, while the latter has a K_a of about 10^{-16} to 10^{-18}. Electron-withdrawing substituents like NO_2 increase the acidity of phenols, while electron-releasing substituents such as —CH_3 decrease the acidity of phenols. Also the position of the (NO_2) substituent (ortho, meta, or para) on the ring influences its stability. NO_2 in the para position is more stable than in the ortho or meta positions. With all this in mind, we can see that (E) is the strongest acid of the compounds given.

93. (B)

$KMnO_4$ is the oxidizing agent that is commonly used to oxidize alcohols to acids. Although oxidation to the aldehyde

$$\left(\begin{array}{c} CH_3 \\ | \\ CH_3CH_2CHCHO \end{array} \right)$$

from the alcohol is possible, $KMnO_4$ is too strong of an oxidizing agent for this to occur.

94. (B)

Aryl halides cannot be used to initiate the process. The other two statements are true.

95. (C)

Nonmetals, not metals, show higher electronegativities. Note that metals more readily donate electrons than nonmetals.

96. (D)

Of all the compounds listed, the only ionic (noncovalent) compound is CsF. Note that Cs is a member of group 1, while F is a member of group 7. These are very good candidates for electrovalent (ionic) bonding. All the other compounds are formed from covalent bonding.

97. (C)

The electronic configuration of an oxygen atom is $1s^2 2s^2 2p^4$. Taking the first shell, $1s^2$, we have N = 1, the superscript indicates that 2 electrons are present. Hence 2 sets of quantum numbers are needed. Because N = 1, and 1 = N − 1, then 1 = 0 for both electrons in this S subshell. Also, because M = +1 to −1, then M = 0 for both electrons also. Now, the quantum numbers for each electron must be different, hence one electron has a spin of $+\frac{1}{2}$ and one has a spin of $-\frac{1}{2}$. The sets of quantum numbers for these two electrons are therefore $1,0,0,+\frac{1}{2}$ and $1,0,0,-\frac{1}{2}$.

By similar reasoning, the sets of quantum numbers for the $2;2s^2$ electrons are $2,0,0,+\frac{1}{2}$ and $2,0,0, -\frac{1}{2}$, not $2,1,1,+\frac{1}{2}$ and $2,1,1,-\frac{1}{2}$. Statement III is correct; the S quantum number does describe the alignment of an electron with a magnetic field.

98. (E)

(E) is the only statement here not true for a carbocation. The carbocation may abstract a hydride ion from an alkane. All the other statements concerning the carbocation are correct.

99. (E)

All the other reactions shown in (A) through (D) require a basic medium to proceed. The reaction shown at (E) is actually an addition reaction, converting acetaldehyde to acetal.

An acidic medium is necessary for this reaction to take place.

(D) represents a crossed Cannizzaro type reaction requiring about 50% NaOH (base). (C) is a reduction requiring NH_2NH_2 base to proceed. Similarly, (A) and (B) require a basic medium to proceed.

(B) shows the conversion of propylene chlorhydrin to propylene oxide; this reaction requires a concentrated basic solution to take place. (A) depicts an esterification process; for this reaction to take place, a base must be present.

100. (E)

Statement II is the only incorrect statement; the product obtained is not a meso product, but a racemic product. If we had started out with trans-2-butene rather than cis-2-butene, we would have obtained meso 2,3-dibromobutane rather than rac-2,3-dibromobutane.

101. (A)

Because francium is a member of the Group 1, it has 1 electron in its outer orbital and would be expected to relinquish (readily) this electron to the electron deficient astatine outer shell. (Astatine is a member of the halogens and requires 1 electron to complete its outer shell.) Thus we would expect the compound FrAt to be formed by electrovalent bonding.

102. (C)

The hydroxides of the group 1 elements (Na, k, etc.) are referred to as alkalis or strong bases.

103. (C)

Na_2CO_3, when dissolved in water, forms the compound $NaHCO_3$ and sodium hydroxide. Both compounds are alkaline. For example,

$$\text{e.g.} \quad Na_2CO_3 + H_2O \rightleftharpoons NaHCO_3 + NaOH$$

(C) is therefore the correct choice here.

104. (C)

To calculate the specific heat of water (standard conditions), we use the following relationship

$$C_p^o = C_v^o + R = 26.0 + 8.3$$

$$= 34.3 \text{ J mol}^{-1} \text{ K}^{-1}$$

105. (A)

$$\text{k.e.} = \frac{1}{2}mv^2, \text{ but } v^2 = 3\frac{kT}{m}$$

$$\therefore \frac{\text{k.e.}_{300}}{\text{k.e.}_{200}} = \frac{\frac{1}{2}m(3\,kT/m)_{300}}{\frac{1}{2}m(3\,kT/m)_{200}} = \frac{573}{473}$$

106. (C)

Note that for this reaction, the activation energy ("hump") for the first part B → C is much smaller than that of C → D. This implies that the rate in the first case is faster than in the second due to the former's smaller activation energy. Hence we would expect k_1 to be greater than k_2.

107. (E)

All three statements concerning the N.M.R. spectrum are accurate.

108. (B)

Statements I and II are correct. Note that even at temperatures of absolute zero, we have the atoms vibrating. If the atoms were at rest, then we could in a definite manner determine their position and momenum. This would most certainly violate the Heisenberg uncertainty principle.

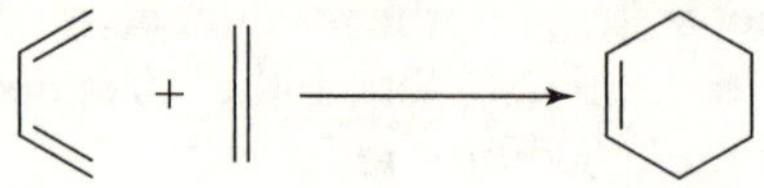

Diene   Dienophile   Adduct

109. (C)

This reaction is an example of cycloaddition—a reaction in which two unsaturated molecules combine, forming a cyclic compound. In the case of the Diels-Alder reaction a [4 + 2] cycloaddition takes place because systems of 4π and 2π electrons are involved. This type of addition yields the structure shown above as an adduct.

110. (E)

All the choices except (E) are true. Hence (E) is the correct choice. Ammonia, along with primary and secondary amines are especially powerful catalysts for the Michael addition. Not only do they abstract a proton from the reagent, generating a carbanion, but they also react with the carbonyl group to form an intermediate that is particularly reactive toward nucleophilic addition.

111. (C)

For the first part of the reaction

$$P + Q \underset{k_2}{\overset{k_1}{\rightleftharpoons}} R$$

we have

Forward   Reverse

$$\frac{dC_R}{dt} = k_1[P][Q] - k_2[R]$$

For the second part of the reaction

$$R + S \xrightarrow{k_3} T$$

$$\frac{dC_R}{dt} = k_2[R][S]$$

Combining the two parts, we have

$$\frac{dC_R}{dt} = k_1[P][Q] - k_2[R] - k_3[R][S]$$

112. (D)

Note that

$$H = E + PV$$

$$\Rightarrow \quad \Delta H = \Delta E + \Delta(PV), \text{ but } P = \text{const.}$$

hence

$$\Delta H = \Delta E + P(\Delta V)$$

$$\therefore \quad P = \frac{\Delta H - \Delta E}{\Delta V}$$

113. (A)

Studies reveal these patterns for a black-body. Classical physics could not account for these patterns. Planck used a quantum hypothesis to explain the black-body radiation.

114. (E)

The structure

is a typical pheromone structure. It is stereospecific, not only toward enantiomers but also toward geometric isomers. Hence it exhibits, not only enantiospecificity but diastereospecificity. Although this compound belongs to the pheromones, it is more specifically a sex attractant of silk moth (10,12-hexadecadien-1-ol). Hence (E) is the correct choice.

115. (D)

The compound is a dicarboxylic acid and, when heated, it yields an anhydride.

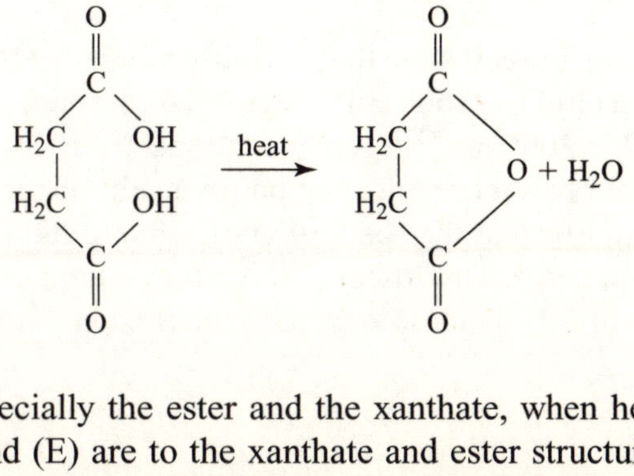

All the other compounds, especially the ester and the xanthate, when heated yield alkenes. Note how similar the structure of (C) and (E) are to the xanthate and ester structure (respectively). This in itself should give us a hint that these compounds would react similarly under similar conditions.

116. (C)

For the mechanism shown, step (1) represents initiation, while steps (2), (3), (4), and (5) represent propagation and termination, respectively. Step (2) is the most difficult step to occur. This step thus limits the overall reaction rate, and we would expect this step to be the rate determining step. Addition of oxygen to the reaction would inhibit, rather than increase, the reaction rate. Oxygen would compete with chlorine, reacting with the methyl radical; step (3). This would slow down the overall reaction because the rate of the propagation step is decreased.

117. (D)

The Paschen lines correspond to $n_1 = 3$, $n_2 = 4, 5, 6, \ldots$

118. (C)

de Broglie's relationship states that the velocity

$$= \frac{h}{\lambda m} = \frac{6.6262 \times 10}{0.06135 \times 10^{-10}(0.300)}$$

119. (B)

$$Q(\text{heat absorbed}) = m \cdot c \cdot \Delta T$$

where $m = \text{mass}$, $\Delta T = T_{final} - T_{initial}$

hence: $Q = 100(4.2)(5 - 25) = -8,400J$

Note that it's not even necessary to convert °C to °K. The difference between temperatures is any scale would be the same.

120. (E)

All the other factors except (E) (thermal) affect the energy content of the system of N molecules.

121. (A)

The Nernst equation is the equation shown in (A).

122. (E)

Only statements I and III are correct. Note that it is absorption due to C—H bonding that occurs at the lower end of the IR spectrum ($1400 - 1600 \, cm^{-1}$ region). Absorption due to C—H stretching occurs at a higher frequency end ($2800 - 3000 \, cm^{-1}$ region) of the spectrum. Statements I and III are correct. It is true that the infrared spectrum gives more information (by itself) about the compound's structure than many other techniques. It is also true that the absorption of infrared light causes the molecules within a compound to change vibration patterns. This effect of the infrared light on the molecules of a compound contributes to the effectiveness of I.R. spectroscopy, particularly compound identification.

123. (E)

This type of reaction is referred to as Markovnikov's addition, and the reaction is in fact an electrophillic addition. The mechanism is as follows:

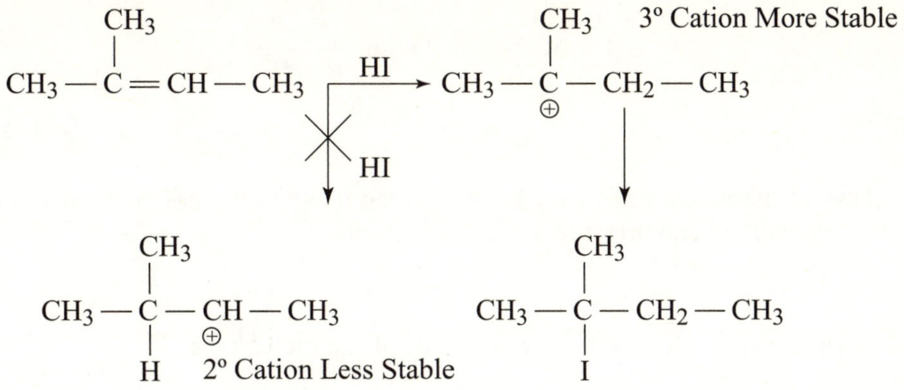

$$
CH_3-\underset{\underset{}{\overset{\overset{CH_3}{|}}{C}}}{}=CH-CH_3 \quad \xrightarrow{\;HI\;} \quad CH_3-\underset{\underset{\oplus}{}}{\overset{\overset{CH_3}{|}}{C}}-CH_2-CH_3 \quad \text{3° Cation More Stable}
$$

(with HI pathway crossed out going down to)

$$
CH_3-\underset{\underset{H}{\overset{}{|}}}{\overset{\overset{CH_3}{|}}{C}}-\underset{\oplus}{CH}-CH_3 \qquad \text{2° Cation Less Stable}
$$

$$
CH_3-\underset{\underset{I}{\overset{}{|}}}{\overset{\overset{CH_3}{|}}{C}}-CH_2-CH_3
$$

124. (C)

Only III is correct here. Hence (C) is the correct choice. As written, the E° for the reaction is $-0.80 + (-0.76) = -1.56V$. The negative sign implies nonspontaneity, the reverse of the reactions shown would, however, be spontaneous.

125. (C)

Note that when the concentration of Y is held constant at 2.0M and the concentration of X is tripled, the rate is tripled. Also, note that when [X] is held constant at 2.0M and [Y] is tripled, the rate is unchanged. Hence the rate is directly related to the concentration of [X] but independent of the concentration of [Y].

126. (A)

The change in Gibbs's free energy is related to ΔH and ΔS by the equation $\Delta G = \Delta H - T\Delta S$. At equilibrium, however, $\Delta G = 0$, and $T = T_{equib}$. Hence $\Delta H = T_{eq}\Delta S$, $T_{equib} = \dfrac{\Delta H}{\Delta S}$.

127. (C)

The Joule-Thompson experiment is carried out for real gases undergoing a throttled adiabatic expansion.

128. (B)

The reactions should proceed as shown below:

(1) $^{241}_{94}Pu \rightarrow ^{241}_{95}X + ^{0}_{-1}e$

(2) $^{241}_{95}X \rightarrow ^{237}_{93}Np + ^{4}_{2}He$

Note: X is actually the element Americium (Am).

129. (C)

The formula for ΔG is $\Delta G = \Delta G° + 2.3\ RT \log Q$, but Q for $N_2(g) + 3H_2(g) \rightarrow 2NH_3(g)$ is $P^2_{NH_3}/(P_{N_2}P^3_{H_2})$. Hence

$$\Delta G = \Delta G° + 2.3\ RT\ \log\ \frac{P^2_{NH_3}}{P_{N_2}P^2_{H_2}}$$

130. (A)

From the laws of thermodynamics, we know that the maximum work is equal to the free energy change, when the temperature and pressure are kept constant.

131. (D)

Graduated cylinders provide crude determinations of sample volumes.

132. (C)

Statements I and III are correct; however, statement II is incorrect. The $—CH_2—$ indeed gives the 1:1 doublet, but the $—CH—$ yields a 1:2:1 triplet, not 1:1:1.

133. (E)

β in this equation represents the compressibility factor of the system.

134. (E)

Note that only I and II are correct statements. At T_1 $\Delta G°$ is on the positive side of the ordinate. Note also that the slope $\left(\dfrac{\delta \Delta G°}{\delta T}\right)_p$ at the minima (T_3), is zero.

135. (C)

All the statements are true—according to the molecular orbital theory, except (C). Molecular orbitals with rotational symmetry about the bond axis are called signal (σ) orbitals.

136. (B)

The only correct choice here is II. Although the two halves of the cell are connected by the salt bridge, which permits a current to flow, the salt bridge does not allow mixing of the two solutions. Note also that only the oxidation of zinc, to zinc ions (Zn^{2+}), occurs at the zinc electrode.

Practice Exam 4

Answer Sheet: Practice Exam 4

1. Ⓐ Ⓑ ⓒ Ⓓ Ⓔ
2. Ⓐ Ⓑ ⓒ Ⓓ Ⓔ
3. Ⓐ Ⓑ ⓒ Ⓓ Ⓔ
4. Ⓐ Ⓑ ⓒ Ⓓ Ⓔ
5. Ⓐ Ⓑ ⓒ Ⓓ Ⓔ
6. Ⓐ Ⓑ ⓒ Ⓓ Ⓔ
7. Ⓐ Ⓑ ⓒ Ⓓ Ⓔ
8. Ⓐ Ⓑ ⓒ Ⓓ Ⓔ
9. Ⓐ Ⓑ ⓒ Ⓓ Ⓔ
10. Ⓐ Ⓑ ⓒ Ⓓ Ⓔ
11. Ⓐ Ⓑ ⓒ Ⓓ Ⓔ
12. Ⓐ Ⓑ ⓒ Ⓓ Ⓔ
13. Ⓐ Ⓑ ⓒ Ⓓ Ⓔ
14. Ⓐ Ⓑ ⓒ Ⓓ Ⓔ
15. Ⓐ Ⓑ ⓒ Ⓓ Ⓔ
16. Ⓐ Ⓑ ⓒ Ⓓ Ⓔ
17. Ⓐ Ⓑ ⓒ Ⓓ Ⓔ
18. Ⓐ Ⓑ ⓒ Ⓓ Ⓔ
19. Ⓐ Ⓑ ⓒ Ⓓ Ⓔ
20. Ⓐ Ⓑ ⓒ Ⓓ Ⓔ
21. Ⓐ Ⓑ ⓒ Ⓓ Ⓔ
22. Ⓐ Ⓑ ⓒ Ⓓ Ⓔ
23. Ⓐ Ⓑ ⓒ Ⓓ Ⓔ
24. Ⓐ Ⓑ ⓒ Ⓓ Ⓔ
25. Ⓐ Ⓑ ⓒ Ⓓ Ⓔ
26. Ⓐ Ⓑ ⓒ Ⓓ Ⓔ
27. Ⓐ Ⓑ ⓒ Ⓓ Ⓔ
28. Ⓐ Ⓑ ⓒ Ⓓ Ⓔ
29. Ⓐ Ⓑ ⓒ Ⓓ Ⓔ
30. Ⓐ Ⓑ ⓒ Ⓓ Ⓔ
31. Ⓐ Ⓑ ⓒ Ⓓ Ⓔ
32. Ⓐ Ⓑ ⓒ Ⓓ Ⓔ
33. Ⓐ Ⓑ ⓒ Ⓓ Ⓔ

34. Ⓐ Ⓑ ⓒ Ⓓ Ⓔ
35. Ⓐ Ⓑ ⓒ Ⓓ Ⓔ
36. Ⓐ Ⓑ ⓒ Ⓓ Ⓔ
37. Ⓐ Ⓑ ⓒ Ⓓ Ⓔ
38. Ⓐ Ⓑ ⓒ Ⓓ Ⓔ
39. Ⓐ Ⓑ ⓒ Ⓓ Ⓔ
40. Ⓐ Ⓑ ⓒ Ⓓ Ⓔ
41. Ⓐ Ⓑ ⓒ Ⓓ Ⓔ
42. Ⓐ Ⓑ ⓒ Ⓓ Ⓔ
43. Ⓐ Ⓑ ⓒ Ⓓ Ⓔ
44. Ⓐ Ⓑ ⓒ Ⓓ Ⓔ
45. Ⓐ Ⓑ ⓒ Ⓓ Ⓔ
46. Ⓐ Ⓑ ⓒ Ⓓ Ⓔ
47. Ⓐ Ⓑ ⓒ Ⓓ Ⓔ
48. Ⓐ Ⓑ ⓒ Ⓓ Ⓔ
49. Ⓐ Ⓑ ⓒ Ⓓ Ⓔ
50. Ⓐ Ⓑ ⓒ Ⓓ Ⓔ
51. Ⓐ Ⓑ ⓒ Ⓓ Ⓔ
52. Ⓐ Ⓑ ⓒ Ⓓ Ⓔ
53. Ⓐ Ⓑ ⓒ Ⓓ Ⓔ
54. Ⓐ Ⓑ ⓒ Ⓓ Ⓔ
55. Ⓐ Ⓑ ⓒ Ⓓ Ⓔ
56. Ⓐ Ⓑ ⓒ Ⓓ Ⓔ
57. Ⓐ Ⓑ ⓒ Ⓓ Ⓔ
58. Ⓐ Ⓑ ⓒ Ⓓ Ⓔ
59. Ⓐ Ⓑ ⓒ Ⓓ Ⓔ
60. Ⓐ Ⓑ ⓒ Ⓓ Ⓔ
61. Ⓐ Ⓑ ⓒ Ⓓ Ⓔ
62. Ⓐ Ⓑ ⓒ Ⓓ Ⓔ
63. Ⓐ Ⓑ ⓒ Ⓓ Ⓔ
64. Ⓐ Ⓑ ⓒ Ⓓ Ⓔ
65. Ⓐ Ⓑ ⓒ Ⓓ Ⓔ
66. Ⓐ Ⓑ ⓒ Ⓓ Ⓔ

67. Ⓐ Ⓑ ⓒ Ⓓ Ⓔ
68. Ⓐ Ⓑ ⓒ Ⓓ Ⓔ
69. Ⓐ Ⓑ ⓒ Ⓓ Ⓔ
70. Ⓐ Ⓑ ⓒ Ⓓ Ⓔ
71. Ⓐ Ⓑ ⓒ Ⓓ Ⓔ
72. Ⓐ Ⓑ ⓒ Ⓓ Ⓔ
73. Ⓐ Ⓑ ⓒ Ⓓ Ⓔ
74. Ⓐ Ⓑ ⓒ Ⓓ Ⓔ
75. Ⓐ Ⓑ ⓒ Ⓓ Ⓔ
76. Ⓐ Ⓑ ⓒ Ⓓ Ⓔ
77. Ⓐ Ⓑ ⓒ Ⓓ Ⓔ
78. Ⓐ Ⓑ ⓒ Ⓓ Ⓔ
79. Ⓐ Ⓑ ⓒ Ⓓ Ⓔ
80. Ⓐ Ⓑ ⓒ Ⓓ Ⓔ
81. Ⓐ Ⓑ ⓒ Ⓓ Ⓔ
82. Ⓐ Ⓑ ⓒ Ⓓ Ⓔ
83. Ⓐ Ⓑ ⓒ Ⓓ Ⓔ
84. Ⓐ Ⓑ ⓒ Ⓓ Ⓔ
85. Ⓐ Ⓑ ⓒ Ⓓ Ⓔ
86. Ⓐ Ⓑ ⓒ Ⓓ Ⓔ
87. Ⓐ Ⓑ ⓒ Ⓓ Ⓔ
88. Ⓐ Ⓑ ⓒ Ⓓ Ⓔ
89. Ⓐ Ⓑ ⓒ Ⓓ Ⓔ
90. Ⓐ Ⓑ ⓒ Ⓓ Ⓔ
91. Ⓐ Ⓑ ⓒ Ⓓ Ⓔ
92. Ⓐ Ⓑ ⓒ Ⓓ Ⓔ
93. Ⓐ Ⓑ ⓒ Ⓓ Ⓔ
94. Ⓐ Ⓑ ⓒ Ⓓ Ⓔ
95. Ⓐ Ⓑ ⓒ Ⓓ Ⓔ
96. Ⓐ Ⓑ ⓒ Ⓓ Ⓔ
97. Ⓐ Ⓑ ⓒ Ⓓ Ⓔ
98. Ⓐ Ⓑ ⓒ Ⓓ Ⓔ
99. Ⓐ Ⓑ ⓒ Ⓓ Ⓔ

Continued

100. Ⓐ Ⓑ Ⓒ Ⓓ Ⓔ
101. Ⓐ Ⓑ Ⓒ Ⓓ Ⓔ
102. Ⓐ Ⓑ Ⓒ Ⓓ Ⓔ
103. Ⓐ Ⓑ Ⓒ Ⓓ Ⓔ
104. Ⓐ Ⓑ Ⓒ Ⓓ Ⓔ
105. Ⓐ Ⓑ Ⓒ Ⓓ Ⓔ
106. Ⓐ Ⓑ Ⓒ Ⓓ Ⓔ
107. Ⓐ Ⓑ Ⓒ Ⓓ Ⓔ
108. Ⓐ Ⓑ Ⓒ Ⓓ Ⓔ
109. Ⓐ Ⓑ Ⓒ Ⓓ Ⓔ
110. Ⓐ Ⓑ Ⓒ Ⓓ Ⓔ
111. Ⓐ Ⓑ Ⓒ Ⓓ Ⓔ
112. Ⓐ Ⓑ Ⓒ Ⓓ Ⓔ

113. Ⓐ Ⓑ Ⓒ Ⓓ Ⓔ
114. Ⓐ Ⓑ Ⓒ Ⓓ Ⓔ
115. Ⓐ Ⓑ Ⓒ Ⓓ Ⓔ
116. Ⓐ Ⓑ Ⓒ Ⓓ Ⓔ
117. Ⓐ Ⓑ Ⓒ Ⓓ Ⓔ
118. Ⓐ Ⓑ Ⓒ Ⓓ Ⓔ
119. Ⓐ Ⓑ Ⓒ Ⓓ Ⓔ
120. Ⓐ Ⓑ Ⓒ Ⓓ Ⓔ
121. Ⓐ Ⓑ Ⓒ Ⓓ Ⓔ
122. Ⓐ Ⓑ Ⓒ Ⓓ Ⓔ
123. Ⓐ Ⓑ Ⓒ Ⓓ Ⓔ
124. Ⓐ Ⓑ Ⓒ Ⓓ Ⓔ
125. Ⓐ Ⓑ Ⓒ Ⓓ Ⓔ

126. Ⓐ Ⓑ Ⓒ Ⓓ Ⓔ
127. Ⓐ Ⓑ Ⓒ Ⓓ Ⓔ
128. Ⓐ Ⓑ Ⓒ Ⓓ Ⓔ
129. Ⓐ Ⓑ Ⓒ Ⓓ Ⓔ
130. Ⓐ Ⓑ Ⓒ Ⓓ Ⓔ
131. Ⓐ Ⓑ Ⓒ Ⓓ Ⓔ
132. Ⓐ Ⓑ Ⓒ Ⓓ Ⓔ
133. Ⓐ Ⓑ Ⓒ Ⓓ Ⓔ
134. Ⓐ Ⓑ Ⓒ Ⓓ Ⓔ
135. Ⓐ Ⓑ Ⓒ Ⓓ Ⓔ
136. Ⓐ Ⓑ Ⓒ Ⓓ Ⓔ

Practice Exam 4

Time: 170 Minutes
136 Questions

Directions: ***Choose the best answer for each question and mark the letter of your selection on the corresponding answer sheet.***

1. Which of the following compounds contains no covalent bonds?

$$KCl, PH_3, O_2, B_2H_6, H_2SO_4$$

(A) KCl, B_2H_6, PH_3
(B) KCl, H_2SO_4
(C) O_2, PH_3, B_2H_6
(D) KCl
(E) KCl, B_2H_6

2. A neutral element Y has the electronic configuration $1s^22s^22p^63s^1$. It will gain or lose electrons to form an ion of valence

(A) -2
(B) -1
(C) $+1$
(D) $+2$
(E) $+3$

3. Which of the following is a Lewis acid?

(A) CCl_4
(B) BF_3
(C) I_2
(D) Na^+H^-
(E) $(CH_3)_3N$

4. An ionic bond is formed between two ions. Which of the following has *no* effect on the strength of the bond?

I. Doubling the charge on both ions
II. Doubling the temperature
III. Doubling the radii of both ions

(A) I only
(B) II only
(C) I and II
(C) I, II, and III
(E) None of the choices has any effect

5. Based on the following half-cell reactions, which of the following statements are correct?

$$Mg^{2+} + 2e^- \rightarrow Mg \qquad E° = -2.38V \qquad\qquad (1)$$

$$Cu^{2+} + 2e^- \rightarrow Cu \qquad E° = 0.34V \qquad\qquad (2)$$

$$Ag^+ + e^- \rightarrow Ag \qquad E° = 0.80V \qquad\qquad (3)$$

I.   Magnesium is a better reducing agent.

II. Under standard conditions, a reaction will occur spontaneously when half-cell (2) is coupled with a hydrogen half-cell.

III. When copper metal is added to a section of $AgNO_3$, silver metal will precipitate.

IV. If $2Ag^+ + 2e^- \rightarrow 2Ag$, then $E = 2(0.80) = 1.60V$

(A) I, II, and III
(B) I and II
(C) II and III

(D) I, III, and IV
(E) I, II, and IV

6.

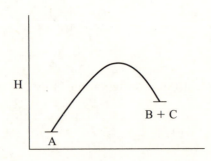

The reaction profile above for the reaction $A \rightarrow B + C$ indicates that

(A) a catalyst would not be useful.
(B) the reaction liberates a large quantity of heat.
(C) the reaction is reversible.
(D) the reaction is endothermic at constant pressure.
(E) the reaction occurs spontaneously.

7. Which of the following regions of the spectrum would be used to determine the structure of crystalline solids?

(A) Microwave
(B) Infrared
(C) Visible

(D) Ultraviolet
(E) X-ray

8.

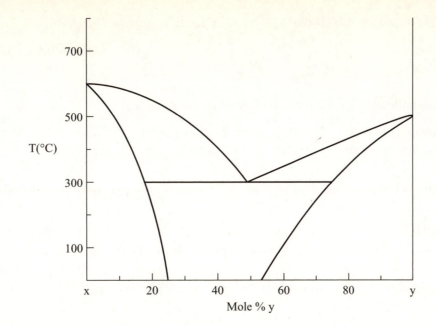

The figure above is a phase diagram for two substances, X and Y, that are partially miscible in the solid state. The phases coexisting in equilibrium at 200°C, if a mixture 80-mole percent in Y is cooled from 600°C to 200°C, are

(A) an unsaturated solution of solid Y in X.
(B) an unsaturated solution of solid X in Y.
(C) a saturated solid solution of Y in X and a saturated solid solution of X in Y.
(D) a liquid and a saturated solid solution of Y in X.
(E) a liquid and a saturated solid solution of X in Y.

9. Which of the following most closely represents an ideal gas?

(A) H_2 (C) O_2 (E) Ne
(B) He   (D) CO_2

10. Which of the following elements has the highest ionization potential?

(A) H   (C) Na   (E) Cl
(B) Li   (D) F

11. Metallic potassium could not be prepared from a potassium iodide solution by means of a chemical reducing agent because

(A) metallic potassium is unstable.   (D) potassium ion is a strong oxidizing agent.
(B) potassium ion is strongly hydrated.   (E) potassium is a strong reducing agent.
(C) potassium is a strong oxidant.

12. All of the following are products of the electrolysis of an aqueous potassium iodide solution or the reaction of the products with water *except* (assume that H_2O is not reduced)

(A) H_2 (C) K   (E) KOI
(B) I_2 (D) KOH

13. Which of the following salts is the most basic in aqueous solution?

    (A) $Al(CN)_3$ (C) $FeCl_3$ (E) $Pb(C_2H_3O_2)_2$
    (B) $KC_2H_3O_2$ (D) KCl

14. Which of the following should have the largest dipole moment?

    (A) carbon tetrachloride   (C) trans-dichloroethylene   (E) trans-stilbene
    (B) cis-dichloroethylene   (D) cis-stilbene

15. Which of the following has a bond formed by the overlap of an sp^2 hybrid orbital with an sp hybrid orbital?

    (A) CH_3CH_3 (C) $CH_2=CHCH_3$ (C) $CH_3C\equiv CCH_2CH_3$
    (B) $CH_2=CH_2$ (D) $CH_2=C=CH_2$

16. Which of the following pairs of isomers are most nearly of equal stability?

    (A)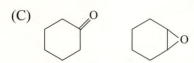

    (D)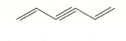

    (B)

    (E)

    (C)

17. The gas phase decomposition of A was experimentally determined to be first order. If the initial pressure of A is 2000 torr, what time is required for the pressure to decrease to 250 torr if it decreases to 500 torr after 7.8 minutes?

    (A) 3.9 minutes   (C) 15.6 minutes   (E) 31.2 minutes
    (B) 11.7 minutes   (D) 27.3 minutes

18. Which of the following reactions would be expected to involve the largest increase in entropy?

    (A) $H_2O_{(l)} \rightarrow H_2O(g)$ (C) $H_{2(l)} \rightarrow H_{2(g)}$ (E) $He_{(l)} \quad He_{(g)}$
    (B) $H_2O(s) \rightarrow H_2O(\ell)$ (D) $H_{2(s)} \rightarrow H_{2(l)}$

19. Which of the following is *not* evoked in quantum theory?

    (A) Boltzmann distribution   (D) The particle in a box
    (B) Schrödinger equation   (E) The rigid rotor approximation
    (C) The simple harmonic oscillator

20. The heat capacity of a substance at constant volume is directly related to the

    (A) enthalpy, H.   (D) internal energy, U or E.
    (B) entropy, S.   (E) Helmholz free energy, A.
    (C) free energy, G.

21. Which of the following compounds exhibits two sharp peaks in its proton NMR spectrum that are separated by approximately 10 ppm?

    (A) $CH_3CH_2CH_3$ (C) CH_3CHO (E) CH_3COOH
    (B) CH_2O (D) CH_3OH

22. What is the principal product of the following reaction?

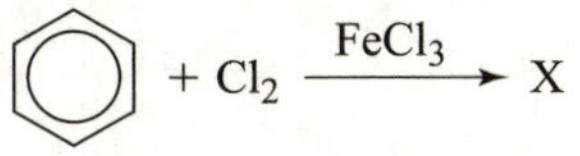

    (A)

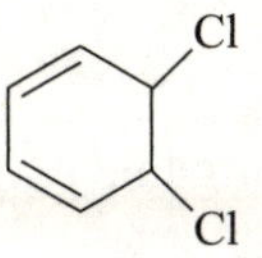

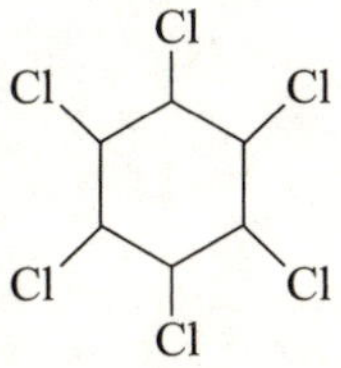

    (C)

    (E) chlorobenzene

    (B)

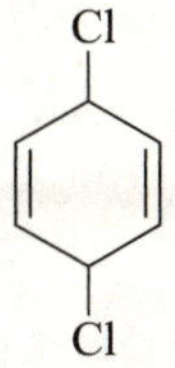

    (D) 1,2,3-trichlorobenzene

23. What is the product if the following compound undergoes acid-catalyzed halogenation? (X_2 is a diatomic halogen.)

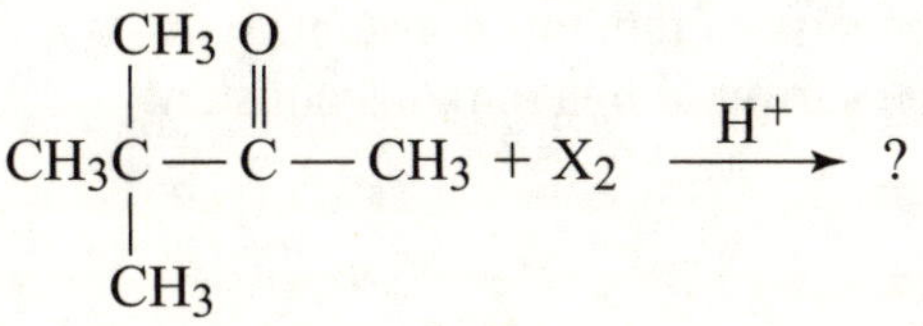

    (A)

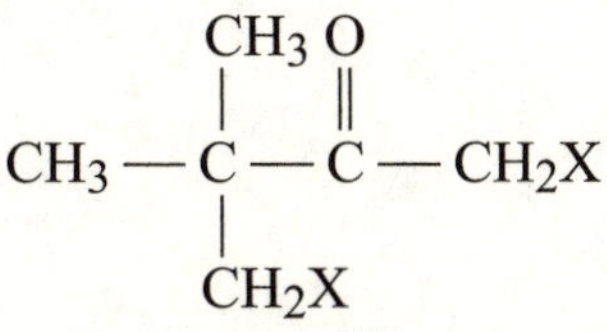

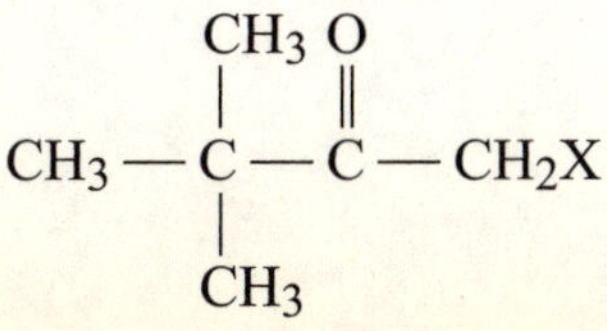

    (D)

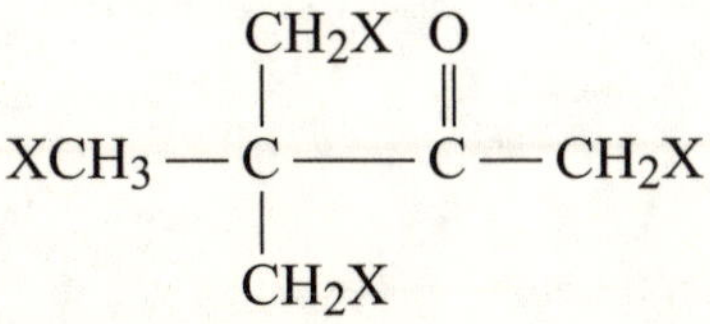

    (B)

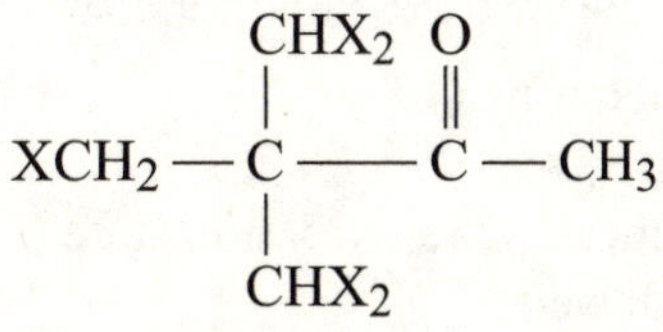

    (E) None of the above

    (C)

24. Which of the following statement(s) is (are) correct for the Diels-Alder reaction shown below?

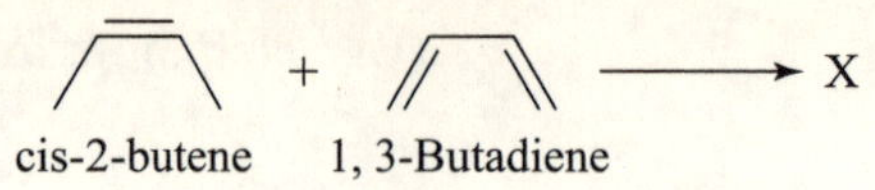

cis-2-butene   1, 3-Butadiene

    I.   cis-2-Butene acts as a dienophile.

   II. This reaction is used to form a six-membered ring.

  III. Compound X is a cyclic alkene.

  IV. Compound X is a 1,2 dimethylcyclohexane.

(A) I and II
(B) III and IV
(C) I, II, and III

(D) I, II, and IV
(E) All of the above

25. 2,2'-Dinitrobiphenyl is to be synthesized from 0-iodonitrobenzene. Which inorganic reagent should be used?

(A) $AlCl_3$
(B) Cu
(C) $KMnO_4$

(D) CH_3Li
(E) I_2

26. Which of the following is *true* of an isothermal reversible gas expansion?

(A) No heat is exchanged between the system and the surroundings.
(B) Heat is given off to the surroundings.
(C) The temperature of the system remains constant.
(D) The temperature of the surroundings remains constant.
(E) Both C and D.

27. During a redox reaction, an oxidizing agent

(A) gains electrons.
(B) is oxidized.
(C) has an increase in oxidation state.
(D) is hydrolyzed.
(E) loses electrons.

28. The simple harmonic oscillator is used as a basis for determining molecular vibrational spectra. Of the following plots, choose the one that best depicts the simple harmonic oscillator plot of potential energy versus internuclear distance.

(A)

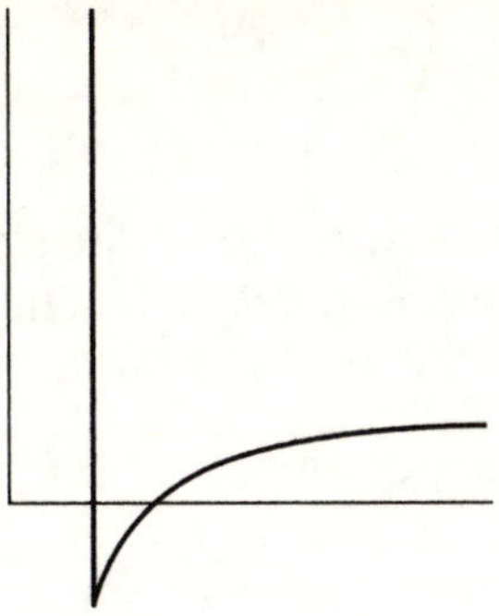

(D)

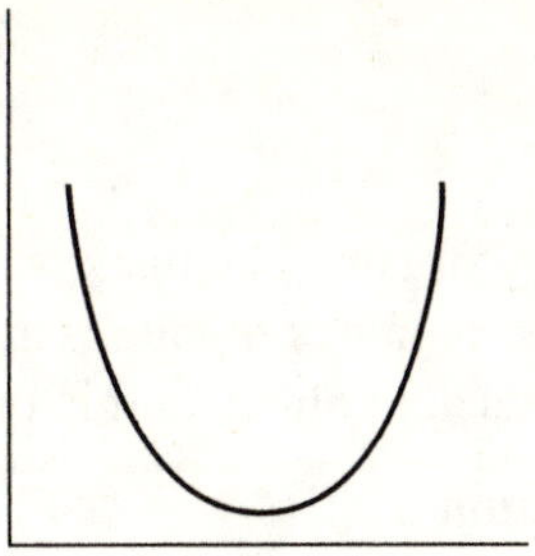

(B)

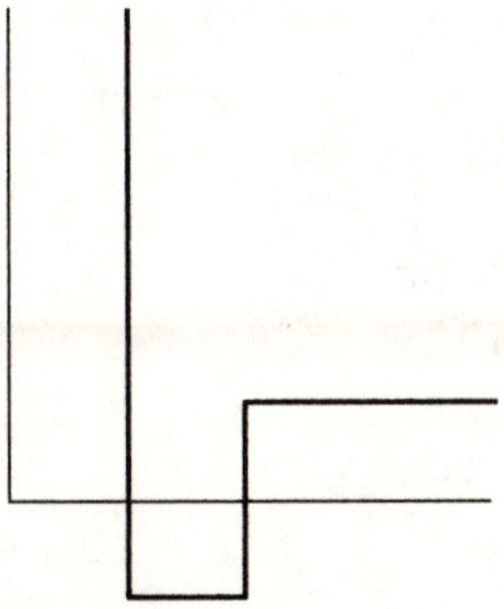

(E)

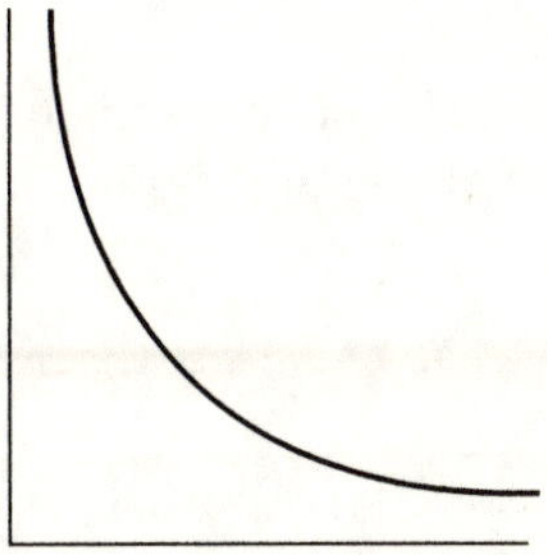

(C)

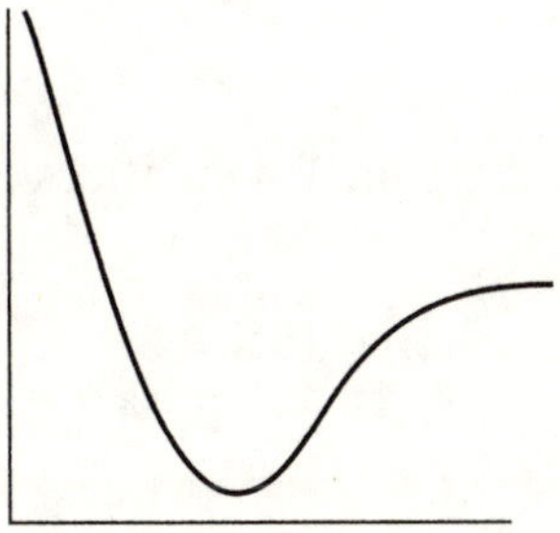

29. $$C_2H_5OH + Br^- \rightleftarrows C_2H_5Br + OH^-$$

This equilibrium will proceed to the right with the addition of:

(A) heat.

(B) H_2SO_4.

(C)

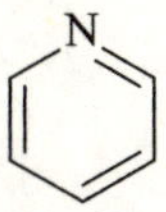

(D) Pt.

(E) light.

30. The equilibrium constant for the protolysis of ammonium ion

$$NH_4^+ + H_2O \rightleftarrows NH_3 + H_3O^+$$

is 5.6×10^{-10} at 25°C. The pH of a 1.0M NH_4Cl solution is closest to which of the following?

(A) 9
(B) 7
(C) 5
(D) 3
(E) 1

31. A buffer solution containing H_2CO_3 and $NaHCO_3$ is to be produced to maintain a pH of 7. What must the ratio $[NaHCO_3]/[H_2CO_3]$ be in order to realize such a pH if the K_a of carbonic acid is 4.3×10^{-7}?

(A) 43   (C) .43   (E) 1.29
(B) 4.3   (D) 86

32. A problem faced by organic chemists is reacting organic compounds with species present in aqueous media because organic compounds are generally immiscible with water. Which of the following methods could be used to alleviate this problem?

(A) Phase separation   (D) Catalytic hydrogenation
(B) Phase-transfer catalysis   (E) Hydrolysis
(C) Ion exchange

33. A sample containing aluminum weighing 10.0 grams yielded 2.0 grams of aluminum sulfide. What is the percentage of aluminum (atomic weight 26.98) in the sample?

(A) $\dfrac{2.0}{10.0} \times 100$

(B) $\dfrac{2.0}{10.0} \times \dfrac{26.98}{150.14} \times 100$

(C) $\dfrac{2.0}{10.0} \times \dfrac{150.14}{3 \times 26.98} \times 100$

(D) $\dfrac{2.0}{10.0} \times \dfrac{2 \times 26.98}{150.14} \times 100$

(E) None of the above

34. What is the normality of a sulfuric acid solution if 50 milliliters completely neutralizes 1.00 liter of a 0.1M potassium hydroxide solution?

(A) 1.0N   (C) 2.0N   (E) 10N
(B) 0.1N   (D) 0.2N

35. A mixture of furfural, (furan ring)–CHO and propanal in dilute sodium hydroxide solution reacts to produce

(A) furan ring with CHO and CH(CH₃)CHO substituents

(B) furan ring with CHO, and CH(OH)(C₂H₅) substituent

(C) furan ring with CH(OH)—CH₂CH₂CH₃ substituent

(D) furan ring with CH(OH)—CH₂—CH₂—CHO substituent

(E) furan ring with CH=C(CH₃)—CHO substituent

36. Which of the following gives three monochlorinated benzene derivatives, assuming that the reaction occurs at any unsubstituted position?

(A)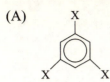

(C)

(E)

(B)  X

O

X

(D) 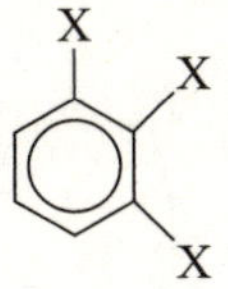 X

X

X

37. Which of the following reactions involves a carbene reaction intermediate?

(A)

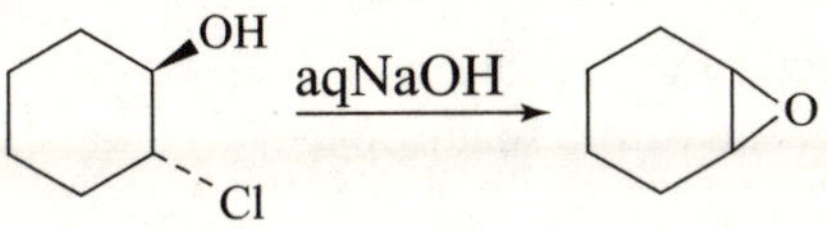

(B) $(CH_3)_3CBr$ $\xrightarrow{EtOH}$ $(CH_3)_3COC_2H_5$

(C) $CH_4 + 4Cl_2$ $\xrightarrow{hv}$ $CCl_4 + 4HCl$

(D)

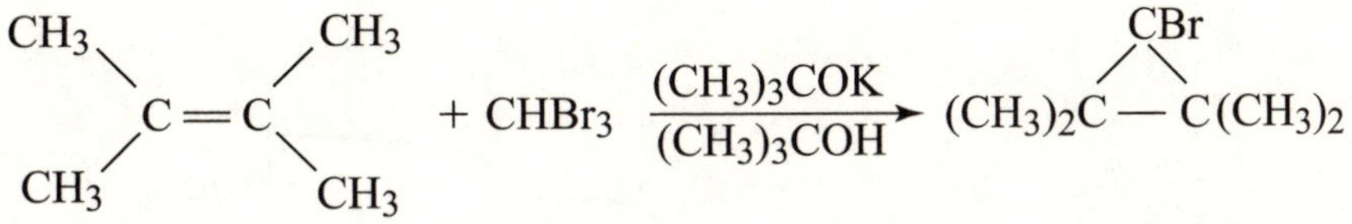

$\begin{array}{c} CH_3 \\ \\ CH_3 \end{array} C = C \begin{array}{c} CH_3 \\ \\ CH_3 \end{array}$ $+ CHBr_3$ $\xrightarrow[(CH_3)_3COH]{(CH_3)_3COK}$ $(CH_3)_2C \overset{CBr}{\underset{}{\triangle}} C(CH_3)_2$

(E)

$\xrightarrow{150°}$ +

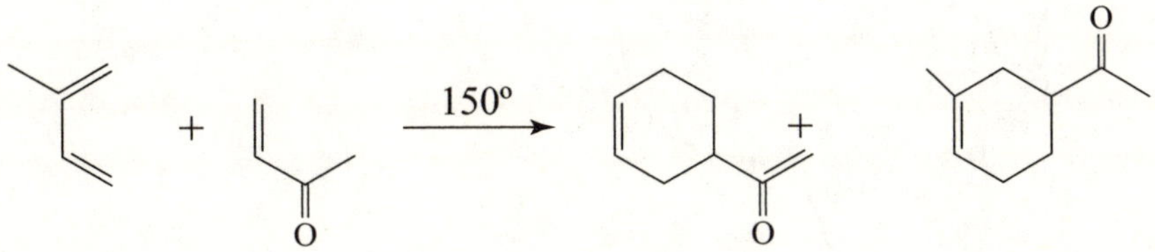

38. Which of the following compounds is most basic?

(A) NH_3

(B) CH_3NH_2

(C) $CH_3CH_2NH_2$

(D) $(CH_3)_3N$

(E) $(CH_3CH_2)_3N$

39. Which of the following reactions will yield t-pentyl bromide?

I.

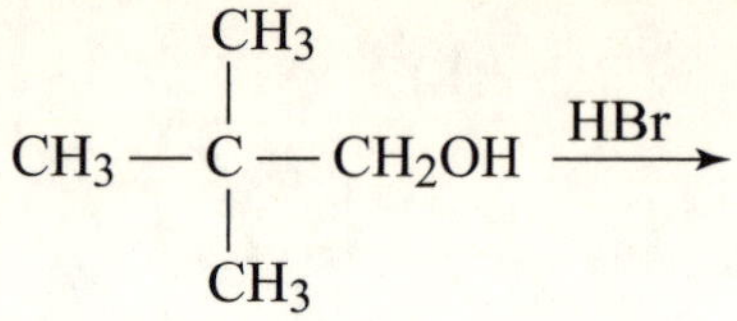

$$CH_3 - \underset{\underset{CH_3}{|}}{\overset{\overset{CH_3}{|}}{C}} - CH_2OH \xrightarrow{HBr}$$

II. $CH_3CHCHOHCH_3 \xrightarrow{HBr}$
   $\quad\quad\underset{|}{\;}$
   $\quad\quad CH_3$

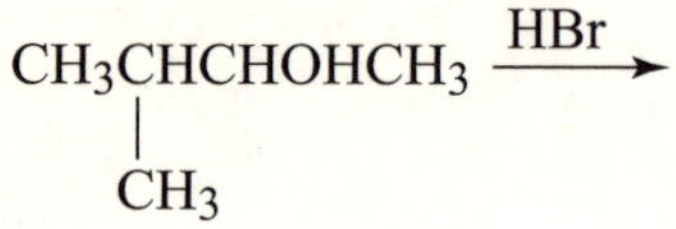

III.

$$CH_3 - \underset{\underset{CH_3}{|}}{\overset{\overset{OH}{|}}{C}} - CH_2CH_3 \xrightarrow{HBr}$$

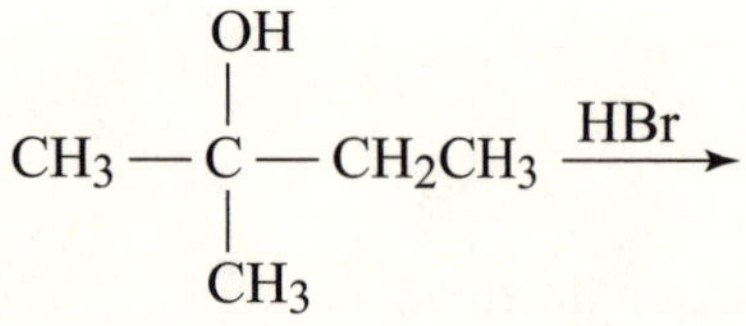

(A) III only
(B) II and III only
(C) I and III only

(D) All of the reactions
(E) None of the reactions

40. An aqueous solution that may have contained HCl, H_2SO_4, and/or H_3PO_4 was titrated with 0.1M NaOH and gave the following titration curve:

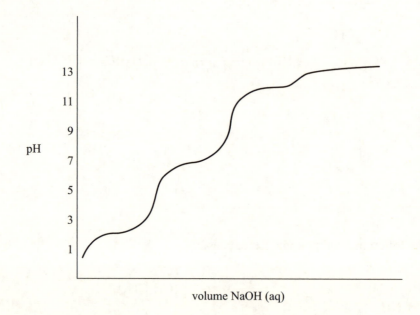

volume NaOH (aq)

The sample probably contained

(A) pure HCl.
(B) pure H_2SO_4.
(C) pure H_3PO_4.

(D) HCl and H_2SO_4.
(E) HCl and H_3PO_4.

41. Which of the following may be deduced from the ultraviolet spectrum of a molecule?

    (A) The presence of conjugated double bonds
    (B) The presence of halides
    (C) The structure of regular crystals
    (D) The vibrational energy states of the molecule
    (E) The rotational energy states of the molecule

42. Consider the two reactions below:

$$H_2O(s) \rightarrow H_2O(l); \qquad \Delta H = 6.0 \text{ kJ} \hspace{3cm} \text{(a)}$$

$$CaCO_3(s) \rightarrow CaO(s) + CO_2(g); \Delta H = 178 \text{ kJ} \hspace{2cm} \text{(b)}$$

    Which of the following statements concerning these reactions is (are) correct?

    (I)   The reactions are spontaneous and exothermic.

    (II) Both reactions occur with an increase in the system's disorder.

    (III) The entropy change ($\Delta S°$) for equation (A) is most likely positive.

    (A) (1) only   (D) None of the statements
    (B) (1) and (2) only   (E) All of the statements
    (C) (2) and (3) only

43.

$$C_2H_5C \equiv CC_2H_5 \rightarrow$$

with product: C_2H_5 and C_2H_5 on carbons, $C=C$, H and H below

    Which of the following conditions can produce the reaction above in good yield?

    (A) $\xrightarrow{\text{H}_2/\text{Pt}}$ (D) $\xrightarrow{\text{KMnO}_4}$

    (B) $\xrightarrow[\text{liq. NH}_3]{\text{Na}} \xrightarrow{\text{NH}_4\text{OH}}$ (E) $\xrightarrow{\text{HCl}}$

    (C) $\xrightarrow[\text{quinoline}]{\text{H}_2/\text{Pd/BaSO}_4}$

44. The area under a plot of heat capacity at constant pressure versus the absolute temperature is directly related to

    (A) ΔW.   (D) ΔA.
    (B) ΔU.   (E) ΔG.
    (C) ΔH.

45. Lithium aluminum hydride may be used to effect all of the following conversions *except*

(A) $CH_3CH_2I \rightarrow CH_3CH_3$

(B) $CH_3C\equiv N \rightarrow CH_3CH_2NH_2$

(C) $CH_3COOCH_3 \rightarrow$
$CH_3CH_2OH + CH_3OH$

(D)
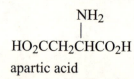

(E) $CH_3CHCHO \longrightarrow CH_3CHCH_2OH$
           | |
           CH_2CH_3 CH_2CH_3

46. Of the following compounds, which has the shortest carbon-halogen bond?

(A) CH_3F (C) CH_3Br (E) CH_3A^+

(B) CH_3Cl (D) CH_3I

47.

$\overset{①\ ②\ ③}{CH_2CH_2CH_3}$
④
⑤

In the structural formula above, which of the numbered hydrogens is most susceptible to substitution by bromine radicals via a free radical mechanism?

(A) ①   (C) ③   (E) ⑤

(B) ②   (D) ④

48. Which of the following statements correctly describes the migratory aptitude of aspartic acid during electrophoresis ($pK_1 = 1.99$, $pK_2 = 3.0$, $pK_3 = 10.00$)?

$$\overset{\displaystyle NH_2}{\underset{\displaystyle |}{HO_2CCH_2CHCO_2H}}$$

apartic acid

(A) At a pH of 1.00, aspartic acid migrates to the positive electrode.

(B) At a pH of 3.00, aspartic acid migrates to the negative electrode.

(C) At a pH of 5.00, aspartic acid does not migrate.

(D) At a pH of 7.00, aspartic acid migrates to the positive electrode.

(E) At a pH of 9.00, aspartic acid migrates to the negative electrode.

49. A solution contains an unknown concentration of Ba^{2+}. When 50ml of a 1M solution of Na_2SO_4 is added, $BaSO_4$ just begins to precipitate. The final volume is 500ml. The solubility product of $BaSO_4$ is 1×10^{-10}. What is the original concentration of Ba^{2+}?

    (A) 5×10^{-9}M
    (B) 2×10^{-9}M
    (C) 9.0×10^{-10}M
    (D) 1.0×10^{-9}M
    (E) 1.1×10^{-9}M

50. A plot of the reciprocal concentration of NO_2 versus time for the decomposition of NO_2 was found to be linear. From this information, it may be concluded that NO_2 decomposition

    (A) is a zeroth-order reaction.
    (B) is a first-order reaction.
    (C) is a second-order reaction.
    (D) is a third-order reaction.
    (E) cannot be evaluated with the given information.

51. The quantum numbers for a given orbital are n = 2, 1 = 1, m = 0. We would usually represent this as

    (A) 1s
    (B) 2_s
    (C) $1p_z$
    (D) $2p_z$
    (E) $1d_{xy}$

52. A 3p orbital has

    (A) two nonspherical nodes.
    (B) two spherical nodes.
    (C) one spherical node and one nonspherical node.
    (D) one spherical node and two nonspherical nodes.
    (E) two spherical nodes and one nonspherical node.

53.

$$\frac{1}{2}N_{2(g)} + \frac{3}{2}H_{2(g)} \leftrightarrows NH_{2(g)}$$

ΔG_f° for $NH_{3(g)}$ is -16.6 kJ/mol. If we assume that this reaction occurs with ideal gases at standard conditions (T = 298°K), what is the equilibrium constant K_{eq}?

    (A) $K_{eq} = \exp(16.6/R \cdot 298)$
    (B) $K_{eq} = \exp(-16.6/R \cdot 298)$
    (C) $K_{eq} = \exp(R \cdot 298/-16.6)$
    (D) $K_{eq} = \ln(-16.6/R \cdot 298)$
    (E) Cannot be determined with given information

54. For any system, the difference between the enthalpy and the internal energy can be expressed as

    (A) $\dfrac{C_p - C_v}{nR}$
    (B) RT
    (C) PV
    (D) C_p
    (E) C_v

55. The solvation energy (H) of an ion can be expressed in terms of the charge on the ion (z), the ionic radius (r), and the dielectric constant of the solvent (ε). Which of the following could be a proper expression for H?

(A) $H = -z^2 \cdot r \cdot \varepsilon^2$

(D) $H = \dfrac{-z^2}{2r}\left(1 - \dfrac{1}{\varepsilon}\right)$

(B) $H = \dfrac{-\varepsilon}{z^2 r}$

(E) $H = \dfrac{-z^2}{2r(\varepsilon + 1)}$

(C) $H = \dfrac{-z^2}{r2}\left(\dfrac{1}{\varepsilon} + 1\right)$

56. An ionic crystal MX has a lattice energy U. The separate ions M^+ and X^- have solvation energies H_1 and H_2. U, H_1, and H_2 are negative, that is, exothermic. MX will be most soluble if

(A) $H_1 + H_2 - U < 0$
(B) $U - H_1 + H_2 < 0$
(C) $H_1 + H_2 = U$

(D) $U + H_1 + H_2 < 0$
(E) $H_1 \cong H_2$

57. Glass is an example of an amorphous solid that can be characterized as

(A) a malleable solid.
(B) crystal-like in structure.
(C) a good conductor.

(D) a molecular solid.
(E) a very viscous fluid.

58. A p-type germanium semiconductor is doped with

(A) selenium
(B) gallium.

(C) arsenic.
(D) silicon.

(E) tin.

59.

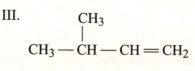

The significant product(s) of this reaction is (are)

I.
$$CH_3 - \underset{\underset{Cl}{|}}{\overset{\overset{CH_3}{|}}{CH}} - CH - CH_3$$

III.
$$CH_3 - \overset{\overset{CH_3}{|}}{CH} - CH = CH_2$$

II.
$$CH_3 - \overset{\overset{CH_3}{|}}{C} = CHCH_3$$

(A) I only
(B) II and III only

(C) I and II only
(D) I, II, and III

(E) None of these

60. $CH_3CH_2Br + KI \xrightarrow{\text{acetone}} CH_3CH_2I + KBr \downarrow$

    In the transition state of the reaction above, the C—C bond is formed by the overlap of what hybrid obitals?

    (A) $s - s$

    (B) $sp^3 - sp^3$

    (C) $sp^3 - sp^2$

    (D) $sp^3 - sp$

    (E) $sp^3 - s$

61. $n - C_7H_{15}CH_2OH \longrightarrow n - C_7H_{15}CHO$

    The oxidation above can be accomplished with

    (A) H_2O_2/acetone

    (B) $KMnO_4/H_2O$, NaOH

    (C) $CrO_3(C_5H_5N)_2/CH_2Cl_2$

    (D) $Na_2Cr_2O_7/H_2SO_4$

    (E) H_2CrO_4/H_2SO_4

62. In the UV spectrum, which of the following would be expected to have the highest λ_{max}?

    (A)

    (D)

    (B)

    (E)

    (C)

63. The reactions $A + B \rightarrow C$ and $C \rightarrow A + B$ have the same transition state. This is due to the

    (A) Pauli exclusion principle.

    (B) Boltzmann distribution function.

    (C) Third Law of Thermodynamics.

    (D) Newton's third law.

    (E) principle of microscopic reversibility.

64. The van der Waals equation of state for nonideal gases differs from the ideal gas law in that it accounts for

    I. the mass of each molecule of the gas.

    II. the volume of each molecule of the gas.

    III. the attractive forces between molecules of the gas.

    (A) I and II only

    (B) II and III only

    (C) I and III only

    (D) I, II, and III

    (E) None of the above

65.

$[A]_o$	$[B]_o$	Time required for [C] to increase by 0.01M
.5M	.5M	80 sec
1.0M	.5M	40 sec
.5M	1.0M	20 sec

At 25°C these rate data were obtained for the reaction $A + B \rightarrow C$. The rate law for the reaction is

(A) $\dfrac{d[C]}{dt} = k[A][B]^2$

(D) $\dfrac{d[C]}{dt} = k[A]^3[B]$

(B) $\dfrac{d[C]}{dt} = k[A]^2[B]$

(E) $\dfrac{d[C]}{dt} = k[A][B]^3$

(C) $\dfrac{d[C]}{dt} = k[A]^2[B]^2$

66.

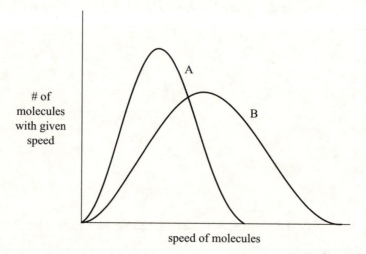

speed of molecules

The above graph represents the Maxwell-Bolztman distribution of molecular speeds of two samples of $O_2(g)$, A and B. Which statement is *true* about these two samples?

(A) A and B are at equal pressure.
(B) A and B have equal kinetic energy.
(C) A is at higher temperature than B.
(D) B is at a higher temperature than A.
(E) Sample A is dissociated into 0 atoms.

67. What is *not* true of the lanthanide metals?

(A) They form 3^+ cations.
(B) They are good reducing agents.
(C) They have high atomic masses.

(D) They are radioactive.
(E) They are difficult to separate.

68. The number of vibrational degrees of freedom for CO_2 is

    (A) 2
    (B) 3
    (C) 4
    (D) 5
    (E) 9

69. Ideally, the molar heat capacity of H_2 gas should be greater than that of He by a factor of

    (A) 6
    (B) $\dfrac{13}{7}$
    (C) $\dfrac{3}{2}$
    (D) 2
    (C) $\dfrac{7}{3}$

70. For a given oxidation-reduction reaction, the equilibrium constant is K, the standard potential is E°, and the standard free energy change is ΔG°. If the reaction proceeds spontaneously, which of the following sets of conditions is satisfied?

    (A) $\Delta G° > 0$ $K > 1$ $E° > 0$
    (B) $\Delta G° > 0$ $K < 1$ $E° < 0$
    (C) $\Delta G° < 0$ $K > 1$ $E° < 0$
    (D) $\Delta G° < 0$ $K < 1$ $E° < 0$
    (E) $\Delta G° < 0$ $K > 1$ $E° > 0$

71. When ΔG for an isolated system is equal to zero, the system is said to be

    (A) ideal.
    (B) in equilibrium.
    (C) adiabatic.
    (D) in a phase transition.
    (E) inert.

72. Which of the following is *not* a possible molecule as written?

    (A) OF_2
    (B) SF_2
    (C) OF_4
    (D) SF_4
    (E) O_2F_2

73. The structure of IF_5 is based on which configuration?

    (A) Tetrahedral
    (B) Trigonal bipyramidal
    (C) Square antiprismic
    (D) Octahedral
    (E) Pentagonal bipyramidal

74. According to molecular orbital theory, which of the following could *not* be a viable molecule?

    (A) He_2^{2+}
    (B) He_2^{+}
    (C) H_2^{-}
    (D) H_2^{2-}
    (E) H_2^{+}

75. Which of the following is *not* an example of electrophilic aromatic substitution?

(A) 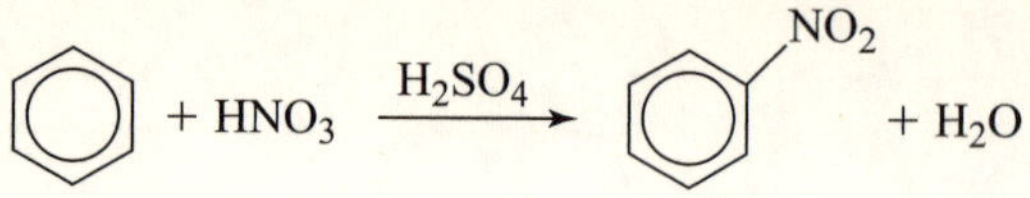 + HNO$_3$ $\xrightarrow{\text{H}_2\text{SO}_4}$ + H$_2$O

(B) 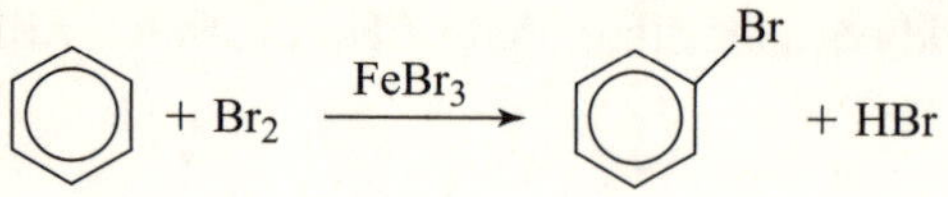 + Br$_2$ $\xrightarrow{\text{FeBr}_3}$ + HBr

(C) 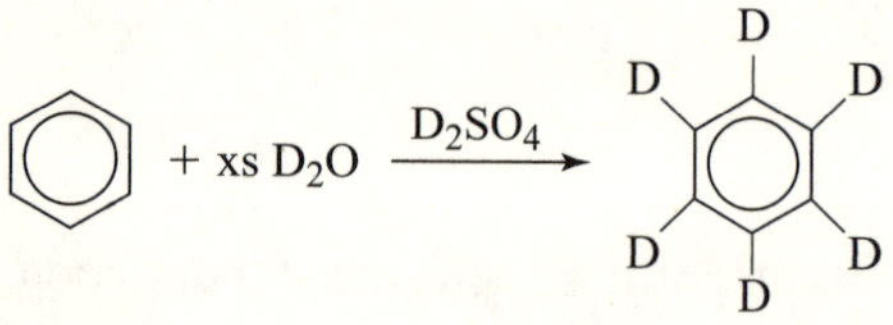 + xs D$_2$O $\xrightarrow{\text{D}_2\text{SO}_4}$

(D) + (CH$_3$)$_3$ CCl $\xrightarrow{\text{FeCl}_3}$

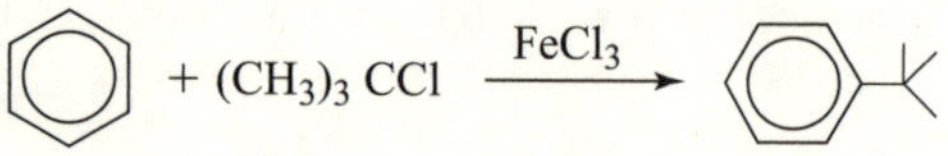

(E) 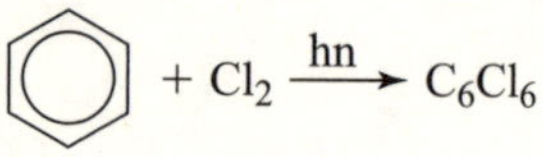 + Cl$_2$ $\xrightarrow{\text{hn}}$ C$_6$Cl$_6$

76. Which of the following structures is misnamed?

(A) 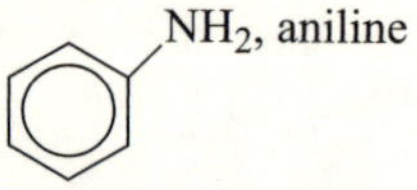 NH$_2$, aniline

(B) 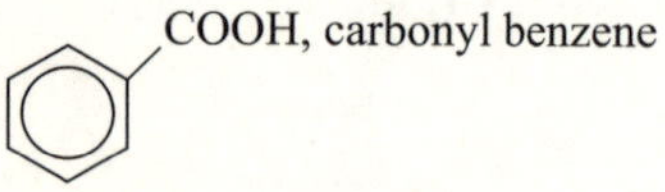 COOH, carbonyl benzene

(C) 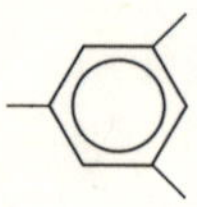 , mesitylene

(D) 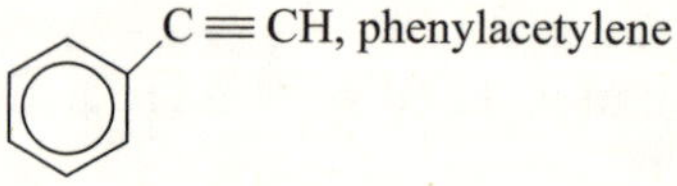 C≡CH, phenylacetylene

(E) 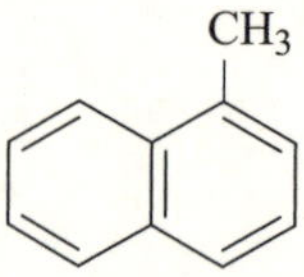 CH$_3$, 1-methylnapthalene

77. The hydrolysis of an ester proceeds most slowly under conditions of

(A) high acidity.
(B) neutrality.
(C) high basicity.

(D) pH being irrelevant.
(E) high temperature.

78. + LiAlH$_4$ $\longrightarrow$

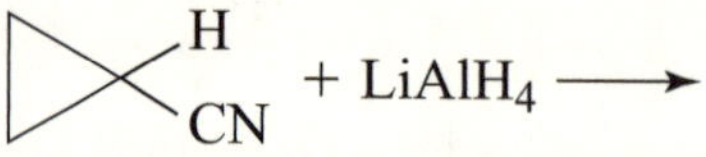

The product of the reaction above is

(A)

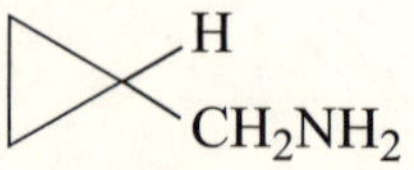

(D) CH$_3$CH$_2$CH$_2$CN

(B) CH$_3$CHCH$_2$NH$_2$ with CH$_3$

(E) None of the above

(C) CH$_3$CH$_2$CH$_2$CH$_2$NH$_2$

79. The statement that heat cannot spontaneously flow from a colder to a hotter body is a result of

    (A) the First Law of Thermodynamics.
    (B) the Second Law of Thermodynamics.
    (C) the Third Law of Thermodynamics.
    (D) Le Chatelier's Principle.
    (E) Henry's Law.

80. Which of the following has the lowest Third Law entropy at 25°C?

    (A) H_2O
    (B) Sucrose
    (C) H_2
    (D) Br_2
    (E) C_6H_{12}

81. Which of the following sets of conditions describes a system undergoing a reversible change?

	ΔS_{system}	$\Delta S_{surroundings}$	ΔS_{total}
(A)	positive	zero	positive
(B)	positive	negative	zero
(C)	negative	positive	positive
(D)	positive	positive	zero
(E)	negative	zero	negative

82. Rutherford's scattering experiment demonstrated the

    (A) existence of X-rays.
    (B) existence of α-particles.
    (C) nature of blackbody radiation.
    (D) mass-to-charge ratio of the electron.
    (E) nuclear model of the atom.

83. For octahedral complexes of Fe^{2+}, the difference in ligand field splitting energy for the high-spin and low-spin states is which of the following? (Assume Dq to be equal in both cases.)

    (A) $-4Dq$
    (B) $-16Dq$
    (C) $-20Dq$
    (D) $-24Dq$
    (E) $-28Dq$

84. Iron (atomic number = 26) is not paramagnetic as

    (A) Fe^{2+} in a strong field octahedral complex.
    (B) Fe^{2+} in a weak field octahedral complex.
    (C) Fe^{3+} in a strong field octahedral complex.
    (D) Fe^{3+} in a weak field octahedral complex.
    (E) metallic Fe.

85. The change in the Gibbs function for the mixing of two gases A and B can be expressed as

    (A) $\Delta G = n_A RT \ln(P_A/P_B) + n_B RT \ln(P_B/P_A)$
    (B) $\Delta G = nRT \ln(P_A/P_B)$
    (C) $\Delta G = RT \ln(n_A/n_B)$
    (D) $\Delta G = -nRT(\ln(P_A + P_B)/p)$
    (E) $\Delta G = RT(P_A/p) + RT(P_B/p)$

86.

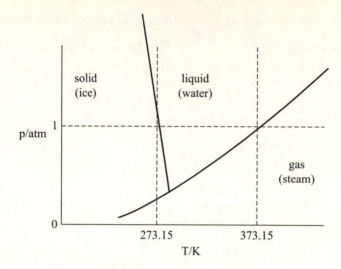

The solid-liquid line in the phase diagram for H_2O has a negative slope because

(A) the freezing process is exothermic.
(B) ice contracts on melting.
(C) H_2O has a high entropy of fusion.
(D) ice can exist in several forms.
(E) the triple-point pressure is very low.

87. The triple-point pressure for H_2O is 4.58mm Hg and the triple-point temperature is 273.16°K. From this we can conclude that

(A) steam cannot exist at temperatures below 273.16°K.
(B) the vapor pressure of ice is 4.58mm Hg for temperatures below 273.16°K.
(C) the vapor pressure of water is less than 4.58mm Hg in most cases.
(D) water cannot exist at pressures below 4.58mm Hg.
(E) ice cannot exist at pressures below 4.58mm Hg.

88. In a one-component system, there is one degree of freedom

(A) when only one phase is present.
(B) when two phases are in equilibrium.
(C) when three phases are in equilibrium.
(D) at all times.
(E) never.

89. The "tunnel effect" refers to the

(A) migration of conducting electrons in a magnetic field.
(B) use of lasers in surveying.
(C) ability of electrons to exist on both sides of a large energy barrier.
(D) existence of cathode rays in a vacuum.
(E) use of X-rays in medicine.

90. The energy levels for a particle in a cubic box with sides of length a are given by the equation

    (A) $E = \dfrac{n^2 h^2}{8ma^2}$

    (B) $\psi(x,y,z) = A\sin\left(\dfrac{n_x \pi X}{a}\right)\sin\left(\dfrac{n_y \pi Y}{a}\right)\sin\left(\dfrac{n_x \pi Z}{a}\right)$

    (C) $E = \dfrac{h^2 n^2}{4m^2 a^2}$

    (D) $E = \dfrac{8ma^2}{h^2 n_x^2 n_y^2 n_z^2}$

    (E) $E = \dfrac{h^2 n_x^2 n_y^2 n_z^2}{8ma^2}$

91. Compared to the potential function for a harmonic oscillator, the Morse potential function

    (A) has more closely spaced vibrational energy levels.
    (B) predicts different equilibrium internuclear distances.
    (C) accounts for the dissociation of molecules.
    (D) All of the above
    (E) None of the above

92. 50ml of a KOH solution is titrated to the phenolphthalien endpoint with 7.50 ml of 1.0M HCl. The concentration of the KOH solution is

    (A) .67M
    (B) 7.5M
    (C) .75M
    (D) .15M
    (E) 1.125M

93. Which of the following is most basic?

    (A) CH_3OH
    (B) CH_3NH_2
    (C) NH_3
    (D) H_2O
    (E) ⬡$-NH_2$

94. Amines cannot be formed by reduction of

    (A) nitriles
    (B) oximes
    (C) thiols
    (D) imines
    (E) amides

95. $CH_3CH_2Br + NH_3 \rightarrow \xrightarrow{\text{NaOH}} CH_3CH_2NH_2$

    The reaction above is not a practical synthetic route for primary amines because

    (A) bromide is more nucleophilic than ammonia.
    (B) many side reactions yield a complex mixture of products.
    (C) the reaction rate is very slow.
    (D) ammonia is insoluble in nonpolar solvents.
    (E) the reactants are expensive and dangerous to work with.

96. Base hydrolysis is fastest for which of the following coordination compounds?

(A) $[Co(NH_3)_5Cl]^{2+}$
(B) $[Co(CN)_5Br]^{3-}$
(C) $[Co(py)_4Cl_2]^+$
(D) $[Co(CN)_4Br_2]^{3-}$
(E) $[Co(py)_4Br_2]^+$

97. For ligand substitution reactions, a D (dissociative) stoichiometric mechanism can be distinguished from an I_d (dissociative interchange) stoichiometric mechanism by

(A) the order of the entering ligand in the rate law.
(B) the order of the original complex in the rate law.
(C) the effect on rate of changing the leaving ligand.
(D) the detection of an intermediate of reduced coordination number.
(E) None of the above.

98.

Which of the following best describes the diagram above of a molecular orbital?

(A) A nonbonding orbital
(B) A bonding σ orbital
(C) An antibonding σ orbital
(D) A bonding π orbital
(E) An antibonding π orbital

99. The proton NMR spectrum of compound X is δ, 0.9(d,9H); 1.5 (m,1H). X could be which of the following?

(A) $CH_3CH_2CH_2CH_2CHBr_2$

(B)  ⬡–⬡–$CHBr_2$

(C) 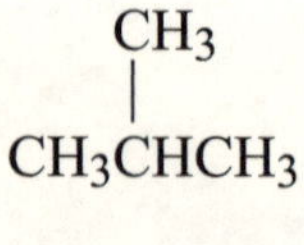 CH_3
      |
   CH_3CHCH_3

(D) 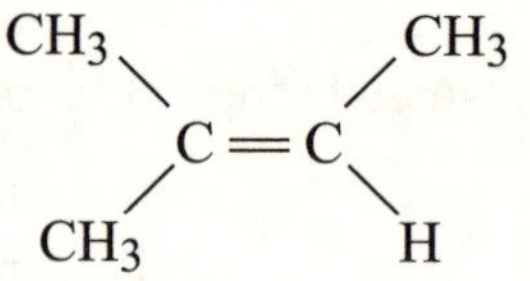
$$\begin{array}{c} CH_3 \\ \diagdown \\ C=C \\ \diagup \\ CH_3 \end{array} \begin{array}{c} CH_3 \\ \diagup \\ \\ \diagdown \\ H \end{array}$$

(E) 1,1-dichloro-2,2-dimethyl-propane

100. The proton NMR spectrum of 1,1,2-trichloropropane would most likely be

(A) δ, 1.7(d,3H); 4.3(m,2H)
(B) δ, 1.7(t,3H); 4.3(d,2H)
(C) δ, 1.7(d,3H); 4.3(m,1H); 5.8(d,1H)
(D) δ, 1.7(d,3H); 4.3(m,1H); 5.8(s,1H)
(E) δ, 1.7(t,3H); 5.8(d,2H)

101. CMR is less sensitive than proton NMR because

    (A) carbon is heavier than hydrogen.
    (B) ^{13}C has a low natural abundance.
    (C) spectra are taken at lower frequencies.
    (D) C—C splitting is not observed.
    (E) the carbon nucleus contains neutrons.

102. A theoretical link between quantum mechanics and thermodynamics is

    (A) spectroscopic analysis.
    (B) electrochemistry.
    (C) statistical thermodynamics.
    (D) the kinetic theory of gases.
    (E) the van der Waals gas law.

103. All of the following share the same crystal structure *except*

    (A) LiCl
    (B) NaCl
    (C) KCl
    (D) RbCl
    (E) CsCl

104. Which of the following does *not* show a tetrahedral structure?

    (A) Diamond
    (B) LiF
    (C) Ice
    (D) Zinc blende (ZnS)
    (E) Wurtzite (ZnS)

105.
$$\begin{array}{cc} I & II \end{array}$$
$$H—N—N—N$$

In hydrogen azide above, the bond orders of bonds I and II are

	I	II
(A)	2	2
(B)	<2	>2
(C)	>2	<2
(D)	>2	>2
(E)	<2	<2

106. Which of the following molecules is linear?

    (A) H_2O
    (B) ClO_2^-
    (C) NO_2^-
    (D) NO_2
    (E) NO_2^+

107.

$$\underset{CH_3}{\overset{CH_3}{>}}CH\underset{Br}{CH}CH_3 \xrightarrow[ether]{Mg} X \xrightarrow{H_2O} Y$$

Compound Y in the reaction above is an

    (A) alkane
    (B) alkene
    (C) alcohol
    (D) alkylhalide
    (E) organometallic haloalcohol

108.

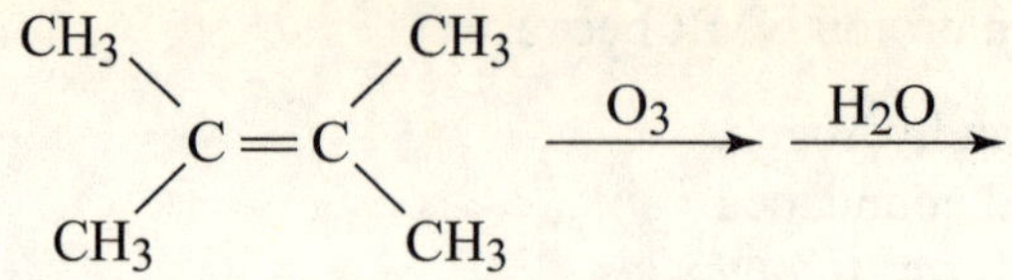

$$CH_3\text{-}C(CH_3)=C(CH_3)\text{-}CH_3 \xrightarrow{O_3} \xrightarrow{H_2O}$$

The product of the above reaction is

(A)

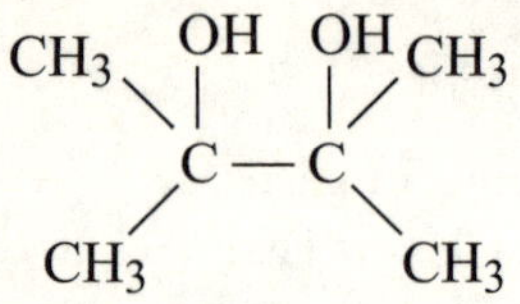

$$CH_3\text{-}C(OH)(CH_3)\text{-}C(OH)(CH_3)\text{-}CH_3$$

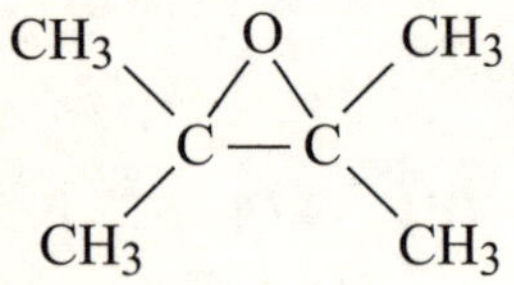

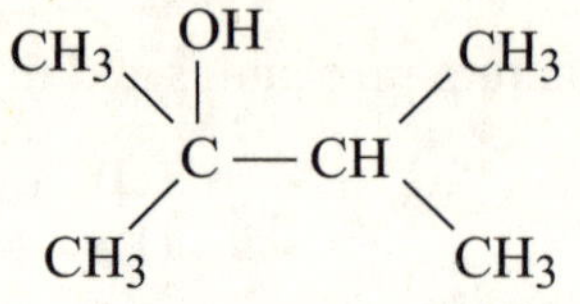

(C)

$$CH_3\text{-}C(OH)(CH_3)\text{-}CH(CH_3)$$

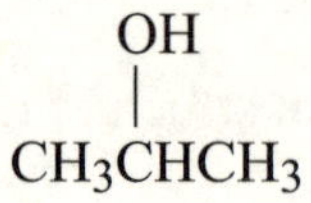

(E)

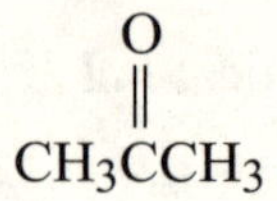

$$CH_3CCH_3 \; (O)$$

(B)

$$CH_3\text{-}C(CH_3)\text{-}C(CH_3) \; (epoxide, O)$$

(D)

$$OH$$
$$CH_3CHCH_3$$

109.

$$\xrightarrow{D_2O/NaOD} X$$

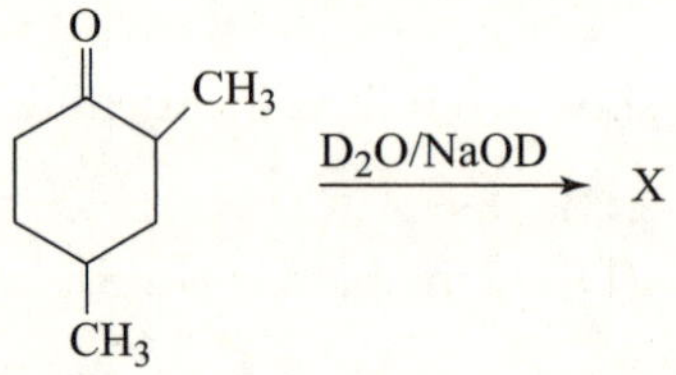

In the reaction above, product X is

(A)

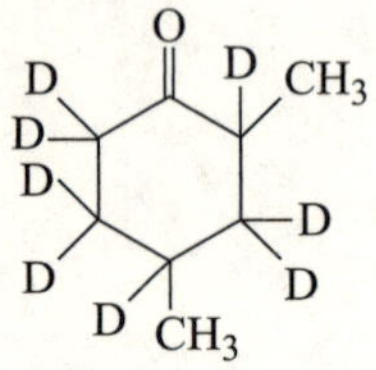

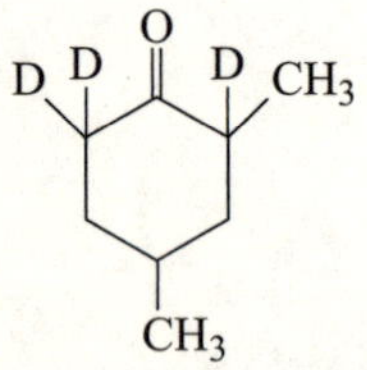

(C)

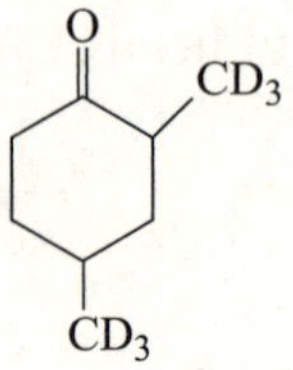

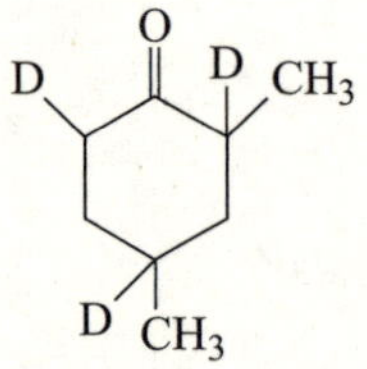

(E)

(B)

(D)

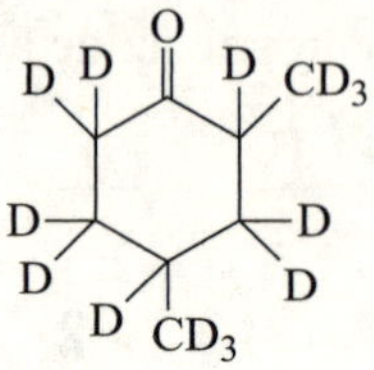

110. $CH_2 = CH_2 + CH_3CH = CH_2 \xrightarrow{\Delta} X$

Product X in the reaction above is

(A)   methylcyclobutane
(B)   pentane

(C)   2-pentene
(D)   1-pentene

(E)   no reaction occurs

111. Which of the following is designated dimethylaminoethane under IUPAC rules of nomenclature?

    (A) $CH_3CH_2N(CH_3)_2$

    (B) 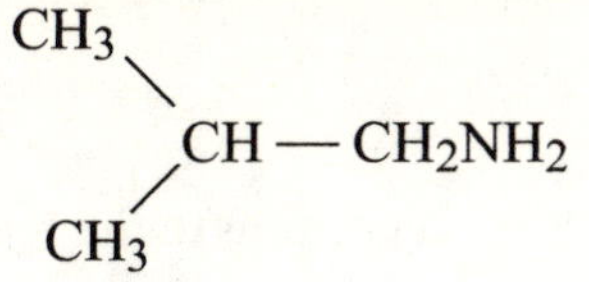
    $$CH_3 \diagdown$$
    $$\qquad CH - CH_2NH_2$$
    $$CH_3 \diagup$$

    (C) $(CH_3)_3CNH_2$

    (D) 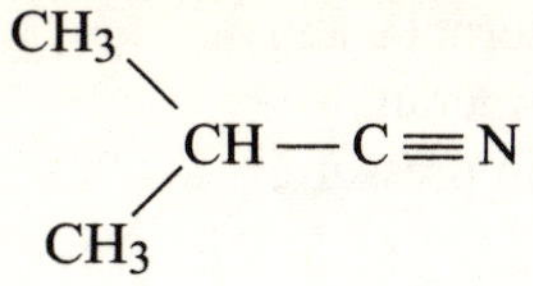
    $$CH_3 \diagdown$$
    $$\qquad CH - C \equiv N$$
    $$CH_3 \diagup$$

    (E) None of the above

112. Which of the following is an R enantiomer of a chiral compound?

    (A) 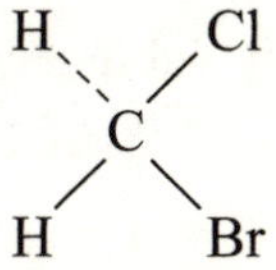 H ⋯ C ⋯ Cl, H, Br

    (B) CH_3 ⋯ C, H, CH_3CH_2, Cl

    (C) CH_3, C ⋯ H, Br, Cl

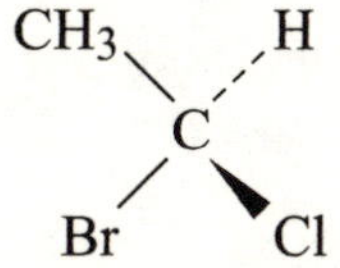

    (D) 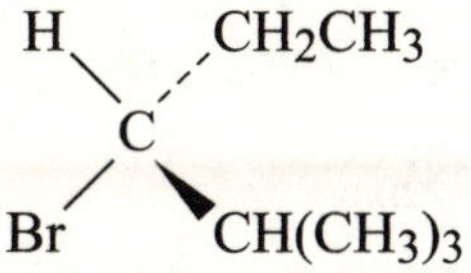 H, C ⋯ CH_2CH_3, Br, $CH(CH_3)_3$

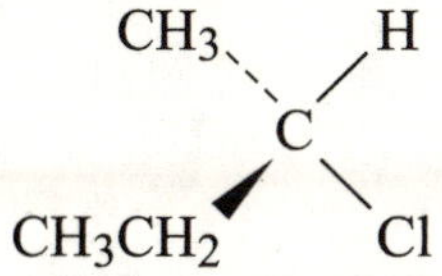

    (E) None of the above

113. Which of the following is a dextrorotatory compound?

    (A) 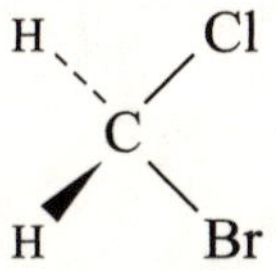 H ⋯ C, Cl, H, Br

    (B) CH_3 ⋯ C, H, Br, Cl

    (C) Br ⋯ C, H, CH_3, Cl

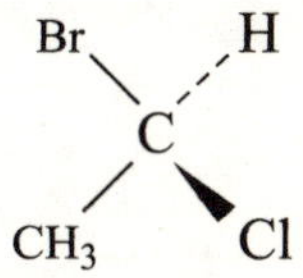

    (D) None of the above

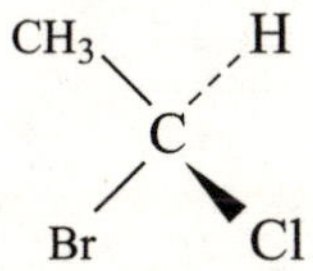

    (E) Cannot be decided by structure alone

114. Which of the following is *not* optically active?

    (A) 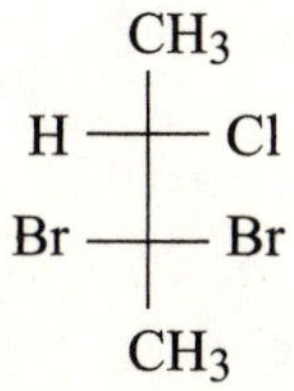
    $$CH_3$$
    $$H - Cl$$
    $$Br - Br$$
    $$CH_3$$

    (B) 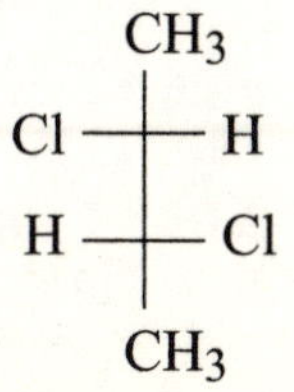
    $$CH_3$$
    $$Cl - H$$
    $$H - Cl$$
    $$CH_3$$

    (C) 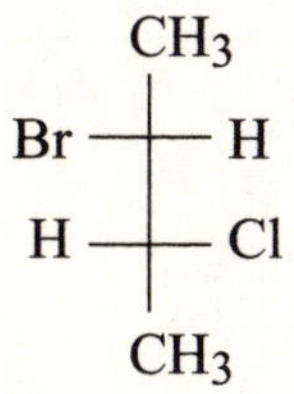
    $$CH_3$$
    $$Br - H$$
    $$H - Cl$$
    $$CH_3$$

    (D) 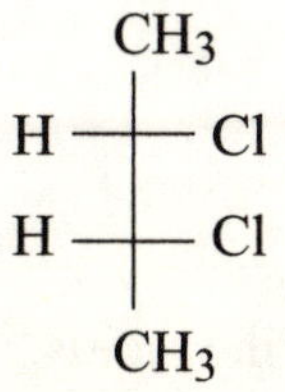
    $$CH_3$$
    $$H - Cl$$
    $$H - Cl$$
    $$CH_3$$

    (E) 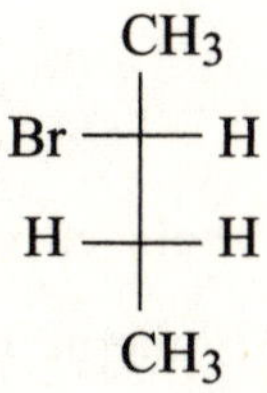
    $$CH_3$$
    $$Br - H$$
    $$H - H$$
    $$CH_3$$

115. How many aldohexose stereoisomers exists?

    (A) 8
    (B) 10
    (C) 16
    (D) 64
    (E) 48

116. If an ideal gas is allowed to expand adiabatically, the work done by the gas is equal to

    (A) the loss of internal energy.   (D) the loss of entropy.
    (B) the rise in temperature.   (E) None of the above
    (C) the decrease in pressure.

117. Ammonia gas is made from nitrogen gas and hydrogen gas at 525°C according to the reaction

$$\frac{1}{2}N2_{(g)} + \frac{3}{2}H2_{(g)} \rightarrow NH3_{(g)}$$

ΔH_4° for $NH_{3(g)}$ at 298°K is −46 kJ/mole. Using the following heat capacity values, what is ΔH for the reaction at 525°C?

	C_p (J/K · mole)
$NH_{3(g)}$	26
$N_{2(g)}$	27
$H_{2(g)}$	29

    (A) −46 kJ/mole   (D) −30 kJ/mole
    (B) −88 kJ/mole   (E) −102 kJ/mole
    (C) −62 kJ/mole

118.

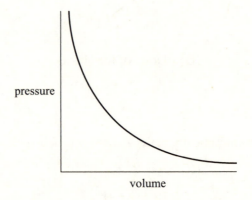

The hyperbolic curve above represents

    (A) An isotherm for an ideal gas.
    (B) An adiabat for an ideal gas.
    (C) A line of constant enthalpy for a real gas.
    (D) A line of constant fugacity for a real gas.
    (E) None of the above

119. Which of the following has the smallest ionic radius?

    (A) Li^+ (C) K^+ (E) Cs^+
    (B) Na^+ (D) Rb^+

120. Which of the following has the highest lattice energy?

    (A) LiCl   (C) KCl   (E) CsCl
    (B) NaCl   (D) RbCl

121. The Madelung constant for a crystal could be changed by varying

    (A) the radii of the ions in the crystal.
    (B) the geometry of the crystal.
    (C) the electron density surrounding the ions in the crystal.
    (D) the heat of formation of the crystal.
    (E) Avagadro's number.

122. Which of the following is *least* inert?

    (A) Helium   (C) Argon   (E) Xenon
    (B) Neon   (D) Krypton

123. Bromine can be prepared by oxidation of a bromide with

    (A) Cl_2 (D) All of the above
    (B) I   (E) None of the above
    (C) H_3PO_4

124. Which of the following elements would you expect to have the highest electronegativity?

    (A) Boron   (C) Aluminum   (E) Zinc
    (B) Carbon   (D) Silicon

125. Which of the following pairs of elements does *not* have approximately the same electronegativity?

    (A) C, S   (C) B, Al   (E) Fe, Ni
    (B) Co, Ni   (D) U, Pu

126. Two highways run between city A and city B. When an accident slows traffic on one highway, more drivers than usual take the other highway. This situation might be taken as an example of

    (A) the Heisenburg Uncertainty Principle.
    (B) Charles's Law.
    (C) Faraday's Laws.
    (D) Le Châtelier's Principle.
    (E) Hund's Rule

127. Which of the following is the strongest acid?

    (A) CH_3COOH (C) FCH_2COOH (E) $C_6H_5CH_2COOH$
    (B) $ClCH_2COOH$ (D) CH_3CH_2COOH

128. Which of the following is a naturally occuring wax?

(A) 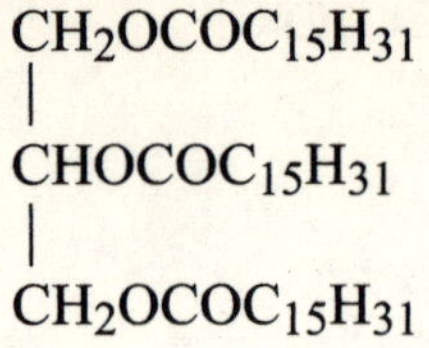 $CH_2OCOC_{15}H_{31}$
      |
      $CHOCOC_{15}H_{31}$
      |
      $CH_2OCOC_{15}H_{31}$

(B)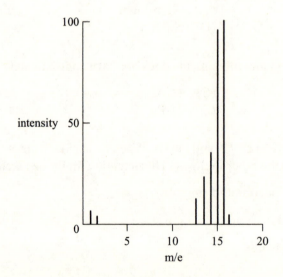
      CH_3CH_2 ... CH_2 ... CH_2 ... $(CH_2)_7COOH$ ... $C=C$ ... $C=C$ ... $C=C$ ... H ... H H ... H H ... H

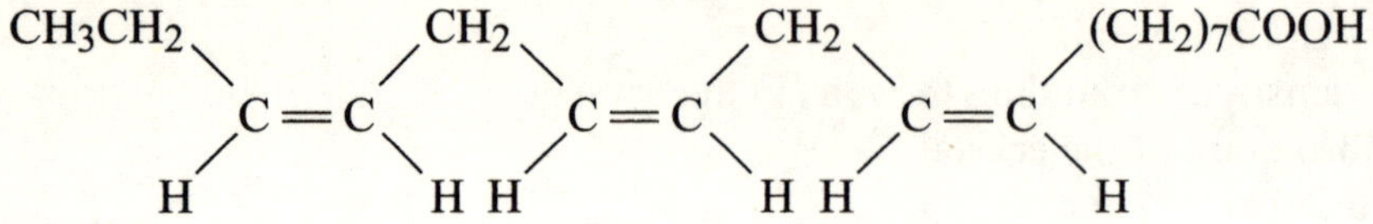

(C) $\overset{+}{N}H_3CH_2CH_2O-\underset{\underset{O^-}{|}}{\overset{\overset{O}{\|}}{P}}-O-CH_2$
      $CHOCOC_{15}H_{31}$
      $CH_2OCOC_{15}H_{31}$

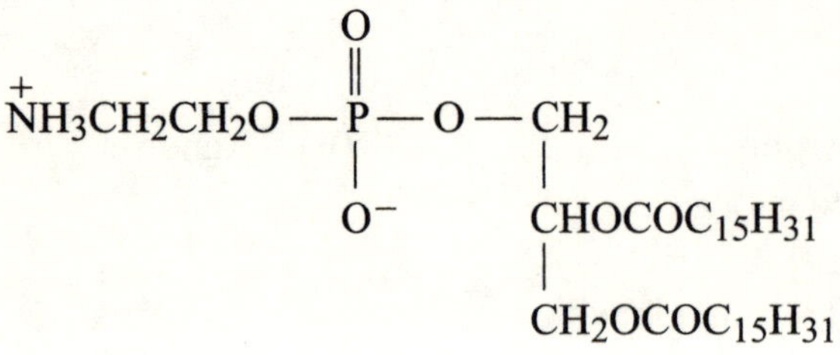

(D) $CH_2OHCHOHCH_2OH$

(E) 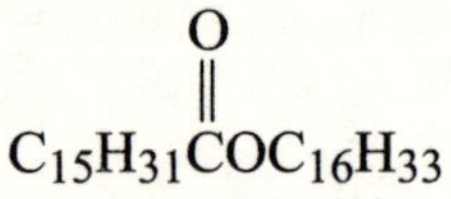 $C_{15}H_{31}\overset{\overset{O}{\|}}{C}OC_{16}H_{33}$

129.

The mass spectrum above is most likely that of

(A) CH_4 (D) O_2
(B) NH_3 (E) N_2
(C) H_2O

130. Which of the following should have the lowest boiling point?

(A) HO—⟨ ⟩—Cl

(C) [structure with OH and Cl on benzene ring]

(E) HO, HO—[benzene ring]—OH

(B) HO—[benzene ring]—Cl

(D) HO—⟨ ⟩—OH

131.

$$CH_2 = CH_2 \xrightarrow[\Delta, \text{ high pressure}]{\text{trace peroxides}}$$

The product of the reaction above is

(A) benzene
(B) ethane
(C) linear polyethylene

(D) branched polyethylene
(E) cyclobutane

For problems 132 to 135, take the speed of light at 3×10^{10} cm · sec^{-1} and Planck's constant as 6.6×10^{-34} J · sec.

132. What is the frequency of light at wavelength 3×10^{-3} cm?

(A) 1×10^{13}
(B) 2.2×10^{-31}
(C) 1×10^{7}

(D) 9×10^{7}
(E) 2.64×10^{-36}

133. What energy (in Joules) would a photon of light have at wavelength 3×10^{-3} cm?

(A) 2.64×10^{-36}
(B) 2.2×10^{-31}
(C) 6.6×10^{-47}

(D) 6.6×10^{-27}
(E) 6.6×10^{-21}

134. Light of wavelength 3×10^{-3} cm falls in which band?

(A) Microwave
(B) Infrared
(C) Visible

(D) Ultraviolet
(E) X-ray

135. One emission line in the spectrum of the hydrogen atom occurs at a wavenumber of 23,032. Assuming the Rydberg constant is 109,678, the line represents a transition between which two quantum levels?

(A) $n = 5 \rightarrow n = 2$
(B) $n = 5 \rightarrow n = 1$
(C) $n = 4 \rightarrow n = 1$

(D) $n = 3 \rightarrow n = 1$
(E) $n = 2 \rightarrow n = 1$

136. If butadiene is polymerized by a free radical synthesis, the product contains which repairing units?

I. 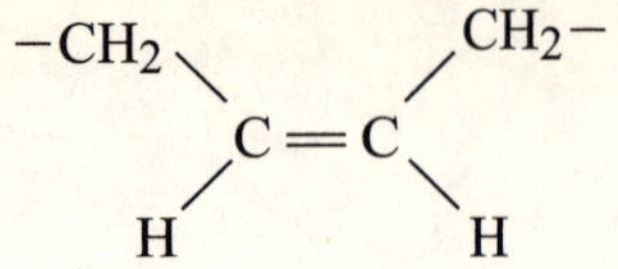 $-CH_2$ $C=C$ CH_2- with H and H

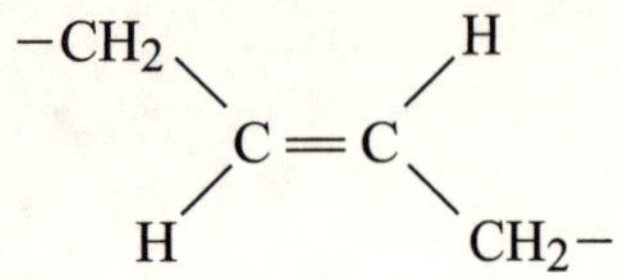

III. $-CH_2-CH$ with $CH=CH_2$

II. $-CH_2$ $C=C$ H with H and CH_2-

IV. $-CH_2-CH_2-CH_2-CH_2-$

(A) I and II only
(B) I, II, and III only
(C) I, II, III, and IV

(D) III only
(E) IV only

Answer Key

1. D	24. C	47. A	70. E	93. B	116. A
2. C	25. B	48. D	71. B	94. C	117. C
3. B	26. C	49. E	72. C	95. B	118. A
4. B	27. A	50. C	73. D	96. A	119. A
5. A	28. D	51. D	74. D	97. D	120. A
6. D	29. B	52. C	75. E	98. E	121. B
7. E	30. C	53. A	76. B	99. C	122. E
8. B	31. B	54. C	77. B	100. C	123. A
9. B	32. B	55. D	78. A	101. B	124. B
10. D	33. D	56. A	79. B	102. C	125. C
11. E	34. C	57. E	80. A	103. E	126. D
12. E	35. E	58. B	81. B	104. B	127. C
13. B	36. C	59. D	82. E	105. B	128. E
14. B	37. D	60. C	83. C	106. E	129. A
15. D	38. E	61. C	84. A	107. A	130. C
16. B	39. D	62. C	85. A	108. E	131. D
17. B	40. C	63. E	86. B	109. B	132. A
18. A	41. A	64. B	87. D	110. E	133. E
19. A	42. C	65. A	88. B	111. A	134. B
20. D	43. C	66. D	89. C	112. D	135. A
21. E	44. C	67. D	90. E	113. E	136. B
22. E	45. D	68. C	91. D	114. D	
23. C	46. A	69. E	92. D	115. C	

Practice Exam 4

Detailed Explanations of Answers

1. (D)

A covalent bond is one in which electrons are shared between two atoms. If there is a great difference in the electronegativities of the two atoms (say, greater than 1.7), the bond becomes ionic.

	Electronegativity Values		Difference
KCl	K = 0.9	Cl = 2.8	1.9 ionic
PH_3	P = 2.1	H = 2.1	0.0 covalent
O_2	O = 3.5	O = 3.5	0.0 covalent
B_2H_6	B = 2.0	H = 2.1	0.1 covalent
H_2SO_4	S = 2.4	O = 3.5	1.1 covalent

Although the H—O bonds in H_2SO_4 are ionic, the S—O bonds are covalent.

2. (C)

Neutral atoms will gain or lose electrons to form ions with noble-gas electron configurations. Often this means achieving a complete octet of valence electrons. Element Y has one valence electron. To achieve a stable noble-gas configuration, it must either gain seven electrons or lose one. It is far easier to lose one electron and form an ion of charge $+1$.

3. (B)

A Lewis acid is defined as any species that acts as an electron pair acceptor. An advantage of the Lewis theory is that it identifies as acids certain nonhydrogen-containing substances that have the same function that the common hydrogen-containing acids have. For example,

$$(CH_3)_3N: + BF_3 \rightarrow (CH_3)_3N:BF_3$$

4. (B)

When two ions come together to form an ionic bond, energy is released. The more energy released, the stronger the ionic bond. The amount of energy released is determined by the equation

$$E = 1.44 \frac{q_1 q_2}{r^2}$$

where E = energy in eV, q_1 and q_2 are the charges on each ion, and r is the distance between the two nuclei. While changes in ionic charge and ionic radius affect the energy of the bond, changes in temperature do not.

5.   **(A)**

Statements I–III are correct. Statement IV is incorrect because electric potential is not dependent on the quantity of material reacted.

6.   **(D)**

The reaction path identifies that $\Delta H > O$; therefore, heat is absorbed by the reactants to give the products, and the reaction is endothermic.

7.   **(E)**

The crystalline structure of a solid is best examined through X-ray crystallography.

8.   **(B)**

The areas of the diagram are labeled below with the answers to question 8:

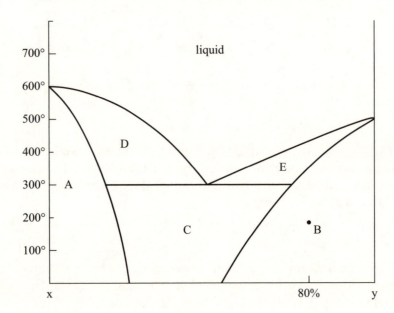

At 80 mole-percent Y and 200°, we are in area B, which is an unsaturated solution of solid X in Y.

9.   **(B)**

An ideal gas is composed of molecules that have no attraction for each other and do not occupy any space in the containing vessel. These criteria are best satisfied by a small monatomic molecule with a complete electronic valence shell.

10. **(D)**

The ionization potential of an element is defined as the energy required to remove the most loosely bound electron from an atom to produce a singly charged positive ion and a free electron. Ionization potential generally increases from left to right along a period of the periodic table and decreases from top to bottom in a group.

11. **(E)**

The reduction of K^+ to K cannot be feasibly undertaken with the use of a chemical reducing agent because metallic potassium is itself a strong reducing agent.

12. **(E)**

The reaction proceeds as follows:

$$2I^- \longrightarrow I_2 + 2e^- \text{ (anode reaction)}$$

$$K^+ + e^- \longrightarrow K \text{ (cathode reaction)}$$

$$2K + 2H_2O \longrightarrow 2KOH + H_2$$

13. **(B)**

A basic solution will be produced if the salt is hydrolyzed to produce a weak acid and a strong base.

$$Al(CN)_3 + 3H_2O \longrightarrow 3HCN + Al(OH)_3$$
weak acid   weak base

$$KC_2H_3O_2 + H_2O \longrightarrow HC_2H_3O_2 + KOH$$
weak acid   strong base

$$FeCl_3 + 3H_2O \longrightarrow 3HCl + Fe(OH)_3$$
strong acid   weak base

$$KCl + H_2O \longrightarrow HCl + KOH$$
strong acid   strong base

$$Pb(C_2H_3O_2)_2 + 2H_2O \longrightarrow 2HC_2H_3O_2 + Pb(OH)_2$$
weak acid   weak base

14. **(B)**

Carbon tetrachloride will have a net dipole moment of zero because the individual dipole moments cancel each other.

$$
\begin{array}{c}
Cl \\
\uparrow \\
Cl \longleftarrow C \longrightarrow Cl \\
\downarrow \\
Cl
\end{array}
$$

Cis-dichloroethylene has an effective dipole moment

$$
\begin{array}{ccc}
Cl & & Cl \\
\nwarrow & & \nearrow \\
& C = C & \\
\diagup & & \diagdown \\
H & & H
\end{array}
$$

while the net dipole moment of trans-dichloroethane is partially cancelled.

$$
\begin{array}{ccc}
H & & Cl \\
\diagdown & & \nearrow \\
& C = C & \\
\diagup & & \diagdown \\
Cl & & H
\end{array}
$$

The dipole moment of cis-stilbene is not as large as that of cis-dichloroethylene because the difference in electron attraction between carbon and chlorine is greater than that between carbon and a phenyl group. The dipole of trans-stilbene is less than that of the cis-isomer for the same reason as that given above.

15. **(D)**

$$
\begin{array}{cc}
sp^3 & sp^3 \\
H_3C & - CH_3
\end{array}
$$

$$
\begin{array}{cc}
sp^2 & sp^2 \\
H_2C & = CH_2
\end{array}
$$

$$
\begin{array}{ccc}
sp^2 & sp^2 & sp^3 \\
H_2C & = CH & - CH_3
\end{array}
$$

$$
\begin{array}{ccc}
sp^2 & sp & sp^2 \\
H_2C & = C & = CH_2
\end{array}
$$

$$
\begin{array}{ccccc}
sp^3 & sp & sp & sp^3 & sp^3 \\
H_3C & - C & \equiv C & - CH_2 & - CH_3
\end{array}
$$

16. **(B)**

Cyclopropane suffers from a great deal of ring strain, making it far less stable than propene. Cyclohexanone is far more stable than the ring structure of the oxirane. The meta- and para-xylenes are approximately equal in stability. Benzene is far more stable than a multiply unsaturated compound, and cyclopentane is significantly more stable than 1-ethylcyclobutene due to the ring strain in the latter.

17. **(B)**

Successive half-lives for first-order reactions are equal. To determine the half-life of the reaction, we note that the pressure of A decreases from 2000 torr to 500 torr in 7.8 minutes. We find that this decrease corresponds to two half-lives:

$$2000 \text{ torr} \xrightarrow[\text{half-life}]{\text{first}} 1000 \text{ torr} \xrightarrow[\text{half-life}]{\text{second}} 500 \text{ torr}$$

Therefore, we find that the half-life of the reaction is

$$\frac{7.8 \text{ minutes}}{2} = 3.9 \text{ minutes}$$

A decrease in pressure from 500 to 250 torr corresponds to another half-life. The amount of time that is required for the pressure to decrease from 2000 to 250 torr is therefore

$$3 \times 3.9 \text{ minutes} = 11.7 \text{ minutes}$$

18. **(A)**

The largest increase in entropy corresponds with the largest loss of order. As expected, this occurs when water makes the transition from a strongly hydrogen-bonded liquid to a free gas.

19. **(A)**

The Boltzmann distribution law is based on statistical thermodynamics.

20. **(D)**

The heat capacity at constant volume, Cv, is directly related to the internal energy, U, as

$$C_v = \left(\frac{\delta U}{\delta T}\right)_v \text{ or } \Delta U = \int C_v dT$$

21. (E)

The approximate chemical shifts of the —OH, —CHO and —COOH protons are 3.5, 9.5, and 11.5, respectively. The spectra of each of the compounds given may be approximated as follows:

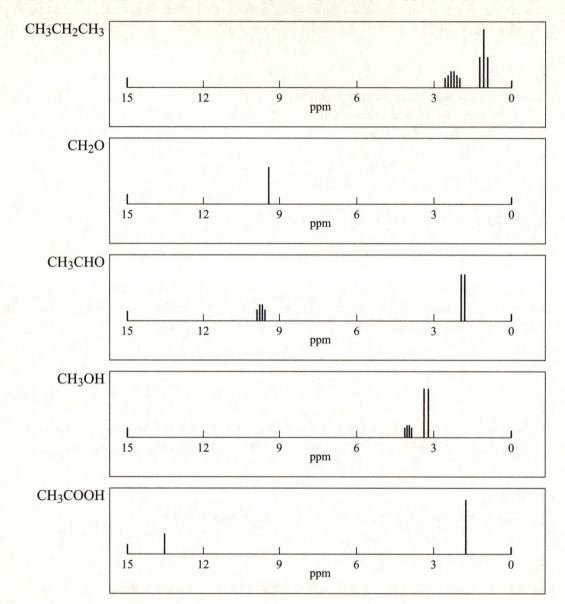

22. (E)

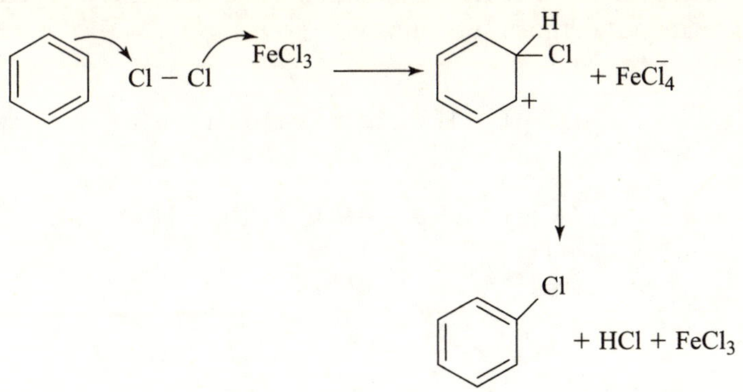

23. (C)

Acid- or base-catalyzed halogenation of ketones produces α-halo-ketones.

24. (C)

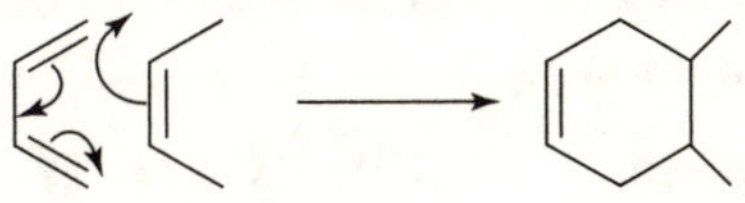

25. (B)

This reaction is known as the Ullmann reaction:

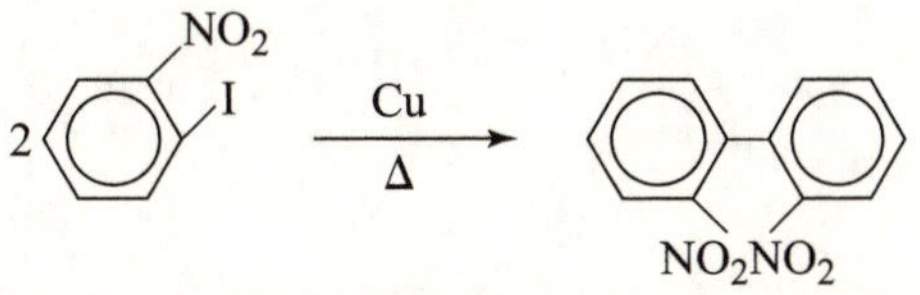

26. (C)

The temperature of the system remains constant, but that of the surroundings may change in an isothermal process. The equation for an isothermal reversal expansion of a gas $Q_{rev}^{sys} = n^{rt} \ln \left(\dfrac{V_f}{V_i} \right)$ shows that if $V_f > V_i$, then q will be positive and heat will be absorbed by the system.

27. (A)

An oxidizing agent is a compound that oxidizes (takes electrons from) another compound. The oxidizing agent accepts these electrons and is thereby reduced.

28. (D)

The simple harmonic oscillator approximation assumes a potential of $\frac{1}{2}kx^2$ where $x = R - R_e$. R is the internuclear distance and R_e is the equilibrium nuclear distance. This equation gives a parabola with an energy minimum occurring at $R = R_e$.

29. (B)

While the equilibrium generally lies far to the left, the addition of H_2SO_4 changes the alcohol to an alkoxonium ion, which readily undergoes substitution.

$$C_2H_5OH + H^+ \rightleftharpoons C_2H_5\overset{+}{O}H_2$$

$$Br^- \curvearrowright CH_2 \curvearrowright OH_2 \longrightarrow C_2H_5Br + H_2O$$
$$\underset{\underset{CH_3}{|}}{}$$

30. (C)

Let x = number of moles of NH_4^+ dissociated per liter of solution; then x = moles of H^+ and of NH_3 per liter. The NH_4^+ concentration then equals $1.0 - x$. Therefore, we have

$$NH_4^+ \rightleftharpoons NH_3 + H^+$$

initial concentrations	1.0	0	0
equilibrium concentrations	1.0 − x	x	x

We now have

$$Ka = \frac{[H^+][NH_3]}{[NH_4^+]} = \frac{(x)(x)}{1.0 - x} = 5.6 \times 10^{-10}$$

Note that the concentration of water has been omitted because it remains relatively constant. To simplify the calculation, we may say that $1.0 - x$ approximately equals 1.0 because x is very small in the case of a weak acid. Thus

$$\frac{(x)(x)}{1.0} = 5.6 \times 10^{-10}$$

$$x^2 = 5.6 \times 10^{-10}$$

$$x \cong [H^+] = 2.4 \times 10^{-5}$$

Recalling that $pH = -\log[H^+]$, we find that $pH \cong 5$.

31. (B)

A solution whose pH is 7 will have a hydrogen ion concentration of

$$[H^+] = 10^{-7}$$

Substitution of this $[H^+]$ value into the K_a expression for carbonic acid gives

$$Ka = \frac{[H^+][HCO_3^-]}{[H_2CO_3]} = 4.3 \times 10^{-7}$$

$$(10^{-7})\frac{[HCO_3^-]}{[H_2CO_3]} = 4.3 \times 10^{-7}$$

$$\frac{[HCO_3^-]}{[H_2CO_3]} = \frac{4.3 \times 10^{-7}}{10^{-7}} = 4.3$$

Thus, the ratio of $[HCO_3^-]/[H_2CO_3]$ required to maintain a pH of 7 is 4.3 to 1.

32. (B)

Phase-transfer catalysis takes advantage of the fact that certain compounds, such as alkylammonium hydroxides, are soluble in both aqueous and organic phases. The catalyst can greatly increase the solubilities of ionic species in the organic phase.

33. (D)

The weight fraction of aluminum sulfide in the sample is given by

$$\frac{2.0\text{g of Al}_2\text{S}_3}{10.0\text{g of sample}}$$

To determine the weight fraction of aluminum in aluminum sulfide, we calculate

$$\frac{\text{weight of Al in one mole of Al}_2\text{S}_3}{\text{weight of one mole of Al}_2\text{S}_3}$$

Recalling that the molar weight of sulfur is 32.06 and, using the given weight of aluminum and the atomic subscripts, we obtain:

$$\frac{2 \times 26.98}{2 \times 26.98 + 3 \times 32.06} = \frac{2 \times 26.98}{150.14}$$

Multiplying the result by 100 (to change from a fraction to a percent scale),

$$\frac{2.0}{10.0} \times \frac{2 \times 26.98}{150.14} \times 100$$

34. **(C)**

The number of moles of hydroxide ion in 1.00 liter of a 0.1M KOH solution is calculated to be

$$\frac{0.1 \text{ mole of OH}^-}{\text{liter}} \times 1.00 \text{ liter} = 0.1 \text{ mole of OH}^-$$

Therefore, we require 0.1 mole of H^+ to exactly neutralize the potassium hydroxide solution. We may now calculate the normality of the KOH solution to be

$$N = \frac{\text{equivalents of solute}}{\text{liters of solution}}$$

where equivalents of solute $= \dfrac{\text{grams of solute}}{\text{grams/equivalent}}$

Because there is one OH^- ion per unit of KOH, the equivalent weight is identical to the molar weight and the molarity equals the normality.

Recalling that $V \times N =$ the number of equivalents and that neutralization requires the number of acid equivalents to equal the number of base equivalents, we have

$$V_{acid} \times N_{acid} = V_{base} \times N_{base}$$

Solving the normality of the acid

$$N_{acid} = \frac{V_{base} \times N_{base}}{V_{acid}} = \frac{1000 \text{ml} \times 0.1N}{50 \text{ml}}$$

$$N_{acid} = 2.0N$$

(Show that this is equivalent to a 1M H_2SO_4 solution.)

35. **(E)**

When an aldehyde or mixture of aldehydes is treated with aqueous sodium hydroxide, an aldol condensation occurs. The initial reaction product may also eliminate a β-hydroxy group to produce an α,β-unsaturated aldehyde. Complex mixtures of aldols usually result when a mixture of aldehydes is used, except in cases where one of the aldehydes cannot form an enolate ion (as in the case of furfural because it does not have any α-proton for the base to abstract). The probable mechanism for this reaction is outlined below:

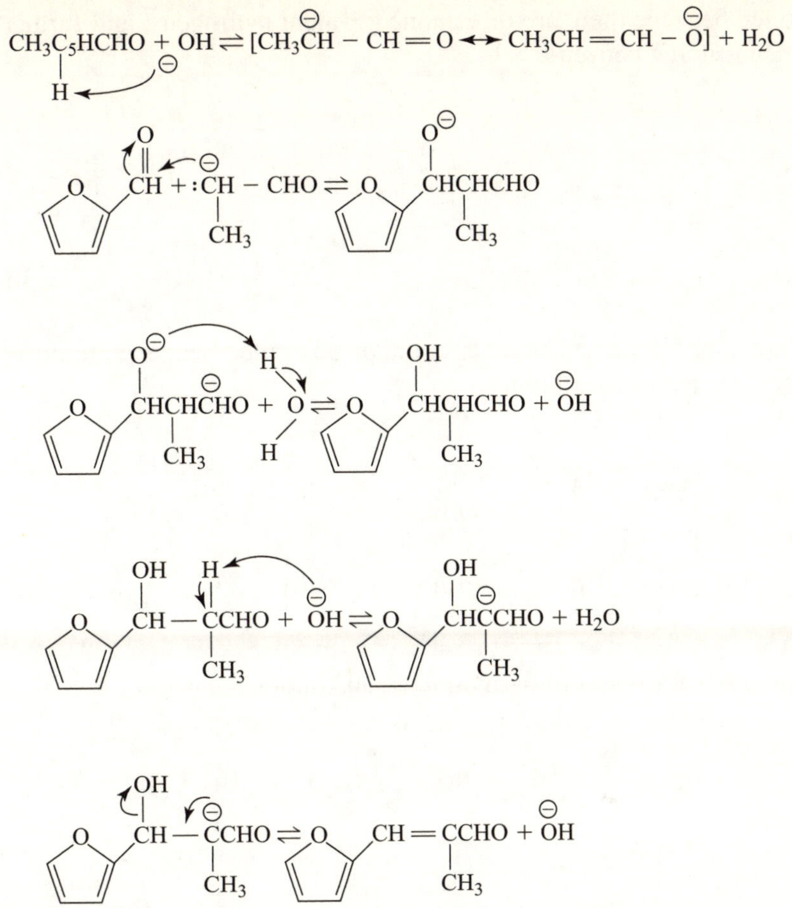

$$CH_3C_5HCHO + OH^{\ominus} \rightleftharpoons [CH_3\overset{\ominus}{C}H - CH = O \longleftrightarrow CH_3CH = CH - \overset{\ominus}{O}] + H_2O$$

36. **(C)**

Körners absolute method may be used to determine the number of trisubstituted benzenes resulting from disubstituted benzenes where both substituents are the same.

Only one trisubstituted benzene can be produced from a para-disubstituted benzene because all four hydrogens are equivalent.

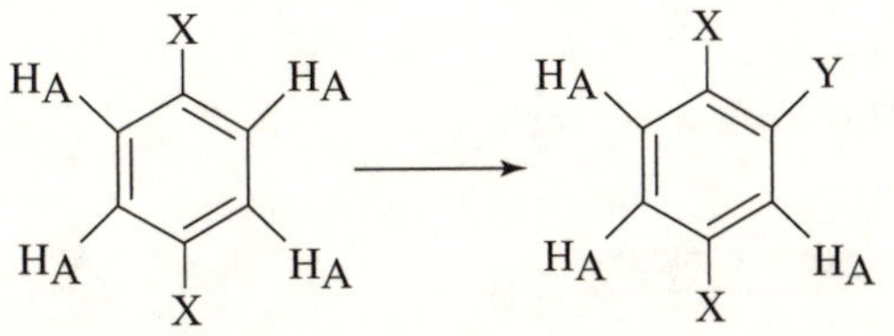

Two trisubstituted benzenes can be produced from an ortho-disubstituted benzene because there are two types of hydrogens.

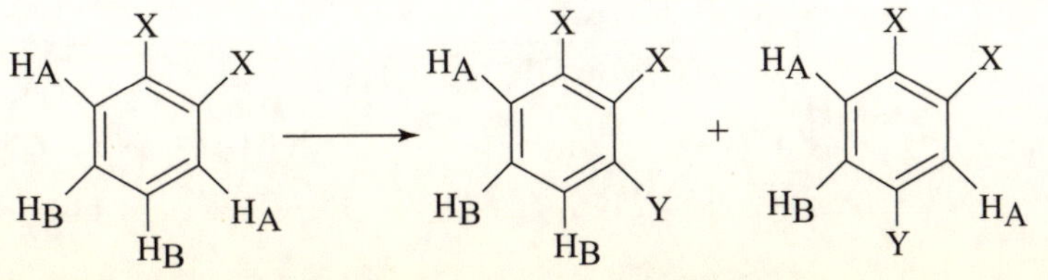

In a meta-disubstituted benzene there are three nonequivalent hydrogens, and further substitution leads to three different trisubstituted benzenes.

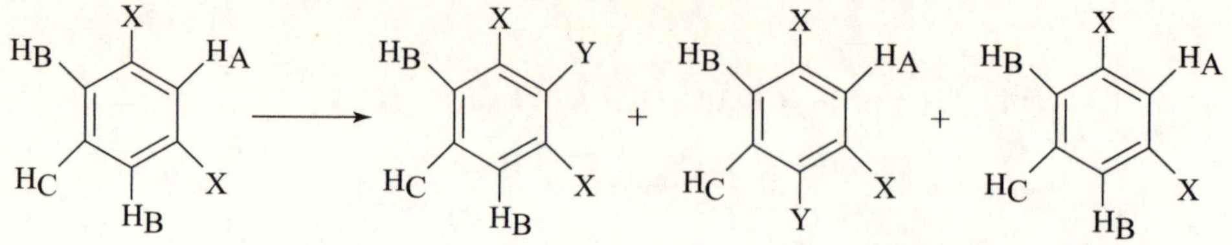

Körners rule does not apply if the substituents in the disubstituted benzene are different and we obtain two different products for para-substitution

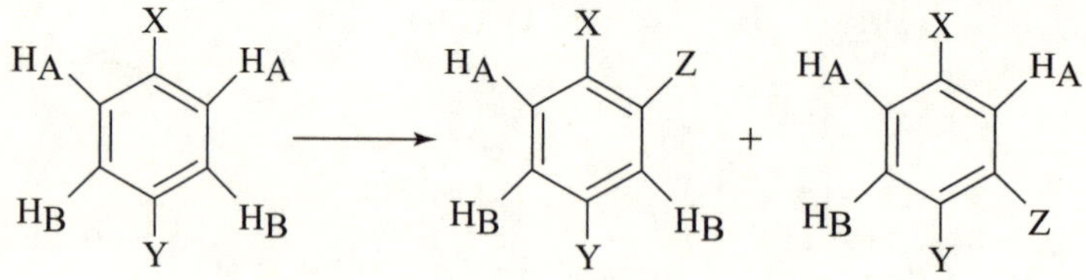

and four different products for both ortho- and meta-substitution.

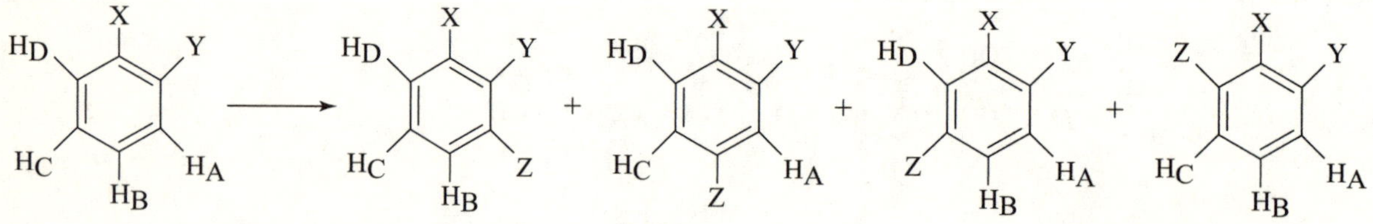

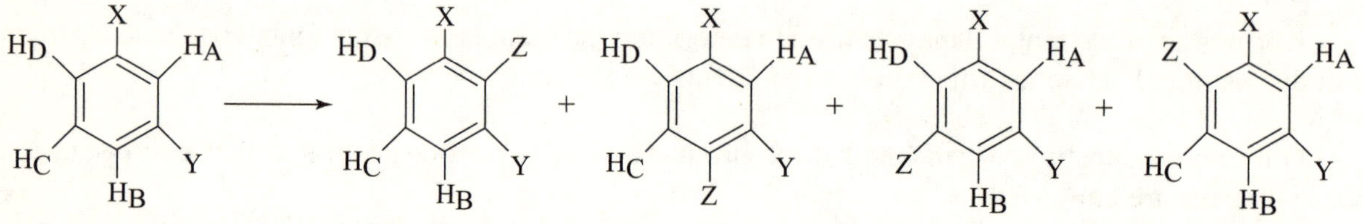

37. (D)

This reaction proceeds in the following manner:

$$Br_3CH \xrightarrow{\text{strong base}} Br_3\overset{\ominus}{C}: \longrightarrow \overset{\ominus}{Br} + Br_2C:$$

bromoform   dibromocarbene

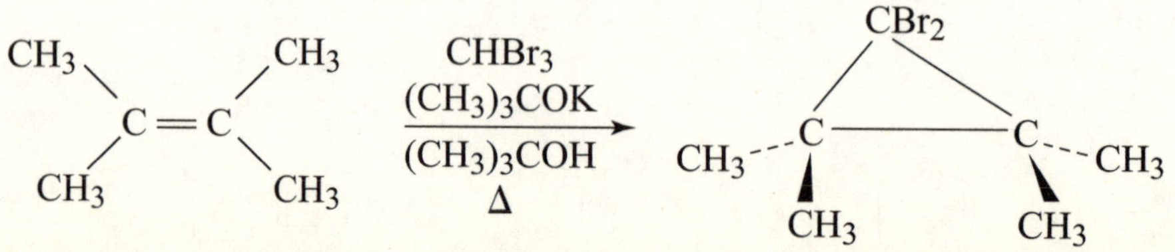

38. (E)

Amines are slightly more basic than ammonia, with tertiary amines being more basic than secondary amines, which in turn are more basic than primary amines (assuming the alkyl groups of these amines is identical). A general trend of increasing basicity is observed when the size of the alkyl group is increased.

39. (D)

I.

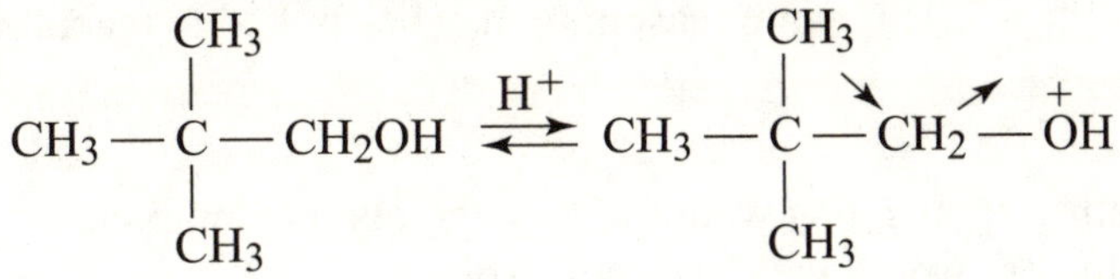

$$CH_3 - \underset{\underset{CH_3}{|}}{\overset{\overset{CH_3}{|}}{C}} - CH_2OH \underset{}{\overset{H^+}{\rightleftharpoons}} CH_3 - \underset{\underset{CH_3}{|}}{\overset{\overset{CH_3}{|}}{C}} - CH_2 - \overset{+}{OH}$$

II.

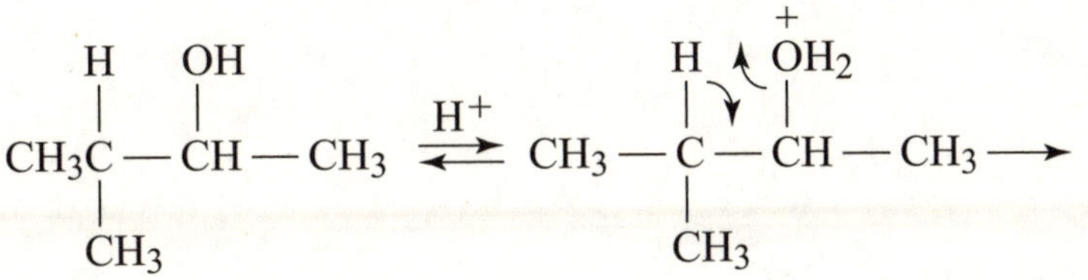

$$CH_3\underset{\underset{CH_3}{|}}{\overset{\overset{H}{|}}{C}} - \overset{\overset{OH}{|}}{CH} - CH_3 \overset{H^+}{\rightleftharpoons} CH_3 - \underset{\underset{CH_3}{|}}{\overset{\overset{H}{|}}{C}} - \overset{\overset{+}{OH_2}}{\underset{|}{CH}} - CH_3 \longrightarrow$$

III.

$$CH_3 - \underset{\underset{CH_3}{|}}{\overset{+}{C}} - CH_2CH_3 \overset{Br^-}{\longrightarrow} CH_3 - \underset{\underset{CH_3}{|}}{\overset{\overset{Br}{|}}{C}} - C_2H_5$$

$$CH_3 - \underset{\underset{CH_3}{|}}{\overset{\overset{OH}{|}}{C}} - C_2H_5 \overset{H^+}{\rightleftharpoons} CH_3 - \underset{\underset{CH_3}{|}}{\overset{\overset{+}{OH_2}}{C}} - C_2H_5$$

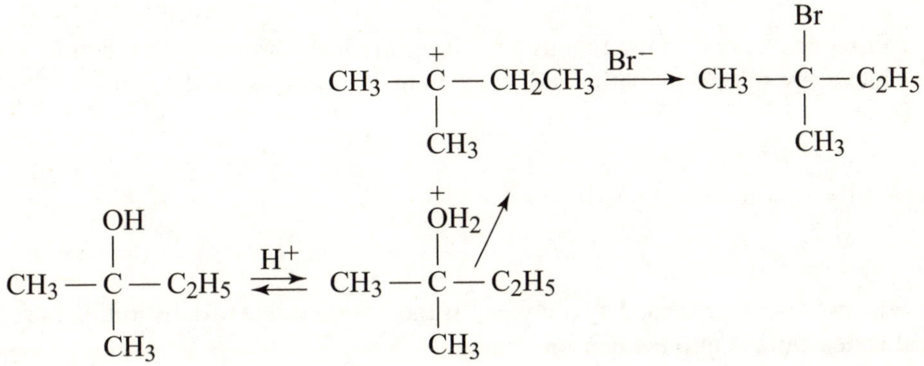

40. (C)

The titration curve indicates three equivalence points at pH 5, 10, and 13. This indicates that three acid protons of different strength are in solution. This rules out answers (A), (B), and (E). When a strong acid is titrated with a strong base, there is an equivalence point near pH 7. Because this does not appear in the graph, we suspect that HCl and H_2SO_4 are not in solution. Very weak acids have equivalence points at very high pH's. Of the choices given, only the third proton of H_3PO_4 could be a weak enough acid to account for the equivalence point at pH 13.

41. (A)

Ultraviolet light quanta are of the right energy to excite electronic transitions in conjugated π-bonding molecular orbitals.

$$\pi \xrightarrow[(uv)]{hv} \pi^*$$

42. (C)

A positive ΔH indicates an endothermic reaction. Hence both reactions are endothermic. The criteria for spontaneity depends on $\Delta H°$ values. Negative ΔH values indicate spontaneity. Water molecules that make up an ice crystal are held in fixed positions in the crystal. When ice melts, the molecules move through the liquid freely (more random distribution of molecules). Thus the amount of order is higher in the solid than in the liquid. By similar reasoning, we conclude that for reaction (B) also, there's an increase in disorderliness. The amount of the disorder is called the system's entropy, and the greater the randomness (or disorder), the greater the entropy. Now, we define $\Delta S°$ as $S°_{H_2O(l)} - S°_{H_2O(s)}$. We would expect $\Delta S°$ to be positive here because $S°_{H_2O(l)} > S°_{H_2O(s)}$. This same reasoning may be applied to reaction (B).

43. (C)

(D) and (E) are not hydrogenating agents. (A) would reduce the alkyne completely to an alkane. (B) could perform the partial reduction but would yield the trans isomer.

44. (C)

$$dH = C_p dT$$

note: $dU = C_v dT$

45. (D)

$LiAlH_4$ will reduce ketones more readily than it will reduce carbon-carbon double bonds. Also, it is difficult to achieve any selectivity with a reducing agent as strong as $LiAlH_4$.

46. (A)

Fluorine has the smallest atomic radius.

47. (A)

The benzylic position represented by number 1 is most susceptible to substitution because the intermediate radical is delocalized into the benzene ring.

48. (D)

At low pH, all three functional groups of aspartic acid are protonated and the molecule has a net charge of $+1$. At pK_1, half of the aspartic acid has lost its most acidic proton, that is

$$\underset{[HOOCCH_2CHCOOH]}{\overset{+NH_3}{|}} = \underset{[HOOCCH_2CHCOO^-]}{\overset{+NH_3}{|}}$$

zwitterionic form

At pH 3, most of the aspartic acid is in the zwitterionic form and has a net charge of 0. At pK_2, aspartic acid is half converted to the form with charge -1 and

$$
\begin{array}{ccc}
{}^+NH_3 & & {}^+NH_3 \\
| & & | \\
[HOOCCH_2CHCOO^-] & = & [^-OOCCH_2CHCOO^-]
\end{array}
$$

At pH's between pK_2 and pK_3 the dominant form of aspartic acid has charge -1 and would migrate toward the positive electrode. At pH's above pK_3, the dominant form of the acid has charge -2:

$$
\begin{array}{c}
NH_2 \\
| \\
{}^-OOCCH_2CHCOO^-
\end{array}
$$

49. (E)

The final concentration of SO_4^{2-} is

$$
\frac{50\text{ml}}{500\text{ml}} \times 1M = .1M
$$

We can find the concentration of Ba^{2+} by using the solubility product because we know that the final solution is just saturated with $BaSO_4$.

$$
K_{sp} = 1 \times 10^{-10} = [Ba^{2+}][SO_4^{2-}]
$$

$$
1 \times 10^{-10} = [Ba^{2+}](.1M)
$$

$$
1 \times 10^{-9} = [Ba^{2+}]
$$

This represents $[Ba^{2+}]$ for the final solution. To find $[Ba^{2+}]$ for the original solution, we must correct for the added volume of SO_4^{2-} solution.

$$
1 \times 10^{-9}M \left(\frac{500\text{ml}}{450\text{ml}} \right) = 1.1 \times 10^{-9}M
$$

50. (C)

The rate expression for a second-order reaction is

$$
\frac{-d[A]}{dt} = k[A]^2
$$

We can rearrange this and take an integral:

$$
\frac{-1}{K} \frac{1}{[A]^2} d[A] = dt
$$

$$
\frac{-1}{K} \int \frac{1}{[A^2]} d[A] = \int dt
$$

$$
\frac{1}{K} \frac{1}{[A]} = t
$$

This equation expresses a linear relationship between $\frac{1}{[A]}$ and t. Because this was the condition of our question, our answer is that the NO_2 decomposition is a second-order reaction. Using the same method as above, we can show that in a third-order reaction, there is a linear relationship between $\frac{1}{[A]^2}$ and t; in a first-order reaction, there is a linear relationship between ln[A] and t; and in a zero-order reaction, there is a linear relationship between [A] and t.

51. (D)

We write the quantum numbers in the order n, 1, m, with the first number given as an integer. The second number is given as a letter: 0 = s, 1 = p, 2 = d, 3 = f. The third number indicates the spacial orientation of the orbital. Here we have chosen to let m = 0 indicate a p-orbital that extends parallel to the z-axis.

52. (C)

An orbital with quantum number n = 3 has (n − 1) = 2 nodes. A p-orbital has one nonspherical node. Therefore, the 3p orbital has one spherical and one nonspherical node.

53. (A)

$\Delta G°$ for the reaction is

$$\Delta G° = \Delta G°_{fNH_3} - \frac{1}{2}\Delta G°_{fNH_2} - \frac{3}{2}\Delta G°_{fNH_2}$$

$$\Delta G° = -16.6 - 0 - 0$$

K_{eq} is related to $\Delta G°$ by

$$-\Delta G° = RT \ln K_{eq}$$

therefore,

$$K_{eq} = \exp(-\Delta G°/RT)$$

$$K_{eq} = \exp(16.6/R \cdot 298)$$

54. (C)

$$H = E + PV$$

A change in the enthalpy of a system is equal to the change of the system's internal energy plus the work done by the system on its surroundings.

55. (D)

More favorable (more exothermic) solvation energy should result from greater attraction between the ion and the solvent. This attraction should increase with increasing ionic charge and decreasing ionic radius. The attraction should also increase with increasing dielectric constant for the solvent. Only answer (D) satisfies these conditions. (D) is known as the Born equation for solvation energy.

56. (A)

MX will be most soluble if $MX_{(s)} \rightarrow M^+_{(aq)} + X^-_{(aq)}$ is exothermic. We can represent this reaction in two steps:

$$MX_{(s)} \xrightarrow{-u} M^+_{(g)} + X^-_{(g)} \xrightarrow{H_1 + H_2} M^+_{(aq)} + X^-_{(aq)}$$

The total energy of solvation is

$$L = H_1 + H_2 - U$$

For MX to be highly soluble, L must be less than 0 (exothermic). Therefore,

$$H_1 + H_2 - U < O$$

57. (E)

Glass can be seen to "flow" over very long periods of time. In very old houses, one can see that the windows have become thicker at the bottom. Glasses exhibit no distinct melting point.

58. (E)

P-type semiconductors contain electron holes that behave like positive charges. To create such holes, atoms of an element with one less electron than Ge must be substituted at various points in the Ge crystal lattice. Ga is the appropriate element. As-doped Ge is an n-type semiconductor.

59. (D)

With a sterically hindered alkyl halide, bimolecular elimination reactions (E2) will compete with S_N2 reactions. In this case, E2 products (II, III) are produced in amounts almost equal to the S_N2 product (I).

60. (C)

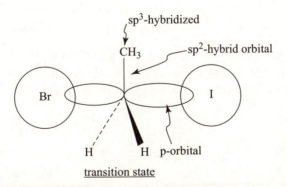

In the transition state of this S_N2 reaction, both the bromide and the iodide form partial overlaps with a p-orbital of the central carbon. This leaves three sp^2 orbitals on the central carbon, one of which forms a bond with the methyl group. The methyl carbon is sp^3 hybridized as usual, and so the C—C bond is $sp^3 - sp^2$.

61. (C)

Only (C) is selective enough to stop at the aldehyde stage and not continue to oxidize the aldehyde to a carboxylic acid.

62. (C)

According to the Woodward-Fieser rules, we would expect these values for λ_{max}:

(A) 220nm
(B) 264nm
(C) 303nm
(D) 274nm

λ_{max} for benzene is 255nm.

63. (E)

64. (B)

The Van der Waals equation is

$$p = \frac{nRT}{(V-nb)} - \frac{an^2}{V^3}$$

where a and b are constants particular to the gas. Compared to the ideal gas law,

$$p = \frac{nRT}{V}$$

the Van der Waals equation has two additional parts. $(V-nb)$ is the volume corrected for the volume of the gas molecules. $\left(-\frac{an^2}{V^2}\right)$ is a factor that corrects for the effects of attractive forces between the molecules of the gas.

65. (A)

When [B] is held constant and [A] is doubled, the rate doubles. Therefore, the rate is in direct proportion to [A]. The rate law is thus first order in A. When [A] is held constant and [B] is doubled, the rate increases four times. Therefore, the rate is in direct proportion to $[B]^2$. The rate law is thus second order in B. The rate law is

$$\frac{-d[C]}{dt} = k[A][B]^2$$

66. (D)

Molecules of sample B have a higher average velocity and thus a higher average kinetic energy.

$$\text{average kinetic energy} = \frac{2}{3}RT$$

Therefore B is at a higher temperature than A.

67. (D)

Stable, nonradioactive isotopes exist for most elements with atomic numbers less than 83. The lanthanides are atomic numbers 57–71.

68. (C)

The total number of degrees of freedom for a molecule made of A atoms is 3A. A linear molecule has 3 translational degrees of freedom, 2 rotational degrees of freedom, and (3A − 5) vibrational degrees of freedom. CO_2 has $3(3) - 5 = 4$ vibrational degrees of freedom.

69. (E)

According to the equipartition of energy principle, the ideal heat capacity per mole of a gas is

$$C_V = \frac{1}{2}R \left(\begin{array}{c} \text{\# of translational and} \\ \text{rotational degrees of} \\ \text{freedom} \end{array} \right) + R \left(\begin{array}{c} \text{\# of vibrational} \\ \text{degrees of} \\ \text{freedom} \end{array} \right)$$

Thus for H_2,

$$C_V = \frac{1}{2}R(5) + R(1) = \frac{7}{2}R$$

and for He,

$$C_V = \frac{1}{2}R(3) + R(0) = \frac{3}{2}R$$

$$\frac{C_{V_{H_2}}}{C_{V_{He}}} = \frac{\frac{7}{2}R}{\frac{3}{2}R} = \frac{7}{3}$$

70. (E)

K is related to E° by

$$E° = \frac{RT}{F}\ln K$$

K is related to $\Delta G°$ by

$$\Delta G° = -RT \ln K$$

Only (B) and (E) are consistent with these relations. In order for the reaction to proceed spontaneously, $\Delta G°$ must be negative. Therefore, (E) is the correct answer.

71. (B)

Because $\Delta G = 0$, there is no free energy present in the system. It is not a spontaneous reaction, and therefore the system in equilibrium.

72. (C)

Sulfur may form more than two bonds with F by promoting its 3p electrons to the empty 3d orbitals to form an expanded octet. Oxygen cannot do this because "2d" orbitals do not exist.

73. (D)

The central atom of IF_5, I, has five σ bonds and one lone pair around it. The best structure for these six constituents is octahedral.

74. (D)

When two helium or two hydrogen atoms combine, the two 1s orbitals form one bonding and one antibonding orbital. He_2^+ and H_2^- both have three electrons: two in the bonding orbital and one in the antibonding orbital for a net bond order of one-half. He_2^{2+} is isoelectric with H_2 and has a single bond. It is not very stable, however, due to the repulsion of the two positively charged nuclei. H_2^+ has a single electron in the bonding orbital for a bond order of one-half. H_2^{2-} would have zero bond order and thus would be unviable. This is because it would have four electrons, and so both the bonding and the antibonding orbitals would be completely filled.

75. (E)

Answer (E) is an example of free radical chlorination.

76. (B)

—COOH is benzoic acid.

77. (B)

Ester hydrolysis can be either base- or acid-catalyzed. The hydrolysis is slowest when both catalysts are in low concentration.

78. (A)

$LiAlH_4$ reduces nitriles but not alkenes or cyclopropane.

79. (B)

The spontaneous flow of heat from a colder to a hotter body would represent a decrease in the entropy of the universe. This would violate the second law, which states that in a spontaneous process, the entropy of the universe can only increase.

80. (A)

Water is strongly hydrogen-bonded as a liquid and retains some ice-like structure.

81. (B)

For a reversible reaction, ΔS_{total} must be zero. This is an ideal; in nature, all processes have a positive value for ΔS_{total}, in accordance with the second law of thermodynamics.

82. (E)

83. (C)

For the high-spin case, Fe^{2+} has two of its six d electrons in the higher-energy e_g orbitals and four in the lower-energy t_{2g} orbitals. The LFSE for the e_g orbitals is $6D_q$ and the LFSE for the t_{2g} orbitals is $-4D_q$. The total LFSE is

$$2(6D_q) + 4(-4D_q) = -4D_q$$

For the low-spin case, all six d electrons are in the t_{2g} orbitals. Thus the LFSE is

$$6(-4D_q) = -24D_q$$

The difference is $-24D_q - (-4D_q) = -20D_q$. In an actual application, D_q would be larger in the low-spin case than in the high-spin case. (The difference in LFSE would be greater than $-20D_q$ high-spin.)

84. (A)

Fe^{2+} has six d electrons. In a strong field octahedral complex, the ion is in a low-spin state and the six electrons occupy the three t_{2g} orbitals. This leaves no unpaired electrons, and so the ion is not paramagnetic.

85. (A)

The mixing of two gases is (almost) always a spontaneous process. Therefore $\Delta G < 0$. Equation (A) is the only choice that necessarily yields a negative value for ΔG.

86. (B)

Because ice takes up more volume than an equal molar amount of water (at the freezing point), higher pressures favor the water phase.

87. (D)

4.58mmHg is the lowest pressure at which water can be observed. Below this point ice sublimes directly into steam.

88. (B)

In a one component system

$$(\text{degrees of freedom}) = 3 - (\text{number of phases})$$

One degree of freedom exists along the phase boundary lines where two phases are in equilibrium, e.g., ice and water. We can specify either temperature or pressure but not both. If we specify a pressure of one atmosphere, the temperature is necessarily given as $273.15°K$.

89. (C)

Tunneling refers to the ability of particles to "leak" through zones, such as a high-energy barrier, forbidden by classical mechanics. Therefore, (C) is the correct response. The other responses do not relate to the "tunneling effect."

90. (E)

Answer choice (E) is the correct expression for the energy levels of a particle confined in a three dimensional space of length a. Answer choice (A) is correct for one dimension. Answer choice (B) is an expression of a wave function, not energy levels.

91. (D)

The potential functions for a harmonic oscillator and the Morse potential for an anharmonic oscillator can be depicted as

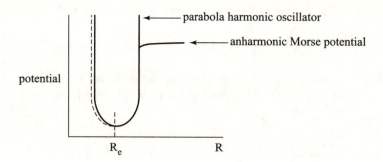

At high vibrational excitations, the Morse curve is less confining than the parabola of the harmonic oscillator, and the energy levels can become less widely spaced. When several vibrational transitions can be detected (i.e., $2 \leftarrow 0$, $3 \leftarrow 0$, etc.) that are forbidden in harmonics by $\Delta v = \pm 1$, an extrapolation can be used to determine the dissociation energy. The Morse potential also allows for dissociation at high energy and, hence, different intermolecular distances.

92. (D)

$$(7.50ml)(1.0M) - (50ml)x$$

where x is the molarity of KOH.

$$x = \frac{(750ml)(1.0ml)}{(50ml)} = 1.5M \ KOH$$

93. (B)

Amines are more basic than alcohols and water because nitrogen is less electronegative than oxygen, and therefore the lone pair on nitrogen is more available to react with a proton. Arylamines are less basic than alkylamines because protonating the nitrogen of the arylamine requires breaking the hyperconjugation between the phenyl π-system and the nitrogen lone pair. Finally, amines are all slightly more basic than ammonia (NH_3, $pK_b = 4.76$; CH_3NH_2, $pK_b = 3.38$).

94. (C)

Thiols are sulfur-containing compounds of the general form R-SH. All of the other choices contain nitrogen and can be reduced to amines:

$$\text{nitriles} \qquad R - C \equiv N$$

oximes

$$R - \overset{\displaystyle \overset{N-OH}{\|}}{C} - R'$$

imines

$$R - \overset{\displaystyle \overset{N-R''}{\|}}{C} - R'$$

amides

$$R - \overset{\displaystyle \overset{O}{\|}}{C} - N \overset{\displaystyle R'}{\underset{\displaystyle R''}{}}$$

R' and R'' can be hydrogen.

95. (B)

Side reactions yield a mixture of primary, secondary, and tertiary amines along with the quaternary ammonium compound.

96. (A)

Base hydrolysis is highly facilitated by the presence of a moderately acidic proton on a ligand of the starting complex. The substitution can then proceed by the following mechanism:

$$[Co(NH_3)_5Cl]^{2+} + OH^- \rightleftharpoons [Co(NH_3)_4(NH_2)Cl]^+ + H_2O$$

$$[Co(NH_3)_5OH]^{2+} \xleftarrow{\;H_2O\;} [Co(NH_3)_4(NH_2)]^{2+} + Cl^-$$

97. (D)

For the D mechanism, the entering ligand does not form a bond to the complex until the leaving ligand has left completely. For the I_d mechanism, the entering ligand begins to form a bond to the complex before the leaving ligand is completely dissociated. The most conclusive method of demonstrating the D mechanism is to detect an intermediate without both the leaving and entering ligands.

98. (E)

The combination of two p orbitals produces a π orbital. The combination of two orbitals of opposite sign produces an antibonding orbital.

99. (C)

Only (C) and (E) contain nine equivalent protons (H's) that could account for the peak at 0.9ppm. The chemical shifts for (E), however, would be farther downfield than 0.9 and 1.5 (they would be about 1.8ppm and 4.0ppm). Compound X must be (C).

100. (C)

$$CH_3 - \underset{\underset{}{\overset{\overset{Cl}{|}}{CH}}}{} - \underset{\underset{\underset{Cl}{|}}{\overset{\overset{Cl}{|}}{CH}}}{}$$

The three equivalent methyl hydrogens should be shifted downfield to 1.7ppm by the chlorine on the neighboring carbon. The peak should be split into a doublet by the hydrogen on the neighboring carbon. The hydrogen on the second carbon should show a peak shifted downfield to 4.3ppm by the chlorines. The peak is a multiplet (it is split into four by the methyl hydrogens and then eight by the hydrogen on the third carbon). The peak for the hydrogen on the third carbon should be shifted farthest downfield because two chlorines are attached to the third carbon. The peak should be split into a doublet by the hydrogen on the second carbon.

101. (B)

NMR can only detect nuclei that have magnetic moments, such as ^1H and ^{13}C. The natural abundance of ^1H is 99.88%, while only 1.1% of carbon atoms are ^{13}C. Special techniques must be used to increase the sensitivity of CMR spectrometers.

102. (C)

Statistical thermodynamics provides a link between quantum mechanics and thermodynamics because it is based on the principle that thermodynamic observables are averages of molecular properties and attempts to calculate these averages. The other responses do not combine both ideas, the molecular and the general observation, in this way.

103. (E)

LiCl, NaCl, KCl, and RbCl all have the 6PO(NaCl) structure. Because of the large ionic radius of Cs, CsCl takes on the 3.2PTOT(CsCl) structure.

104. (B)

LiF has the octahedral NaCl structure.

105. (B)

Contributing structures to the resonance-stabilized hydrogen azide molecule are

(A) $H - \overset{..}{N} = \overset{(+)}{N} = \overset{(-)}{\underset{..}{N}}:$

(B) $H - \overset{(-)}{N} - \overset{(+)}{N} \equiv N:$

(C) $H - \overset{(+)}{N} \equiv \overset{(+)}{N} - \overset{(2-)}{\underset{..}{N}}:$

The most important structures are (A) and (B). (C) is less important because it necessitates placing positive formal charges on two adjacent molecules and creating a double negative charge. The actual bond orders are partway between those shown in structures (A) and (B). Thus bond I has a bond order between two and one, and bond II has a bond order between two and three.

106. (E)

Lewis structures for these compounds are

(A)

$$:O:$$
$$H \qquad H$$

(B)

$$\overset{..}{Cl}\overset{\ominus}{:}$$
$$:O: \qquad :O:$$

(C)

$$\overset{..}{N}$$
$$\overset{\ominus}{:O:} \qquad :O:$$

(D)

$$\overset{\cdot}{N}\overset{\oplus}{}$$
$$\overset{\ominus}{:O:} \qquad :O:$$

(E)

$$:\overset{\cdot}{O} = \overset{\oplus}{N} = \overset{\cdot}{O}:$$

(A) to (D) all have at least one nonbonding electron on the central atom. The repulsion of the nonbonding electrons necessarily pushes the bonding electrons out of a linear arrangement. Alternately, we can say that the presence of nonbonding electrons necessitates nonlinear sp^2 or sp^3 hybridization on the central atom. NO_2^+ has no nonbonding electrons on the central atom. The σ N—O bonds involve sp hybrid orbitals, which are linear.

NO_2^+ is isoelectric with CO_2.

107. (A)

$$\underset{CH_3}{\overset{CH_3}{\diagdown}}CH\underset{Br}{\overset{|}{C}}HCH_3 \xrightarrow[\text{ether}]{Mg} \underset{CH_3}{\overset{CH_3}{\diagdown}}CH\underset{MgBr}{\overset{|}{C}}HCH_3 \xrightarrow{H_2O} \underset{CH_3}{\overset{CH_3}{\diagdown}}CHCH_2CH_3 + HOMgBr$$

Organometallic reagents hydrolyze to form alkanes and metal hydroxides.

108. (E)

Although oxidative cleavage of double bonds can also be accomplished with concentrated $KMnO_4$, better yields are available by ozonization. If reduction conditions are used in decomposing the intermediate ozonide, alcohols and aldehydes can be isolated.

109. (B)

Protons α to the ketone group are fairly acidic and thus open to substitution with deuterium.

110. (E)

This reaction would be an example of a $\pi_2 + \pi_2$ thermal cycloaddition, which is not allowed. Ethylene can polymerize, but high pressure and temperature are required as well as peroxides or other free-radical initiators.

111. (A)

is designated dimethylaminoethane because the two methyl groups on the N give dimethylamino and because the main chain is two C's long, giving the base name ethane.

112. (D)

(A) is not a chiral compound and (B) and (C) represent S enantiomers.

113. (E)

The relationship between the direction of optical activity of a molecule and the absolute configuration of the molecule follows no simple rules. Although either (B) or (C) must be dextrorotatory, only experimental evidence can determine which is.

114. (D)

(D) is known as a meso compound. Although it has two asymmetric carbons, a center of symmetry exists between these two carbons. This can be seen by rotating the mirror image of (D) 180°. (D) shows no optical activity because it is not chiral.

115. (C)
Aldohexoses have the general form

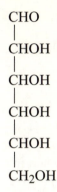

CHO
|
CHOH
|
CHOH
|
CHOH
|
CHOH
|
CH₂OH

Each of the four intermediate carbons has two possible configurations, R or S. The total number of aldehexoses is thus

$$2^4 = 16$$

116. (A)
In an adiabatic process, $\Delta q = 0$. Because $\Delta E = \Delta q - \Delta w$, Δw is now equal to $-\Delta E$, the loss in internal energy.

117. (C)

$$
\begin{array}{ccc}
T_1 & R \xrightarrow{\;I\;} P \\
& \downarrow \quad \uparrow \\
T_2 & R \xrightarrow{\;II\;} P
\end{array}
$$

Reaction path I and reaction path II should have the same ΔH. Thus to find ΔH for our reaction at 798°K (525°C), we can sum the changes in enthalpy involved in cooling the reactants to 298°K, forming the products, and heating the products to 798°K.

$$-\left[\left(\frac{1}{2}C_{pN_2} + \frac{3}{2}C_{pH_2}\right)\Delta T\right] + \Delta H_f^\circ + \left[C_{pNH_3} \times \Delta T\right] = \Delta H_{798}$$

$$-[(13.5 + 43.5)(798 - 298)] + (-46 \text{kJ/mole}) + [26(798 - 298)] = \Delta H_{798}$$

$$-[28,500 \text{J/mole}] + (-46 \text{kJ/mole}) + [13,000 \text{J/mole}] = \Delta H_{798}$$

$$-28.5 \text{kJ/mole} - 46 \text{kJ/mole} + 13 \text{kJ/mole} = \Delta H_{798}$$

$$-62 \text{kJ/mole} = \Delta H_{298}$$

118. (A)

PV = nRT = constant at constant temperature.

PV = C is an equation for a hyperbola.

Adiabats are similar in appearance but follow the curve $PV^Y = C$, where $Y = C_p/C_v$.

119. (A)

In the alkali metal family, the smallest ion has the smallest atomic number, $_3$Li.

120. (A)

The lattice energy is the energy released when free ions are brought together in a crystal lattice. It is conventional to represent lattice energy as a positive number. The lattice energy is inversely proportional to the interatomic distance of the ions in the crystal. (If oppositely charged ions can be brought more closely together, they achieve a lower potential energy and thus release more lattice energy.) The interatomic distance decreases with decreasing ionic radius. Because Li$^+$ has the smallest ionic radius of all the cations listed, LiCl has the highest lattice energy.

121. (B)

The Madelung constant is a factor in calculating the potential energy of an ion in a crystal. It is the sum of an infinite series that represents the effects on the ion of its neighboring ions. The Madelung constant reflects the relative positions of ions in the crystal, and hence it is dependent on the geometry of the crystal.

122. (E)

Xenon has been shown to form several compounds, including XeF_6, XeF_4, and XeF_2. Ionization energies increase with decreasing atomic number. Although KrF_2 is known, stable compounds of the other noble gases are unknown and unexpected.

123. (D)

The oxidation of a bromide with chlorine is a standard industrial preparation. Iodine, being less electronegative than bromine, would not oxidize a bromide. Phosphoric acid is a very weak oxidizing agent and is used to form HBr from NaBr.

124. (B)

In general, electronegativity increases from the left to the right and from the bottom to the top of the periodic table. Of the choices given, carbon is the closest to the top right corner.

125. (C)

Fe, Co, and Ni are all fourth period members of group VIII and thus likely to have similar characteristics. The same is true for U and Pu because they are both actinides. Sulfur is on the next higher period from carbon but it is also farther to the right. In fact, they have equal electronegativity according to Allred's values. Boron and aluminum are members of the same group but in different periods. The electronegativity values are 2.0 and 1.6.

126. (D)

Le Châtelier's Principle states:

When an external stress affects a system at equilibrium, the equilibrium shifts to counter the effects of the stress. In this case, the accident causes the distribution of traffic between the two highways to shift toward a restoration of the original traffic flow rate.

127. (C)

Electronegative substituents on an acid increase the strength of the acid. In fluoracetic acid, FCH_3COOH, the F—C bond has a dipole character because electrons are held more closely by fluorine than by carbon. The positive end of this dipole, on the carbon, is close to the negatively charged carboxy group. The ngative charge is stabilized by the attraction of the dipole. Fluorine is the most electronegative substituent of the choices given.

128. (E)

Waxes are esters of long-chain carboxylic acids with long-chain acids. (A) is a glyceride or fat; (B) is the fatty acide, linolenic acid; (C) is a phosphoglyceride; and (D) is glycerol.

129. (A)

H_2O, O_2, and N_2 would all show molecular ion peaks above 17. NH_3 would show a stronger peak at 17. The peak at 17 is due to the molecule ion of methane with the ^{13}C isotope, $[^{13}CH_4]^+$. In addition, NH_3 would not show a peak at 12, which represents the ion $[C]^+$.

130. (C)

In every case, intermolecular hydrogen bonding would be a factor in raising the boiling point. However, choice (C) can also form an intramolecular hydrogen bond between the chlorine and the hydroxy hydrogen. This reduces intermolecular hydrogen bonding and thus reduces the boiling point.

131. (D)

The peroxides are free radical initiators for the polymerization:

$$Y \cdot + CH_2 = CH_2 \rightarrow Y—CH_2—CH_2 \cdot$$

$$Y—CH_2—CH_2 \cdot + CH_2 = CH_2 \rightarrow Y—CH_2—CH_2—CH_2—CH_2 \cdot$$

etc.

Branching occurs probably by this mechanism:

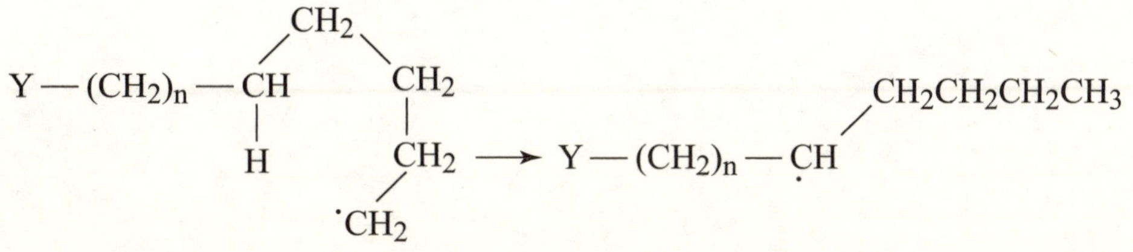

Polymerization continues at the radical carbon. Linear polyethylene is made with a process involving organometallic catalysts.

132. (A)

$$v = \frac{c}{\lambda} = \frac{3 \times 10^{10} cm \times sec^{-1}}{3 \times 10^{-3} cm} = 1 \times 10^{13} sec^{-1}$$

133. (E)

$$E = hv = (6.6 \times 10^{-34} J \cdot sec)(1 \times 10^{13} sec^{-1})$$

$$= 6.6 \times 10^{-21} J$$

134. (B)

The IR band is between $7 \times 10^{-5} cm$ and about 10^{-2} cm.

135. (A)

$$\bar{v} = R_H \times \left(\frac{1}{n_1^2} \ \frac{1}{n_2^2} \right)$$

$$23,032 = 109,678 \left(\frac{1}{n_1^2} \ \frac{1}{n_2^2} \right)$$

$$\frac{23,032}{109,678} = \left(\frac{1}{n_1^2} \ \frac{1}{n_2^2} \right)$$

(A) is the only plausible answer because (B) to (D) would yield $v < \frac{1}{2} R_H$.

136. (B)

The free radical synthesis is unselective between repeating units I, II, and III. More selective syntheses can be made with metal catalysts.

Practice Exam 5

Answer Sheet: Practice Exam 5

1. Ⓐ Ⓑ Ⓒ Ⓓ Ⓔ
2. Ⓐ Ⓑ Ⓒ Ⓓ Ⓔ
3. Ⓐ Ⓑ Ⓒ Ⓓ Ⓔ
4. Ⓐ Ⓑ Ⓒ Ⓓ Ⓔ
5. Ⓐ Ⓑ Ⓒ Ⓓ Ⓔ
6. Ⓐ Ⓑ Ⓒ Ⓓ Ⓔ
7. Ⓐ Ⓑ Ⓒ Ⓓ Ⓔ
8. Ⓐ Ⓑ Ⓒ Ⓓ Ⓔ
9. Ⓐ Ⓑ Ⓒ Ⓓ Ⓔ
10. Ⓐ Ⓑ Ⓒ Ⓓ Ⓔ
11. Ⓐ Ⓑ Ⓒ Ⓓ Ⓔ
12. Ⓐ Ⓑ Ⓒ Ⓓ Ⓔ
13. Ⓐ Ⓑ Ⓒ Ⓓ Ⓔ
14. Ⓐ Ⓑ Ⓒ Ⓓ Ⓔ
15. Ⓐ Ⓑ Ⓒ Ⓓ Ⓔ
16. Ⓐ Ⓑ Ⓒ Ⓓ Ⓔ
17. Ⓐ Ⓑ Ⓒ Ⓓ Ⓔ
18. Ⓐ Ⓑ Ⓒ Ⓓ Ⓔ
19. Ⓐ Ⓑ Ⓒ Ⓓ Ⓔ
20. Ⓐ Ⓑ Ⓒ Ⓓ Ⓔ
21. Ⓐ Ⓑ Ⓒ Ⓓ Ⓔ
22. Ⓐ Ⓑ Ⓒ Ⓓ Ⓔ
23. Ⓐ Ⓑ Ⓒ Ⓓ Ⓔ
24. Ⓐ Ⓑ Ⓒ Ⓓ Ⓔ
25. Ⓐ Ⓑ Ⓒ Ⓓ Ⓔ
26. Ⓐ Ⓑ Ⓒ Ⓓ Ⓔ
27. Ⓐ Ⓑ Ⓒ Ⓓ Ⓔ
28. Ⓐ Ⓑ Ⓒ Ⓓ Ⓔ
29. Ⓐ Ⓑ Ⓒ Ⓓ Ⓔ
30. Ⓐ Ⓑ Ⓒ Ⓓ Ⓔ
31. Ⓐ Ⓑ Ⓒ Ⓓ Ⓔ
32. Ⓐ Ⓑ Ⓒ Ⓓ Ⓔ
33. Ⓐ Ⓑ Ⓒ Ⓓ Ⓔ

34. Ⓐ Ⓑ Ⓒ Ⓓ Ⓔ
35. Ⓐ Ⓑ Ⓒ Ⓓ Ⓔ
36. Ⓐ Ⓑ Ⓒ Ⓓ Ⓔ
37. Ⓐ Ⓑ Ⓒ Ⓓ Ⓔ
38. Ⓐ Ⓑ Ⓒ Ⓓ Ⓔ
39. Ⓐ Ⓑ Ⓒ Ⓓ Ⓔ
40. Ⓐ Ⓑ Ⓒ Ⓓ Ⓔ
41. Ⓐ Ⓑ Ⓒ Ⓓ Ⓔ
42. Ⓐ Ⓑ Ⓒ Ⓓ Ⓔ
43. Ⓐ Ⓑ Ⓒ Ⓓ Ⓔ
44. Ⓐ Ⓑ Ⓒ Ⓓ Ⓔ
45. Ⓐ Ⓑ Ⓒ Ⓓ Ⓔ
46. Ⓐ Ⓑ Ⓒ Ⓓ Ⓔ
47. Ⓐ Ⓑ Ⓒ Ⓓ Ⓔ
48. Ⓐ Ⓑ Ⓒ Ⓓ Ⓔ
49. Ⓐ Ⓑ Ⓒ Ⓓ Ⓔ
50. Ⓐ Ⓑ Ⓒ Ⓓ Ⓔ
51. Ⓐ Ⓑ Ⓒ Ⓓ Ⓔ
52. Ⓐ Ⓑ Ⓒ Ⓓ Ⓔ
53. Ⓐ Ⓑ Ⓒ Ⓓ Ⓔ
54. Ⓐ Ⓑ Ⓒ Ⓓ Ⓔ
55. Ⓐ Ⓑ Ⓒ Ⓓ Ⓔ
56. Ⓐ Ⓑ Ⓒ Ⓓ Ⓔ
57. Ⓐ Ⓑ Ⓒ Ⓓ Ⓔ
58. Ⓐ Ⓑ Ⓒ Ⓓ Ⓔ
59. Ⓐ Ⓑ Ⓒ Ⓓ Ⓔ
60. Ⓐ Ⓑ Ⓒ Ⓓ Ⓔ
61. Ⓐ Ⓑ Ⓒ Ⓓ Ⓔ
62. Ⓐ Ⓑ Ⓒ Ⓓ Ⓔ
63. Ⓐ Ⓑ Ⓒ Ⓓ Ⓔ
64. Ⓐ Ⓑ Ⓒ Ⓓ Ⓔ
65. Ⓐ Ⓑ Ⓒ Ⓓ Ⓔ
66. Ⓐ Ⓑ Ⓒ Ⓓ Ⓔ

67. Ⓐ Ⓑ Ⓒ Ⓓ Ⓔ
68. Ⓐ Ⓑ Ⓒ Ⓓ Ⓔ
69. Ⓐ Ⓑ Ⓒ Ⓓ Ⓔ
70. Ⓐ Ⓑ Ⓒ Ⓓ Ⓔ
71. Ⓐ Ⓑ Ⓒ Ⓓ Ⓔ
72. Ⓐ Ⓑ Ⓒ Ⓓ Ⓔ
73. Ⓐ Ⓑ Ⓒ Ⓓ Ⓔ
74. Ⓐ Ⓑ Ⓒ Ⓓ Ⓔ
75. Ⓐ Ⓑ Ⓒ Ⓓ Ⓔ
76. Ⓐ Ⓑ Ⓒ Ⓓ Ⓔ
77. Ⓐ Ⓑ Ⓒ Ⓓ Ⓔ
78. Ⓐ Ⓑ Ⓒ Ⓓ Ⓔ
79. Ⓐ Ⓑ Ⓒ Ⓓ Ⓔ
80. Ⓐ Ⓑ Ⓒ Ⓓ Ⓔ
81. Ⓐ Ⓑ Ⓒ Ⓓ Ⓔ
82. Ⓐ Ⓑ Ⓒ Ⓓ Ⓔ
83. Ⓐ Ⓑ Ⓒ Ⓓ Ⓔ
84. Ⓐ Ⓑ Ⓒ Ⓓ Ⓔ
85. Ⓐ Ⓑ Ⓒ Ⓓ Ⓔ
86. Ⓐ Ⓑ Ⓒ Ⓓ Ⓔ
87. Ⓐ Ⓑ Ⓒ Ⓓ Ⓔ
88. Ⓐ Ⓑ Ⓒ Ⓓ Ⓔ
89. Ⓐ Ⓑ Ⓒ Ⓓ Ⓔ
90. Ⓐ Ⓑ Ⓒ Ⓓ Ⓔ
91. Ⓐ Ⓑ Ⓒ Ⓓ Ⓔ
92. Ⓐ Ⓑ Ⓒ Ⓓ Ⓔ
93. Ⓐ Ⓑ Ⓒ Ⓓ Ⓔ
94. Ⓐ Ⓑ Ⓒ Ⓓ Ⓔ
95. Ⓐ Ⓑ Ⓒ Ⓓ Ⓔ
96. Ⓐ Ⓑ Ⓒ Ⓓ Ⓔ
97. Ⓐ Ⓑ Ⓒ Ⓓ Ⓔ
98. Ⓐ Ⓑ Ⓒ Ⓓ Ⓔ
99. Ⓐ Ⓑ Ⓒ Ⓓ Ⓔ

Continued

Answer Sheet: Practice Exam 5 (Continued)

100. Ⓐ Ⓑ Ⓒ Ⓓ Ⓔ
101. Ⓐ Ⓑ Ⓒ Ⓓ Ⓔ
102. Ⓐ Ⓑ Ⓒ Ⓓ Ⓔ
103. Ⓐ Ⓑ Ⓒ Ⓓ Ⓔ
104. Ⓐ Ⓑ Ⓒ Ⓓ Ⓔ
105. Ⓐ Ⓑ Ⓒ Ⓓ Ⓔ
106. Ⓐ Ⓑ Ⓒ Ⓓ Ⓔ
107. Ⓐ Ⓑ Ⓒ Ⓓ Ⓔ
108. Ⓐ Ⓑ Ⓒ Ⓓ Ⓔ
109. Ⓐ Ⓑ Ⓒ Ⓓ Ⓔ
110. Ⓐ Ⓑ Ⓒ Ⓓ Ⓔ
111. Ⓐ Ⓑ Ⓒ Ⓓ Ⓔ
112. Ⓐ Ⓑ Ⓒ Ⓓ Ⓔ

113. Ⓐ Ⓑ Ⓒ Ⓓ Ⓔ
114. Ⓐ Ⓑ Ⓒ Ⓓ Ⓔ
115. Ⓐ Ⓑ Ⓒ Ⓓ Ⓔ
116. Ⓐ Ⓑ Ⓒ Ⓓ Ⓔ
117. Ⓐ Ⓑ Ⓒ Ⓓ Ⓔ
118. Ⓐ Ⓑ Ⓒ Ⓓ Ⓔ
119. Ⓐ Ⓑ Ⓒ Ⓓ Ⓔ
120. Ⓐ Ⓑ Ⓒ Ⓓ Ⓔ
121. Ⓐ Ⓑ Ⓒ Ⓓ Ⓔ
122. Ⓐ Ⓑ Ⓒ Ⓓ Ⓔ
123. Ⓐ Ⓑ Ⓒ Ⓓ Ⓔ
124. Ⓐ Ⓑ Ⓒ Ⓓ Ⓔ
125. Ⓐ Ⓑ Ⓒ Ⓓ Ⓔ

126. Ⓐ Ⓑ Ⓒ Ⓓ Ⓔ
127. Ⓐ Ⓑ Ⓒ Ⓓ Ⓔ
128. Ⓐ Ⓑ Ⓒ Ⓓ Ⓔ
129. Ⓐ Ⓑ Ⓒ Ⓓ Ⓔ
130. Ⓐ Ⓑ Ⓒ Ⓓ Ⓔ
131. Ⓐ Ⓑ Ⓒ Ⓓ Ⓔ
132. Ⓐ Ⓑ Ⓒ Ⓓ Ⓔ
133. Ⓐ Ⓑ Ⓒ Ⓓ Ⓔ
134. Ⓐ Ⓑ Ⓒ Ⓓ Ⓔ
135. Ⓐ Ⓑ Ⓒ Ⓓ Ⓔ
136. Ⓐ Ⓑ Ⓒ Ⓓ Ⓔ

Practice Exam 5

Time: **170 Minutes**
       136 Questions

Directions: *Choose the best answer for each question and mark the letter of your selection on the corresponding answer sheet.*

1. Which of the following postulates was *not* part of Bohr's model of the atom?

    (A) The quantization of electromagnetic radiation
    (B) The quantization of an electron's angular momentum
    (C) The quantization of an electron's spin
    (D) The nuclear model of the atom
    (E) That electrons travel in circular orbits

2. Uranium-238 decays to thorium-234 by the process of

    (A) alpha radiation   (D) fission
    (B) beta radiation   (E) fusion
    (C) gamma radiation

3. Which of the following nuclei might be measured with nuclear magnetic resonance?

    (A) $^{12}_{6}C$ (D) $^{20}_{10}Ne$
    (B) $^{18}_{8}O$ (E) $^{52}_{24}Cr$
    (C) $^{19}_{9}F$

4. A solution 0.10M in H_2CO_3 and 0.10M in $NaHCO_3$ is made, and then 0.01 mole of HCl is added to a liter of this solution. The pH of the resulting solution should be closest to which of the following? (Note: For H_2CO_3, pKa = 6.37.)

    (A) 6.37   (D) 4.35
    (B) 6.28   (E) 2.10
    (C) 5.84

5. The oxidation states of Ni atomic number (a.n.) = 28 most closely resemble those of

    (A) Pd, a.n.45   (D) Cu, a.n.27
    (B) Pt, a.n.78   (E) Zn, a.n.30
    (C) Fe, a.n.26

6. Which of the following pairs of representations does not indicate the same molecule?

(A)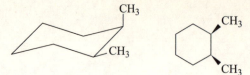

(B)

(C)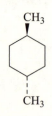

(D)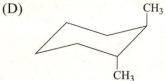

(E) $(CH_3)_3C$ ⬡ $C(CH_3)_3$ $(CH_3)_3C$ ⬡ $C(CH_3)_3$

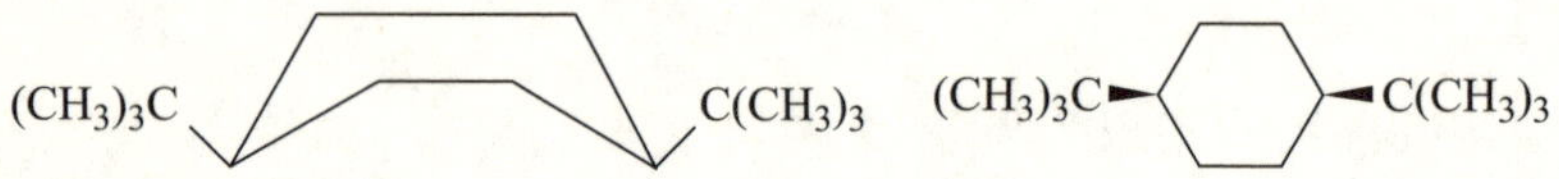

7. Which of the following is *not* a free radical process?

(A) Cracking of alkanes
(B) High-temperature polymerization of ethylene
(C) Alkene $+ Br_2 \rightarrow$ dibromoalkane
(D) Photochemical isomerization of alkenes
(E) Norrish reactions

8. Which of the following is (are) valid as resonance structures of the pentadienyl cation?

I. $CH_2 = CH - CH = CH - \overset{\oplus}{C}H_2$

II. $CH_2 = CH - \overset{\oplus}{C}H - CH = CH_2$

III. $CH_3 - CH = CH - CH = \overset{\oplus}{C}H$

IV. $CH_2 = CH - CH = \overset{\oplus}{C} - CH_3$

(A) I only   (D) III and IV only
(B) I and II only   (E) I, II, III, and IV
(C) II and III only

9. Which of the following is the most stable carbocation?

(A) $(CH_3)_3C^{\oplus}$

(C) [benzene ring]—$CH_2^{\oplus}$

(E) [cycloheptatrienyl cation structure] $+$

(B) $CH_3^{\oplus}$

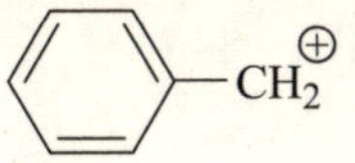

(D) 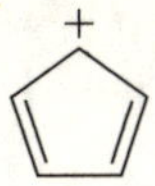 [cyclopentadienyl cation structure] $+$

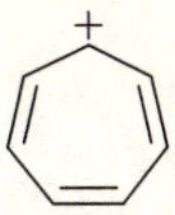

10. $CH_3CH_2I + Br^- \xrightarrow{\text{acetone}} CH_3CH_2Br^+I^-$

In the transition state of the reaction above, the C—C bond is formed by the overlap of which types of orbitals?

(A) sp^3—sp^3

(D) sp^3—s

(B) sp^3—sp^2

(E) sp^3—p

(C) sp^3—sp

11.

[structure: C with D and H, CH₃CH₂ and Br] $+$ KI $\xrightarrow{\text{acetone}}$

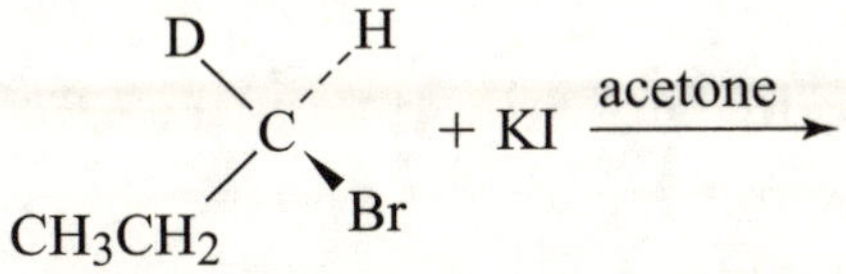

The reaction above goes to completion and shows second-order kinetics. The major product is

(A) $CH_3CH=CH_2$

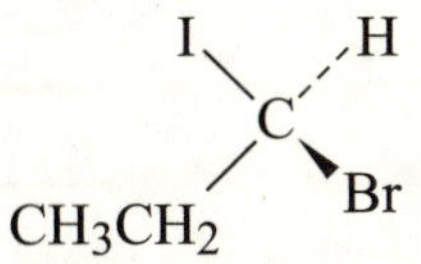

(D) 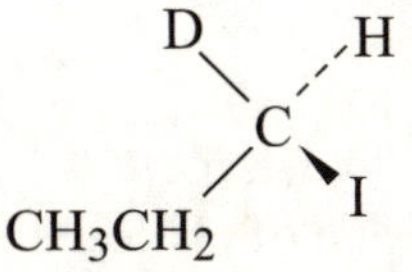 [structure: C with D and H, CH₃CH₂ and I]

(B) [structure: C with D and I, CH₃CH₂ and Br]

(C) [structure: C with I and H, CH₃CH₂ and Br]

(E) 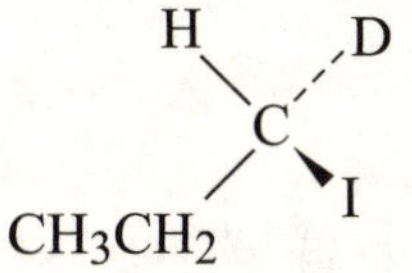 [structure: C with H and D, CH₃CH₂ and I]

12.

[structure: cyclohexane with Cl] $\xrightarrow[\text{ether}]{\text{Mg}}$ $\xrightarrow{CH_3COCH_3}$ $\xrightarrow{H^+, H_2O}$ X

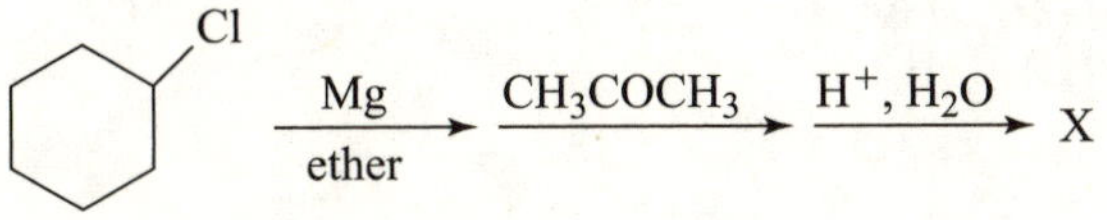

Product X for the reaction above is

(A) [structure: cyclohexane with CH₂C(=O)CH₃]

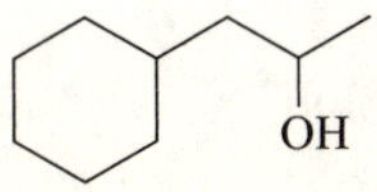

(C) 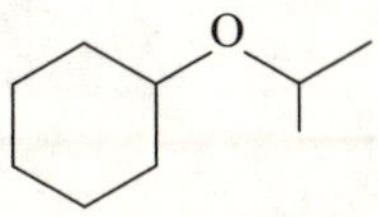 [structure: cyclohexane with O-isopropyl]

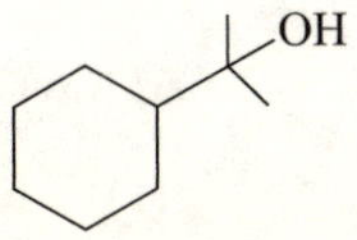

(E) 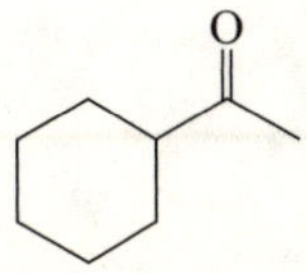 [structure: cyclohexane with C(=O)CH₃]

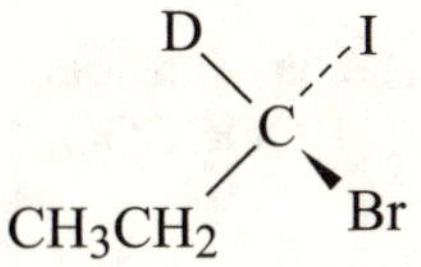

(B) 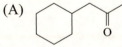 [structure: cyclohexane with CH₂CH(OH)CH₃]

(D) [structure: cyclohexane with C(CH₃)(OH)CH₃]

13. Ethers are generally inert to which reagent(s)?

    I.   KOH   II. HBr   III. $NaBH_4$

    (A) III only
    (B) I and II only
    (C) I and III only
    (D) II and III only
    (E) I, II, and III

14. Alkynes can be partially hydrogenated to alkenes by use of metal catalysts and H_2 gas. The resulting alkenes have which stereostructure?

    (A) cis
    (B) trans
    (C) mixture of cis and trans
    (D) stereostructure varies with temperature of reaction
    (E) stereostructure varies with pressure of reaction

15. We have a solution of 0.01M in Ag^+ and 0.01M in Ca^{2+}. To selectively precipitate the silver, we could add which anion?

    (A) SO_4^{2-} ($K_{sp}CaSO_4 = 2.4 \times 10^{-5}$, $K_{sp}Ag_2SO_4 = 1.2 \times 10^{-5}$)
    (B) OH^- ($K_{sp}Ca(OH)_2 = 1.3 \times 10^{-6}$, $K_{sp}AgOH = 2.0 \times 10^{-8}$)
    (C) PO_4^{3-} ($K_{sp}Ca_3(PO_4)_2 = 1.3 \times 10^{-32}$, $K_{sp}Ag_3PO_4 = 1.8 \times 10^{-18}$)
    (D) Any of the above
    (E) None of the above

16. For oxalic acid, HOOCCOOH, $pK_{a1} = 1.23$ and $pk_{a2} = 4.19$. Suppose you have an aqueous solution of oxalic acid. Which value of pH leads to the greatest concentration of $[HOOCCOO^-]$?

    (A) 1.23
    (B) 4.19
    (C) 7.55
    (D) 2.71
    (E) 14.00

17. Which of the following is the strongest Lewis base?

    (A) BH_3
    (B) CH_4
    (C) NH_3
    (D) H_2O
    (E) HF

18. How many orbitals exist with principal quantum number 3?

    (A) 2
    (B) 3
    (C) 4
    (D) 8
    (E) 9

19. Which of the following nuclei might be inclined toward spontaneous fission?

    (A) ^3_1H
    (B) $^{14}_6C$
    (C) $^{222}_{86}Rn$
    (D) $^{238}_{92}U$
    (E) $^{251}_{98}Cf$

20. Which of the following represents a stable nucleus?

    (A) $^{239}_{94}Pu$ (D) $^{97}_{48}Tc$
    (B) $^{210}_{85}At$ (E) $^{14}_{6}C$
    (C) $^{118}_{50}Sn$

21. Which element has the highest second ionization energy?

    (A) He   (D) Cs
    (B) Li   (E) I
    (C) F

22. Which of the following is an ionic oxide?

    (A) Mn_2O_7 (D) H_2O_2
    (B) ZnO   (E) H_2CrO_4
    (C) CO

23. Which of the following elements is the most electronegative?

    (A) Li   (D) Be
    (B) Na   (E) Ca
    (C) K

24. Which of the following atoms in the given oxidation state has the highest electronegativity?

    (A) Mo(II)   (D) Mo(V)
    (B) Mo(III)   (E) Mo(VI)
    (C) Mo(IV)

25. A neutral atom of $^{14}_{6}C$ contains, respectively, how many protons, neutrons, and electrons?

    (A) 6, 14, 14   (D) 6, 8, 6
    (B) 6, 14, 6   (E) 6, 8, 8
    (C) 8, 6, 6

26. The mass spectrum of CH_4 shows a small peak at an (m/e) ratio of 17. This peak is probably

    (A) due to imprecision of   (D) due to $^{12}C^1H_3^2H$
        the spectrometer   (E) None of the above
    (B) the molecular ion peak
    (C) due to $^{13}C^1H_4$

27. The differences in energy between different states of bond vibration in a molecule correspond to light in which region?

    (A) Microwave   (D) Ultraviolet
    (B) Infrared   (E) X-ray
    (C) Visible

28. A student weighs an amount of NaCl placed on a piece of filter paper. The paper weighs 0.455g and the total weight is 11.085g. She dissolves the salt in distilled water in a 200ml volumetric flask and then adds water to the line. What is the concentration of NaCl in moles/liter (atomic weight Na = 22.99, atomic weight Cl = 35.45)?

(A) $\dfrac{(11.085 - .455)(22.99 + 35.45)}{200}$

(D) $\dfrac{(11.085 - .455)}{(22.99 + 35.45)} \times \dfrac{1000}{200}$

(B) $\dfrac{(11.085 - .455)(22.99 + 35.45)}{200} \times 1000$

(E) $\dfrac{(11.085 - .455)}{(22.99 + 35.45)} \times \dfrac{200}{1000}$

(C) $\dfrac{(11.085 - .455)}{(22.99 + 35.45)} \times \dfrac{1}{200}$

29. A student measures a phenomenon seven times and obtains these results: 10, 14, 16, 11, 17, 14, 9. The difference between the median and the mean of these numbers is

(A) 1 (C) 4 (E) 6
(B) 0 (D) 5

30. A student isolates 35.8g of AgCl from a photographic emultion. What is the maximum amount of silver metal he could recover from this (atomic weight Ag = 108, atomic weight Cl = 35.5)?

(A) 17.9g (C) 21.6g (E) 0.6g
(B) 26.9g (D) 0.2g

31.

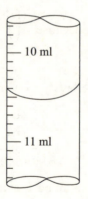

10 ml

11 ml

The burret above reads:

(A) 11.45ml (C) 10.5ml (E) 10.4ml
(B) 10.54ml (D) 10.40ml

32. 50ml of a solution of H_2SO_4 with unknown concentration is titrated to the phenolphthalein endpoint with 10.0ml of 1.00M of NaOH. The concentration of the H_2SO_4 is

(A) 5.0M (C) 0.5M (E) 0.1M
(B) 1.0M (D) 0.2M

33. Which parameter of a chemical reaction will change with the use of a catalyst?

    (A) ΔG, the change in Gibbs energy
    (B) ΔS, the change in entropy
    (C) K_{eq}, the equilibrium constant
    (D) k, the rate constant
    (E) ΔA, the change in Helmholtz energy

34. Which of the following are components of the kinetic theory model of gases?

    I. The gas is a collection of particles in constant random motion.

    II. The particles have negligible size.

    III. The particles do not interact except by elastic collisions.

    (A) I only
    (B) I and II only
    (C) I and III only
    (D) II and III only
    (E) I, II, and III

35. The Maxwell distribution of speeds of particles in an ideal gas ($f(v)$) is proportional to which of the following expressions (m is the mass of a single particle)?

    (A) $\exp(-mv^2/2kT)$
    (B) $\exp(-mv^2/2RT)$
    (C) $\exp(-mv/2kT)$
    (D) $\exp(-mv/2RT)$
    (E) $\exp(-mv/T)$

36. The existence of H_2^{2-} is not possible because

    (A) it would be disproportioned.
    (B) it would be radioactive.
    (C) it would violate the Pauli exclusion principle.
    (D) no H—H bond would form.
    (E) hydrogen is too electropositive.

37. $$A \xrightarrow{\text{STP}} B$$

    $\Delta G°$ for the reaction above is 15 kJ/mol. At standard conditions, the reaction will

    (A) be endothermic.
    (B) be exothermic.
    (C) proceed slowly.
    (D) proceed quickly.
    (E) not go forward.

38. At 25°C the entropy of diamond is 2.44 $JK^{-1} mol^{-1}$ and the entropy of diamond-structure tin is 44.8 $JK^{-1} mol^{-1}$. As the temperature is reduced to 0°K, the difference in entropy between these substances will

    (A) increase to infinity.
    (B) increase to a finite number.
    (C) remain constant.
    (D) decrease to a nonzero number.
    (E) decrease to zero.

39.
$$C_2H_{6(g)} + \frac{7}{2}O_{2(g)} \rightarrow 2CO_{2(g)} + 3H_2O_{2(l)}$$

	ΔH_f°(kJ/mol)
$C_2H_{6(g)}$	-85
$CO_2(g)$	-394
$H_2O_{(l)}$	-286

Given the ΔH_f° values above, ΔH° for the reaction above is

(A) $\Delta H^\circ = -85 + 394 + 286$
(B) $\Delta H^\circ = -394 - 286 + 85$
(C) $\Delta H^\circ = -85 - 2(-394) - 3(-286)$
(D) $\Delta H^\circ = 2(-394) + 3(-286) - (-85)$
(E) ΔH° cannot be calculated with the given information

40. Which of the following is an intensive property of a system?

(A) p, the pressure
(B) m, the mass
(C) H, the enthalpy
(D) V, the volume
(E) None of the above

41. Which of the following is *not* a state function of a system?

(A) H, the enthalpy
(B) S, the entropy
(C) w, the work
(D) p, the pressure
(E) A, the Helmholtz energy

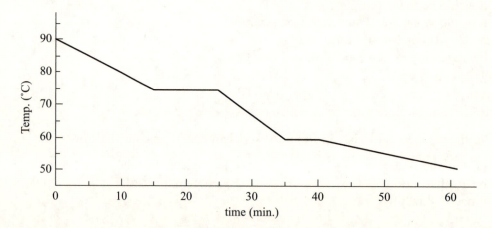

The graph above is a cooling curve for compound Y, beginning with gaseous Y. Use this curve to answer questions 42, 43, and 44.

42. The melting point of compound Y is

(A) 90°C
(B) 75°C
(C) 60°C
(D) 50°C
(E) None of the above

43. If the graph represents a 2 mole sample of the compound Y losing heat at a rate of 100 calories/min., what is the heat of vaporization of Y?

    (A) 250 cal./mol.
    (B) 500 cal./mol.
    (C) 750 cal./mol.

    (D) 1000 cal./mol.
    (E) 1500 cal./mol.

44. Given the conditions of question 43 and that the sample is at constant pressure, what is the constant-pressure heat capacity of liquid Y?

    (A) 33 cal//°C · mol.
    (B) 50 cal/°C · mol.
    (C) 67 cal/°C · mol.

    (D) 100 cal/°C · mol.
    (E) 200 cal/°C · mol.

45.

    The compound above is an important component of

    (A) protein
    (B) DNA

    (C) heme
    (D) cellulose

    (E) aspirin

46. Which of the following Kekulé structures is the most likely representation of ozone?

    (A) $O = O = O$

    (B) $\overset{\ominus}{O} - \overset{\oplus}{O} - \overset{\ominus}{O}$

    (C)

    (D) $\overset{\oplus}{O} - \overset{\ominus}{O} = O$

    (E) $O = \overset{\oplus}{O} - \overset{\ominus}{O}$

47. The HXH bond angle is greatest at which of the following compounds?

    (A) CH_4
    (B) NH_3

    (C) H_2O
    (D) PH_3

    (E) H_2S

48. Which of the indicated bonds is the shortest?

    (A) $CH_3 - H$
    (B) $CH_3 - CH_3$
    (C) $CH_3 - NH_2$

    (D) $CH_3 - OH$
    (E) $CH_3 - F$

49.

$$A \xrightarrow[\text{10 atm.}]{\text{catalyst}} B$$

For the reaction above, a plot of the concentration of A as a function of time yields a straight line. The rate according to which this reaction takes place is of

(A) zero order in A.
(B) first order in A.
(C) second order in A.
(D) third order in A.
(E) fourth order in A.

50.

cyclohexene + $Br_2 \rightarrow$ dibromocyclohexane

Which of the following represents the most stable conformation of the product of the reaction above?

(A)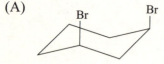

(B)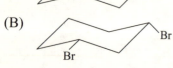

(C)

(D)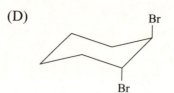

(E)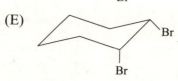

51. Entropy and randomness are related by which of the following models?

(A) Statistical mechanics
(B) Classical thermodynamics
(C) Quantum mechanics
(D) Kinetic theory of gases
(E) Intuition only

52. Which of the following is *not* a properly balanced redox reaction?

(A) $5H_2O + 3SO_3^{2-} + 2CrO_4^{2-} \rightarrow 3SO_4^{2-} + 2Cr(OH)_3 + 4OH^-$
(B) $6Fe^{2+} + ClO_3^- + 6H^+ \rightarrow 6Fe^{3+} + Cl^- + 3H_2O$
(C) $2CoCl_2 + 4OH^- + OCl^- + H_2O \rightarrow 2Co(OH)_3 + 5Cl^-$
(D) $3I_2 + 4Cr_2O_7^{2-} + 2OH^+ \rightarrow 6IO_3^- + 8Cr^{3+} + 10H_2O$
(E) $2MnO_4^- + 3H_2O_2 \rightarrow 2MnO_2 + 3O_2 + 2H_2O + 2OH^-$

53.

$$N_{2(g)} + 3H_{2(g)} \rightleftharpoons 2NH_{3(g)}$$

$\Delta H^\circ_{298} = -46.19 \text{ kJ} \cdot \text{mol}^{-1}$ for the reaction above. Which statement is *true* about the equilibrium constant Keq for this reaction?

(A) Keq increases with increasing temperature.
(B) Keq decreases with increasing temperature.
(C) Keq increases with increasing pressure.
(D) Keq decreases with increasing pressure.
(E) Keq is independent, of temperature and pressure.

54.

Half-reaction	Standard Reduction Potentials
$Fe^{2+} + 2e^- \rightarrow Fe$	-0.41
$Cu^{2+} + 2e^- \rightarrow Cu$	0.34
$Ni^{2+} + 2e^- \rightarrow Ni$	-0.23
$Zn^{2+} + 2e^- \rightarrow Zn$	-0.76

Refer to the table above. Which metal(s) could be used as "sacrificial metal" to prevent corrosion of iron?

(A) Cu only
(B) Ni only
(C) Zn only
(D) Cu and Ni only
(E) Ni and Zn only

55. A certain reaction has an equilibrium constant of 10 at 300°K and 100 at 400°K. The ratio of ΔG at 300°K to ΔG at 400°K is

(A) 1/10
(B) 3/8
(C) 1/2
(D) 3/4
(E) 2

56.
$$2SO_{2(g)} + O_{2(g)} \rightleftharpoons 2SO_{3(g)}$$

The equilibrium constant for the reaction above is 3.47. SO_2, O_2, and SO_3 are in equilibrium in a closed vessel. The partial pressures of SO_2 and O_2 are 2.0 atm. and 1.0 atm., respectively. The partial pressure of SO_3 is

(A) $2\sqrt{3.47}$ atm.
(B) $2/\sqrt{3.47}$ atm.
(C) $4\sqrt{3.47}$ atm.
(D) $3.47/4$ atm.
(E) $2(3.47)$ atm.

57. What will occur if a block of copper metal is dropped into a beaker containing a solution 1M of $ZnSO_4$?

(A) The copper will dissolve with no other change.
(B) The copper will dissolve and zinc metal will be deposited.
(C) The copper will dissolve with evolution of H_2 gas.
(D) The copper will dissolve with evolution of O_2 gas.
(E) No reaction will occur.

58.

	Standard Reduction Potential
$PbSO_{4(s)} + 2e^- \rightleftharpoons Pb_{(s)} + SO_4^{2-}$	-0.36
$PbO_{2(s)} + 4H^+ + SO_4^{2-} + 2e^- \rightleftharpoons PbSO_{4(s)} + 2H_2O$	1.69

The two half-reactions above are involved in the discharge of a lead storage battery. The potential of a single-cell lead storage battery with unit activity of the solutes is

(A) 1.33 volts
(B) 2.05 volts
(C) 2.66 volts
(D) 4.10 volts
(E) None of the above

59.

Initial Concentrations		Initial Rate
[X]	[Y]	$d[XY_2]/dt$
.010M	.010M	$1.0 \times 10^{-5} M \cdot sec^{-1}$
.030M	.010M	$1.0 \times 10^{-5} M \cdot sec^{-1}$
.030M	.030M	$9.0 \times 10^{-5} \cdot sec^{-1}$

The rate data above was measured for the reaction $X + 2Y \rightarrow XY_2$. The initial rate of XY_2 formation is

(A) first order in both X and Y.
(B) zero order in X and first order in Y.
(C) zero order in X and second order in Y.
(D) first order in X and second order in Y.
(E) second order in both X and Y.

60. The rate constant for the rection $X + 2Y \rightarrow XY_2$ above is

(A) $1.0 \times 10^{-3} sec^{-1}$
(B) $1.0 \times 10^{-5} M sec^{-1}$
(C) $1.0 \times 10^{-1} M^{-1} sec^{-1}$
(D) $9 \times 10^{-3} M^{-1} sec^{-1}$
(E) $9 \times 10^{-3} M^{-2} sec^{-1}$

61. For the reaction $X + 2Y \rightarrow XY_2$ above, the most likely rate-limiting set is

(A) $\cdot Y + \cdot Y \rightarrow Y_2$
(B) $X + \cdot Y \rightarrow XY$
(C) $X + \cdot Y + \cdot Y \rightarrow XY_2$
(D) $XY + \cdot Y \rightarrow XY_2$
(E) $Y_2 + X \rightarrow XY_2$

62. Carbon-14 decays to nitrogen-14 and has a half-life of 5,570 years. The initial decay rate of C-14 is 15.3 cpm/g. A sample of charcoal from an ancient cave shows a C-14 decay rate of 4.1 cpm/g. How old is the charcoal?

(A) $t = 5570 \left(\dfrac{15.3}{4.1} \right)$ years

(B) $t = 5570 \left(\dfrac{15.3 - 4.1}{15.3} \right)$ years

(C) $t = 5570 \left(\dfrac{1}{\ln 2} \right) \ln \left(\dfrac{15.3 - 4.1}{15.3} \right)$ years

(D) $t = 5570 \left(\dfrac{1}{\ln 2} \right) \ln \left(\dfrac{15.3}{4.1} \right)$ years

(E) $t = 5570 \ln \left(\dfrac{15.3}{4.1} \right)$ years

63. Two energy states are available to a system of particles in thermal equilibrium. The difference in energy between these states is $5.0 \text{ kJ} \cdot \text{mol}^{-1}$. The temperature is 0°C. According to the Boltzman distribution, what proportion of particles will be in the higher energy state (take $R = 8.3 \text{ J} \cdot \text{K}^{-1} \cdot \text{mol}^{-1}$)?

(A) $\exp(-8.3 \times 273/5.0 \times 1000)$
(B) $\exp(8.3 \times 273/5.0 \times 1000)$
(C) $\exp(5.0 \times 1000/8.3 \times 273)$
(D) $\exp(-5.0 \times 1000/8.3 \times 273)$
(E) $\exp(-5.0 \times 1000 \times 273/8.3)$

64. The root mean square velocity of particles of an ideal gas is directly proportional to which of the following expressions of absolute temperature?

(A) T^3 (D) $\sqrt{T}$
(B) T^2 (E) $\sqrt[3]{T}$
(C) T

65. For an atom of hydrogen, which of the following pairs of orbitals have equal energies (ignoring electron spin)?

I. $1s, 2s$ II. $2p_0, 2p_{+1}$ III. $2s, 2p_0$

(A) II only   (D) I and II only
(B) II and III only   (E) I, II, and III
(C) I only

66.

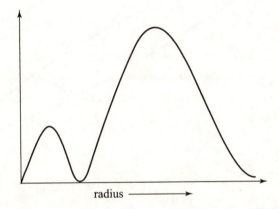

radius →

The graph above represents a radial probability distribution for an electron in an atomic orbital. Which of the following orbitals might this graph represent?

(A) 2p   (D) 1s
(B) 3p   (E) 4s
(C) 4p

67. 3-pentanol is produced by which of the following reactions?

I. $CH_3CH_2Br \xrightarrow[\text{ether}]{Mg} \xrightarrow{CH_3CH_2CHO} \xrightarrow[\text{H}_2\text{O}]{H^+}$

II. $HC \equiv CH \xrightarrow{NaNH_2} \xrightarrow{CH_3CH_2CHO} \xrightarrow[\text{H}_2\text{O}]{H^+}$

III. $(CH_3CH_2)_2CO \xrightarrow[\text{ether}]{LiAlH_4} \xrightarrow[\text{H}_2\text{O}]{H^+}$

(A) I only
(B) I and II only
(C) I and III only
(D) II and III only
(E) I, II, and III only

68. Consider a mixture of two liquids A and B in a nonideal solution. Under which conditions will Henry's Law accurately describe the vapor pressure of component B?

(A) The vapor pressures of pure A and pure B are very similar.
(B) The vapor pressure of pure A is very low.
(C) The vapor pressure of pure B is very low.
(D) The mole fraction of B in the mixture is close to zero.
(E) The mole fraction of B in the mixture is close to unity.

69.

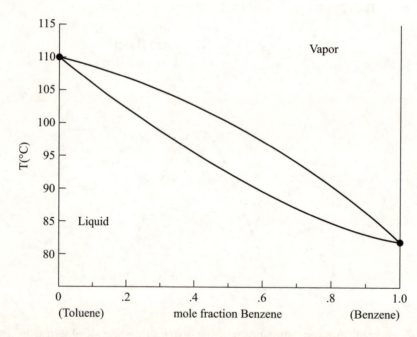

The graph above is a temperature-composition diagram for mixtures of benzene and toluene at 1 atm. pressure. Given a 50 mole % mixture of the two liquids, we could obtain a mixture that is 25 mole % benzene by

(A) simple distillation.
(B) fractional distillation with two theoretical plates.
(C) fractional distillation with three theoretical plates.
(D) boiling in an open flask until the boiling point reaches 100°C.
(E) boiling in an open flask until the boiling point reaches 106°C.

70.

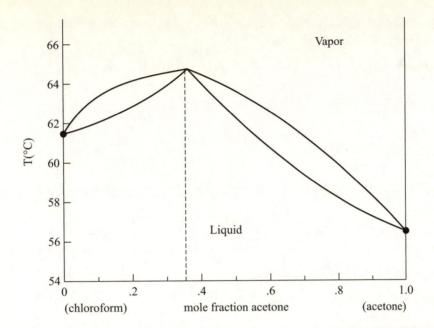

The graph above is a temperature-composition diagram for mixtures of chloroform and acetone at 1 atm. pressure. Efficient fractional distillation of 4:1 mixture of chloroform and acetone will yield

(A) pure chloroform.

(B) pure acetone.

(C) 35 mole % acetone in chloroform.

(D) 35 mole % chloroform in acetone.

(E) None of the above

71. Under conditions of constant temperature and pressure, a system will be in equilibrium when which of the following quantities is at a minimum?

(A) Internal energy (E or U)

(B) Enthalpy (H)

(C) Helmholtz energy (A)

(D) Gibbs energy (G)

(E) None of the above

72. The Helmholtz energy, A, is defined by which expression?

(A) $PV - TS$

(B) $H - E$

(C) $E + PV$

(D) $q + PV$

(E) $E - TS$

73. One liter of an ideal gas at 10 atm pressure is allowed to expand irreversibly against a pressure of one atm. The temperature of the gas is held constant at 0°C. Which of the following is the correct value of q (the heat entering the system) for this expansion (1 liter · atm = 101J)?

(A) 909J

(B) 10.1J

(C) $[(101)\ln 10]J$

(D) zero

(E) Cannot be determined with the given information

74. The change in enthalpy (ΔH) of a system is equal to the heat flow between the system and its surroundings (q) under which conditions?

(A) Constant volume
(B) Constant pressure
(C) Constant temperature
(D) Adiabatic conditions
(E) None of the above

75.

$$CH_3COCH_3CH_2CH_2CH_2Br \xrightarrow[H^+ - H_2O]{HOCH_2CH_2OH} > \xrightarrow[ether]{Mg} > \xrightarrow{CH_3CHO} >$$

$$\xrightarrow{H_3O^+} >$$

Which of the following is the product of the series of reactions above?

(A)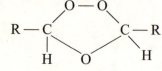

(B)

(C)

(D) Br

(E) None of the above

76. Alkenes can best be converted to alkynes by way of which intermediate?

(A)
```
        O — O
       /     \
  R — C       C — R
      |   O   |
      H       H
```

(B)
```
      O   O
      ‖   ‖
  R — C — C — R
```

(C)
```
      O
      ‖
  R — C — CH₂ — R
```

(D)
```
          BR₂
          |
  R — CH₂ — CH — R
```

(E)
```
      Br    Br
      |     |
  R — CH — CH — R
```

77. A compound with molecular formula $C_3H_6Cl_2$ shows these peaks in its NMR spectrum: δ, 1.3(triplet); δ, 2.0(octet); δ, 4.5 (triplet). The compound could be which of the following?

(A) $ClCH_2CH_2CH_2Cl$
(B) $ClCH_2CHClCH_3$
(C) $Cl_2CHCH_2CH_3$
(D) $CH_3CCl_2CH_3$
(E) None of the above

78. In the coordination compound $Fe(CO)_n$, n is most probably

(A) 4
(B) 5
(C) 6
(D) 7
(E) 8

79.

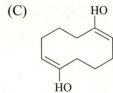

base
$\xrightarrow{\text{H}_2\text{O}}$ x

Product X for the reaction above is

(A)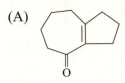

(C)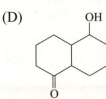

(E) No reaction occurs

(B)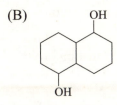

(D)
OH

O

80. In an octahedral coordination complex, the ligand field splitting energy is related to the difference in energy (10 Dq) between two groups of degenerate molecular orbitals. These two groups can be described as

(A) bonding and bonding.
(B) bonding and antibonding.
(C) antibonding and antibonding.
(D) nonbonding and bonding.
(E) nonbonding and antibonding.

81. H.G.J. Moseley demonstrated a direct relation between the frequency of X-rays emitted by an element bombarded with electrons and what characteristic of the element?

(A) Degree of ionization
(B) Electron configuration
(C) Number of unfilled d-orbitals
(D) Atomic mass
(E) Atomic number

82. In the reaction

$$^{223}_{87}\text{Fr} \rightarrow {}^{223}_{88}\text{Ra} + \text{X}$$

particle X is a(n)

(A) neutron
(B) proton
(C) alpha particle
(D) electron
(E) positron

83. The H-NMR spectrum of 1,1,2-trichloroethane should show

(A) two singlet peaks.
(B) a singlet and a doublet.
(C) two doublets.
(D) a doublet and a triplet.
(E) two triplets.

84. A chemist adds 0.1000 mole of KCl to 1.000 liter of distilled water at 25°C. The concentration of the resulting solution is

(A) 7.455M
(B) 1.000M
(C) 0.1000M

(D) >0.1000M and <1.000 M
(E) <0.1000M

85. Li^+, Na^+, and K^+ ions in acidified solution can best be separated by

(A) gas chromatography
(B) liquid chromatography
(C) thin layer chromatography

(D) ion-exchange chromatography
(E) distillation

86. The acid concentration of solution A is roughly measured to be 0.95N ± 10%. When equal amounts of solution A and a standardized 1.00M KOH solution are mixed, the resulting solution will be

(A) slightly basic
(B) slightly acidic
(C) strongly basic

(D) strongly acidic
(E) cannot tell from the information given

87. Which of the following indicators could be used in a titration of $KOH_{(aq)}$ with $HCl_{(aq)}$ without introducing an error?

I. Bromcresol green, pKa ~ 4.7

II. Bromthymol blue, pKa ~ 6.8

III. Phenolphthalein, pKa ~ 9.0

(A) I only
(B) II only
(C) III only

(D) II and III only
(E) I, II, and III

88. The largest peak in the mass spectrum of 3-ethylpentane should be at m/e

(A) 100
(B) 85

(C) 71
(D) 41

(E) 29

89. Which of the following protons will show the *smallest* downfield shift in proton-NMR?

(A) CH_3CH_2—H

(B) $(CH_3)_2CH$—H

(C) $(CH_3)_3C$—H

(D) CH_3CH—H
    |
    Br

(E) CH_2CH_2—H
    |
    Br

90. Electrons in a molecule can be promoted from σ bonding orbitals to σ^* antibonding orbitals by light "carrying" the appropriate energy. This light has wavelengths around 150nm (1.5×10^{-5}cm). Spectroscopy of compounds is difficult in this band because

    (A) it must be done in a vacuum.
    (B) generation of light at this wavelength is difficult.
    (C) the apparatus must be shielded with ten inches of lead.
    (D) it must be done at temperatures below 10°K.
    (E) it must be done at very high temperatures.

91. $$RCH{=}CH_2 + HBr \rightarrow RCH_2CH_2Br$$

    The reaction above requires the addition of

    (A) acid
    (B) $KOC(CH_3)_3$
    (C) peroxides
    (D) $Hg(OAc)_2$
    (E) reducing agents

92. Consider the ion pairs listed below. In which pair does the second ion have a larger ionic radius than the first one?

    (A) Na^+, Mg^{2+}
    (B) S^{2-}, Cl^-
    (C) Br^-, Cl^-
    (D) Cs^+, K^+
    (E) Ni^{2+}, Fe^{2+}

93.

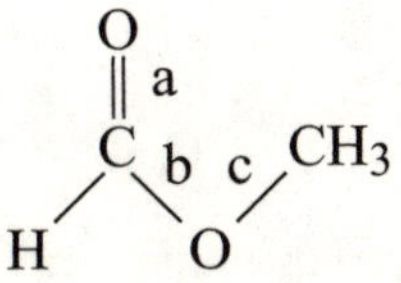

    Methyl formate has three C—O bonds, labeled in the diagram above. Which of the following is a correct list of these bonds in order of increasing length?

    (A) $a < b < c$
    (B) $a < c < b$
    (C) $b < a < c$
    (D) $b < c < a$
    (E) $c < b < a$

94. How long should a 500 A current flow, in the electrolysis of $AlCl_3$, in order to deposit 2.7g of aluminum metal at the cathode (M.W. Al = 27; Faraday's constant = 96,485 coulombs $\cdot$ mole^{-1})?

    (A) $\dfrac{2.7}{27} \times \dfrac{96,485}{} \times 500$
    (B) $\dfrac{2.7}{27} \times \dfrac{96,485}{500}$
    (C) $\dfrac{2.7}{27} \times 3 \times 96,485 \times 500$
    (D) $\dfrac{2.7}{27} \times 3 \times \dfrac{96,485}{500}$
    (E) $\dfrac{2.7}{27} \times 3 \times \dfrac{500}{96,485}$

95.

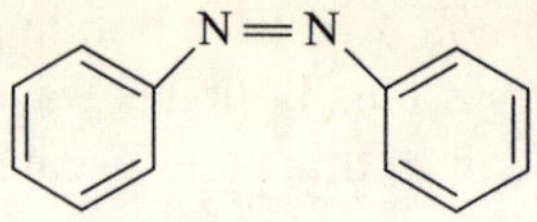

cis-azobenzene

The isomeric compound above is rarely seen because it

(A) rapidly rearranges to form

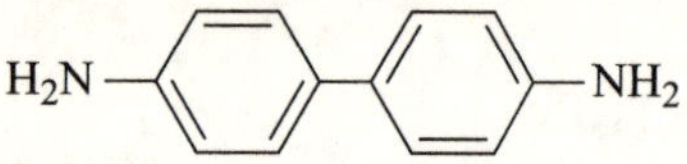

H_2N— —NH_2

(B) rapidly decomposes to N_2 and benzene
(C) oxidizes in air to nitrosobenzene
(D) is easily reduced to aniline
(E) converts easily to the trans isomer

96. The electron configuration of gallium, atomic number 31, is

(A) $[Ar]3s^23d^{10}3p^3$
(B) $[Ar]4s^23d^{10}4p^3$
(C) $[Ar]4s^23d^{10}4p^1$
(D) $[Kr]4s^23d^{10}4p^1$
(E) $[Kr]4s^23d^{10}4p^3$

97. In anhydrous HF solvent, which of the following is an acid?

(A) HNO_3
(B) ZnO
(C) BF_3
(D) H_2SO_4
(E) NH_3

98. Which of the following electron configurations is (are) correct?

I. $_{29}Cu:[Ar]4s^13d^{10}$

II. $_{46}Pd:[Kr]5s^04d^{10}$

III. $_{26}Fe:[Ar]4s^23d^54p^1$

(A) I only
(B) I and II only
(C) I and III only
(D) II and III only
(E) None of them

99. In describing his or her work, which scientist wrote, "It was . . . as if you fired a 15-inch shell at a piece of tissue paper and it came back at you."

(A) Albert Einstein
(B) J.J. Thomson
(C) Wilhelm Röntgen
(D) Marie Curie
(E) Ernest Rutherford

100. A student prepares 500ml of a 0.100M solution of HNO_2 (pKa = 3.34). The pH of the solution is then adjusted to 3.34 by addition of NaOH. What is the concentration of NO_2^-?

(A) 0.200M
(B) 0.100M
(C) 0.050M

(D) 0.010M
(E) Cannot tell from the information given

101. Which of the following pairs of compounds cannot undergo Diels-Alder cycloaddition?

(A) $CH_2 = CH - CH = CH_2$,

$$COOC_2H_5$$
$$|$$
$$C$$
$$|||$$
$$C$$
$$|$$
$$COOC_2H_5$$

(B) $CH_2 = CH - CHO$, $CH_2 = CH - CHO$

(C) 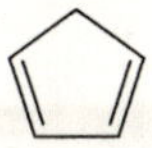 , $CH_2 = CH - COOCH_3$

(D) $CH_2 = CH - CH = CH_2$, $CH_2 = CH - CH = CH_2$
(E) $CH \equiv CH$, $CH_2 = CH_2$

102. Which ionization energy is greatest?

(A) First for Li
(B) First for Be
(C) Second for Be

(D) First for Mg
(E) Second for Mg

103. Which of the following conversions is most difficult to carry out?

(A)

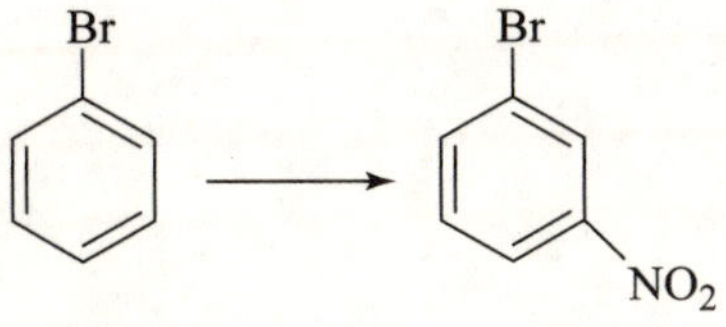

(B)

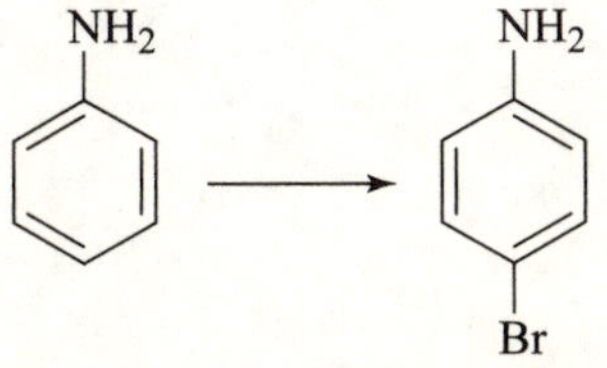

(C)

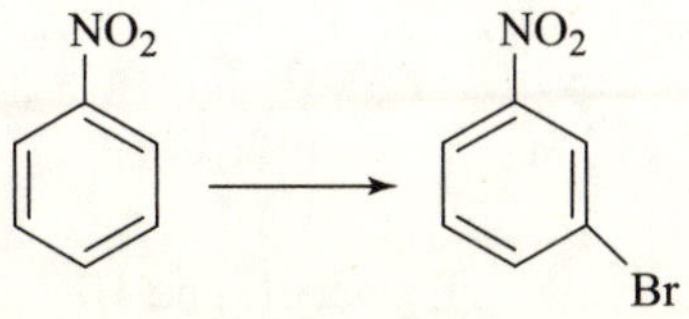

(D)

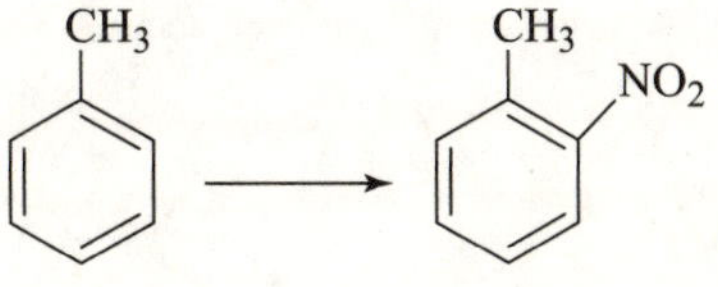

(E)

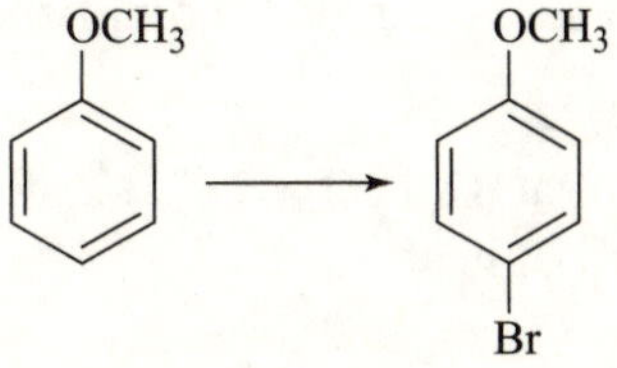

104. Which of the following is the most reactive in SN_2 reactions?

    (A) $(CH_3)_3CCN$
    (B) $(CH_3)_2CHCN$
    (C) CH_3CH_2CN

    (D) $(CH_3)_3CCl$
    (E) CH_3CH_2Cl

105.

$$CH_3COOH \longrightarrow CH_3COOCH_3$$

The conversion above can be accomplished best with which reagents and solvents?

    (A) $K^+{}^{\ominus}OCH_3$, CH_3OH
    (B) H^+, CH_2OH
    (C) $K^+{}^{\ominus}OCH_3$, H_2O

    (D) H^+, CH_3OH, H_2O
    (E) KOH, CH_3OH

106.

$$R - C \equiv N \longrightarrow R - COOH$$

The conversion above can be accomplished with

    I. H_2O, H_2SO_4 II. H_2O, KOH III. $KMnO_4$

    (A) I only
    (B) II only
    (C) III only

    (D) I or II only
    (E) I, II, or III

107. Elemental alkali metals and halides can both be prepared from their naturally occurring forms by

    (A) reduction
    (B) oxidation
    (C) acidification

    (D) ion-exchange
    (E) electrolysis

108.

The conversion above can be accomplished with

    (A) $HlCl$, H_2O
    (B) H_2NNH_2, $NaOH$, heat
    (C) H_2O_2, $NaOH$, heat

    (D) $LiAlH_4$
    (E) H_2, Pt catalyst

109. Which of the following represent(s) existing compounds?

    I. NF_5 II. PF_5 III. AsF_5

    (A) I only
    (B) II only

    (C) I and II only
    (D) II and III only

    (E) I, II, and III

110. Dichlorocarbene adds readily to propene to form

(A) $CH_3CH_2CH_2CHCl_2$

(B) 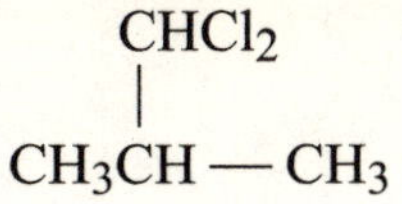
$$CH_3CH \overset{\overset{\displaystyle CHCl_2}{|}}{-} CH_3$$

(C) 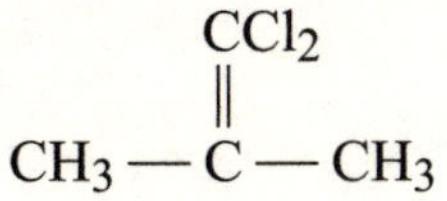
$$CH_3 - \overset{\overset{\displaystyle CCl_2}{\|}}{C} - CH_3$$

(D) $CH_3 - CHCl - CH_2Cl$

(E) 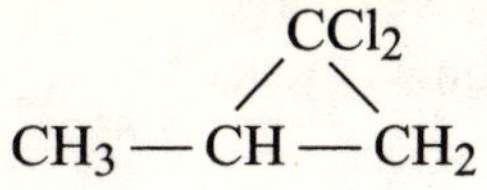
$$CH_3 - CH \overset{\displaystyle CCl_2}{\underset{\diagdown}{\diagup}} CH_2$$

111. How many different values can m_1 assume in the electron subshell designated by quantum numbers $n = 5, 1 = 4$?

(A) 3
(B) 4
(C) 5
(D) 8
(E) 9

112.

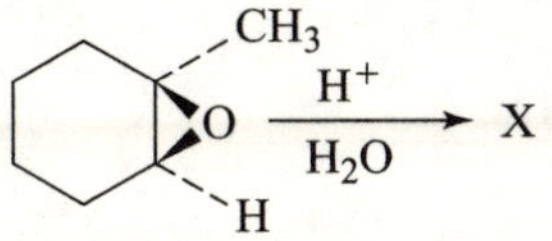

The product X for the reaction above is

(A)

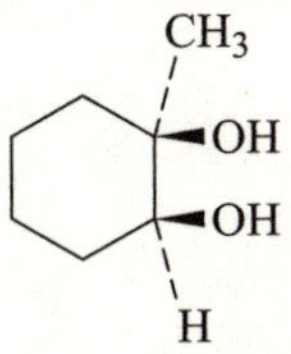

(B)

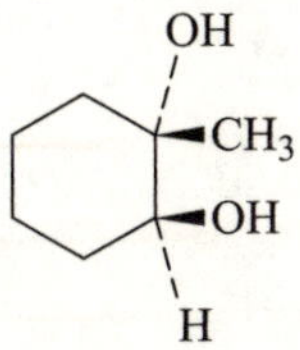

(C)

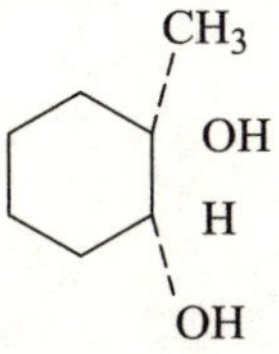

(D)

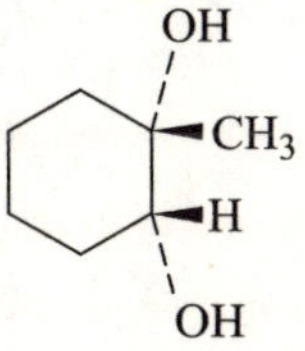

(E) No reaction occurs

113. One mole of an ideal gas expands irreversibly from a volume of 5 liters to a volume of 20 liters at a constant temperature of 3000K. ΔS for the gas in this process is

(A) (300)R ln4
(B) R ln4/300
(C) R ln4
(D) (300)R ln(.25)
(E) Cannot be determined from the information given

114. An HNMR spectrum is taken for a sample of ethanol. The spectrum shows a triplet at δ 1.2, a multiplet at δ 3.6, and a triplet at δ5.3. Which statement is *true* about this sample of ethanol?

(A) It is very pure.
(B) It is contaminated with some acid.
(C) It is contaminated with some water.
(D) It is contaminated with some base.
(E) It is contaminated with some inert solvent.

115. As a ligand, CN^- has very high ligand field strength because

    (A) it is highly electronegative
    (B) it carries a negative charge
    (C) it forms high-spin complexes

    (D) it forms π bonds with the metal atom
    (E) None of the above

116.
$$(CH_3)_2CHCHOHCH_3 \xrightarrow{\text{HBr}} X$$

For the reaction above, product X is

    (A) $(CH_3)_2CHCHBrCH_3$
    (B) $(CH_3)_2CHCH_2CH_2Br$
    (C) $(CH_3)_2CBrCH_2CH_3$

    (D)
    $$(CH_3)_2\,CHCH \overset{\displaystyle CH_3}{\underset{\displaystyle |}{}} \!\!-\!\! CHCH\,(CH_3)$$
    with CH_3 substituents

    (E) No reaction occurs

117. Nitrogen dioxide gas exists in equilibrium primarily with:

    (A) N_2O_4
    (B) HNO_3

    (C) $N_2 + O_2$
    (D)

    (E) $NO + NO_3\ NO_2^- + NO_2^+$

118. Compounds X and Z are completely miscible in the liquid phase and insoluble in each other in the solid phase. Which of the following cooling curves would you expect for a non-eutectic mixture of X and Z as it solidifies?

(A)
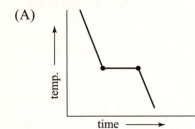

(D)

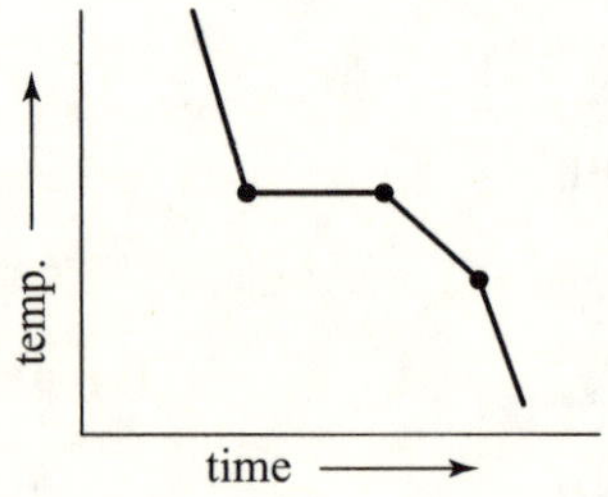

(B)
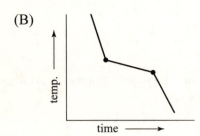

(E)

(C)
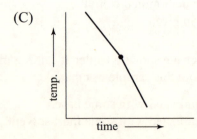

119. Which of the following pairs of compounds would be expected to have approximately the same absorption peak in the UV region?

(A) $CH_2\!=\!CH\!-\!CH\!=\!CH_2$,

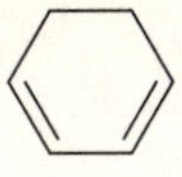

(B)

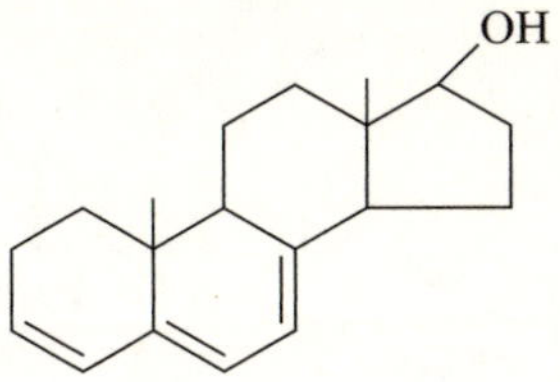

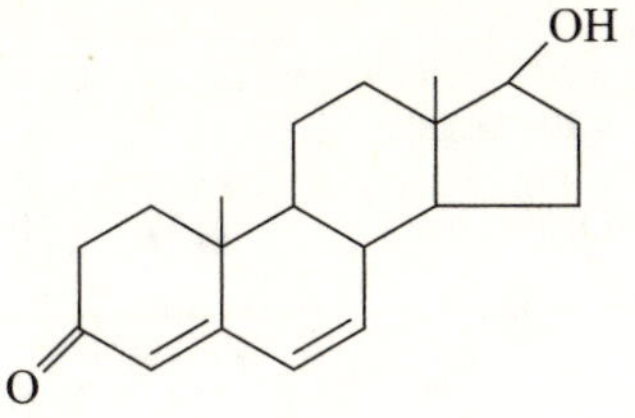

(C)

$CH_3\!-\!CH\!=\!CH\!-\!CH\!=\!CH\!-\!CH\!=\!CH\!-\!CH_3$,

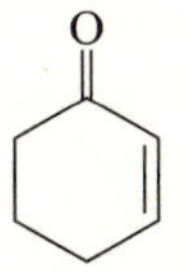

(D)

$CH_3\!-\!\overset{\overset{\displaystyle O}{\|}}{C}\!-\!CH\!=\!CH\!-\!CH_3, CH_3\!-\!CH\!=\!CH\!=\!CH\!-\!CH_3$,

(E)

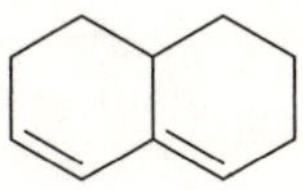

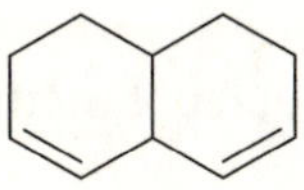

120. An unknown amine is treated with an excess of methyl iodide. Two equivalents of methyl iodide react with the amine. The amine is then treated with silver oxide and water, and then heated to 120°C. The resulting products are trimethylamine and ethylene. The unknown amine is probably

(A) $CH_3CH_2NHCH_3$
(B) $CH_3CH_2NH_2$
(C) $CH_2\!=\!CHNHCH_3$
(D) $CH_2\!=\!CHNH_2$
(E)

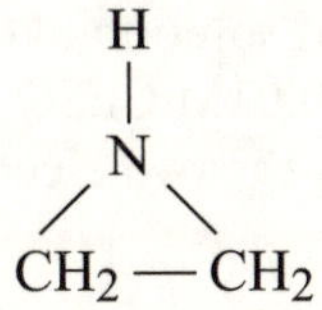

$$\underset{\displaystyle CH_2\!-\!CH_2}{\overset{\displaystyle H}{\underset{}{N}}}$$

121. (R)-3-phenyl-2-butanone is dissolved in a water/ethanol mixture containing NaOH. When this solution is in equilibrium, which optical rotation should it show?

(A) Dextrorotation
(B) Levorotation
(C) No rotation
(D) Cannot predict the direction of rotation without knowing concentration
(E) Cannot predict the direction of rotation before measuring it

122. Which of the following metals might not be considered a transition element?

(A) Cr
(B) Mn
(C) Fe
(D) Ni
(E) Zn

123. Electrons may generate transitions between atomic orbitals by emitting photons. Which of the following transitions is forbidden for a hydrogen atom?

(A) $4p \rightarrow 3d$
(B) $3d \rightarrow 2p$
(C) $4p \rightarrow 2s$
(D) $4p \rightarrow 3s$
(E) $3p \rightarrow 2p$

124. Which of the following is *not* a terpene?

(A)

(B)

(C)

(D)

(E)

125. Which of the following statements comparing the nucleophilicity of I^- and Cl^- is *true*?

(A) I^- is always more nucleophilic than Cl^-.
(B) I^- is usually more nucleophilic than Cl^-.
(C) I^- and Cl are approximately equal in nucleophilicity.
(D) I^- is usually less nucleophilic than Cl^-.
(E) I^- is always less nucleophilic than Cl^-.

126. A beaker containing a 1.00M solution of $CuSO_4$ is connected by a salt bridge to another beaker containing an equal amount of 0.01M $CuSO_4$ solution. If copper electrodes are placed in both beakers, the voltage measured across the two electrodes should be

(A) $-(RT/F)\ln(.01/1.0)$
(B) $-(RT/2F)\ln(.01/1.0)$
(C) $-RT \ln(.01/1.0)$
(D) $-2RT \ln(.01/1.0)$
(E) $\varepsilon° - FRT \ln(.01/1.0)$

127.

$$CO_{(g)} + \tfrac{1}{2}O_{2(g)} \rightarrow CO_{2(g)}$$

The change in internal energy for the reaction above, ΔE (or ΔU), is -282 kJ $\cdot$ mol^{-1} at 300°K. What is ΔH for the same reaction, assuming the gases are ideal (R = 8.3 J $\cdot$ mol^{-1} $\cdot$ K^{-1})?

(A) -282 kJ/mol
(B) -283 kJ/mol
(C) -285 kJ/mol
(D) -1245 kJ/mol
(E) -1527 kJ/mol

128. The mass of a neutron is 1.0087 a.m.u. and the mass of a proton-electron pair is 1.0078 a.m.u. The mass of a deuterium atom is closest to

(A) 2.0190 a.m.u.   (C) 2.0140 a.m.u.   (E) 1.0078 a.m.u.
(B) 2.0165 a.m.u.   (D) 2.0000 a.m.u.

129. Ortho-chlorotoluene is heated with aqueous NaOH and then acidified. The product is a mixture of ortho- and meta-methylphenol. The reactive intermediate of this reaction is

(A)   (C)   (E) None of the above

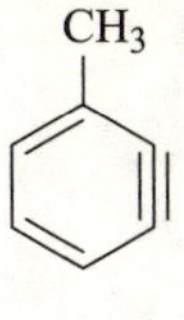

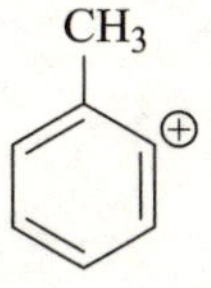

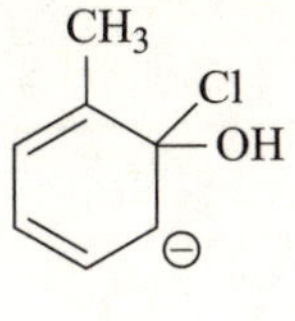

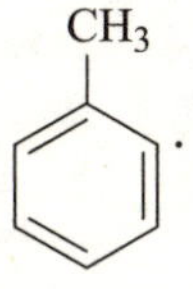

(B)   (D)

130.

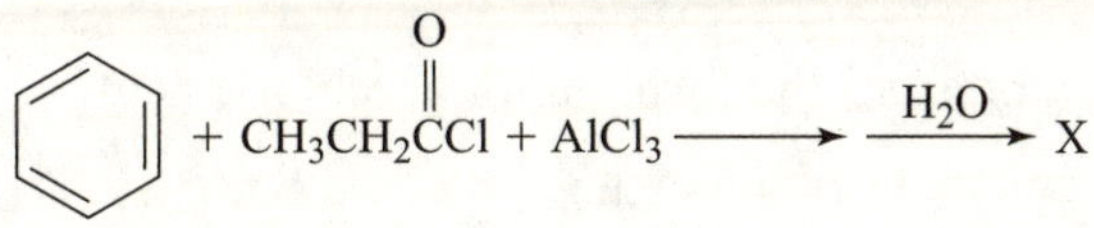

The product X for the reaction above is

(A)   (D)

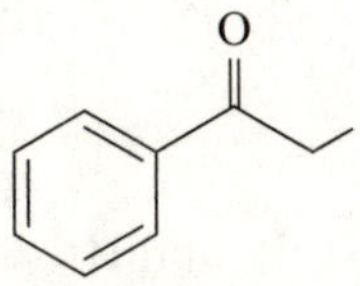

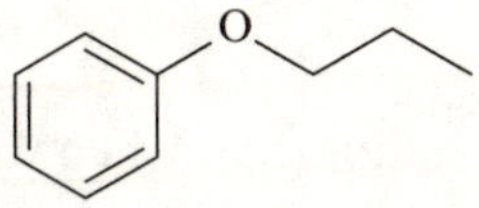

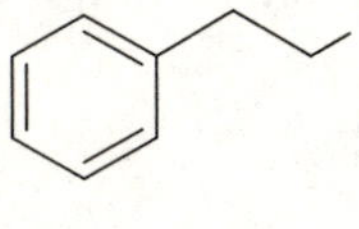

(B)   (E)

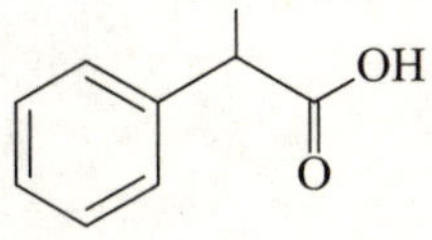

(C)

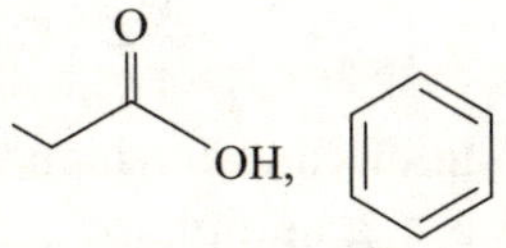

131. $$A_{(g)} \rightleftharpoons 2B_{(g)}$$

Determine the partial pressure of A, after gases have reached equilibrium in a sealed tank, if pure A is pumped into a tank with pressure of 1 atmosphere and temperature of 298K. Assume that a catalyst is used to facilitate the reaction. Also assume that K = 2.

(A) 0.25 atm   (C) 0.50 atm   (E) 1.00 atm
(B) 0.33 atm   (D) 0.67 atm

132. $CH_2=CH-O-CH_2-CH=CH_2$

Upon heating, the compound shown above will rearrange to form which of the following?

(A)
$$\overset{\displaystyle O}{\underset{}{\overset{\|}{HC}}}-CH_2-CH_2-CH=CH_2$$

(B)
$$\overset{\displaystyle O}{\underset{}{\overset{\|}{HC}}}-CH=CH-CH=CH_2$$

(C)
$$\overset{\displaystyle OH}{\underset{}{\overset{\|}{CH_2}}}-CH=CH-CH=CH_2$$

(D) $CH_2=CH-O-CH=CH-CH_3$

(E)

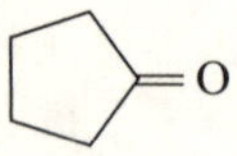

133. Which of the following represents the formula for perchloric acid?

(A) HCl   (C) $HClO_2$ (E) $HClO_3$
(B) HOCl   (D) $HClO_4$

134. Which of the following should be major peaks in the mass spectrum of 3-heptanone?

I. m/e 57   II. m/e 85   III. m/e 72

(A) I only   (C) III only   (E) I, II, and III
(B) II only   (D) I and II only

135. Under adiabatic conditions and constant volume a system will be in equilibrium when which of the following quantities is at a minimum?

(A) Internal energy (E or U)   (D) Gibbs energy (G)
(B) Enthalpy (H)   (E) None of the above
(C) Helmholtz energy (A)

136.

THF

You find an old bottle of THF in the lab. Before you use it, you should

(A) distill it.   (D) test for acidity.
(B) filter it.   (E) dry it in a desiccator.
(C) test for peroxides.

Answer Key

1. C	24. E	47. A	70. A	93. A	116. C
2. A	25. D	48. A	71. D	94. D	117. A
3. C	26. C	49. A	72. E	95. E	118. E
4. B	27. B	50. C	73. A	96. C	119. D
5. C	28. D	51. A	74. B	97. C	120. A
6. C	29. A	52. D	75. C	98. B	121. C
7. C	30. B	53. B	76. E	99. E	122. E
8. B	31. B	54. C	77. C	100. C	123. E
9. E	32. E	55. B	78. B	101. E	124. C
10. B	33. D	56. A	79. A	102. C	125. B
11. E	34. E	57. E	80. E	103. A	126. B
12. D	35. A	58. B	81. E	104. E	127. B
13. C	36. D	59. C	82. D	105. B	128. C
14. A	37. E	60. C	83. D	106. D	129. A
15. B	38. E	61. A	84. E	107. E	130. A
16. D	39. D	62. D	85. D	108. B	131. C
17. C	40. A	63. D	86. E	109. D	132. A
18. E	41. C	64. D	87. E	110. E	133. D
19. E	42. C	65. B	88. C	111. E	134. E
20. C	43. B	66. B	89. A	112. B	135. A
21. B	44. A	67. C	90. A	113. C	136. C
22. B	45. B	68. D	91. C	114. A	
23. D	46. E	69. D	92. E	115. D	

Practice Exam 5

Detailed Explanations of Answers

1. (C)

Bohr's postulates about the atom included the quantization of electromagnetic radiation and the quantization of an electron's angular momentum, but did not speak of the quantization of an electron's spin. It also said that an electron moves in circular orbits around the nucleus and in general provided the nuclear model of the atom.

2. (A)

A uranium-238 nuclear can emit an alpha particle (a helium nucleus) to become a thorium 234 nucleus:

$$^{238}_{92}U \rightarrow ^{234}_{90}Th \rightarrow ^{4}_{2}He$$

The change of atomic weight by four indicates that an alpha radiation took place.

3. (C)

The only nuclei that can be measured with nuclear magnetic resonance are the ones that have a spin and a magnetic moment. This happens only to nuclei that do not have an even number of both protons and neutrons. In this case, pairs of protons and neutrons have opposed spin, and the net nuclear spin is zero. The only choice with an odd number of protons or neutrons is $^{19}_{9}F$.

4. (B)

A solution of a weak acid and its conjugate base is a buffer solution (resists changes in pH). A convenient equation for calculating the pH of a buffer solution is the Henderson-Hasselbach equation:

$$pH = pK_a + \log_{10} \frac{[A^-]}{[HA]}$$

Assuming all the added HCl will protonate bicarbonate ions, the resulting pH should be

$$pH = 6.37 + \log \left(\frac{.10 - .01}{.10 + .01} \right)$$

$$pH = 6.37 - 0.09 = 6.28$$

The added HCl changes the pH by only 0.09 pH points.

5. (C)

Characteristic oxidation states are: Ni, II and III; Pd, II and IV; Pt, II and IV; Fe, II and III; Cu, I and II; Zn, II. Nickel and iron both belong to group VIII, along with paladium and platinum. The similarities are greatest in this group along horizontal triads. Nickel and iron both belong to the iron triad.

6. **(C)**

The two molecules represented in (C) are trans-1,4-dimethylcyclohexane and cis-1,4-dimethylcyclohexane.

7. **(C)**

The reaction proceeds as follows:

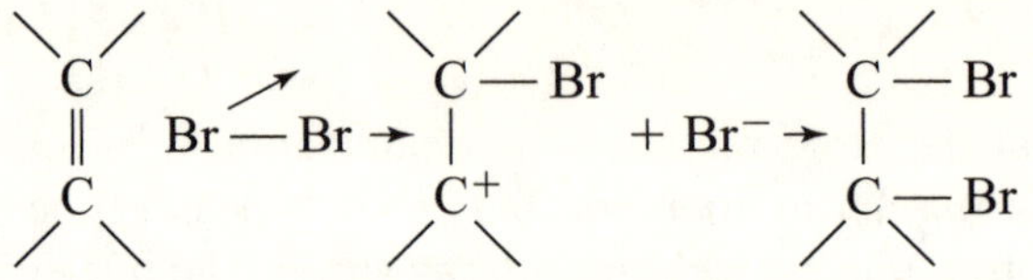

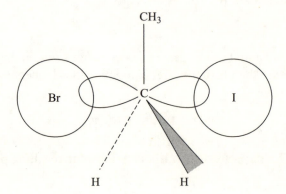

8. **(B)**

(III) and (IV) are unstable vinyl cations that would rearrange to form the genuine conjugated pentadienyl cation. (II) is available from (I) by a simple movement of electrons:

$$CH_2 = CH - CH = CH - \overset{\oplus}{C}H_2 \longleftrightarrow CH_2 = CH - \overset{\oplus}{C}H - CH = CH_2$$

9. **(E)**

(E) is the most stable because it satisfies the Hückel $4n+2$ rule for aromaticity; it has 6π electrons.

10. **(B)**

In the SN_2 reaction shown, the transition state is

The methyl carbon is sp^3 hybridized. The central carbon is sp^2 hybridized because the two H's and the methyl are co-planar and because one p orbital is partially bound to the incoming and outgoing groups.

11. **(E)**

The reaction occurs by the SN_2 mechanism, which involves reversal of stereochemistry.

12. (D)

The first step is the formation of a Grignard reagent (cyclohexylmagnesium bromide). This reacts with ketone as shown below:

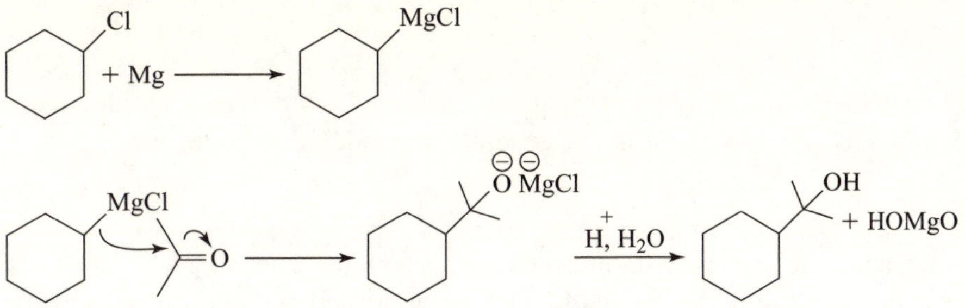

13. (C)

Ethers are inert to base and to reducing agents, but react with strong acids:

$$CH_3CH_2OCH_2CH_3 + 2HBr \xrightarrow{\Delta} 2CH_3CH_2Br + H_2O$$

14. (A)

With a very few exceptions, catalytic hydrogenation involves syn addition of hydrogen. Both hydrogen atoms add to the same side of the multiple bond. This is thought to be the result of the way in which the hydrogen and the alkene or alkyne bond to the metal catalyst:

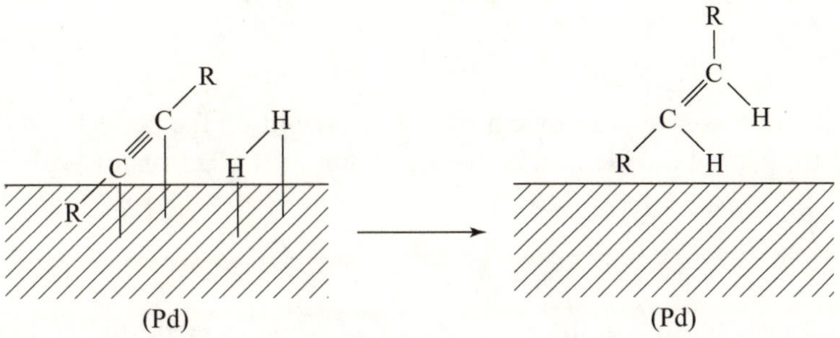

15. (B)

To selectively precipitate the Ag^+, we need an anion whose solubility with Ag^+ is significantly less than with Ca^{2+}. There should be a difference in K_{sp} of ~ 100 or more. OH^- is the only correct choice.

16. (D)

At pH 1.23 [HOOCCOOH] = [HOOCCOO$^-$] and at pH 4.19 [HOOCCOO$^-$] = [$^-$OOCCOO$^-$]. Midway between these points [HOOCCOO$^-$] reaches a maximum, at pH 2.71.

17. (C)

BH_3 acts as an electron acceptor or Lewis acid. CH_3 is a poor electron acceptor or donor. The three remaining choices can act as Lewis bases. The strongest of them is ammonia because the less electronegative nitrogen can more easily donate its pair of electrons.

GRE CHEMISTRY

18. (E)

For principal quantum number n = 3, there are three subshells: 3s, 3p, and 3d. These correspond to values for quantum number 1 of 0, 1, and 2. The 3s subshell contains one orbital; the 3p, three; and the 3d, five, for a total of nine. A simple rule is that shell n contains n^2 orbitals.

19. (E)

Only the heavy elements decay by spontaneous fission. U-238 decays by alpha emission. While α decay is technically a fission process, it is not generally considered to be fission.

20. (C)

Because no stable nuclei exist with atomic number greater than 83, (A) and (B) can be ruled out. C-14 is a radioisotope used in dating archeological artifacts, and technetium is an artificially produced element that has no stable isotopes. $^{118}_{50}Sn$ is a stable isotope.

21. (B)

In all cases we are removing an electron from an ion of charge $+1$, so the ionization energy will be relatively high. In the case of lithium, we are also removing an electron from an ion of very small radius and we are destroying the noble gas electron configuration ($1s^2$). These considerations contribute to explain why the second IE of lithium is the highest of all.

22. (B)

Oxygen binds covalently with nonmetals and metals in high oxidation states, e.g., Mn^{7+} or Cr^{6+}. ZnO, however, is an ionic compound of Zn^{2+} and O^{2-}.

23. (D)

Electronegativity increases as we move up and to the right on the periodic table. Be is in the upper right-hand corner of the periodic table and is therefore the most electronegative element of the choices given.

24. (E)

Electronegativity is a measure of the attraction of an atom for electrons. In higher oxidation states, atoms are more electron deficient and their electronegativity increases.

25. (D)

The atomic number is 6, so it contains 6 protons. The mass number is 14, so it contains $14 - 6 = 8$ neutrons. Because the atom is neutrally charged, it contains as many electrons as protons: six.

26. (C)

The molecular ion peak should appear at m/e 16 because nearly 99% of the methane should be composed of ^{12}C and ^1H. There should be an observable isotope peak at m/e 17, however. Because ^{13}C has a natural abundance of 1.107% and ^2H has a natural abundance of 0.015%, most of the isotope peak should be due to $^{13}C^1H_4$.

27. (B)

The energy differences are in the range 1–10 kcal/mole, corresponding to light wavelengths of 3×10^{-4} to 3×10^{-3} cm, the infrared region.

28. **(D)**

The net weight of NaCl is

$$11.085g - .445g$$

The number of moles of NaCl is

$$\frac{(11.085g - .445g)}{M.W.NaCl(moles/g)} = \frac{(11.085g - .445g)}{(22.99 + 35.45)moles/g}$$

The concentration is the number of moles of solute divided by the volume of the solution in liters:

$$\frac{(11.085g - .445g)}{(22.99 + 35.45)moles/g} \times \frac{1000ml/1}{200ml} = .91 \text{ moles}/1$$

29. **(A)**

The mean is the average:

$$\frac{10 + 14 + 16 + 11 + 17 + 14 + 9}{7} = \frac{91}{7} = 13$$

The median is the "middle" value; in a set of seven values, it is the fourth value. In this case it is 14.

The difference is $14 - 13 = 1$.

30. **(B)**

The molecular weight of AgCl is $108 + 35.5 = 143.5$. The weight of Ag per gram of AgCl is

$$108g \text{ Ag/mole}/143.5 \text{ AgCl/mole}$$

In 35.8g $AgCl_2$ there is

$$35.8 \text{ AgCl} \times \frac{108g \text{ Al}}{143.5 \text{ AgCl}} = (.25)(108g \text{ Ag})$$

$$= 26.9 \text{ Ag}$$

31. **(B)**

The burret should be read from the bottom of the meniscus (the curve in the liquid surface). Tenths of milliliters can be read off the scale and hundredths should be estimated. Notice that the volume measured increases going down the scale.

32. (E)

10.0ml of 1.00M NaOH contains

$$(10.0ml)(1.00 \text{ mole/liter}) = 10.0 \text{ mmoles OH}^-$$

This should neutralize 5.0 mmoles of H_2SO_4 because H_2SO_4 is a diprotic acid (two H^+'s). The concentration is thus

$$\frac{5.0 \text{ moles}}{50ml} = 0.1 \text{ mole/liter}$$

33. (D)

Only k is affected by a catalyst.

34. (E)

All three of these idealized assumptions are part of the kinetic theory model of an ideal gas.

35. (A)

To find the right expression, one could use dimensional analysis (check the units of each of the expressions).

Considering that the distribution of speeds of particles has to be dimensionless and that K is expressed in JK^{-1}, R in $JK^{-1}mol^{-1}$ and $1J = 1Kg \times m^2 \times sec^{-2}$, the only expression that has all expressions cancelled out is (A):

$$\frac{mv^2}{2KT} = \frac{Kg \times (m \, sec^{-1})^2}{JK^{-1}K} = \frac{Kgm^2 sec^{-2}}{Kgm^2 sec^{-2}}$$

36. (D)

The H_2^{2-} ion would contain four electrons. According to molecular orbital theory, the first two would fall into a sigma bonding molecular orbital. The second two electrons would fall into the next lowest energy level, a sigmal antibonding orbital. The net bond order would be zero.

H_2 ions might be possible to construct. H_2^+ ions have been observed. Both would have a net bond order of one-half.

37. (E)

Endothermic and *exothermic* are terms that describe the direction of ΔH. Positive ΔH corresponds to an endothermic reaction, and negative ΔH indicates an exothermic reaction.

The rate of a reaction is not related to ΔG values. ΔG values can tell us whether a reaction at constant temperature and pressure will tend to go forward or not. Negative ΔG values indicate reactions that are favored in the forward direction.

38. (E)

The third law states that all perfect crystals have the same entropy at $0°K$.

39. (D)

$$\Delta H° = \Delta H°_{f(products)} - \Delta H°_{f(reactants)}$$

$\Delta H°_f$ values must be multiplied by the molar amount of the reactant or product involved in the reaction:

$$\Delta H° = 2(\Delta H°_f CO_{2(g)}) + 3(\Delta H°_f H_2O_{(l)}) - (\Delta H°_f C_2H_{6(g)})$$

$\Delta H°_f$ for substances in their elemental state, e.g., $O_{2(g)}$, is by definition zero.

40. (A)

Extensive properties depend on the amount of material present, e.g., mass, internal energy, or volume. Intensive properties are independent of the amount of material present, e.g., pressure, temperature, or molar heat capacity.

41. (C)

The work obtained from a system is not solely a function of the state of the system. It is also dependent on the "path" travelled by the system. For example, more useful work is done in the reversible expansion from V_1 to V_2 than in the irreversible expansion. For a system expanding against a vacuum, no work is done at all.

42. (C)

At both the boiling and melting points, the temperature remains constant while Y is undergoing a phase transition. The first transition on the graph is liquification and the second is solidification.

43. (B)

Compound Y takes 10 minutes to change from gas to liquid. In this time it loses (10 min. × 100 cal./min.) = 1000 cal. of heat. Because this is for two moles of Y, we must divided by two:

$$1000cal./2 \text{ moles} = 500cal./mol.$$

44. (A)

The liquid portion of the curve is the second sloping section. The two moles of liquid lose 1000 calories of heat and 15°C of temperature. Combining these terms, the heat capacity is

$$\frac{1000cal.}{15° \times 2 \text{ mol.}} = 33 \text{ cal.}/°C \times \text{mol}$$

45. (B)

The compound is adenine, a purine base that is a component of DNA or RNA nucleotides.

46. (E)

(A), (B), and (D) do not adequately account for the octet rule. (C) is a highly strained and unlikely structure. An acceptable structure would be a resonance hybrid of (E) and its mirror image:

$$O = \overset{\oplus}{O} - \overset{\ominus}{O} \longleftrightarrow \overset{\ominus}{O} - \overset{\oplus}{O} = O$$

47. (A)

Actual angles are: CH_4, 109.5°; NH_3, 107.1°; H_2O, 104.5°. Only CH_4 shows the expected tetrahedral angle of 109.5°. In the other cases, the bonding orbitals are not exactly sp^3 hybrids. They have less s character because the lone pair of electrons has more s character. In PH_3 and H_2S, there is even more p character in the bonding orbitals. Because the second row elements are larger, the repulsion between bonding orbitals is smaller. The HPH angle is only 93°.

48. (A)

The CH_3—H bond is smallest because hydrogen has the smallest atomic radius. The bond lengths are approximately

CH_3—H	1.10Å
CH_3—CH_3	1.53Å
CH_3—NH_2	1.47Å
CH_3—OH	1.42Å
CH_3—F	1.38Å

49. (A)

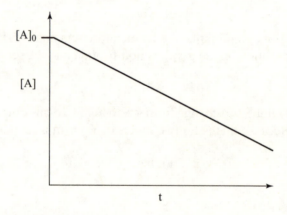

The rate law takes the general form:

$$\frac{-d[A]}{dt} = k[A]^n$$

where n is the order of the rate law in A. From inspection of the graph, we can see that d[A]/dt is constant. Therefore n = 0 nd k is the slope of the line.

For a first-order reaction, we obtain a straight line by graphing ln[A] versus t. For a second-order reaction, we must graph 1/[A] versus t; for a third order reaction, $1/[A]^2$; etc.

50. (C)

The product is trans-1,2-dibromocyclohexane, which is represented by (C) or (D). The conformation with both bromines equatorial (C) instead of axial (D) is more stable because interactions with hydrogens are reduced.

51. (A)

(C) and (D) are not directly related to entropy. In classical thermodynamics, entropy is defined by the relation

$$dS = \frac{q_{reversible}}{T}$$

In statistical mechanics, entropy is defined by the relation

$$S = k\ln W$$

where k is Boltzman's constant and W is the number of possible states that may be taken by a collection of molecules. Randomness increases with W; there are many possible random states but only one or a few ordered states.

52. (D)

Answer (D) is incorrectly balanced with respect to charge and electron transfer. The net charge on the left side of the reaction is 12+, but on the right side it is 18+. We also do not have the proper ratio of oxidizing agent to reducing agent. Each $Cr_2O_7^{2-}$ gains six electrons when reduced to $2Cr^{3+}$. Each I_2 loses ten electrons when oxidized to $2IO_3^-$. The coefficients should reflect conservation of charge and electrons:

$$3I_2 + 5Cr_2O_7^{2-} + 34H^+ \rightarrow 6IO_3^- + 10Cr^{3+} + 17H_2O$$

53. (B)

Because ΔH is negative, the reaction is exothermic. We might consider the reaction in this way:

$$N_{2(g)} + 3H_{2(g)} \quad 2NH_{3(g)} + heat$$

Increasing the temperature drives the reaction to the left, and thus K_{eq} decreases with increasing T. K_{eq} is independent of pressure; it varies only with temperature.

54. (C)

Only zinc is more easily oxidized than iron; that is, its reduction potential is less than that of iron. If iron must be in contact with water, e.g., an iron ship hull, it can be put in electrical contact with zinc using a wire. The zinc then becomes an anode and the iron a cathode. The zinc corrodes and must be replaced, but the iron stays intact.

55. (B)

K_{eq} and ΔG are related:

$$\Delta G = -RT\ln K_{eq}$$

$$\Delta G = -2.303RT\log K_{eq}$$

We are looking for the ratio:

$$\frac{\Delta G_{300}}{\Delta G_{400}} = \frac{2.303R(300)\log 10}{2.303R(400)\log 100} = \frac{(300)(1)}{(400)(2)} = \frac{3}{8}$$

56. **(A)**

The proper expression for K_{eq} is

$$K_{eq} = \frac{PSO_3^2}{PSO_2^2 PO_2}$$

Substituting known values,

$$3.47 = \frac{PSO_3^2}{(4)(1)}$$

$$PSO_3 = \sqrt[2]{3.47} \text{ atm.}$$

57. **(E)**

Copper is easily reduced and hence can be found in nature in its metallic state. Zinc and hydrogen are both more difficult to reduce, as reflected by their standard reduction potentials:

	ε°
$Cu^{2+} + 2e^- \rightarrow Cu$	0.34
$2H^+ + 2e^- \rightarrow H_2$	0.00
$Zn^{2+} + 2e^- \rightarrow Zn$	-0.76

Because metallic copper cannot act to oxidize water and cannot dissolve, no reaction will occur.

58. **(B)**

To find the overall reaction and potential, we must reverse the half-reaction with the smaller potential and add:

	ε°
$Pb_{(s)} + SO_4^{2-} \rightleftharpoons PbSO_{4(s)} + 2e^-$	0.36v
$PbO_{2(s)} + 4H^+ + SO_4^{2-} + 2e^- \rightleftharpoons PbSO_{4(s)} + 2H_2O$	1.69v
$PB_{(s)} + PbO_{2(s)} + 4H^+ + 2SO_4^{2-} \rightarrow 2PbSO_{4(s)} + 2H_2O$	2.05v

59. **(C)**

The rate $d[XY_2]/dt$ is unaffected by changes in $[X]$. Therefore, it is zero order in X. Tripling $[Y]$ causes the rate to increase nine times, that is, by a factor of 3^2. Because the rate increases with the square of the increase in $[Y]$, the rate is second order in Y. The rate law is

$$d[XY_2]/dt = k[Y]^2$$

60. **(C)**

The rate law for the reaction is

$$d[XY_2]/dt = k[Y]^2$$

We can substitute data from the table in the previous problem:

$$1.0 \times 10^{-5}M \cdot sec^{-1} = k(.010M)^2$$

$$k = \frac{1.0 \times 10^{-5}}{(.010)^2}M^{-1}sec^{-1}$$

$$k = 1.0 \times 10^{-1}M^{-1}sec^{-1}$$

61. **(A)**

Because the overall rate law is zero order in X, the rate limiting step most probably does not involve X. Answer (A) satisfies this condition.

62. **(D)**

For a first-order reaction such as radioactive decay,

$$\frac{-dC}{dt} = kC$$

where C is the concentration of the reactant. By rearranging and integrating, we obtain

$$\frac{-1}{k} \times \frac{1}{C} \times dC = dt$$

$$\frac{1}{k} \ln\left(\frac{C_o}{C}\right) = tt_o$$

Setting $t_o = 0$,

$$t = \frac{1}{k} \ln\left(\frac{C_o}{C}\right)$$

Knowing the half-life, $t_{\frac{1}{2}}$, we can determine k:

$$t_{\frac{1}{2}} = \frac{1}{k} \ln\left(\frac{1}{.5}\right)$$

$$\frac{\ln 2}{t_{\frac{1}{2}}}$$

We can substitute this value in the equation above:

$$t = \frac{t_{\frac{1}{2}}}{\ln 2} \ln \left(\frac{C_o}{C} \right)$$

Because the amount of C-14 is directly proportioanl to the disintegration rate ($C_o/C \propto 15.3/4.1$), we can write

$$t = \frac{5570}{\ln 2} \ln \left(\frac{15.3}{4.1} \right) = 10,582 \text{ years}$$

63. (D)

For states i and j, the proportion of particles in each state is

$$\frac{N_i}{N_j} = \exp \left[- \left(E_i - E_j \right) / RT \right]$$

By substituting the values given, we obtain the expression below.

$$\frac{N_i}{N_j} = \exp \left[-5 \times 1000/8.3 \times 273 \right] = 0.11$$

64. (D)

The root mean square velocity can be expressed in kinetic theory as

$$\sqrt{<v^2>} = \sqrt{\frac{3RT}{mL}}$$

65. (B)

The hydrogen atom is the only atom that has orbitals whose energy depends only on the principal quantum number n. Its orbitals with the same value of n (e.g., 2s and $2p_o$) have the same energy.

66. (B)

The orbital pictured has one radial node. An orbital with quantum numbers n and l has (n − 1) nodes. Some of these may be angular nodes that would not appear on this graph. The number of angular nodes is given by l. Thus the possible answers are n = 2, l = 0(2s); n = 3, l = 1(3p); n = 4, l = 2(4d); etc. 3p is correct.

67. (C)

Reaction (II) would produce $CH_3CH_3CHOHC \equiv CH$. This could be hydrogenated to produce 3-pentanol.

68. **(D)**

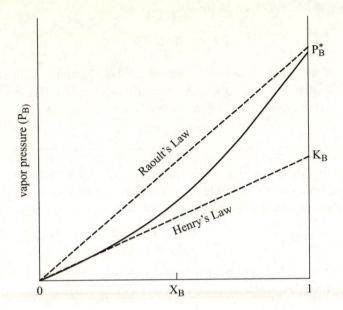

The graph above shows the vapor pressure of component B for nonideal mixtures of A and B, where X_B is the mole fraction of B. For X_B close to unity, Raoult's Law applies:

$$P_B = X_B P_B^*$$

where P_B^* is the vapor pressure of pure B. For X_B close to zero, Henry's Law applies:

$$P_B = X_B K_B$$

where K_B is an experimentally determined constant.

69. **(D)**

As we boil the mixture, the escaping vapor contains more of the more volatile component, benzene. The remaining liquid becomes richer in toluene. According to the graph, a liquid mixture 25 mole% in benzene will boil at ~100°C. As we boil the liquid, its composition and boiling point move to the left and up on the "boiling point line" until we reach the desired point.

70. **(A)**

For a mixture that is less than 35 mole % acetone, boiling will produce a vapor phase that is richer in chloroform. Fractional distillation will isolate more or less pure chloroform. For mixtures greater than 35 mole % in acetone, distillation will isolate fractions richer in acetone. In both cases, the boiling liquid in the pot will tend toward the azeotropic composition of 35 mole % acetone.

71. (D)

The Gibbs energy can be expressed as follows:

$$dG = -SdT + VdP$$

With T and P constant, $dG = 0$ and so G is at an extremal. This extremal is in fact a minimum. If G is perturbed from this value, it will return to the same equilibrium value. Because most laboratory reactions are carried out at fairly constant T and P, tables of G are widely available.

72. (E)

The Helmholtz energy, $A = E - TS$, is analogous to the Gibbs energy, $G = H - TS$. The Gibbs energy represents the maximum work available from a system at constant T and P. The Helmholtz energy gives us the maximum work at constant T and V.

73. (A)

For an ideal gas at constant temperature $dE = 0$. Therefore, $q = -w$. For an irreversible expansion, $w = -P_{(opposing)} \Delta V$. Thus we have

$$q = P_{opp} \Delta V = (1 \text{ atm})(V_2 - 1 \text{ liter})$$

Because T is constant,

$$V_2 = \frac{P_i V_i}{P_2} = 10 \text{ liters}$$

$$q = (1 \text{ atm})(10\ell - 1\ell) = 9\ell \cdot \text{atm.} = 909J$$

74. (B)

Enthalpy is defined as the constant-pressure heat of reaction. The constant-volume heat of reaction is the internal energy (E or U). The two are related as shown below:

$$H = E + PV$$

$$\Delta H = \Delta E + P\Delta V + V\Delta P \tag{1}$$

Taking the constant pressure case ($\Delta P = 0$), and substituting $\Delta E = q - P_{(opposing)} \Delta V$ into (1):

$$\Delta H = q - P_{opp}\Delta V + P_{sys}\Delta V + 0$$

At constant pressure, the pressure of the system is equal to the pressure opposing the system throughout the reaction; that is, $P_{opp} = P_{sys}$. Therefore,

$$\Delta H = q \text{ at constant pressure}$$

75. (C)

The first step is the addition of a protecting group to the carboxy function to form

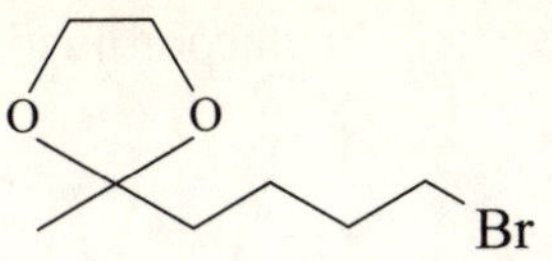

The compound can now form a Grignard reagent with Mg and react with acetaldehyde to form

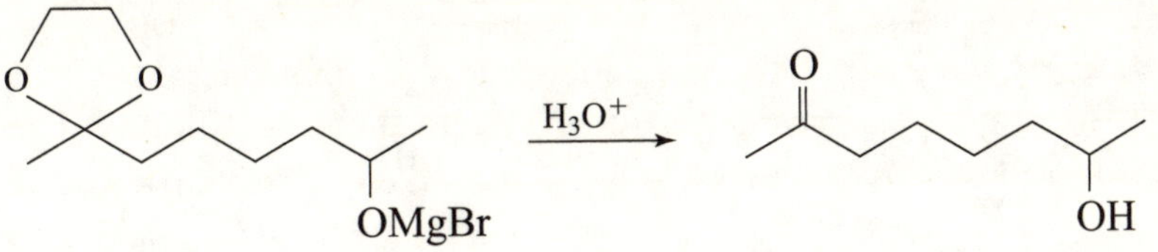

Hydrolysis with acid yields the final product.

76. (E)

The reaction would proceed as follows:

The second step requires a strong base such as $NaNH_2$.

77. (C)

(D) can be eliminated because it would show only a single peak. (A) can be eliminated because it would show only two peaks. In both cases, the protons on the terminal carbons are equivalent—they appear in a single peak. From the splitting, we can conclude that we have two groups that are adjacent to a two-hydrogen group. From the chemical shifts, we can conclude that one of these two groups is adjacent to the chlorines and the other is distant from them. The only plausible structure is

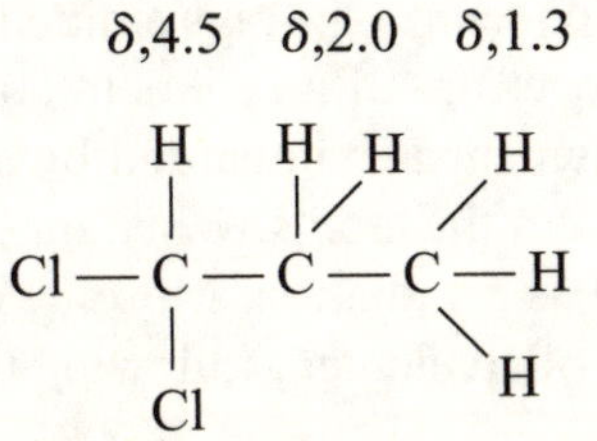

$\delta,4.5 \quad \delta,2.0 \quad \delta,1.3$

The octet splitting on the middle group (δ, 2.0) results from the peak being split in four by the methyl protons and again in two by the proton with the chlorines.

78. (B)

If possible, we would like the effective atomic number (EAN) of Fe to achieve a noble gas state. Fe (a.n. = 26) is in oxidation state O, so it has 8 valence electrons. To achieve the noble gas configuration of Kr, it needs 10 more electrons in its outer shell. Each coordinating CO group donates a pair of electrons, so five CO groups are needed.

79. (A)

This is an intramolecular aldol condensation:

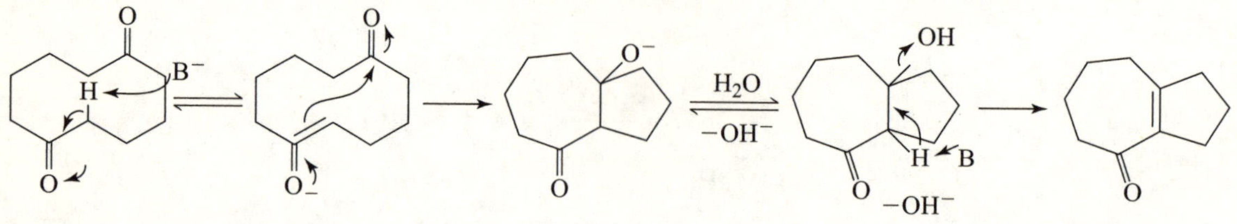

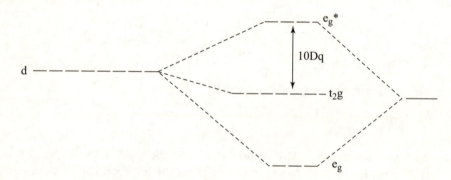

80. (E)

In an octahedral complex, the metal's $d_{x^2-y^2}$ and d_{z^2} orbitals are directed toward the ligands and involved in bonding, while the d_{xy}, d_{xz}, and d_{yz} orbitals are not. The d orbitals combine with two of the "ligand group orbitals" as shown below:

$$e_g^*$$

$$10Dq$$

$$t_{2g}$$

$$d$$

$$e_g$$

The e_g^* orbitals are antibonding and the t_{2g} orbitals are nonbonding.

81. (E)

In 1912, Moseley observed that frequency of x-rays emitted from elements could be correlated with atomic number. Therefore, the x-ray spectrum of an element contains information about the electronic energy levels of the atom. When an element is bombarded by a beam of electrons, electrons from the innermost levels or shells are ejected from the atoms. When outer electrons jump into the vacancies left by ejected electrons, energy is emitted as x-radiation. Moseley discovered that the frequency of x-rays emitted varies with the atomic number of an element following the relationship below:

$$v = c(2 - b)$$

where v = frequency of x-rays emitted

2 = atomic number

b, c = refer to a specific x-ray line and are the same for all elements

82. (D)

X must have negligible mass because the mass of the reacting nucleus remains unchanged. X must have a charge of -1 because the nuclear charge increases by one. An electron is the only choice that fits this description.

83. (D)

The two protons marked y are equivalent. They will appear as a doublet because they are split by the proton H_X. H_X will appear further downfield as a triplet because it is split by both of the H_y protons.

$$\begin{array}{ccccc} & H_X & & H_y & \\ & | & & | & \\ Cl - & C & - & C & - Cl \\ & | & & | & \\ & Cl & & H_y & \end{array}$$

84. (E)

The molarity of a solution is the number of moles of solute per liter of solution, not solvent. Adding the salt to the solvent increases its volume. Because the final volume is greater than 1.000 liter, the final concentration is

$$\frac{0.1000 \text{ mole}}{> 1.000 \text{ liter}} = < 0.1000M$$

85. (D)

Ion-exchange chromatography separates materials based on their affinity to an ionic immobile solid. Anionic resins are suitable for separating cations such as Li^+, Na^+, and K^+. It has been widely used in the separation of lanthanides and actinides.

Gas chromatography is impractical because the ions would have to be vaporized. Liquid and thin layer chromatography would not distinguish well between the cations.

86. (E)

Our very rough measurement of the normality of solution A tells us that the true value could be anywhere between $0.95 - 10\%$ and $0.95 + 10\%$, that is, .86N and 1.05N. If the normality of A is less than 1.00, the final mixture will be basic; if it is greater than 1.00, acidic. Because we are not certain, the correct answer is (E).

87. (E)

In the titration of a strong base with a strong acid, the pH of the solution changes very rapidly in the region of the equivalence point. Indicators that change color between pH 4 and pH 10 will all give nearly identical results.

88. (C)

$$CH_3$$
$$|$$
$$CH_2$$
$$|$$
$$CH_3CH_2CHCH_2CH_3$$

During mass spectrometry, alkanes cleave especially easily at branch points because this produces secondary carbocations. These are more stable than primary carbocations. The principal fragment for 3-ethylpentane should be

$$CH_3CH_2\overset{+}{C}HCH_2CH_3 \qquad M.W. = 71$$

The peak for this fragment is much larger than the molecular ion peak.

89. (A)

Alkyl groups, as well as halogens, cause a downfield shift when attached to the same carbon as the proton is being measured. A halogen removed by one carbon, as in (E), still has a significant effect.

90. (A)

Like most mixtures of compounds, air will absorb strongly in this band. Air must be completely evacuated from the apparatus and the spectrum must be taken in a vacuum. Light in the region near 150nm is known as the vacuum ultraviolet band.

91. (C)

Because the reaction shows anti-Markovnikov addition, it must proceed by a free radical mechanism. This requires a free radical initiator such as a peroxide.

92. (E)

Between two isoelectronic ions, as in (A) and (B), the ion with the higher atomic number has the smaller ionic radius. Within a family, as in (C) and (D), the ion with the higher atomic number has the larger atomic radius. Among the transition elements, there is a tendency for ionic radii to decrease with increasing atomic number, even for ions of the same charge.

93. (A)

Bond (a) is in fact a double bond and is thus the shortest and strongest bond. Bond (b) has some double bond character and is thus shorter than bond (c). The double bond character in (b) can be seen as resulting from the resonance structure on the right:

The measured bond lengths are: (a) 1.20Å, (b) 1.33Å, (c) 1.44Å.

94. **(D)**
We wish to deposit

$$2.7\text{g}/27\text{g} \cdot \text{mole}^{-1} = 0.1 \text{ mole Al}_{(s)}$$

Because aluminum ions have a charge of $3+$, this will require

$$0.1 \text{ mole Al}_{(s)} \times 3 = 0.3 \text{ mole electrons}$$

The charge on 0.3 mole of electrons is 0.3 faraday. Because one faraday = 96,485 coulombs,

$$0.3 \text{ faraday} \cdot 96,485 \text{ coulombs/faraday} = 28,945.5 \text{ coulombs}$$

Because one ampere = one coulomb/second, the time required for a 500 amp current to pass 28,945.5 coulombs of electricity is

$$28,945.5 \text{ coulombs}/500 \text{ coulombs} \cdot \text{sec}^{-1} = 57.89 \text{ sec}$$

Bringing together the steps above, we obtain answer (D):

$$\frac{2.7}{27} \times 3 \times \frac{96.485}{500} = 57.89 \text{ seconds}$$

95. **(E)**
Azobenzene compounds are frequently used as dyes and are not unstable. The cis isomer, however, is easily converted to the more stable trans isomer. At room temperature the conversion has a half-life of between one and three hours.

96. **(C)**
Gallium lies between argon (a.n. 18) and krypton (a.n. 36) so we can abbreviate the configurate of the first 18 electrons with [Ar]. Gallim is in the fourth period because it follows argon, so the first sub-shell to fill will be $4s^2$. The $3d^{10}$ subshell is then filled and we are left with one electron to go in the 4p subshell. The complete configuration is thus

$$[\text{Ar}]4s^23d^{10}4p^1$$

97. **(C)**
In HF solvent, no proton donating acids are known. The only acids known are fluoride acceptors:

$$\text{HF} + \text{BJ}_3 \rightleftharpoons \text{H}^+ + \text{BF}_4^-$$

98. **(C)**
In order to complete a d subshell, electrons from s orbitals can be promoted to d orbitals because their energies are similar. However, electrons are not promoted to the next p subshell to avoid pairing because the pairing energy is small compared with the difference between the d and p subshells.

99. (E)

Rutherford is best known for establishing the nuclear model of the atom. The decisive experiments involved the scattering of a beam of alpha particles by metal foil. Rutherford was shocked to find that a few particles were reflected directly backward by the foil, whereas most passed through. He concluded that most of the mass and all of the positive charge of the atom must be concentrated in the center of the atom, in a nucleus. It was Thomson's model of the atom that Rutherford disproved. Rontgen discovered X-rays and Marie Curie isolated radioactive elements (and died of leukemia).

100. (C)

When the pH of the solution is equal to the pKa of the dissolved acid, $[HA] = [A^-]$. This can be shown as follows:

$$K_a = \frac{[H^+][A^-]}{[HA]}$$

$$pK_a = pH + \log \frac{[A^-]}{[HA]}$$

Because $pK_a = pH$,
$$0 = pK_a - pH = \log \frac{[A^-]}{[HA]}$$

$$\therefore \frac{[A^-]}{[HA]} = 1 \text{ or } [A^-] = [HA]$$

Because $[HNO_2] + [NO_2^-] = 0.100M$ and $[HNO_2] = [NO_2^-]$, $[NO_2^-] = 0.050M$.

101. (E)

Diels-Alder reactions involve the addition to a diene of a dienophile, usually a multiple bond. One of the two double bonds on the diene can be a carboxyl group, as in (B).

102. (C)

Ionization energies generally increase as we move up and to the right on the periodic table. Be is above Mg and to the right of Li. Second ionization energies are greater than first ionization energies as a rule because we are removing an electron from an atom that already has a charge of $+1$.

103. (A)

To predict the possible products of an electrophilic aromatic substitution, it is necessary to classify the group attached to the ring as ortho-para director or metal director. In (B), $-NH_2$ is ortho-para, in (C) $-NO_2$ is meta, in (D) $-CH_3$ is ortho-para, and in (E) $-OCH_2$ is ortho-para. The only one that is very unlikely to occur is (A) because $-Br$ is ortho-para, not meta as shown.

104. (E)

Primary alkyl groups are more reactive than secondary or tertiary groups. We are left with answers (C) and (E). Chloride is a much better leaving group than cyanide. It is the conjugate base of a stronger acid, so it is more stable as a free anion. (E) is the most reactive.

105. (B)

In the presence of a strong base, the acid will be deprotonated and no further reaction will occur. The acid catalyzed esterification is an equilibrium process and involves the formation of water. For this reason, we wish to have a high concentration of the reactant CH_3OH in order to drive the equilibrium forward. We should add no H_2O in order to avoid driving the equilibrium backward.

106. (D)

Nitriles are hydrolyzed to carboxylic acids under acidic or basic conditions. They are unreactive in oxidative conditions but form many reduction products.

107. (E)

Both families of elements occur naturally in their ionic forms, e.g., Na^+ or Cl^-. Alkali metals must be reduced and halides must be oxidized to obtain the elemental form. Electrolysis of salts is a common procedure for isolating these elements.

108. (B)

This is known as the Wolff-Kishner reduction.

109. (D)

Nitrogen cannot form an expanded octet, whereas phosphorus and arsenic can. All three have valence shells of configuration ns^2np^3. In order to form an expanded octet, an electron must be promoted to the nd subshell. For nitrogen, $n = 2$. Because no 2d subshell exists, nitrogen cannot form an expanded octet.

110. (E)

The reaction is

$$CH_3-CH=CH_2 + :CCl_2 \longrightarrow CH_3-\overset{\displaystyle CCl_2}{\overset{\diagup \diagdown}{CH-CH_2}}$$

:CCl_2 is prepared by the action of a strong base on chloroform:

$$CHCl_3 + RO^- \rightleftharpoons ROH + Cl_3C:^- \longrightarrow Cl^- + :CCl_2$$

111. (E)

m_l can be any integer such that $-1 \leq m_l \leq 1$. In the case of $l = 4$, m_l can be $-4, -3, -2, -1, 0, 1, 2, 3,$ or 4. These nine values correspond to the nine orbitals in the g subshell.

112. (B)

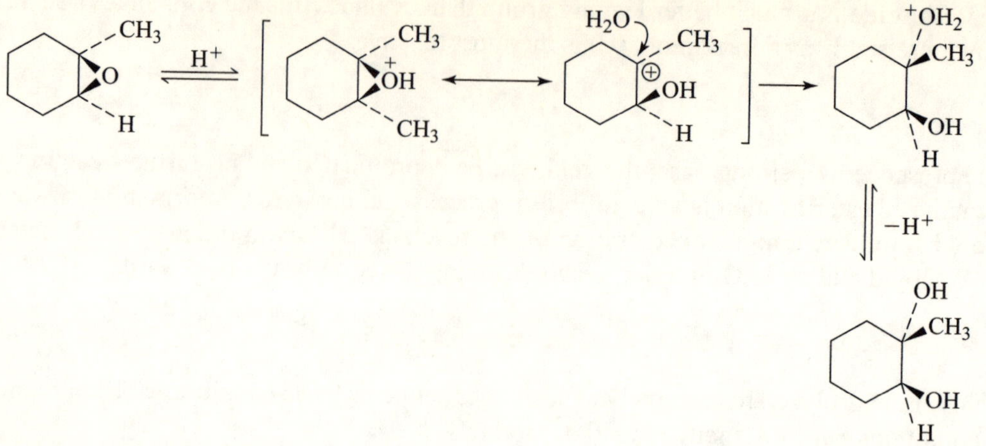

The acid-catalyzed ring opening of an oxirane yields a trans-diol, with the incoming group on the more substituted carbon.

113. (C)

Entropy is defined by the relation

$$\Delta S \cong \frac{q(\text{reversible})}{T}$$

If the process is carried out irreversibly, the entropy can still be calculated. Because entropy is a state function, it is the same for any two processes that share the same initial and final states. We can calculate ΔS for a reversible expansion equivalent to the expansion in our problem.

For an ideal gas at constant temperature, $dE = 0$. Therefore, $q = -w$. For a reversible expansion

$$w = -RT \ln \frac{V_2}{V_1}$$

Therefore,

$$q_{rev} = RT \ln \frac{V_2}{V_1}$$

Because

$$\Delta S = \frac{q_{rev}}{T}$$

$$\Delta S = R \ln \frac{V_2}{V_1} = R \ln \frac{20}{5} = R\ln 4$$

114. (A)

Only in extremely pure samples of alcohols will the hydroxy hydrogen ($\delta 5.3$) appear as a triplet. In other cases, proton exchange is so rapid that the hydroxy proton cannot be resolved as a triplet but appears as a broad, featureless *mesa*.

115. (D)

CN^- can form π bonds in which the metal t_{2g} electrons are donated to antibonding orbitals of the CN^- ion. This lowers the energy of the t_{2g} orbitals, thus increasing the 10Dq or splitting energy.

116. (C)

This SN_1 reaction proceeds via a carbocation intermediate that rearranges itself:

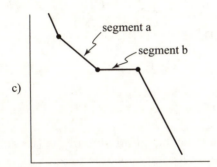

The tertiary carbocation is more stable than the secondary carbocation.

117. (A)

NO_2 dimerizes easily to N_2O_4. The equilibrium is highly dependent on temperature and pressure.

118. (E)

The cooling curve for an eutectic mixture would resemble that of a pure substance. All other mixtures will resemble choice (E).

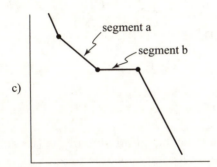

For a non-eutectic mixture rich in compound X, segment a of the curve represents pure X solidifying out of the melt. The melt becomes richer in Z and so its freezing point continues to become depressed. When we reach segment b, we have a liquid eutectic mixture of X and Z and we have solid X. The eutectic mixture is that which has the lowest freezing point of any X-Z mixture. At this point, the temperature drop halts as all the eutectic mixture solidifies.

For a pure eutectic mixture, segment a of curve (c) is eliminated and we have curve (a).

119. (D)

According to the Woodward-Fieser rules, we should expect the following λ_{max} for the given answers.

(A) 214nm, 263nm
(B) 313nm, 270nm
(C) 254nm, 225nm
(D) 225nm, 224nm
(E) 234 nm, (absorbs only in the "vacuum UV," that is $\lambda < 200$nm)

120. (A)

This process is known as the Hoffman degradation. For our unknown amine, the reaction goes as follows:

$$CH_3CH_2NHCH_3 + 2CH_3I \rightarrow CH_3CH_2\overset{\oplus}{N}(CH_3)_3I^{\ominus} + HI$$

$$CH_3CH_2\overset{\oplus}{N}(CH_3)_3I \xrightarrow[H_2O]{\overset{\ominus}{Ag_2O}} CH_3CH_2\overset{\oplus}{N}(CH_3)_3\overset{\ominus}{O}H$$

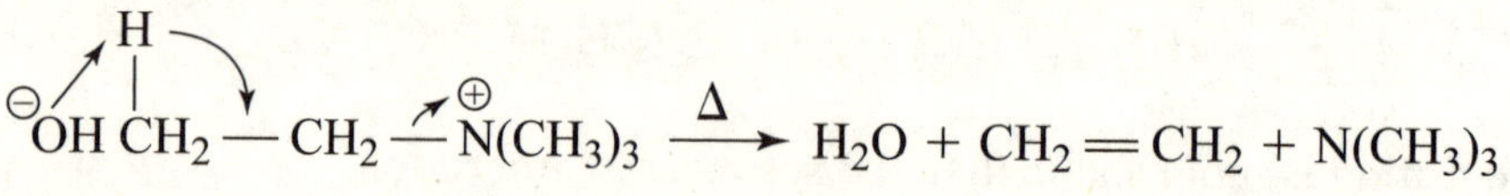

$$\overset{\ominus}{O}H \; CH_2 - CH_2 - \overset{\oplus}{N}(CH_3)_3 \xrightarrow{\Delta} H_2O + CH_2=CH_2 + N(CH_3)_3$$

Because two equivalents of CH_3I are consumed, our amine must be secondary. Because the product amine is trimethyl amine, one of the original alkyl groups must be methyl. Considering the mechanism above, the other alkyl group must be ethyl.

121. (C)

In strong base, this ketone would racemize via the enol form:

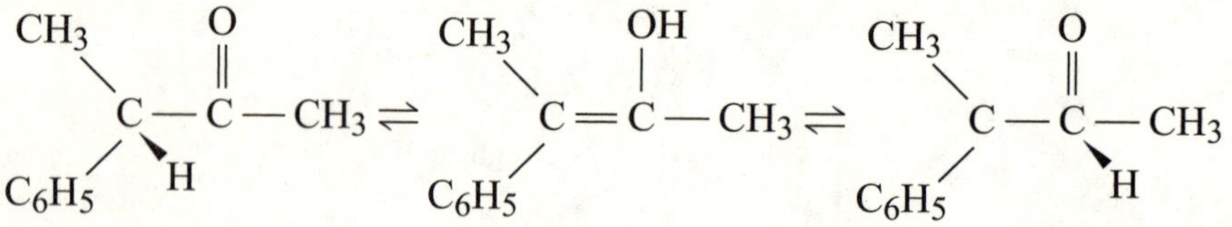

(R) enantiomer   (S) enantiomer

At equilibrium, the solution would be an equal mixture of the (R) and (S) enantiomers. The effects of both forms would cancel out and the net rotation would be zero.

122. (E)

Transition elements are often defined as elements with incompletely filled d orbitals. This definition excludes zinc, which has the electron configuration shown below:

$$[Ar]4s^23d^{10}$$

123. (E)

The allowed transitions are given by the spectral selection rules:

$$\Delta\ell = \pm 1$$

$$\Delta n = \text{any integer}$$

All photons possess angular momentum (spin) of magnitude one. Because angular momentum must be conserved, electrons must change their angular momentum by ± 1 when emitting a photon. For answer (E), $\Delta\ell = 0$.

124. (C)

Terpenes are natural products that are generally constructed from five-carbon isoprene units:

$$C - C - C - C$$
(with a C branch above the second carbon)

Choice (C) is a 13-carbon compound.

125. (B)

I^- is more nucleophilic than Cl^-, except in special circumstances, such as in DMF (a polar aprotic solvent).

126. (B)

According to the Nernst equation:

$$\varepsilon = \varepsilon^\circ - \frac{RT}{nf} \ln Q$$

In the given situation, $\varepsilon^\circ = 0$ because both half-cells are identical, except for differences in concentration. Q is the ratio of concentrations, .01/1.0; n is the number of electrons involved, in this case, two; f is Faraday's constant.

127. (B)

H and E are related by the equation

$$\Delta H = \Delta E + \Delta(PV)$$

For ideal gases and constant temperature,

$$\Delta(PV) = \Delta(nRT) = \Delta n \cdot RT$$

therefore, $\Delta H = \Delta E + \Delta n \cdot RT$

$\Delta H = -282 \text{ kJ/mol} + (-\frac{1}{2})(8.3 \text{J/mol} \cdot \text{K})(300\text{K})$

$\Delta H = -282 \text{ kJ/mol} - 1245 \text{ J/mol}$

$\Delta H = -282 \text{ kJ/mol} - 1.245 \text{ kJ/mmol}$

$\Delta H = -283 \text{ kJ/mol}$

128. (C)

The mass of the atom is slightly less than the sum of the masses of the particles involved. In forming the nucleus, some of the mass of the nucleons is converted to energy in accordance with Einstein's formula, $E = mc^2$. This is called the binding energy, and it is the energy that must be added in order to split the atom.

129. (A)

Answer (C) would represent an addition-elimination mechanism, which would not allow the incoming hydroxy group to shift to the meta position. (B) would not form without light or a free radical initiator. (A) is the accepted intermediate. It is very reactive because it is highly strained.

130. (A)

This is an example of a Friedel-Crafts reaction.

131. (C)

The proper expression for the equilibrium constant is

$$K = \frac{P_{B^2}}{P_A}$$

At equilibrium, an amount x of A has been converted to an amount 2x of B. Because the amount is (ideally) proportional to the partial pressure, and the initial pressure of A is 1 atm.,

$$K = \frac{(2x)^2}{1-x}$$

We can substitute K = 2.0 and find x using the quadratic equation:

$$2 = \frac{4x^2}{1-x}$$

$$2 - 2x = 4x^2$$

$$0 = 4x^2 + 2x - 2$$

$$x = \frac{-2 \pm \sqrt{4+32}}{8} = \frac{-2 \pm 6}{8} = -1, \frac{1}{2}$$

Taking the positive root,

$$P_A = 1 - \tfrac{1}{2} = \tfrac{1}{2} \text{ atm.}$$

$$P_B = 2(\tfrac{1}{2}) = 1 \text{ atm.}$$

132. (A)

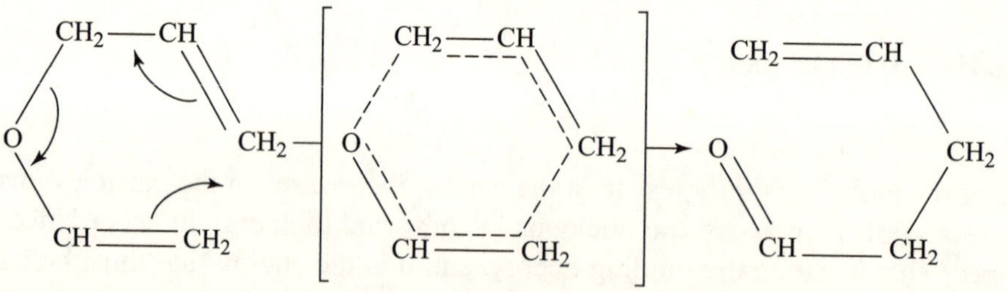

This reaction uses a six-atom, six-electron cyclic intermediate that is common in rearrangements.

The Claisen and Cope rearrangements are related reactions.

133. (D)

$HClO_4$ is perchloric acid. HCl is hydrochloric acid. HOCl is hypochlorous acid. $HClO_2$ is chlorous acid, and $HClO_3$ is chloric acid.

134. (E)

The peaks at m/e 57 and m/e 85 result from fragmentation, which yields an oxomium ion:

$$\left[CH_3CH_2CH_2CH_2 \overset{\overset{O}{\|}}{C} CH_2CH_3 \right]^+ \longrightarrow CH_3CH_2CH_2CH_2 + CH_3CH_2C\equiv O^+$$
$$\text{m/e 57}$$

This is typical of ketones, as is the McLafferty Rearrangement:

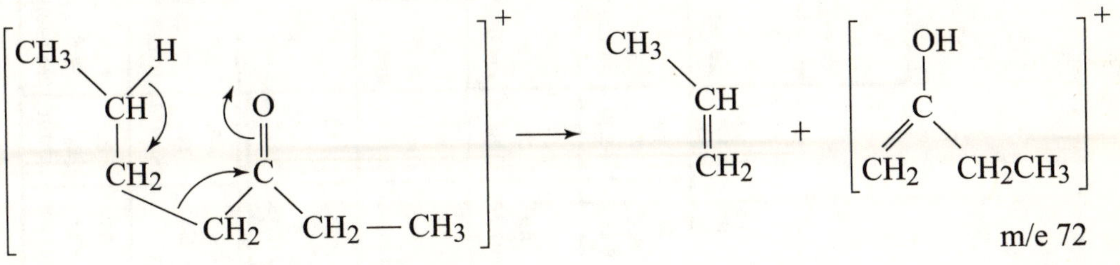

135. (A)

E can be expressed in the following form:

$$dE = TdS - PdV$$

When S and V are constant, that is, no heat or expansion work can leave the system, dE = 0. E is then at an extremal, which is in fact a minimum. E for the system will tend toward this value at which the system is in equilibrium.

136. (C)

Ethers have a tendency to undergo autoxidation when they are in contact with any air. They can form peroxides, which are explosive and dangerous. The peroxides can be eliminated by reduction with ferrous sulfate.

THE PERIODIC TABLE

KEY

Group Classification → 4 / IVA / IVB
Symbol → 22 Ti
Atomic Number
Atomic Weight → 47.88
( ) indicates most stable or best known isotope

METALS | NONMETALS

TRANSITIONAL METALS

§ Not yet named

Alkali Metals — Alkaline Earth Metals — Halogens — Noble Gases

1 IA	2 IIA	3 IIIA/IIIB	4 IVA/IVB	5 VA/VB	6 VIA/VIB	7 VIIA/VIIB	8 VIIIA/VIII	9 VIIIA/VIII	10 VIIIA/VIII	11 IB	12 IIB	13 IIIB/IIIA	14 IVB/IVA	15 VB/VA	16 VIB/VIA	17 VIIB/VIIA	18 VIII/0
1 H 1.008																	2 He 4.003
3 Li 6.941	4 Be 9.012											5 B 10.811	6 C 12.011	7 N 14.007	8 O 15.999	9 F 18.998	10 Ne 20.180
11 Na 22.990	12 Mg 24.305											13 Al 26.982	14 Si 28.086	15 P 30.974	16 S 32.066	17 Cl 35.453	18 Ar 39.948
19 K 39.098	20 Ca 40.078	21 Sc 44.956	22 Ti 47.88	23 V 50.942	24 Cr 51.996	25 Mn 54.938	26 Fe 55.847	27 Co 58.933	28 Ni 58.693	29 Cu 63.546	30 Zn 65.39	31 Ga 69.723	32 Ge 72.61	33 As 74.922	34 Se 78.96	35 Br 79.904	36 Kr 83.8
37 Rb 85.468	38 Sr 87.62	39 Y 88.906	40 Zr 91.224	41 Nb 92.906	42 Mo 95.94	43 Tc (97.907)	44 Ru 101.07	45 Rh 102.906	46 Pd 106.4	47 Ag 107.868	48 Cd 112.411	49 In 114.818	50 Sn 118.710	51 Sb 121.757	52 Te 127.60	53 I 126.905	54 Xe 131.29
55 Cs 132.905	56 Ba 137.327	57 La 138.906	72 Hf 178.49	73 Ta 180.948	74 W 183.84	75 Re 186.207	76 Os 190.23	77 Ir 192.22	78 Pt 195.08	79 Au 196.967	80 Hg 200.59	81 Tl 204.383	82 Pb 207.2	83 Bi 208.980	84 Po (208.982)	85 At (209.982)	86 Rn (222.018)
87 Fr (223.020)	88 Ra (226.025)	89 Ac (227.028)	104 Rf (261.11)	105 Db (262.114)	106 Sg (263.118)	107 Bh (262.12)	108 Hs (265)	109 Mt (266)	110 § (269)	111 § (272.153)	112 § (277)						

LANTHANIDE SERIES

58 Ce 140.115	59 Pr 140.908	60 Nd 144.24	61 Pm (144.913)	62 Sm 150.36	63 Eu 151.965	64 Gd 157.25	65 Tb 158.925	66 Dy 162.50	67 Ho 164.930	68 Er 167.26	69 Tm 168.934	70 Yb 173.04	71 Lu 174.967

ACTINIDE SERIES

90 Th 232.038	91 Pa 231.036	92 U 238.029	93 Np 237.048	94 Pu 244.064	95 Am 243.061	96 Cm 247.070	97 Bk 247.070	98 Cf 251.080	99 Es 252.083	100 Fm 257.095	101 Md 258.1	102 No 259.101	103 Lr 262.11

336

TABLE OF INFORMATION

Below are various physical constants and several conversion factors among SI units. A similar table appears in the GRE Chemistry Test booklet.

Electron rest mass	$m_e = 9.11 \times 10^{-31}$ kilogram
Proton rest mass	$m_p = 1.672 \times 10^{-27}$ kilogram
Neutron rest mass	$m_n = 1.675 \times 10^{-27}$ kilogram
Magnitude of the electron charge	$e = 1.60 \times 10^{-19}$ coulomb
Bohr radius	$a_n = 5.29 \times 10^{-11}$ meter
Avogadro number	$N_A = 6.02 \times 10^{23}$ per mol
Universal gas constant	$R = 8.314$ joules/(mol $\cdot$ K) $= 0.0921$ L $\cdot$ atm/(mol $\cdot$ K) $= 0.08314$ L $\cdot$ bar/(mol $\cdot$ K)
Boltzmann constant	$k = 1.38 \times 10^{-23}$ joule/K
Planck constant	$h = 6.63 \times 10^{-34}$ joule second
Speed of light	$c = 3.00 \times 10^8$ m/s $= 3.00 \times 10^{10}$ cm/s
1 atmosphere press	1 atm $= 1.0 \times 10^5$ newtons/meter^2 $= 1.0 \times 10^5$ pascals (Pa)
Faraday constant	$F = 9.65 \ 10^4$ coulombs/mol
1 atomic mass unit (amu)	1 amu $= 1.66 \times 10^{-27}$ kilogram
1 electron volt (eV)	1eV $= 1.602 \times 10^{-19}$ joule
Volume of 1 mole of ideal gas at 0°C, 1 atmosphere	$= 22.4$ liters

Notes

Notes

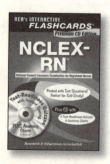

INSTALLING REA's TestWare®

SYSTEM REQUIREMENTS

Pentium 75 MHz (300 MHz recommended) or a higher or compatible processor; Microsoft Windows 98 or later; 64 MB available RAM; Internet Explorer 5.5 or higher.

INSTALLATION

1. Insert the GRE Chemistry TestWare® CD-ROM into the CD-ROM drive.
2. If the installation doesn't begin automatically, from the Start Menu choose the RUN command. When the RUN dialog box appears, type d:\setup (where d is the letter of your CD-ROM drive) at the prompt and click OK.
3. The installation process will begin. A dialog box proposing the directory "Program Files\REA\GREChem" will appear. If the name and location are suitable, click OK. If you wish to specify a different name or location, type it in and click OK.
4. Start the GRE Chemistry TestWare® application by double-clicking on the icon.

REA's GRE Chemistry TestWare® is **EASY** to **LEARN** AND USE. To achieve maximum benefits, we recommend that you take a few minutes to go through the on-screen tutorial on your computer. The "screen buttons" are also explained there to familiarize you with the program.

SSD ACCOMMODATIONS FOR STUDENTS WITH DISABILITIES

Many students qualify for extra time to take the GRE Chemistry, and our TestWare® can be adapted to accommodate your time extension. This allows you to practice under the same extended-time accommodations that you will receive on the actual test day. To customize your TestWare® to suit the most common extensions, visit our website at *www.rea.com/ssd*.

TECHNICAL SUPPORT

REA's TestWare® is backed by customer and technical support. For questions about **installation or operation of your software**, contact us at:

> **Research & Education Association**
> **Phone: (732) 819-8880 (9 a.m. to 5 p.m. ET, Monday–Friday)**
> **Fax: (732) 819-8808**
> **Website: *www.rea.com***
> **E-mail: info@rea.com**

Note to Windows XP Users: In order for the TestWare® to function properly, please install and run the application under the same computer administrator-level user account. Installing the TestWare® as one user and running it as another could cause file-access path conflicts.